BRITISH EVANGELICAL THEOLOGIANS OF THE TWENTIETH CENTURY

An enduring legacy

Edited by
Thomas A. Noble and Jason S. Sexton

APOLLOS (an imprint of Inter-Varsity Press)
36 Causton Street, London SW1P 4ST, England
Website: www.ivpbooks.com
Email: ivp@ivpbooks.com

First published 2022

British Library Cataloguing-in-Publication Data
A catalogue record for this book is available from the British Library.

ISBN: 978–1–78974–379–1
eBook ISBN: 978–1–78974–380–7

Produced on paper from sustainable sources.

Set in Minion Pro 10.75/13.75 pt

Typeset in Great Britain by CRB Associates, Potterhanworth, Lincolnshire
Printed and bound in Great Britain by Ashford Colour Press

Inter-Varsity Press publishes Christian books that are true to the Bible and that communicate the gospel, develop discipleship and strengthen the church for its mission in the world.

IVP originated within the Inter-Varsity Fellowship, now the Universities and Colleges Christian Fellowship, a student movement connecting Christian Unions in universities and colleges throughout Great Britain, and a member movement of the International Fellowship of Evangelical Students. Website: www.uccf.org.uk. That historic association is maintained, and all senior IVP staff and committee members subscribe to the UCCF Basis of Faith.

In memoriam

Thomas Vance Findlay

Faithful preacher, stimulating teacher, caring pastor,
enthusiastic scholar, erudite bibliophile and
forthright Scot

Contents

Contributors   ix

Introduction   1
   Thomas A. Noble

1 James Orr   11
   A. T. B. McGowan

2 James Denney   33
   Thomas V. Findlay

3 Peter Taylor Forsyth   51
   Trevor Hart

4 W. H. Griffith Thomas   71
   Andrew Atherstone

5 H. R. Mackintosh   93
   David L. Rainey

6 W. E. Sangster   113
   Andrew J. Cheatle

7 Martyn Lloyd-Jones   133
   David Ceri Jones

8 John R. W. Stott   155
   Ian M. Randall

9 James I. Packer   176
   Don J. Payne

10 Thomas F. Torrance   197
   Robert T. Walker

11 Lesslie Newbigin   220
   Donald LeRoy Stults

Contents

12 Colin E. Gunton   240
   John E. Colwell

Coda: looking back to look forwards   260
   Jason S. Sexton

Index of names   267

Contributors

Andrew Atherstone is Latimer Research Fellow at Wycliffe Hall, Oxford, and a member of the University of Oxford's Faculty of Theology and Religion. His research focuses on the history of evangelicalism, especially within the Church of England, and his recent books include (as co-editor) *Making Evangelical History: Faith, Scholarship and the Evangelical Past* (2019) and *Transatlantic Charismatic Renewal, c.1950–2000* (2021).

Andrew J. Cheatle is Principal Lecturer in Theology and Pastoral Theology at Liverpool Hope University, where he serves as Assistant Subject Lead (Assistant Head of Department) and Senior University Pastor. He has been a Methodist presbyter since 2008, before which he pastored both in the UK and Denmark. His research interests are the life and theology of W. E. Sangster, homiletics and preaching. His latest book on Sangster is entitled *W. E. Sangster: Sermons in America* (2018).

John E. Colwell was Tutor in Christian Doctrine and Ethics at Spurgeon's College in London, serving previously as a Baptist minister and subsequently as the pastor of Budleigh Salterton Baptist Church in Devon. Among his publications are *Living the Christian Story: The Distinctiveness of Christian Ethics* (2002) and the volume of Colin Gunton's sermons, which he co-edited with Sarah Gunton, *The Theologian as Preacher* (2007).

The late **Thomas V. Findlay** lectured in biblical studies at European Nazarene Bible College in Büsingen, near Schaffhausen on the Swiss–German border, and was subsequently a pastor in the Swiss Reformed Church in the parishes of Feuerthalen-Laufen near the Rhine Falls and in Andelfingen, both in the canton of Zürich.

Trevor Hart taught theology in the University of Aberdeen, and then became Professor of Divinity in the University of St Andrews. He edited a collection of essays on P. T. Forsyth, *Justice the True and Only Mercy* (1995), and his recent publications include *In Him Was Life: The Person and Work of Christ* (2019). He is the rector of St Andrews Episcopal Church, St Andrews.

List of contributors

David Ceri Jones is Reader in Early Modern History at Aberystwyth University in Wales. He is the co-editor of *Engaging with Martyn Lloyd-Jones: The Life and Legacy of 'the Doctor'* (2011), co-author of *The Elect Methodists: Calvinistic Methodism in England and Wales, 1735–1811* (2012) and editor and co-author of *A History of Christianity in Wales* (2022). He is writing a new life of Martyn Lloyd-Jones for the Eerdmans 'Library of Religious Biography' series.

A. T. B. McGowan is Director of the Rutherford Centre for Reformed Theology and Professor of Theology in the University of the Highlands and Islands. He is President of the Scottish Evangelical Theology Society. He also serves as Vice Chairman of the World Reformed Fellowship and chairs its Theological Commission. His publications include *Always Reforming: Explorations in Systematic Theology* (2006), *The Divine Spiration of Scripture: Challenging Evangelical Perspectives* (2007), *The Person and Work of Christ: Understanding Jesus* (2012), and *Adam, Christ and Covenant: Exploring Headship Theology* (2016).

Thomas A. Noble is Research Professor of Theology at Nazarene Theological Seminary in Kansas City, Missouri, and a Senior Research Fellow at Nazarene Theological College, Manchester. His publications include *Tyndale House and Fellowship: The First Sixty Years* (2006) and *Holy Trinity: Holy People: The Theology of Christian Perfecting* (2013). He has co-edited several books including the second edition of the IVP *New Dictionary of Theology* and chairs the Christian Doctrine study group of the Tyndale Fellowship.

Don J. Payne is Vice-President of Academic Affairs, Academic Dean and Professor of Theology at Denver Seminary. He pastored in Tennessee and Colorado and completed his doctoral studies at the University of Manchester. Among his publications are *The Theology of the Christian Life in J. I. Packer's Thought* (2006), *Surviving the Unthinkable* (2015) and *Already Sanctified* (2020).

David L. Rainey was Senior Lecturer in Theology at Nazarene Theological College, Manchester, where he supervised doctoral research for the University of Manchester. He served previously as a Nazarene minister in British Columbia and Alberta. His research under Colin Gunton at King's College London was on the theology of John Wesley and he has published articles on Wesley and Jürgen Moltmann.

Ian M. Randall is a Research Associate, Cambridge Centre for Christianity Worldwide. He was Lecturer in Church History and Spirituality at Spurgeon's

College, London, and Director of Baptist and Anabaptist Studies at the International Baptist Theological Seminary, Prague. He has published numerous works on evangelical history and spirituality, most recently a study of the Bruderhof community, *A Christian Peace Experiment* (2018).

Jason S. Sexton completed his doctoral studies at the University of St Andrews and is Visiting Research Scholar and Lecturer at the University of California, Los Angeles. He co-chairs the American Academy of Religion's Evangelical Studies Unit and the Tyndale Fellowship Christian Doctrine group. His publications include *The Trinitarian Theology of Stanley J. Grenz* (2013), several edited volumes, and articles at the intersection of theology and culture.

Donald LeRoy Stults served as a missionary in South Korea, Philippines and Germany and as the pastor of a Nazarene church in Washington, DC. He completed his doctoral studies at the University of Manchester and has been a lecturer in theology and missiology in South Korea, Germany and in the USA. His publications include *Developing an Asian Theology* (1989/2001) and *Grasping Truth and Reality: Lesslie Newbigin's Theology of Mission in the Western World* (2008).

Robert T. Walker studied theology with his uncle, T. F. Torrance, and, much later, edited Torrance's lectures for publication as *Incarnation: The Person and Life of Christ* (2008) and *Atonement: The Person and Work of Christ* (2009). Having taught theology at Edinburgh University and outdoor sports at Firbush Point, its Highland Outdoor Centre, he is now an honorary fellow in systematic theology, New College, University of Edinburgh.

Introduction

THOMAS A. NOBLE

We are still so close to the twentieth century that it is only now becoming possible to understand its events and developments in perspective. For evangelical Christians, that includes the understanding of the development of our own thinking in an ongoing tradition. Evangelical Christianity is growing enormously in the Global South and East, and is almost alone in resisting the decline among the churches of the increasingly secular West. But growing popularity can mean superficiality and it is therefore important to see the depth and strength of the tradition of evangelical theology. This study of twelve twentieth-century British evangelical theologians aims to do that and it will be helpful first to gain a longer perspective on what we mean by the word 'evangelical' and on the evangelical tradition.

A brief historical overview

The word 'evangelical' was originally coined in German: *evangelische*. It was the word chosen to refer to those branches of the Church Catholic that had been reformed in the Protestant Reformation in order to centre on the preaching of the gospel, the evangel, the good news (*euangelion*). That gospel was centred in 'Christ crucified', a message to be received by 'faith alone' (*sola fide*) as a result of the initiative of God, that is, by 'grace alone' (*sola gratia*). As the sixteenth-century debate with Rome widened into a question of authority, the Reformers also asserted the principle of 'Scripture alone' (*sola scriptura*), meaning that the doctrines of the church had to be based on Holy Scripture. But at the heart of the theology of the Reformers was the concern that Christ alone (*solus Christus*) should be central, the one and only Mediator between God and humankind.

In the succeeding centuries, through all the theological disputes and factions among the traditions of the Reformation, the German Pietists and the English Puritans emphasized that evangelical faith was not only a matter of true doctrine. As Luther had put it, faith was 'the wedding ring' that unites us to Christ the heavenly bridegroom so that our sins become his and his righteousness ours.[1] As Calvin had emphasized, true faith was 'a firm and sure knowledge of the divine favour toward us, founded on the truth of a free promise in Christ, and revealed to our minds and sealed upon our hearts by the Holy Spirit'.[2] 'The word', he wrote, 'is not received in faith when it merely flutters in the brain, but when it has taken deep root in the heart.'[3]

It was this emphasis on *Herzensreligion*, the 'religion of the heart', that characterized the rightly named 'Evangelical *Revival*' of the eighteenth century. This 'Great Awakening' began with the ministry of Jonathan Edwards and New England Puritanism, followed by the ministry of George Whitefield, the clergyman of the Church of England who was welcomed by Scottish Presbyterians and New England Congregationalists. If they represented the continuing tradition traced back through the Reformed tradition, the brothers John and Charles Wesley represented the tradition of Anglican Arminianism and also drew on the Lutheran tradition through German Pietism. Calvinist and Arminian traditions united (despite their theological disputes) in urging the centrality of Christ and the necessity of the new birth. The evangelical movement opposed both dead orthodoxy and the increasing influence of the new deism that was undermining the doctrines of the faith.[4]

In the early nineteenth century, Charles Simeon, Fellow of King's College, Cambridge, became the leading figure in establishing the evangelical tradition in the Church of England.[5] In Scotland, the evangelical wing of the national church, led by Thomas Chalmers, seceded to form the Free Church of Scotland. Evangelical cooperation across denominational boundaries led to the modern missionary movement, the abolition of the slave trade and slavery itself, and humanitarian reform. In the USA, the evangelical tradition developed the subculture of 'revivalism', notably in the ministries of Charles Finney and D. L. Moody, but also in the ministry of the Methodist laywoman Phoebe Palmer.[6] Revivalism was evident too in the UK in the ministry of William and Catherine Booth, uniting evangelism with social action. The founding of the interdenominational Evangelical Alliance in London in 1846 was to lead to the international World Evangelical Alliance in the twentieth century.

---

[1] *Luther's Works*, ed. J. Pelikan (St. Louis: Concordia, 1955–), vol. 22, p. 334.

[2] J. Calvin, *Institutes of the Christian Religion* (Peabody, MA: Hendrickson, 2011), 3.2.7.

[3] Ibid., 3.2.36.

[4] For the history of evangelicalism in the eighteenth century, see Mark A. Noll, *The Rise of Evangelicalism: The Age of Edwards, Whitefield and the Wesleys* (Leicester: Inter-Varsity Press, 2004).

[5] See Oliver R. Barclay and Robert Horn, *From Cambridge to the World* (Leicester: Inter-Varsity Press, 2002), for the emergence of the evangelical student movement from its roots in Cambridge.

[6] See Donald W. Dayton and Robert K. Johnston (eds.), *The Variety of American Evangelicalism* (Downers Grove, IL: InterVarsity Press, 1991).

Evangelicalism has always been notable for the way in which Christians of different traditions – Anglican, Baptists, Congregationalists, Presbyterians, Methodists, Pentecostals, Mennonites and so many more – unite in what they consider to be the heart of the gospel.[7]

The aim of the student missionary movement at the end of the nineteenth century was encapsulated in the title of the book published by John R. Mott in 1900, *The Evangelization of the World in This Generation*. Mott chaired the Edinburgh Missionary Conference of 1910, which brought together an international and interdenominational consultation now regarded as the launching of the ecumenical movement. But evangelicalism was entering stormy waters. The late nineteenth century had seen the spreading influence of the theological liberalism of Ritschl and Harnack from the German universities. At the same time the development of the historical-critical method in biblical studies and the questions raised by Darwin and Darwinism posed serious intellectual questions about the authority of the Bible. In the USA this led to the disaster of fundamentalism, a grassroots movement among evangelicals characterized by an obscurantist opposition to modern science and a millennialist and dispensationalist approach to eschatology, the doctrine of the last things.[8] Opposition to the 'social gospel' of Walter Rauschenbusch also led fundamentalists to react against the social action that had always been part of the evangelical tradition.[9]

In the middle of the twentieth century the 'New Evangelicals' emerged in the USA, led by the evangelist Billy Graham and the theologian Carl F. Henry. Henry encouraged evangelicals to reunite social action with evangelism. Graham sponsored the development of the Lausanne Movement for World Evangelism in which the British preacher John R. W. Stott became the leading theological influence. Many conservative evangelicals were suspicious of trends in the ecumenical movement and particularly in the World Council of Churches. All evangelicals were committed to biblical authority, but in America there was division over the concept of biblical 'inerrancy'. There too the developing concern for moral issues such as the looser sexual mores and

---

[7] For the history of evangelicalism in the nineteenth century, see John Wolffe, *The Expansion of Evangelicalism: The Age of Wilberforce, More, Chalmers and Finney* (Nottingham: Inter-Varsity Press, 2006); and David W. Bebbington, *The Dominance of Evangelicalism: The Age of Spurgeon and Moody* (Leicester: Inter-Varsity Press, 2005).

[8] It should be noted that not all the contributors to *The Fundamentals*, a series of booklets published in Chicago between 1910 and 1915, were 'fundamentalists' in the sense of the word that developed in the 1920s.

[9] See George M. Marsden, *Understanding Fundamentalism and Evangelicalism* (Grand Rapids, MI: Eerdmans, 1991). For evangelicalism in the early twentieth century, see Geoff Treloar, *The Disruption of Evangelicalism: The Age of Mott, Machen and McPherson* (Nottingham: Inter-Varsity Press, 2017).

the easier availability of abortion led in the 1970s to an increasing involvement of the 'moral majority' in politics and the emergence of the so-called culture wars. This has led more recently to a reaction among some evangelicals, who are more concerned with other social issues such as poverty and racial prejudice against the identification of evangelicalism with what they perceive as 'right-wing' politics.[10] These American debates were largely irrelevant however to the vast growth of evangelical Christianity outside the USA in the Global South and East. *Evangélicos* in Brazil and evangelical Anglicans in Nigeria became increasingly strong and culture-shaping communities, while the vibrant Christianity of South Korea is evangelical in character.[11] In post-Christian Europe (as we have noted), evangelicalism is almost the only form of Christianity that is not in steep decline.

Against the background of this great growth of evangelicalism in the Global South and East, the rugged persistence of evangelicalism in Europe and the travails of American evangelicals in the culture wars of the USA, how are we to understand the theological character of this increasingly powerful movement in world Christianity?

Evangelical theology

The historian David Bebbington famously defined the evangelical movement by identifying four characteristics: conversionism, activism, biblicism and crucicentrism.[12] That is a useful checklist for a historian, but for the theologian it is not an entirely satisfactory account. Undoubtedly, all evangelicals since the eighteenth century have stressed the need for evangelism and conversion, although dramatic conversion experiences are no longer stressed the way they used to be. Evangelicals have always been active in evangelism and social action. Perhaps more at the centre of much evangelical thought throughout the twentieth century than in previous centuries was the authority of the Bible. In what amounted to an evangelical manifesto in 1958,[13] James Packer identified catholic traditions as those which gave ultimate authority to church tradition, theological 'liberals' as those who made reason or experience of the

---

[10] See Mark Labberton, *Still Evangelical? Insiders Reconsider Political, Social and Theological Meaning* (Downers Grove, IL: InterVarsity Press, 2018).

[11] See Brian Stanley, *The Global Diffusion of Evangelicalism: The Age of Billy Graham and John Stott* (Nottingham: Inter-Varsity Press, 2013).

[12] David Bebbington, *Evangelicalism in Modern Britain: A History from the 1730s to the 1980s* (London: Routledge, 1989).

[13] J. I. Packer, *'Fundamentalism' and the Word of God* (London: IVF, 1958). The quotation marks in the title are significant.

individual the final authority and evangelicals as those who gave final authority to the Bible. That was not to be dismissed as 'fundamentalism', he argued, but was the historic position of the church.

But if the authority of the Bible was a key issue for theologians, 'cruci-centrism', the centrality of 'Christ crucified', was more evident in the preaching, evangelism and worship of evangelical churches. The theme of the cross often dominated the hymnody of the classical evangelical hymn writers, the gospel song tradition and the new generation of contemporary praise songs that developed towards the end of the century. In contrast to various forms of 'liberal' theology, the atonement was a dominating theme in all evangelical theology, worship and preaching.

Other doctrines were held in common. No evangelical would question the doctrine of the Trinity, but that was a formal badge of orthodoxy rather than a living concern in the life of the churches. While there were differences on eschatology, the doctrine of the last things, all held to final judgment and the final destinies of heaven or hell. The coming general resurrection was agreed, but popular theology focused more on eternal life in heaven. A strong focus on the second coming was typical of those who saw the world as declining into greater wickedness ('premillennialism'), and certainly to those who embraced dispensationalism, but the older evangelical theology favoured 'postmillennialism', the view that the gospel would spread throughout the world through missions until the millennium dawned, leading to the second coming of Christ. The theologically well informed knew however that amillennialism, the rejection of any idea of a literal millennium on earth, was the older Augustinian tradition of the magisterial Reformers.

Differences clearly existed over the doctrines of the church and sacraments, but those were generally ignored when evangelicals from different traditions cooperated in evangelism or social action. There was some debate too over Christian sanctification. While all agreed on justification by faith, the Reformed tradition tended to see Christian sanctification in terms of 'growth in grace' and the spiritual disciplines, while Methodism and the holiness movement (either as understood by the Salvation Army and other holiness churches or at the Keswick Convention) saw a place for a 'second blessing'. Pentecostal denominations developed their own understanding of 'the baptism of the Spirit' marked by the gift of tongues, and Pentecostalism grew enormously across South America and Africa. In the 1960s, the charismatic movement with its emphasis on the gifts of the Spirit grew strongly, developing a new variety of evangelical Christianity and influencing the established churches.

Twelve theologians

It is against that background of evangelical history and doctrine that we will try to view the twelve theologians we have chosen to represent the British evangelical tradition through the twentieth century. We could easily examine twelve evangelical biblical scholars, and our list would stretch from Denney (who was primarily a New Testament scholar) through F. F. Bruce to a significant group of scholars towards the end of the century. But our focus here is on theology as the exploration and defence of Christian doctrine. The first six on our list represent the early twentieth century and were both preachers and academic theologians. James Orr taught systematic theology in the United Presbyterian College in Edinburgh and then, after the union of the United Presbyterian Church and the Free Church of Scotland in 1900, he taught at what became the United Free College in Glasgow. He addressed the controversial theological issues dividing evangelical theology from the dominant liberal theology of Ritschl and Harnack. He published works on the authority of the Bible, the relationship of God to the world as it was then understood by science, and the question of whether the Christian doctrines of Christ and the Trinity were really (as alleged by Harnack) the 'Hellenization' of Christianity.

Orr's colleague James Denney was primarily a New Testament scholar, but also a theologian who defended as biblical the doctrine of the atonement as understood by Anselm and the Reformers. He briefly held the chair of Systematic and Pastoral Theology at the college of the Free Church of Scotland in Glasgow before moving to the chair of New Testament Language, Literature and Theology. His passionate focus on the atoning death of Christ had a significant influence on some of the later theologians in the book, including those who were more conservative in their view of Scripture. P. T. Forsyth, a contemporary of Orr and Denney, was a Scottish Congregationalist who certainly saw 'Christ crucified' at the centre of his theological vision. He is notable for rejecting his earlier commitment to Ritschlian liberalism, being turned (as he put it) 'from a Christian to a believer, from a lover of love to an object of grace'.[14] After twenty-five years in pastoral ministry, he became Principal of Hackney College in London. Belonging to the same generation, W. H. Griffith Thomas represents the Anglican evangelical tradition of the early twentieth century. After serving as Principal of Wycliffe Hall, Oxford, he taught theology at Wycliffe College, Toronto, moving then to Philadelphia, where he gave leadership to 'Victorious Life' conferences in the Keswick tradition. His posthumous

---

[14] P. T. Forsyth, *Positive Preaching and the Modern Mind* (London: Hodder & Stoughton, 1907), p. 281.

publication *The Principles of Theology: An Introduction to the Thirty-Nine Articles* was influential for decades after his death.

A younger contemporary of these four, H. R. Mackintosh is less well known today, but he too like Forsyth turned away from Ritschlian liberalism in his mature years. As Professor of Christian Dogmatics at New College, Edinburgh, he carried on the evangelical tradition of the United Free Church of Scotland into the reunited Church of Scotland that emerged from the union of 1929. He was notable for his work on Christology, *The Person of Jesus Christ*, and his relating of the atonement to forgiveness in *The Christian Doctrine of Forgiveness*.

In the mid-century, we concentrate on two preachers who never held university chairs, but whose preaching drew thousands in London during the Blitz and in the period after the Second World War. Martyn Lloyd-Jones abandoned a promising medical career in Harley Street to become the pastor of a Welsh mission, being then invited to succeed the notable preacher G. Campbell Morgan, at London's Westminster Chapel. His example of expository preaching over many decades and his admiration for the theology of B. B. Warfield, the Calvinist theologian of Princeton, had a long-term influence. At Westminster Central Hall the somewhat more popular style of W. E. Sangster drew even larger congregations. Sangster represented an evangelical Methodism that rejected fundamentalism and attempted to defend the Christian doctrine of sin in the face of the popular humanist use of Darwin. Popular contemporary thought was also the context in which he tried to understand Christian sanctification in a way that was both biblical and enlightened by twentieth-century psychology. His theology was not concerned with the central dogmatic mysteries of the incarnation and Trinity, but with wrestling to present the realities of heaven and hell to a generation living daily with death and destruction.

As we move farther into the second half of the century, we consider five influential figures. John Stott became the young rector of All Souls, Langham Place, in London in 1950 and has been said to be one of the most influential Anglicans of the twentieth century. Standing in the tradition of Charles Simeon, he exemplified expository preaching and had worldwide influence through his university missions, and later his role in the Lausanne Movement. His university addresses, published as *Basic Christianity*, sold in millions, his book on the atonement presented a biblical theology of the cross, and his concern with social issues in the contemporary world was influential. His Anglican contemporary James Packer was converted as a student at Oxford and, developing a deep interest in Puritan theology, was more committed to the traditional doctrines of Calvinism, but, in addition to the defence of evangelical Christianity we have already noted, he published widely read books such as *Knowing God* and *A Passion for Holiness*. Emigrating to Canada to teach at Regent College in Vancouver, he became widely influential in North America and remained active in teaching well into the present century.

With T. F. Torrance, we return to Presbyterian Scotland and to the intellectual world of the leading universities. Born in China into an evangelical missionary family, Torrance studied under Mackintosh and then under the Basle theologian Karl Barth. Serving as Professor of Christian Dogmatics at Edinburgh's New College for almost thirty years, he is reckoned by many to be the greatest English-speaking theologian of the century. He engaged with the relationship between theology and the natural sciences at a much deeper methodological level than most. He was a strong advocate of the theology of Calvin (though not of scholastic Calvinism) but his championing of the theology of Barth brought strong disapproval from some evangelicals. Torrance was mainly concerned not just to relate theology to science, but to dig in depth into the theology of the church fathers. This was not only to bring him into significant theological conversations with Eastern Orthodoxy, but was intended to place the Reformation and evangelical concern with 'Christ crucified' in the context of a deeper understanding of the gospel of the incarnation and the trinitarian faith of the church.

Lesslie Newbigin had a similar theological stance. Like Torrance, he was an evangelical who remained committed to the ecumenical movement, and also an English Presbyterian who became a bishop in the newly united Church of South India. His greatest theological impact came however after he 'retired' back to Britain and published a series of books addressing the church's mission in the Western world and helping to shape the new discipline of missiology. Finally, Colin Gunton of the United Reformed Church was a preacher and professional theologian. He served as Professor of Christian Doctrine at King's College London, promoting the study and teaching of systematic theology through his founding of the Research Institute in Systematic Theology and the *International Journal of Systematic Theology*. He published a significant book on the doctrine of the atonement, but his most notable writings were on the doctrine of creation and the doctrine of the Trinity.

These twelve theologians represent the tradition of British evangelical theology at its best. Thomas, Lloyd-Jones, Stott and Packer represent the more 'conservative' evangelicals. The others might not entirely have agreed with their way of defending biblical authority or the way in which Lloyd-Jones and Packer embraced traditional Calvinism. But they were all 'conservative' in comparison even with the 'liberal evangelicals' of the 1920s. They were all centred on 'Christ crucified', for all of them the Bible was in fact authoritative for faith and doctrine, and all of them were truly 'evangelical' in developing their preaching, teaching and writing out of the central evangel of the Christian faith. While all of them wrote on many theological topics, we have intentionally highlighted their views on the atonement and the authority of Scripture, two topics that particularly concerned evangelicals. The chapters have been written not primarily for experts and professional theologians, but for students, pastors and interested laypeople. Where possible, appropriate personal reminiscences have been included in the later chapters (particularly in Robert Walker's vivid memories of his uncle and John Colwell's delightful essay on Colin Gunton), reminding us that these theologians were not merely leading thinkers, but men of flesh and blood engaged in Christian ministry. Some were senior professors writing academic theology (though also preachers): others were primarily preachers or wrote mainly for the wider church.

There are of course other doctrinal or systematic theologians who could have been included. Daniel Lamont and G. T. Thomson of New College, Edinburgh, come to mind. John Murray was a Scot who served as Professor of Theology at Princeton before leaving with the conservative minority to found Westminster Theological Seminary in Philadelphia, where he taught from 1930 to 1966. James Torrance, Peter Toon, Philip Hughes, H. D. McDonald, Bruce Milne, David Watson, Tom Smail, Michael Green and Donald Macleod could also have been included. Geoffrey Wainwright was a Yorkshire Methodist who served as a professor of theology at Duke Divinity School in North Carolina and was noted particularly for his one-volume theology *Doxology*. One leading theologian whom readers might expect to be included is John Webster, but in fact his major publications came only at the beginning of the twenty-first century. That is true too of the systematic theologies published by Anthony Thiselton and Gerald Bray. Alan Torrance, William Abraham and Stephen Williams also belong to this next generation. J. H. S. Burleigh, R. Newton Flew, R. Tudur Jones, Arthur Skevington Wood, David F. Wright, Andrew Walls, A. N. S. Lane and Alister McGrath must be regarded as historical rather than systematic theologians, and Paul Helm as a philosophical theologian.

From today's perspective, we will also be struck by the absence of women. But while we might mention the significant contribution of two college principals, Ruth Etchells at St John's, Durham, and (at the very end of the century) Christina Baxter at St John's, Nottingham, the all-male group of twelve accurately reflects the fact that evangelical theology in the twentieth century was (like so much else) almost exclusively male. For some evangelical traditions (though not for all) that was linked to the belief that only men should be ordained to the Christian ministry. From our twenty-first-century perspective, we will also be reminded that our use of language has changed quite suddenly and recently. But we must use our historical imagination to understand that for almost all of the twentieth century, words such as 'man' and 'men' were regarded as gender inclusive. That assumption was indeed as old as language itself and has changed only in the last two or three decades. We observe the new usage of course, but will not falsify the historical record by changing what was then the common usage in quotations from these theologians.

Finally, this book had its origin in a study group of the Tyndale Fellowship for Biblical and Theological Research in Cambridge in 2011. One of the contributors then was the late Thomas V. Findlay, a New Testament scholar who lectured from 1976 to 1988 at European Nazarene Bible College near Schaffhausen (where Dr Andrew Cheatle was his student) and served from 1991 to 1998 as a pastor in the Swiss Reformed Church. Sadly, Tom Findlay died suddenly a few months after the meeting of the study group. I have edited his paper on James Denney for publication (adding two paragraphs that tie it in with the theme of the book), and would like to dedicate the book to his memory. All of us who contribute are increasingly aware that life is short, but we write our chapters as tributes to these twelve evangelical theologians who shaped our generation and were such exemplars of faith seeking understanding.

1
James Orr

A. T. B. McGOWAN

James Orr was born in Glasgow on 11 April 1844 and died in Glasgow on 6 September 1913.[1] His father was an engineer and work took him to Manchester and then Leeds. The young James Orr began his schooling in these cities but both his parents died when he was about 9 years old and he returned to Glasgow to live with relatives. Later, he found work as an apprentice bookbinder. His introduction to evangelical Christianity came through three institutions: the Young Men's Christian Association (YMCA), the Glasgow City Mission and Sydney Place United Presbyterian Church. The YMCA stimulated his mind with lectures and opportunities for study, the Glasgow City Mission enabled him to engage in practical Christianity, working in the poor Calton area of the city. Although Alan Sell says that Orr's home church was Parliamentary Road United Presbyterian Church, it was the Sydney Place United Presbyterian congregation where, as a young man, he was nurtured. This congregation was large and very significant within the denomination, not least in producing candidates for its ministry, one of whom was James Orr. Hence the United Presbyterian Church became the denomination he would serve as a member, a minister and as a professor in its theological college until the Union of 1900.

Orr's church background

To understand James Orr and the United Presbyterian Church, we need a little background on Scottish Presbyterianism at the end of the nineteenth century.[2]

---

[1] Sources for this personal information: D. W. Bebbington, 'Orr, James (1844–1913), theologian', in *Oxford Dictionary of National Biography*, article published 2004; Alan P. F. Sell, *Defending and Declaring the Faith: Some Scottish Examples 1860–1920* (Exeter: Paternoster Press, 1987); Glen G. Scorgie, *A Call for Continuity: The Theological Contribution of James Orr* (Macon, GA: Mercer University Press, 1988).

[2] Sources for this section include J. H. S. Burleigh, *A Church History of Scotland* (London: Oxford University Press, 1960); Andrew L. Drummond and James Bulloch, *The Church in Late Victorian Scotland 1874–1900* (Edinburgh: The St Andrew Press, 1978); and J. K. S. Reid, *Presbyterians and Unity* (London: A. R. Mowbray, 1962).

At that time there were three large Presbyterian churches in Scotland: the Church of Scotland, the Free Church of Scotland and the United Presbyterian Church. The Free Church came into being in 1843 at the so-called 'Disruption', when a large number of ministers and congregations left the Church of Scotland, substantially over the issue of patronage, whereby lairds, heritors and elders chose ministers, rather than the members of a congregation. The United Presbyterian Church came into existence in 1847, as a result of a union between the United Secession Church and the Relief Churches. These two churches were themselves largely the result of earlier schisms from the Church of Scotland, but came together as the United Presbyterian Church in 1847.

There were attempts between 1863 and 1873 to bring about a union between the Free Church and the United Presbyterian Church but these discussions failed. One major stumbling block was that the United Presbyterian Church did not believe in the 'Establishment Principle', which the Free Church upheld. When the Free Church left the Church of Scotland in 1843, it stated that, although leaving the Church of Scotland, it maintained its convictions regarding the 'Establishment Principle'. The United Presbyterian Church, however, was 'voluntarist' in its ecclesiology and opposed all state recognition of, interference with, or funding of, the church.

The other factor that hindered the relations between the United Presbyterians and the Free Church was that the United Presbyterian Church was less strict in its adherence to the Westminster Confession of Faith. Indeed, it was the first church in Scotland to adopt 'Declaratory Articles' in relation to confessional subscription. These articles, adopted in 1879, clarified the Church's affirmation of the *Westminster Confession of Faith*.[3] The key declaratory article and the one that would later be adopted by the Free Church and later again by the Church of Scotland stated:

> That, in accordance with the practice hitherto observed in this Church, liberty of opinion is allowed on such points in the Standards, not entering into the substance of faith, as the interpretation of the 'six days' in the Mosaic account of the creation: the Church guarding against the abuse of this liberty to the injury of its unity and peace.

The key expression here is 'liberty of opinion is allowed on such points in the Standards, not entering into the substance of faith'. Both of these hindrances

---

[3] For a copy of the Declaratory Articles as proposed by the committee chaired by Professor Cairns and the final text of the document approved by the Church, see <https://theologyinteralia.net/wp-content/uploads/2019/11/UPC-Declaratory-Act-Committee-and-Final-versions-4.pdf> (consulted 3 March 2021).

to union were duly addressed by the Free Church and the ground was clear for the union to take place, which it duly did in 1900, when the two churches came together to form the United Free Church.[4]

Orr the student

James Orr was encouraged by his minister at Sydney Place United Presbyterian Church, John Ker, to register as a student at the University of Glasgow, with a view to becoming a United Presbyterian minister. He duly began his studies in 1865. By all accounts he was a brilliant student, with a strong inclination towards the study of philosophy. At that time in Glasgow there were competing philosophical influences upon the students. On the one hand, there was John Veitch, Professor of Logic and Rhetoric. Veitch was a proponent of Scottish common-sense realism, which had been developed in Aberdeen and then Glasgow by Thomas Reid at the end of the eighteenth century. This was the philosophy that made such an impact on North America, being introduced to the College of New Jersey (later renamed Princeton University) by its President, John Witherspoon, and adopted by many American theologians, including Charles Hodge. On the other hand, there was Edward Caird, Professor of Moral Philosophy, who was an advocate of Hegel's idealist philosophy. Orr immersed himself in his philosophical studies and made great progress. Given the opposing schools of thought he encountered in his studies, it can be said that Orr preferred Veitch's modern version of common-sense realism to Caird's Hegelianism, but he was also somewhat eclectic and took some elements from idealism into his thinking.

Having graduated Master of Arts with first-class honours in philosophy in 1870, Orr won a Ferguson scholarship. Many of those who won that prize used it to travel to Oxford or Cambridge or even overseas, for further study. Orr, however, opted to use it to stay in Glasgow and work towards his Bachelor of Divinity degree. He graduated in 1872 and also won a share of the Lord Rector's prize for an essay on David Hume that was later expanded and published.[5]

In addition to his studies at the University of Glasgow, in order to become a minister of the United Presbyterian Church it was necessary to attend classes

---

[4] Since our focus is on Orr, we must leave the story there, except to note that, in order to facilitate union between the Church of Scotland and the United Free Church, the Church of Scotland adopted its own 'Articles Declaratory of the Constitution of the Church of Scotland'. These are embedded in an Act of Parliament, called the 'Church of Scotland Act 1921'. This paved the way for the union between the Church of Scotland and the United Free Church in 1929.

[5] James Orr, *David Hume and His Influence on Philosophy and Theology* (Edinburgh: T&T Clark, 1903).

at the United Presbyterian Divinity Hall in Edinburgh. Orr did this, alongside his Glasgow studies, attending the Hall from 1868 to 1872. This meant that the major influences on his theological development were Professor John Caird (brother of Edward) in divinity at Glasgow and Professor John Cairns in the United Presbyterian Divinity Hall.

Orr the churchman

After a period as a Probationer in Trinity United Presbyterian Church in Irvine, Orr was called to East Bank United Presbyterian Church in Hawick, where he was inducted on 3 February 1874. In April 1874, he married Hannah Fraser. Trinity was one of the larger and more substantial United Presbyterian congregations, with around 600 attending on a Sunday. The congregation grew under his ministry and by the time he left in 1891 the church building had been expanded to seat around 1,000 people. Orr, by all accounts, was a diligent and well-respected minister of the gospel. He also became very involved in the life of the town of Hawick, including as chairman of the Hawick School Board.

Throughout his life, Orr was also very involved in the life of his denomination. He held firmly to its voluntarist ecclesiology and was an advocate of disestablishment. Being in favour of a measure of theological freedom, he was one of the architects of the Declaratory Articles adopted by the United Presbyterian Church. He was also one of the advocates of union with the Free Church and later became Joint Convenor of the United Presbyterian Union Committee.

In 1890–91, while still the minister in Hawick, Orr was appointed to deliver the first series of Kerr Lectures. These lectures, given in 1891, led to Orr's appointment as Professor of Church History in the United Presbyterian College in Edinburgh. The lectures were published in 1893 as *The Christian View of God and the World*.[6] In this volume, Orr spells out the importance of having a 'world view'. Later, this theological viewpoint would be identified with the Dutch Reformed school of Abraham Kuyper and Herman Bavinck. Indeed, many regard Abraham Kuyper's Stone Lectures, delivered at Princeton University in 1898, as the classic expression of Calvinism presented as a world and life view.[7] Interestingly, however, in the very first footnote of Kuyper's book, he refers appreciatively to Orr's *The Christian View of God and the*

---

[6] James Orr, *The Christian View of God and the World as Centring in the Incarnation* (Edinburgh: Andrew Elliott, 1893).

[7] Abraham Kuyper, *Calvinism: Six Stone Lectures* (Edinburgh: T&T Clark, 1989).

World. In some ways, that earlier volume by Orr is a more sustained and profound treatment than Kuyper's and clearly influenced the direction of Kuyper's thought.[8]

It is a most significant volume coming from the pen of a young scholar at the beginning of his academic career and demonstrates, even at that stage, the breadth and depth of his thinking. As Stephen Williams says in his introduction to a modern edition of the book:

> Orr was an evangelical theologian and apologist. When we take in his work as a whole – and he could write on everything from the detail of Old Testament criticism to the philosophy of David Hume – we are astonished at the scholarship submitted to the service of Christ and gospel. One is tempted to state immediately that this range and depth are simply not possible in our twenty-first century. But such a pronouncement must allow for two riders. Firstly, even if one person can not do it, teams from across the sub-disciplines of theology and philosophy might be encouraged to closer co-operation and collaboration to achieve the same end. Secondly, it is good for a number of individuals to develop the kind of synthetic intuition manifested both in this particular work of Orr's and across his authorship in general, so that we establish and ground a Christian 'world-view' perspective, even if we can not scale the measure of Orr's erudition.[9]

Orr taught church history for nine years in the United Presbyterian College and although his later books attracted most attention, he also published on the history of the early church. When the union between the Free Church and the United Presbyterian Church took place in 1900 and the United Free Church was formed, he transferred to what became the United Free Church College in Glasgow, where he was appointed to the chair of apologetics and dogmatics. One of the first works he published after taking up this chair was *The Progress of Dogma*.[10] These were lectures delivered at the Western Theological Seminary in Allegheny, Pennsylvania, in 1897. While recognizing the importance of holding to the authority of Scripture, Orr sought to establish a firm foundation for Christian doctrine, that Scripture might be interpreted consistently.

---

[8] This view is supported by Peter Heslam, 'Faith and Reason: Kuyper, Warfield and the Shaping of the Evangelical Mind', *Anvil*, vol. 15, no. 4 (1998), pp. 299–313.

[9] James Orr, *The Christian View of God and the World* (Vancouver: Regent College Publishing, 2002).

[10] James Orr, *The Progress of Dogma* (London: Hodder & Stoughton, 1902).

The whole book is set against the background of the critical movement that he believed had seriously damaged confidence in Christian doctrine. Orr argued that the developing history of Christian doctrine down through the centuries followed a logical and dogmatic pattern. Indeed, the order in which the doctrines were settled by the church historically, coincided with the order in which these doctrines would be found in any standard work of systematic theology: prolegomena, doctrine of God, anthropology, Christology, atonement and application of redemption. He argued that those dogmatic decisions are now beyond reversal and act as criteria for orthodoxy. His conclusion was that the work of his own day was to establish the one remaining area of dispute, namely eschatology.

There are many reasons why his thesis was not entirely persuasive, as Stephen Williams points out in the foreword to a modern edition of the book,[11] but it demonstrates, nevertheless, a theologian who was extremely well read in the history and development of dogmatic theology and had a firm grasp of the key movements in the church's decision-making process, not least in the great ecumenical councils of the early centuries, as well as the great doctrinal gains of the Reformation and post-Reformation periods. All of this demonstrated that Orr was a most able dogmatic theologian and helped to enhance his reputation as a scholar. It also demonstrated Orr's willingness to incorporate aspects of philosophy into his dogmatics, not least the Hegelian view learned in his student days. As Scorgie writes:

> Orr did not try, as John Henry Newman had, to vindicate the history of dogma by an appeal to the authority of the Spirit-led Church. Rather, he appealed to forces that he alleged were operating within the larger sphere of history. This theory of dogmatic development, stressing as it did a correspondence between the logical and the historical, manifested some rather obvious affinities to Hegel's philosophy of history. Once again Orr borrowed from idealism, this time in an effort to vindicate the history of dogma and to challenge the iconoclasm of Harnack.[12]

As noted above, throughout the greater part of his life Orr was involved in the life of the church, first the United Presbyterian Church and then the United Free Church. He was no ivory-tower theologian but rather a man who saw theology as primarily the theology of the church. He would have identified with

---

[11] James Orr, *The Progress of Dogma* (Vancouver: Regent College Publishing, 2002).
[12] Scorgie, *Call for Continuity*, p. 77.

Barth, who first called his great project *Christian Dogmatics* before beginning again and calling it *Church Dogmatics*.

Orr and Liberal Theology

Orr began his theological career just as the new higher-critical views of the Bible, which had largely developed in Germany, were beginning to have an impact in Britain. Similarly, theologians were faced with the rise of the Liberal Theology,[13] which was based upon and flowed out of those critical views. Much of his earlier theological work was devoted to analysing and resisting these encroaches and defending a traditional, orthodox theology. This began as early as 1894, while Orr was still a professor in the United Presbyterian College in Edinburgh, when he contributed a chapter to a book entitled *The Supernatural in Christianity: With Special Reference to Statements in the Recent Gifford Lectures*. The other two chapters were written by professors in the New College in Edinburgh, Robert Rainy and Marcus Dods. The occasion for this book, as indicated by the subtitle, was the series of Gifford Lectures that had been delivered by Professor Otto Pfleiderer of the University of Berlin, entitled 'The Philosophy and Development of Religion'. In these lectures, following F. C. Baur, Pfleiderer questioned the historical authenticity of the incarnation, the resurrection and the supernatural acts recorded in the Gospels. A series of lectures arranged to respond to Pfleiderer were subsequently published in that little volume. The ground of dispute was laid bare by Professor A. H. Charteris of the University of Edinburgh, who was unable to deliver a lecture himself for medical reasons but who introduced the first speaker. This introduction became the preface to the book. Charteris stated that he and the three lecturers objected to many things stated in the Gifford Lectures:

> Perhaps I may be allowed to speak for myself, and say that I object to the Lecturer's presupposition that the Incarnation is to be disbelieved because it is not according to his conception of history, founded on our experience. Further, I object to his assumption that all the more marvellous incidents in the Gospel history of Jesus Christ are of later invention than the others. I object to his extraordinary assertion that St. Paul believed in a merely spiritual Resurrection of Jesus Christ.[14]

---

[13] The expression 'Liberal Theology' is used throughout to refer to that school of thought represented by Schleiermacher, Ritschl, Herrmann and others. When a more general comment on the 'liberalizing' of theology is intended, the word 'liberal' will be in lower case.

[14] Robert Rainy, James Orr and Marcus Dods, *The Supernatural in Christianity: With Reference to Statements in the Recent Gifford Lectures* (Edinburgh: T&T Clark, 1894), p. viii.

Orr's contribution was to provide an analysis and assessment of Pfleiderer's views.[15] In doing so, he pointed out that, although many were hailing Pfleiderer as representing the way forwards for Christian theology, in fact the views thus expressed had already been overtaken in Germany by the emerging theology of Ritschl and no longer held sway in the academy![16] Orr's main argument, however, centres on Pfleiderer's rationalist and anti-supernaturalist assumptions. Orr challenges these assumptions and demonstrates that they are arbitrary and not supported even by other sceptics. He also shows that the views of the Gifford lecturer are incompatible with knowing God and enjoying communion with God, incompatible with a doctrine of sin and salvation and, above all, incompatible with the biblical picture of Jesus. Pfleiderer speaks highly of Christ, but it is a natural Christ, a human Christ, not a divine Christ. Certainly, Pfleiderer's Jesus is not the Jesus of the Bible, the Son of the living God.[17]

The views of F. C. Baur and Otto Pfleiderer having given way to the theology of Ritschl, Orr then turned his attention to this latter theology. His book *The Ritschlian Theology and the Evangelical Faith*[18] was his first major contribution to the assessment and critique of Liberal Theology. Scorgie describes it as 'the first book-length assessment of the Ritschlian theology by a British writer'.[19] Orr notes that he wrote as one who 'while conscious of having benefited by its teaching, does not share the standpoint of the school'.[20] What is obvious in the book is the amount of time and careful scholarship Orr expended in seeking to understand Ritschl. Some early evangelical responses to Liberal Theology, either that of Schleiermacher or of Ritschl, were fairly dismissive. This volume of Orr's is different. It is clear that he has made a serious effort to understand the origins and development of Ritschl's thinking. It is also clear that he respects Ritschl. Indeed, it is not until 230 pages have passed that Orr turns from presentation and analysis to summary and critique. When he does so, Orr identifies the key question: 'Is Ritschlianism justified in the absolute separation it makes between theology and metaphysics, or more generally, between "religious" and "theoretic" thought?'[21] Having considered this question, Orr rejects this separation. Another key element of the critique concerns

[15] Otto Pfleiderer, *Philosophy and Development of Religion Being The Gifford Lectures Delivered Before the University of Edinburgh 1894* (Edinburgh: William Blackwood and Sons, 1894), 2 vols. Orr's reply was entitled 'Can Professor Pfleiderer's View Justify Itself?', in Rainy et al., *Supernatural in Christianity*, pp. 33–67.

[16] Rainy et al., *Supernatural in Christianity*, p. 36.

[17] Ibid., pp. 63–67.

[18] James Orr, *The Ritschlian Theology and the Evangelical Faith* (London: Hodder & Stoughton, 1897).

[19] Scorgie, *Call for Continuity*, p. 59.

[20] Orr, *Ritschlian Theology*, p. 8.

[21] Ibid., p. 238.

revelation. Finally, Orr focuses specifically on the various doctrines of the Christian faith and shows how all of them are undermined by the Ritschlian theology.[22]

Towards the end of the book, Orr notes that the Ritschlian theology focuses heavily on the notion of love as the chief characteristic of God, drawing all doctrines out of that starting point. Although the Bible does teach that God is love, Orr sees that such an emphasis undermines other aspects and attributes of God and also undermines major doctrines; for example, the doctrine of justification. He writes:

> Then, as we saw, the remaining attributes of God are viewed in the Ritschlian system as so many phases of this primary attribute of love. Righteousness especially is defined as the consistency of God in carrying out the ends of His love, and is deprived entirely of its judicial and retributive character. This is a point on which, again, we think that the evangelical theology much more exactly conserves the Scriptural truth, while Ritschlianism obscures it.[23]

Finally, Orr brings the book towards a close by highlighting two key doctrines. He writes, 'Without entering into too many details, we propose to test this new theology with reference to two of the greater doctrines of the evangelical faith – the doctrine of the Incarnation, and the doctrine of Reconciliation.'[24] He finds that the new Ritschlian theology undermines the clear teaching of Scripture on these two key doctrines, perhaps especially on the atonement. Thus, he concludes his argument as follows:

> While, therefore, we cheerfully recognise the exceeding ability and earnestness of many of the representatives of the new theology, and gratefully acknowledge the valuable services they have in various ways rendered to theology, we cannot grant that the system they advocate has the superiority over the older evangelical faith they would claim for it, or regard it as likely soon to supplant the latter.[25]

Orr would later write another book on Ritschlianism, in which he not only engaged further with the theology of Ritschl himself but also that of a number

---

[22] Ibid., pp. 254–255.
[23] Ibid., p. 256.
[24] Ibid., p. 262.
[25] Ibid., p. 270.

of other scholars who had adopted Ritschlian theology.[26] Indeed, throughout his academic life, Orr continued to engage with Liberal Theology and to refute its core arguments. Perhaps the most important book of this genre was his *The Problem of the Old Testament*.[27] The subtitle was 'Considered with Reference to Recent Criticism'. The significance of this book lies not just in its material content but in the fact that Orr could write this against the background of heated controversy in the church on the question of what was acceptable for scholars to hold about the Old Testament and the fact that Orr appeared to tolerate more diversity and 'liberalism' than others did.

The book was a response to the theories of Julius Wellhausen and others regarding the text of the Old Testament. Orr made it clear once again that he respected the critics, while disagreeing with their conclusions. Indeed, he expressed opposition to the 'violent and indiscriminating' attacks on the critics by some conservative writers. Instead, he writes, 'The case which the critics present must be met in a calm, temperate, and scholarly way, if it is to be dealt with to the satisfaction of thoughtful Christian people.'[28] That is precisely what he proceeded to do.

In the first chapter he lays out the issues at stake, noting the need for careful discrimination, lest the debate be seen simply as believing scholars versus higher critics. He notes the importance of textual criticism, in establishing the best text of the Bible, based on manuscript evidence and the history and transmission of the texts. He does, however, focus on two themes that lie at the centre of his whole theological project, namely revelation and the supernatural. Orr held to a position that might be called 'believing criticism'. That is to say, he insists that to take the textual issues out of the context of a Christian belief in the supernatural work of God and God's revelation to human beings undermines the need to read the texts as what they are, namely the record of the revelation of God. He goes on to insist that much of the higher criticism stems from a rationalistic approach, rather than from a belief in the God who has chosen to reveal himself. He goes on in chapter 2 to speak of 'The Old Testament from its own point of view', insisting upon its organic character and structural unity, despite the number of books involved. He also demonstrates the evidence for the authority and reliability of the Old Testament through its fulfilment in the New Testament. This leads him on to matters of teleology, namely that the Old Testament must be understood in the context of purpose and end. That is

[26] James Orr, *Ritschlianism: Expository and Critical Essays* (London: Hodder & Stoughton, 1903).
[27] James Orr, *The Problem of the Old Testament* (London: James Nisbet, 1905).
[28] Ibid., p. xv.

to say, he views the Old Testament as a 'history of redemption' that culminates in the coming of Jesus Christ.

After these introductory chapters in which he lays out his key principles, the remainder of the book is spent in a careful analysis of the higher-critical views of the Old Testament, looking in detail at textual issues regarding authorship, date, literary style and construction, influence of other cultures and writings and much more. He takes considerable time in analysing what he describes as the Graf-Wellhausen theory of the origins of the Pentateuch, a documentary hypothesis in which four different sources are identified (J, E, D and P), which was fast becoming the dominant view among Old Testament scholars. He goes through the Old Testament, dealing with other higher-critical views, not least on prophecy and the dating of Old Testament books. The whole work is a detailed analysis that seeks to be fair to the higher critics, while ultimately rejecting their theories.

As well as these more general books covering a wide range of material, Orr also published books on specific controversial issues. Many of those in the Liberal Theology school denied the authenticity of the incarnation and the resurrection, rejecting any supernatural intervention in the natural laws that govern everyday experience. For Orr, the fundamental issue, which pervades all of his writing, is the importance of understanding Christianity to be a super-natural religion, based on a God who has chosen to reveal himself to his creatures. Without an understanding of the supernatural and of revelation we would have to abandon biblical Christianity altogether, which is what he thought many of the critical scholars had done. To rebut these liberal views, Orr wrote on the virgin birth[29] and the resurrection.[30]

His book on the virgin birth was the published version of a series of lectures delivered in April 1907 in Fifth Avenue Presbyterian Church, New York, under the auspices of the Bible Teachers' Training School. In the preface, Orr makes his intentions clear: 'The aim of the lectures is to establish faith in the miracle of the Lord's Incarnation by Birth from the Virgin, to meet objections, and to show the intimate connection of fact and doctrine in this transcendent mystery.'[31] After laying out the essential case for the incarnation and the objections brought against it, Orr proceeds to analyse the texts. He looks at the Gospel witnesses to the incarnation and defends their credibility, looking too at the sources of these narratives. He also answers the objection that the story of the incarnation is found in a very limited number of New Testament

---

[29] James Orr, *The Virgin Birth of Christ* (New York: C. Scribner's Sons, 1907).
[30] James Orr, *The Resurrection of Jesus* (London: Hodder & Stoughton, 1908).
[31] The preface has no pagination.

texts and not even in all four Gospels. He sets the story of the incarnation in the context of the Old Testament revelation and dismisses ideas that it originated in pagan sources. Only after all this does he focus on the doctrinal and theological issues, emphasizing the importance for salvation of the fact that the second Person of the Trinity became a sinless human being. Finally, he sums up his argument in twenty-three propositions, which serve to sum up the argument of the whole book. He concludes:

> In the light of these propositions, I cannot acquiesce in the opinion that the article of the Virgin Birth is one doctrinally indifferent, or that can be legitimately dropped from the public creed of the Church. The rejection of this article would, in my judgement, be a mutilation of Scripture, a contradiction of the continuous testimony of the Church from Apostolic times, a weakening of the doctrine of the Incarnation, and a practical surrender of the Christian position into the hands of the advocates of a non-miraculous, purely humanitarian Christ – all on insufficient grounds.[32]

Orr's book on the resurrection was published a year later (1908) and followed the same general pattern as the book on the virgin birth. First, Orr lays out the objections of the critics to the idea of a bodily resurrection and then devotes a chapter to the idea of miracle and its significance for Christianity. This is followed by looking at the resurrection stories in the Gospels and an analysis of the credibility of those who claimed to have witnessed the risen Christ, as well as the way in which the resurrection of Christ was viewed by the early church. Once again, he dismisses the notion that ideas of resurrection had their origins in pagan myths. Finally, he demonstrates the doctrinal significance of the resurrection. He begins this final chapter by pointing out the intentions of the critics:

> It will probably be evident from the preceding discussion that a movement is at present in process which aims at nothing less than the dissolution of Christianity, as that has hitherto been understood. It is not simply the details of the recorded life of Jesus that are questioned but the whole conception of Christ's supernatural Person and work as set forth in the Gospels and Epistles, which is challenged. If the Virgin Birth is rejected at one end of the history, and the bodily Resurrection

---

[32] Orr, *Virgin Birth*, p. 229.

at the other, not less are the miracles and supernatural claims that lie between.[33]

Orr and evolution

If higher criticism of the Bible and Liberal Theology were the main challenges to orthodox Christianity in Orr's day, the other challenge was Darwinian evolution, which many saw as proving that the book of Genesis could not be relied upon in its account of human origins and particularly in its view that human beings were unique and made in the image of God. Orr engaged with these views in another book, which arose out of the Stone Lectures he gave at Princeton in 1903, published as *God's Image in Man and Its Defacement in the Light of Modern Denials*.[34] In this volume he sought to defend a doctrine of creation and especially the unique creation of human beings in God's image. In doing so, he also defended the biblical teaching on the origins of sin and evil, holding firmly to the doctrines of the fall and of original sin.

Orr was in no doubt that the newly developing views on science and evolution presented a serious challenge to Christian theology. He described this 'modern view' as 'a positively-conceived counter-view of the world, claiming to rest on scientific grounds, ably constructed and defended, yet in its fundamental ideas striking at the roots of the Christian system'.[35] Orr focused his attack on Ernst Haeckel's *The Riddle of the Universe*, which was published in German in 1899 and in English in 1901.[36] Haeckel was a scientist who propagated Darwin's work in Germany and supported Darwin's work by his own scientific researches. Orr sums up Haeckel's arguments in relation to the evolution of human beings:

1 There has been a slow and unbroken process of evolution from the lowest forms of organic life to the highest achievements of nature – Man . . .
2 This evolution is the result of natural causes which do not imply intelligence or purpose.
3 The immediate ancestors of man are the anthropoid apes . . .
4 This law of evolution applies to the mental and moral endowments, not less than to the physical structure of man.

---

[33] Orr, *Resurrection*, p. 265.
[34] Orr, *God's Image in Man and Its Defacement in the Light of Modern Denials* (New York: A. C. Armstrong and Son, 1908).
[35] Ibid., p. 4.
[36] <https://archive.org/details/riddleoftheunive034957mbp/page/n13/mode/2up> (accessed 10 March 2021).

5 The doctrine of the evolution of man from lower animals, by excluding belief in his essential distinction from the animals, is fatal to the assumption of a higher spiritual nature in man, and to belief in personal immortality.[37]

Contrary to what might have been expected, Orr did not offer a 'creationist' defence, or a simple denial of evolutionary theory. Instead, he affirmed what would later be called 'theistic evolution'. Other theologians of his time, including B. B. Warfield, also held this view. Orr believed that evolution was a mechanism used by God in his work of creation. The progress and outcomes of evolution are not to be understood as the results of pure chance but must be understood in the context of God's creative work. He wrote, 'No religious interest, I may take it for granted, is imperilled by a theory of evolution, viewed simply as a method of creation, provided certain conditions are fulfilled, and certain limits are observed.'[38] Orr believed in the unity of truth, arguing that the truth of science (about God's creation through which his general revelation comes) and the truth of Scripture (God's special revelation) can never be in conflict. He thus defended Christianity against those who said that science had disproved the biblical account of creation in Genesis. As a theistic evolutionist, he rejected the notion that human beings were descended from primates and insisted on the 'special creation' of humanity in the image of God, as taught in Scripture.

Orr the popular apologist

Later in his life, Orr gave much more attention to writing for a more general, rather than an academic, readership. Scorgie identifies one main reason for this, namely that his views had largely been rejected by the academic establishment and he was seeking another, more popular audience.[39] It may also be that he was seeing the effects of Liberal Theology in the churches and wanted to counter it with a positive account of traditional evangelical theology. After all, many in the pews were disturbed by the results of higher criticism, Liberal Theology and evolutionary theories and needed some reassurance that they could still trust in the Bible. Whatever the reason, he began to publish books for the general reader, normally made up of addresses given to public meetings or articles that had appeared in popular journals, on both sides of the Atlantic. These included

---

[37] Orr, *God's Image in Man*, pp. 82–83.
[38] Ibid., pp. 87–88.
[39] Scorgie, *Call for Continuity*, p. 140.

The Bible Under Trial,[40] and *Sidelights on Christian Doctrine*.[41] The twelve chapters in *The Bible Under Trial* were originally published in the *Life of Faith* magazine, a popular evangelical journal with close connections to the Keswick movement. In his preface to *Sidelights on Christian Doctrine*, Orr explains the chapters had their origins in addresses 'at various Conferences and Bible Schools in America'. He goes on, 'Perhaps the less formal nature of the Studies will adapt them better to the needs of those whom technical works on theology might repel.'

The subjects covered in these more popular volumes were the same as those addressed in his academic volumes but at a different level and in a different style. In *The Bible Under Trial*, Orr seeks to demonstrate the trustworthiness of the Bible in the face of various attacks. Among other things, he shows how a number of the critical scholars later changed their minds, or their views were rejected by the next generation of scholars. Similarly, difficulties raised by scholars sometimes found their answer in the work of scholars from a different discipline, such as the question of when Quirinius was governor of Syria.[42] Orr brings out many defences of the Bible, including some from science and archaeology. He deals with questions of ethics and also gives examples of discrepancies in Scripture that were later proved not to be such at all. In the end, he affirms trust in the Scriptures and encourages his readership to stand firm.

In *Sidelights on Christian Doctrine*, Orr speaks more directly to the doctrines of the Christian faith, their significance and their connection one with another. He deals with the doctrine of God at some length, in several chapters, defending the orthodox position and challenging the views of the critics. He goes on to do the same with the doctrines of humanity and sin. His chapters on Christ and his atoning work and union with Christ take us to the very heart of his understanding of the faith. He concludes with chapters on the Holy Spirit and then eschatology. It is almost a mini-systematic theology for church members, written in a language they could understand. It provides education, encouragement and spiritual hope.

The supreme example of Orr's determination to speak to a popular audience in the defence of orthodox biblical Christianity came with the invitation to contribute to *The Fundamentals*.[43] These volumes were the vision of two

---

[40] James Orr, *The Bible Under Trial* (London: Marshall Brothers, 1907).

[41] James Orr, *Sidelights on Christian Doctrine* (London: Marshall Brothers, 1909).

[42] Orr, *Bible Under Trial*, p. 33.

[43] The most accessible edition is R. A. Torrey and A. C. Dixon (eds.), *The Fundamentals: A Testimony to the Truth* (Grand Rapids, MI: Baker Book House, 1917). This was reprinted in 1970. It should be noted that the writers of *The Fundamentals* did not all share the extreme views of those who later took the name 'fundamentalist'.

brothers (Lyman and Milton Stewart), who commissioned and published articles that promoted orthodox evangelical theology, in opposition to Liberal Theology. There were sixty-four authors and their work was produced in twelve volumes, which were then distributed free of charge to ministers, missionaries, theological students, academics and many others, all over the world. In 1917, since many of the volumes were out of print, a four-volume edition was produced, containing most but not all of the original articles.

The articles contained in *The Fundamentals* were written by a mixture of significant academic theologians, ministers and some more popular writers. Most of them were living at the time but some articles from the eighteenth and nineteenth centuries were also included. They all agreed on the inspiration and authority of Scripture, although they disagreed on how that authority was to be understood. They also represented a wide range of theological views, including Reformed, Arminian, Dispensationalist and more. Orr contributed four articles to *The Fundamentals*: 'The Virgin Birth of Christ';[44] 'Science and Christian Faith';[45] 'The Early Narratives of Genesis';[46] and 'Holy Scripture and Modern Negations'.[47] As a contributor to *The Fundamentals*, Orr was identified as an evangelical theologian and a defender of orthodox biblical Christianity.

Orr and Scripture

Given that Orr spent most of his life engaged in the battle against Liberal Theology and the defence of orthodox, evangelical Christianity, one might expect that he would be highly regarded by evangelicals then and now. Sadly, that is not the case. Orr's views on Scripture attracted criticism from some of his evangelical contemporaries and continue to do so today. The problem for some was that Orr held to a 'high' view of the inspiration and authority of Scripture but did not hold to 'inerrancy'.[48] Since B. B. Warfield and the Princeton school affirmed inerrancy and since that school of thought held sway among many evangelicals at the time, Orr was regarded with some disappointment and suspicion. As Scorgie writes, 'Princeton spokesman William Brenton Greene, Jr., was predictably disappointed by a number of Orr's concessions.'[49]

---

[44] *The Fundamentals*, vol. 1 (vol. 2 in the 4-vol. 1917 edn). This was the first essay in the first volume of *The Fundamentals*.

[45] Ibid., vol. 4 (vol. 1 in the 4-vol. 1917 edn).

[46] Ibid., vol. 6 (vol. 1 in the 4-vol. 1917 edn).

[47] Ibid., vol. 9 (vol. 1 in the 4-vol. 1917 edn).

[48] See A. T. B. McGowan, 'Inerrancy', in *The Oxford Handbook of Divine Revelation* (Oxford: Oxford University Press, 2021), pp. 85–101.

[49] Scorgie, *Call for Continuity*, p. 99.

Despite the fact that Orr rejected Warfield's teaching on inerrancy, however, they respected one another. Orr spoke at Princeton in 1897, 1903 and 1907 and, as editor of *The International Standard Bible Encyclopaedia*,[50] invited Warfield to contribute the articles on 'Inspiration' and 'Revelation'.

Orr spelled out his doctrine of Scripture in his book *Revelation and Inspiration*.[51] His views on the importance of supernatural revelation, important in his opposition to Ritschlianism in particular and Liberal Theology more generally, played a part in establishing his doctrine of Scripture. Orr argues that revelation precedes inspiration, nevertheless arguing that they are *'closely and inseparably united'*.[52] Indeed, he says that '[r]evelation and inspiration thus go together, and conjointly give to the written word *a quality* which distinguishes it from any product of ordinary human wisdom'.[53] Despite this high view, Orr was very reluctant to use the expression 'verbal inspiration', noting that it 'is one to which so great ambiguity attaches that it is now very commonly avoided by careful writers'.[54] Instead, he preferred the phrase 'plenary inspiration'.[55] That having been said, he understood why some writers used 'verbal inspiration':

> It opposes the theory that revelation and inspiration have regard only to thoughts and ideas, while the language in which these ideas are clothed is left to the unaided faculties of the sacred penman. This is a defective view. Thought of necessity takes shape and is expressed in words. If there is inspiration at all, it must penetrate words as well as thought, must mould the expression, and make the language employed the living medium of the idea to be conveyed.[56]

As noted above, just as Orr was unhappy with the expression 'verbal inspiration', so also he was unhappy with the word 'inerrancy'. He wrote:

> It is urged, *e.g.*, that unless we can demonstrate what is called the 'inerrancy' of the Biblical record, down even to its minutest details, the whole edifice of belief in revealed religion falls to the ground. This, on the face of it, is a most suicidal position for any defender of revelation to take up.[57]

[50] James Orr (ed.), *The International Standard Bible Encyclopaedia* (Chicago: Howard-Severance, 1915).
[51] James Orr, *Revelation and Inspiration* (London: Duckworth, 1909).
[52] Ibid., p. 199.
[53] Ibid., p. 200.
[54] Ibid., p. 209.
[55] Ibid., p. 196.
[56] Ibid., p. 209.
[57] Ibid., pp. 197–198.

He recognized that some writers, such as Warfield, advocated the inerrancy of the Scriptures but urged caution:

> such 'inerrancy' can never be demonstrated with a cogency which entitles it to rank as the foundation of a belief in inspiration. It must remain to those who hold it a doctrine of faith; a deduction from what they deem to be implied in an inspiration established independently of it; not a ground of belief in the inspiration.[58]

One of the reasons for fundamentalists regarding Orr with suspicion was what he said about the 'Limits of Biblical Inspiration'. He writes, 'The limitations attaching to inspiration arise from the causes already specified – the *progressiveness* of revelation, the varying *degrees* of inspiration, and the *fragmentariness* or other defects of the materials with which inspiration deals.'[59] He then spells out in more detail each of these. First, 'inspiration *cannot transcend the existing stage of revelation*'.[60] Second, another limitation 'arises from the recognition of *degrees in inspiration*'.[61] He compares this with the varying degrees of the operation of the Spirit in history, sometimes acting in revival and sometimes 'operating on a lower plane'.[62] Third,

> account has to be taken also of the character and quality of *the sources of information* inspiration has to work with, and of the fact that, while adequate for the ends of revelation, these sources, judged by a literary standard, may be in various ways *defective*.[63]

After pointing out a number of the 'defects' to which he is referring he says:

> Is inspiration to take responsibility for these defects? Or is a supernatural communication to be assumed, in each case, to supply the missing word, or correct the misspelt name or corrupted number? This cannot be reasonably maintained, nor does the result in the books show that such correction was made. It did not need to be for the ends of inspiration.[64]

---

[58] Ibid., p. 199.
[59] Ibid., p. 175.
[60] Ibid.
[61] Ibid., p. 177.
[62] Ibid., p. 178.
[63] Ibid., p. 179.
[64] Ibid., p. 180.

None of this should be taken to mean that Orr did not have a high view of Scripture. Towards the end of the book he can say:

It remains the fact that the Bible, impartially interpreted and judged, is free from demonstrable error in its statements, and harmonious in its teachings, to a degree that of itself creates an irresistible impression of a supernatural factor in its origin.[65]

Indeed, he believes that in their central concerns the defenders of inerrancy are not far away from his own position:

The most searching inquiry still leaves them with a Scripture, supernaturally inspired to be an infallible guide in the great matters for which it was given – the knowledge of the will of God for their salvation in Christ Jesus, instruction in the way of holiness, and the 'hope of eternal life, which God, who cannot lie, promised before times eternal'.[66]

Orr's convictions about the uniqueness of the Scriptures are evident in his book *The Faith of a Modern Christian*,[67] where he addresses a difficult question: Why should Christians regard their Scriptures as of a different order from the holy books of other religions? In affirming the uniqueness of the Christian Scriptures, Orr makes three points about them. First, 'they *claim to embody a special, supernatural* revelation – the discovery of a gracious purpose of God's love for the redemption and blessing of mankind'.[68] Second, 'they *possess a structure and purposefulness* which all other sacred books lack'.[69] Third, Holy Scripture has '*a spiritual quality, force, illumination, in the record itself*, emanating, as it could only do, from a special presence of the Holy Spirit, equipping and qualifying the sacred writers for the special task'.[70]

Orr stands as an example to evangelical theologians today who believe that the word 'inerrancy' tends towards rationalism and fundamentalism and promises more than it delivers. He demonstrates that it is possible to hold to Scripture as the Word of God without following Warfield. In other words, there is more than one evangelical method of holding to the full authority of

---

[65] Ibid., p. 216.
[66] Ibid., p. 217.
[67] James Orr, *The Faith of a Modern Christian* (London: Hodder & Stoughton, 1910).
[68] Ibid., p. 7.
[69] Ibid., p. 11.
[70] Ibid., p. 15.

God's speaking by his Spirit through the Scriptures. Orr was not alone in holding to this position; a similar view of Scripture was also to be found in two of his contemporary European theologians, Abraham Kuyper and Herman Bavinck.[71]

Orr's final years were taken up with the huge task of editing the *International Standard Bible Encyclopaedia*.[72] This was his final contribution to the promotion and defence of conservative, evangelical theology and was published in 1915, two years after his death. It contained articles by over 200 writers and was highly regarded.

Although, as noted above, Orr invited Warfield to contribute the chapters on 'Inspiration' and 'Revelation', he himself contributed many articles, including 'The Bible'. It is in this article that he underlines two points that are important for an understanding of his doctrine of Scripture. First, like Calvin, he is unconcerned about minor apparent conflicts or textual issues; and second, while reaffirming his rejection of inerrancy, he nevertheless upholds the highest view of the authority of Scripture. As he wrote:

> It might be shown that these claims made by New Testament writers for the Old Testament and for themselves are borne out by what the Old Testament itself teaches of prophetic inspiration, of wisdom as the gift of God's spirit, and of the light, holiness, saving virtue and sanctifying power continually ascribed to God's 'law,' 'words,' 'statutes,' 'command-ments,' 'judgments' (see above). This is the ultimate test of 'inspiration' – that to which Paul likewise appeals – its power to 'make wise unto salvation through faith which is in Christ Jesus' (2Ti 3:15) – its profit-ableness 'for teaching, for reproof, for correction, for instruction which is in righteousness' (2Ti 3:16) – all to the end 'that the man of God may be complete, furnished completely unto every good work' (2Ti 3:17). Nothing is here determined as to 'inerrancy' in minor historical, geographical, chronological details, in which some would wrongly put the essence of inspiration; but it seems implied that at least there is no error which can interfere with or nullify the utility of Scripture for the ends specified. Who that brings Scripture to its own tests of inspiration, will deny that, judged as a whole, it fulfils them?

---

[71] For a fuller account of Orr's views on Scripture, see A. T. B. McGowan, *The Divine Spiration of Scripture* (Nottingham: Apollos, 2007), pp. 126–139, from which much of the above is drawn.

[72] See <www.internationalstandardbible.com> (accessed 10 March 2021).

Orr and the atonement

If Orr's view of Scripture was sometimes criticized, no one could doubt his orthodoxy in relation to the atonement. In *God's Image in Man*, he wrote this:

> In various well-known passages in the Gospels Jesus expressly attributes to His sufferings and death a redeeming efficacy, and connects them with the forgiveness of sins and life of the world. More fully and clearly His death is uniformly represented in the Apostolic Gospel as a true propitiatory sacrifice for sin – the one means by which guilt is purged, sin put away, peace made with God, reconciliation effected.[73]

In spelling out this position, Orr affirms his belief that 'the world is in a state of *sin* and *guilt* from which it *needs* redemption'.[74] To obtain such redemption, God has provided a Saviour. In explaining the mechanics of this salvation, Orr points his readers to what Paul teaches in Romans 5, regarding the parallel between Adam and Christ. In other words, those 'in Adam' die and those 'in Christ' will be made alive. As Orr says, 'The representative principle brought us under condemnation; the same representative principle works deliverance.'[75]

Orr is also orthodox in his understanding of the significance of the death of Christ on the cross. He views Christ's submission to death as the 'kernel' of his reconciling work. It was in his death that the judgment of God was expressed upon the sin of the human race.[76] In a later volume, Orr reaffirms his convictions regarding the atonement. He says that 'it is in the *work of atonement* for sins which Christ accomplished by His death that Scripture always concentrates the efficacy of His appearance for our salvation'. To that end, the atonement can be seen as a propitiation for sin by which reconciliation was effected and peace made between human beings and God.[77] Orr goes so far as to say, 'The atonement is the basis on which the whole superstructure of redemption rests. To deny it is, in effect, to take the foundation from the Gospel.'[78] Orr notes that the doctrine of the atonement was no longer central to the preaching of the church in his day and believes that this can be shown to derive from two false convictions. First, the denial of the holiness of God as the just judge (often replaced by weak notions of love and fatherhood) and a denial of the sinfulness

---

[73] Orr, *God's Image in Man*, p. 273.
[74] Ibid., p. 274 (emphasis original).
[75] Ibid., p. 277.
[76] Ibid.
[77] Orr, *Sidelights on Christian Doctrine*, p. 126.
[78] Ibid.

of human beings, through evolutionary ideas about moral development. Orr insists that the doctrine of the propitiatory sacrifice of Christ for sinners as the only way of salvation must be returned to the very centre of preaching if the gospel is not to be lost.[79]

Conclusion

Professor James Orr became a theologian at the very time when higher criticism and Liberal Theology were beginning to have an impact in Scotland and England. He made it his business to read and understand the critics and the Liberal theologians, so that he could respond to them from a conservative, evangelical perspective. His many books, both academic and popular, were designed to challenge Liberal Theology and to uphold the traditional orthodoxy of the church. He recognized the importance of biblical criticism but challenged the rationalistic and anti-supernatural presuppositions of many of its exponents. Instead, he insisted on a proper recognition of the supernatural revelation that has come from God to human beings and that must be determinative of all Christian thought and action. He was one of the most significant apologetic and dogmatic theologians of his day and did a great deal to maintain the faith of many believers, whose convictions about God, the Bible and human salvation had been undermined by the critical scholars.

Scottish Reformed theology has been hugely influenced in the past hundred years by English Puritanism and by the theology of Old Princeton. James Orr is not well known today but he represents an indigenous Scottish theology, which offers an alternative to these other imported strands in Reformed theology and encourages us also to explore connections between his work and that of Dutch Reformed theology. For these reasons, Orr has an important place in the pantheon of twentieth-century British theologians.

---

[79] Ibid., pp. 127–129.

2

James Denney

THOMAS V. FINDLAY[1]

James Denney was an evangelical theologian of the late nineteenth and early twentieth century. He was born in Paisley in 1857, but a few months after his birth the family moved to Greenock on the Firth of Clyde, where his father, a joiner by trade, was a partner in a small business. It was in Greenock that James received his formal education at the Highlanders Academy, while his religious upbringing was within his family, who were active members of the Reformed Presbyterian Church. His father was a leading elder in this small denomination that traced its roots back to the Covenanters of the seventeenth century. It was very conservative in theology, seeking to preserve its members from the 'canker of rationalism' displayed in modern developments in biblical studies that challenged 'in various ways the supreme authority of scripture'.[2] Such was the theological environment in the church in which Denney grew up during his school years and it was with this background that he went to Glasgow University in 1874.

At university, Richard Jebb was Denney's professor of classics. Jebb had studied at Cambridge under the great biblical and classical scholar J. B. Lightfoot, and was a formative influence in teaching Denney to translate, interpret and analyse ancient texts critically. Edward Caird taught philosophy and John Veitch was professor of logic.[3] Denney impressed all three of them and his name is recorded fifteen times in the list of university prizes. It was a different young man who graduated in 1879. He was not at all persuaded by the Hegelian Idealism of Caird, but Jebb had taught him how to read and interpret ancient texts critically, and Veitch had inspired him with a passion for critical thinking

---

[1] In editing this study-group paper for publication, I have deleted introductory remarks, added sentences with fuller background information and two evaluative paragraphs. (T. A. N.)

[2] James M. Gordon, *James Denney (1856–1917): An Intellectual and Contextual Biography* (Milton Keynes: Paternoster Press, 2006), p. 35.

[3] Denney won the class prize for logic in 1877 and excelled in the discipline to such an extent that, on the death of Veitch in 1894, his friend John P. Struthers of Greenock urged him to stand as his successor for the chair. See John Paterson Struthers, *Life and Letters of John Paterson Struthers* (London, n.d.), p. 225.

in the pursuit of truth. For all this, however, he never lost his conviction of the greatness of Christ and this Christocentrism became a standard by which he evaluated the current optimism of Idealism's view of divine–human relations.[4]

The authority of the Bible

While he was a student, the majority in the Reformed Presbyterian Church united with the Free Church of Scotland, formed at the Disruption of 1843 when the evangelicals in the established Church of Scotland, led by Thomas Chalmers, left to form a new denomination free of state control or interference. James Denney thus found himself in a much larger denomination with a vigorous intellectual life. In 1879 the Free Church Presbytery of Greenock accepted Denney as a candidate for the ministry and he entered the Free Church College in Glasgow. He began his theological studies just as the tension between theological orthodoxy and the new discipline of the historical and literary criticism of the Bible had reached its height. To understand Denney's writings on the authority of Scripture, we must understand something of the heated controversy that engulfed the Free Church of Scotland while he was a student.

Criticism and the 'believing critics'

The Free Church was in the throes of theological controversy over the libel action taken against Professor William Robertson Smith of Aberdeen after an anonymous article published against him in 1876 for his article 'Bible' in the ninth edition of the *Encyclopaedia Britannica*. The action dragged on until May 1880, when Smith was acquitted of heresy. His opponents, however, would not let the matter rest; and when a further article by Smith appeared in the next volume of the *Encyclopaedia Britannica* the matter was reignited and after a debate in the Assembly, Smith was removed from his chair in the Free Church College in Aberdeen. Three of Denney's professors at the Free Church College in Glasgow were deeply involved in the controversy, defending Smith: A. B. Bruce, James S. Candlish and T. M. Lindsay. They were all committed to the view that the historical and literary criticism of the Bible was not contrary to orthodox Christian belief and were part of the group of Free Church professors who have become known as 'the believing critics'. We cannot understand James Denney's view of the authority of Scripture without understanding something of this debate that raged during his time as a theology student and

4 Gordon, *James Denney*, pp. 57–61.

in which his teachers were deeply involved. The young student brought to his perspective on the debate the critical thinking he had learned under Jebb and Veitch.

A. B. Bruce, Professor of Apologetics and New Testament Exegesis at the Free Church College in Glasgow, had been the minister at the Broughty Ferry East Free Church from 1868 until 1875 and Denney was to follow in his footsteps from 1886 until 1897, when he too moved to teach in the college in Glasgow. At the final debate in the Assembly in 1881, when Smith was removed from his chair at Aberdeen, Bruce made a final impassioned appeal in his defence 'without any note of theological bitterness', in which he said:

> I cannot sit down without expressing my sorrow and shame at what is about to be done. I never expected to see the day when such a spectacle could be witnessed in our Church. Had I foreseen it, I do not know that I should have been very much inclined to be either a minister or a professor in this Church ... We humbly think she is doing great wrong, but we count surely on a reaction and a noble repentance in which she will cancel the ostracism which she is about to exercise against her ablest servant and devoted son.[5]

In 1891 Bruce edited and published a work of 274 pages entitled *Inspiration and Inerrancy*,[6] containing the inaugural address of Dr Charles A. Briggs,[7] together with two papers supporting Briggs, one by Lewellyn J. Evans and the other by Henry Preserved Smith. Briggs was the leading exponent of 'believing criticism' in the Presbyterian Church in the USA, strongly opposed to the view of B. B. Warfield, that we must not only speak of the inspiration, but of the *inerrancy* of Scripture. Bruce himself contributed a thirty-five-page introduction and no doubt was left in the mind of any as to where he stood on the issue.

It was a similar situation with T. M. Lindsay. Smith and Lindsay had been close friends since their student days at New College, Edinburgh,[8] and in 1870 Lindsay campaigned on Smith's behalf when he applied for the Hebrew Chair at Aberdeen. The *Encyclopaedia Britannica*, in which Smith's article on 'Bible' gave so much cause for alarm, also contained an article by Lindsay on

---

[5] See John Sutherland Black and George Chrystal, *The Life of William Robertson Smith* (London: Adam and Charles Black, 1912), p. 439.

[6] A. B. Bruce, *Inspiration and Inerrancy* (London: James Clark, 1891).

[7] Briggs was inaugurated as Professor of Biblical Theology at Union Theological Seminary in New York in 1891 and his inaugural lecture was on 'The Authority of Holy Scripture'. On the basis of this lecture he was tried for heresy in 1892 by the Presbytery of New York and acquitted.

[8] Black and Chrystal, *Life of William Robertson Smith*, p. 83 and *passim*.

'Inspiration' and although decidedly taking a similar line to Smith, no charge was ever made against him. Lindsay was, if not the most vociferous, certainly the most vocal protagonist of Smith. In his speech to the Assembly in 1881 he declared:

> I take my stand . . . on the critical position. (Cheers.) Another thing is this: that with everything that Professor Smith has said about prophecy except one – in my way, and according to my understanding of what he has said – I agree with him.[9]

The situation was a little different with Candlish. His friendship and support of Smith was as strong as the others', but he was not so publicly demonstrative or vocal. He was, however, Smith's constant advisor and a member of the original subcommittee appointed 'to consider the article "Bible" . . . contributed by Professor Smith to the *Encyclopaedia Britannica*, and to report to the committee at its next meeting'.[10] Candlish also dissented from parts of the report on the ground that 'it is unnecessary and inexpedient for the Committee to express an opinion *as to the force of the evidence* which is supposed to establish the non-Mosaic origin of some of the Deuteronomic laws'.[11]

Denney in debate

To understand James Denney's view of the authority of Scripture, it is important to see the context of the great debate that was dividing the Presbyterian world in his years as a student, and reverberating through other evangelical traditions and denominations. The upshot of examining this background material is to help us to understand that long before Denney became a minister of the United Free Church of Scotland (as it became through union with the United Presbyterian Church in 1900), or a professor in one of its colleges, both his university and college education predisposed him to an approach to the authority of the Scriptures that regarded their inerrancy as unnecessary for the fulfilling of their divine intention for the Christian church. Indeed, before he had to deal with the matter in a formal academic setting at Chicago in 1894, he had already nailed his colours to the mast. In his Bible studies to his congregation at Broughty Ferry, later published in commentary form in the *Expositor's Bible* in

---

[9] Ibid., p. 449.
[10] *Special Report of the College Committee*, Edinburgh, 1877, p. 1.
[11] Ibid., p. 31 (emphasis mine).

the first part of 1894,[12] commenting on the glory of the new covenant (2 Cor. 3:9–11), Denney said:

> These qualities of the Christian Dispensation, which constitute its new-ness, are too readily lost sight of . . . In a Protestant scholasticism this glorious Gospel has . . . been lost oftener than once . . . [I]t is lost . . . when an unlearned piety swears by verbal, even by literal, inspiration, and takes up to mere documents an attitude which in principle is fatal to Christianity.[13]

And even more forcefully, in 1891, in his introduction to the English edition of Charles Augustus Briggs' inaugural lecture, in *Inspiration and Inerrancy*, A. B. Bruce quotes Denney from a debate on the 'Revision of the Confession of Faith' in the General Assembly of the Free Church of Scotland: 'For a mere verbal inerrancy I care not one straw. It is worth nothing to me; it would be worth nothing if it were there and it is not.'[14]

In 1894, while still a parish minister, Denney fulfilled an invitation to give a series of lectures at Chicago Theological Seminary, a Congregational insti-tution. His ninth lecture was on 'Holy Scripture'. Although he was not aware of the educational level of his Chicago audience,[15] Denney was certainly well aware not only of the theological issues involved in the matter of biblical authority in the light of modern criticism, but also of the emotional response it was stirring in the churches. Initially, he had thought on 'one (or two) [lectures] on the Bible, or rather on the word of God as a means of grace and as a spiritual authority',[16] but settled on only one, albeit not the one that was eventually printed.[17] In that unprinted lecture he opens with a short review of the diverse place the Bible occupies in various Protestant creeds, and concludes:

---

[12] See Struthers' *Letters*, p. 218.

[13] James Denney, *The Second Epistle to the Corinthians* (London: Hodder & Stoughton, 1910), pp. 125–126.

[14] A. B. Bruce, *Inspiration and Inerrancy* (London: James Clarke, 1891), p. 4. Bruce identifies Denney as the source of the quotation on p. 5.

[15] See W. Robertson Nicoll (ed.), *Letters of Principal James Denney to W. Robertson Nicoll, 1893–1917* (London: Hodder & Stoughton, 1920), pp. 4–5.

[16] Ibid., p. 4.

[17] See J. Denney, *Studies in Theology* (London: Hodder & Stoughton, 1894), p. v. The original lecture is reproduced by Dr Gordon as Appendix 2, pp. 236–253, of his biography of Denney. Denney writes in *Studies in Theology*, p. 20, 'The next lecture will be on the Bible and its place in the Church. This has been a burning question in Scotland, and is so, I understand, in some of the American churches.' Three years prior to this A. B. Bruce had published his edition of *Inspiration and Inerrancy*, in which Denney was quoted, so Denney must certainly have been aware of the 'battle for the Bible' that was sweeping the American churches.

These phenomena ... show that in the use actually made of the Bible, and in the conclusions actually drawn from it, there may be substantial agreement among men who are not agreed historically about the place Scripture should hold in a dogmatic system, or the precise nature of the authority which should be ascribed to it.[18]

One gets the feeling that Denney was trying to soften the blow of what was to come by demonstrating diversity on the issue within historical Protestantism. If he was, it would seem that he was not entirely successful.

In 1895, Denney was awarded a DD by the University of Glasgow. He had already received the same honour from Chicago and was later to receive honorary doctorates from Aberdeen and Princeton. In 1897, he succeeded J. S. Candlish as Professor of Practical and Systematic Theology at the Free Church College in Glasgow (not without opposition in the General Assembly). Two years later he succeeded A. B. Bruce in the chair of New Testament Language, Literature and Theology, being elected Principal of the college by the General Assembly of the United Free Church in 1915. The first decade of the twentieth century saw the publication of his major works on the atonement, *The Death of Christ* (1902), *The Atonement and the Modern Mind* (1903), *Jesus and the Gospel* (1908). *The Church and the Kingdom* (1910) followed and *The Christian Doctrine of Reconciliation* was published posthumously in 1917.

Denney on biblical authority

What, then, was Denney's view of the authority of Scripture? In the first place, Scripture was, for Denney, a *means of grace*. He said:

> The valuable parts of the [Westminster] Confession, those which still appeal to the Christian conscience and awaken a response in it ... are the parts which treat of the work of Christ ... saving faith and repentance unto life ... Christian liberty and liberty of conscience ... Holy Scripture, or The Word of God, *as the supreme means of grace*.[19]

> The Bible is ... *the* means through which God communicates with man, making him know what is in His heart towards him. It must be known and experienced in this character before we can form a doctrine concerning it. We cannot *first* define its qualities, and *then* use it accordingly;

---

[18] Gordon, *James Denney*, p. 237.
[19] Denney, *Jesus and the Gospel* (London: Hodder & Stoughton, 1908), p. 392 (emphasis added).

we cannot start with its inspiration, and then discover its use for faith or practice. It is through an experience of its power that words like inspiration come to have any meaning.[20]

The authority of the Scriptures is not given to us by any antecedent ecclesiastical dogma, but by the self-authenticating truth 'of the avowedly practical end which scripture has to serve'.[21]

Christ Himself and all the reconciling virtue associated with Him are themselves mediated to us in numberless ways ... But though this is important it is not the main thing. The main thing ... is the New Testament witness to Jesus.[22]

What the testimony of the Spirit does guarantee in our experience is what Luther calls *the Gospel*, or the word of God. That word of God certainly reaches us thro' Scripture; but on the mere ground of the Spirit's testimony to it we cannot say more about Scripture than this. It is the word of God or Gospel which lies behind everything; which has created both the church and the Bible, which is the standard for criticising both, and which give to both whatever authority they have. But for that very reason it cannot be identified, off hand, with either.[23]

In this respect the authority of Scripture parallels that authority of the One of whom it testifies. 'You search the scriptures,' Jesus said, 'because you think that in them you have eternal life; and it is they that bear witness to me' (John 5:39, RSV). And what we find when we search the Scriptures is that the authority of Christ, as distinct from that of the scribes, was 'self-authenticating' and had 'the moral weight of the speaker's personality behind it'.[24] In contrast, that of the scribes 'was a deduction or application of some legal maxim connected with a respectable name'.[25] '[Christ's] precepts are legal in form, but He came to abolish legalism.'[26] The authority of the Scripture does not lie in the recorded words of Jesus:

[20] Denney, *Studies in Theology*, p. 203.
[21] Ibid., p. 21.
[22] Denney, *The Christian Doctrine of Reconciliation* (London: Hodder & Stoughton, 1918), p. 8.
[23] Gordon, *James Denney*, pp. 240–241.
[24] James Denney, 'Authority of Christ', in James Hastings (ed.), *Dictionary of Christ and the Gospels* (Edinburgh: T&T Clark, 1906), vol. 1, p. 146.
[25] Ibid.
[26] Ibid., p. 147.

What commands conscience in the most startling words of Jesus is the truth and love which dictate them, but to recognize the truth and love is to recognize that no form of words is binding of itself . . . Jesus is our authority, but His words are not our statutes; we are not under law, even the law of His words, but under grace – that is under the inspiration of His personality . . . There is an authority in Him to which no words, not even His own, can ever be equal.[27]

It is only as we are sensitive to this aspect of the words of Scripture, words as vehicles of the gospel, that is, of the fact that 'in Christ God was reconciling the world to himself, not counting their trespasses against them' (2 Cor. 5:19, RSV), and realize that 'one has died for all' (2 Cor. 5:14, RSV), that Scripture fulfils the end it was designed to serve:

> To Him bear all the Scriptures witness; and it is as a testimony to Him, the Bearer of sin, the Redeemer who gave His life a ransom for us, that we acknowledge them. This is the burden of the Bible, the one fundamental omnipresent truth to which the Holy Spirit bears witness by and with the word in our hearts. This, at bottom, is what we mean when we say that the Scripture is inspired.[28]

> When we read the New Testament with susceptible minds, we listen to the voice of those who were once themselves estranged from God, but have been reconciled to Him through Christ, and are letting us into the secret of their new life; it is the nearest approach we can make, and therefore the most vital, to the reconciling power which streamed from Christ Himself.[29]

In their controversy with Rome, Protestant theologians found it

> necessary to find an authority which could be conveniently opposed to that of the Pope . . . and betook themselves to the Bible . . . They identified it *simpliciter* with that word of God which had come to Luther through it, which the Spirit had guaranteed to his experience, and which he freely used to criticise all tradition, including the tradition which fixed the canon itself.[30]

---

[27] Ibid., p. 148.
[28] J. Denney, *The Death of Christ* (London: Hodder & Stoughton, 1902), pp. 313–314.
[29] Denney, *Reconciliation*, p. 9.
[30] Denney, Lecture IX Holy Scripture, in Gordon, *James Denney*, p. 241.

Denney endorsed the view of one German scholar:

> So far as is known, the notion of a book fallen direct from heaven[31] ... was never applied to the Bible as such ... Luther's lively piety, like the oldest Christianity, combines faith in divine inspiration with quite human ideas as to the method: he gives a vivid picture of the way in which one prophet uses the writings of the others ... But orthodoxy did not follow him here. It ranged itself on the side of the strictly supernatural idea of inspiration, and carried the view to its extremist consequences. The Biblical authors are only the hands and pens of the Holy Spirit. They are perhaps *notarii et actuarii* but never can they be called *auctores*. That epithet belongs to God or to the Holy Ghost alone. From Him proceeds not only the impulse to write, but also the matter and the method (*suggestio rerum et verborum*). In the end all human participation in the composition of Scripture is denied.[32]

Agreeing with this, Denney declared, in an unguarded and unfortunate (unfortunate considering the theological climate of the times) turn of phrase:

> a more extraordinary perversion than this of the Reformation doctrine of the word of God no ingenuity could imagine. This Protestant doctrine of inspiration is literally the most stupendous example on record of lying for God; of deliberate shutting of the eyes to the most palpable and obtrusive facts.[33]

Denney writes, 'It is a commonplace of modern theology that no doctrine has any value except as it is based on experience.'[34] For Denney the *experience* of the doctrine of the inspiration of Scripture was co-terminus with the experience of the reconciling love of God through the atoning death of Christ:

> We do not believe in inspiration because we find something in Isaiah which we do not find in Æschylus ...; nor because we find something in Paul which we do not find in Plato ...; we believe in inspiration because in the whole Bible ... there is a unity of mind and spirit and purpose which shines out on us at last in the atoning work of Christ ... The Cross dominates everything. It interprets everything. It puts all things in their

---

[31] See Eusebius on the Helkesaites, *Ecclesiastical History* VI, p. xxviii.
[32] Ernst von Dobschütz, 'Bible in the Church', in James Hastings (ed.), *Encyclopaedia of Religion and Ethics* (Edinburgh: T&T Clark, 1909), vol. 2, p. 589.
[33] Gordon, *James Denney*, pp. 241–242.
[34] Denney, *Reconciliation*, p. 7.

true relations to each other. Usually those who are perplexed about the inspiration of the Bible discuss their difficulties with no consideration of what the Bible means as a whole; and yet it is only as a whole that we can attach any meaning to its being inspired. There is no sense in saying every separate sentence is inspired; we know that every separate sentence is not. There are utterances of bad men in the Bible, and suggestions of the devil . . . We never know what inspiration is until Scripture has resolved itself for us into a unity. That unity, I venture to say, will be its testimony to a love in God which we do not earn, which we can never repay, but which in our sins comes to meet us with mercy, dealing, nevertheless, with our sins in all earnest, and at infinite cost doing right by God's holy law in regard to them; a love which becomes incarnate in the Lamb of God bearing the sin of the world, and putting it away by the sacrifice of Himself. It is in its testimony to this that the unity of Scripture and its inspiration consists, and whoever believes in this believes in inspiration in the only sense which can be rationally attached to the word.[35]

He said:

The infallibility of the Scriptures is not a mere verbal inerrancy or historical accuracy, but an infallibility of power to save. The Word of God infallibly carries God's power to save souls. If a man submit his heart and mind to the Spirit of God speaking in it, he will infallibly become a new creature in Christ Jesus. That is the only infallibility I believe in.[36]

Some more conservative evangelicals have found Denney's view of the authority of Scripture hard to stomach.[37] The heirs of Warfield have regarded it as an unstable position, damaging to biblical authority and leading to the slippery slope that ends in outright liberalism, rejecting miracles, denying the atonement and the deity of Christ and ending in some kind of vaguely Christian humanism. But some things may be said to prevent us coming to such a conclusion. First, one must understand the historical context of impassioned controversy. Denney was an intense preacher, passionate for truth and not given to mincing his words. Some allowance must be made for his tendency to use trenchant phrases rather than those that might seek to heal division. That was typical of his generation. Second, it must be noted that the key issue was the

---

[35] Denney, *Death of Christ*, pp. 314–317.
[36] As quoted by Bruce, *Inspiration and Inerrancy*, p. 4.
[37] This is the first of my added paragraphs. (T. A. N.)

validity of biblical criticism. Many of those who voted for the dismissal of W. Robertson Smith or against James Denney's appointment were opposed to biblical criticism as such. That is not the position even of conservative evangelicalism today, but is rather the position that later became known as 'fundamentalism'. A host of biblical scholars such as F. F. Bruce, Donald Guthrie, Howard Marshall and numerous others down to the present day have in fact followed in the footsteps of the 'believing critics' of Denney's day while affirming the full inspiration of Scripture. Third, terminology can confuse the issues. Denney had positive ways of talking about the 'inspiration' of Scripture, even its 'infallibility', and his opposition to the term 'inerrancy', regarded as so important by many evangelicals in the USA, has been shared by most British evangelical biblical scholars.[38] In contrast with his stance on Scripture, Denney's understanding of the apostolic doctrine of the atoning work of Christ has been strongly affirmed by all evangelicals, and to that we now turn.

The apostolic doctrine of the atonement

Denney's treatment of the atonement begins by seeking the answers to two questions. The first is, what does the New Testament teach about the death of Christ? In *Jesus and the Gospel*, Denney says, 'It is in the Church and through its testimony to Jesus that whatever knowledge we have of Him . . . has been preserved.'[39] And so, 'The first [question] is quite simple: is the conception of the Christian religion which prevails and has always prevailed in the Church borne out by the New Testament?'[40]

The second question is, what is it that makes the gospel necessary?

Is it man's distrust of God? Man's dislike, suspicion, alienation? Is it the special direction of vice in human nature, or its debilitating corrupting effects? It is none of these things, nor is it all of them together. What makes the situation serious, what necessitates a gospel, *is that the world, in virtue of its sin, lies under the condemnation of God*. His wrath abides upon it. That wrath is revealed from heaven against all ungodliness and

---

[38] See A. T. B. McGowan, *The Divine Spiration of Scripture: Challenging Evangelical Perspectives* (Nottingham: Apollos, 2007).

[39] Denney, *Jesus and the Gospel*, p. 4.

[40] Ibid., p. 5. See also Denney, *Death of Christ*, pp. v, vi: 'There have been conspicuous examples of . . . treatises on the Atonement, standing in no discoverable relation to the New Testament. The proportions of average current Christianity are not those of apostolic Christianity; and if the latter is in any sense normal, it is desirable that we should rectify our impressions by it. To aid in this, by setting the death of Christ in that relief in which it stands out in the New Testament, is part of the writer's purpose.'

unrighteousness in man; and it is in view of this . . . that the righteousness and love of God are revealed in the Gospel.[41]

And it is with this simple question and its answer that we are plunged into the middle of the New Testament teaching on the atonement. It is the essence of the nature of God as holiness and love that determines his divine reaction in the condemnation of sin:

> For thou art not a God who delights in wickedness;
>   evil may not sojourn with thee.
> (Ps. 5:4, RSV)

We must not misconceive the character of this wrath . . . The wrath of God is no arbitrary passionate outburst; it is not, as wrath so often is with us, a fury of selfish resentment. 'Evil shall not dwell with Thee,' says the Psalmist; and in that simple word we have the root of the matter. *The wrath of God is, as it were, the instinct of self-preservation in the Divine nature; it is the eternal repulsion, by the Holy One, of all evil.*[42]

It is 'the absolute, implacable hostility of the divine holiness to every form of moral evil',[43] the persistent, inexorable, absolute repulsion of God of all that is evil; and it is because of his holy nature that God's reaction to sin can *only be* one of eradication and annihilation. Toleration, indulgence or lenity would not be an expression of compassion or understanding, but the divine demise. The result of such wrath is seen in 2 Samuel 6:6–7:

> And when they came to the threshing floor of Nacon, Uzzah put out his hand to the ark of God and took hold of it, for the oxen stumbled. And the anger of the LORD was kindled against Uzzah; and God smote him there because he put forth his hand to the ark; and he died there beside the ark of God.
> (RSV)

Man's sin came into contact with divine holiness and the result was death. God does not – indeed he cannot – treat sin as a mere shortcoming or misdemeanour

---

[41] Denney, *Studies in Theology*, pp. 102–103 (emphasis added).

[42] Comment on 1 Thess. 1:10, in James Denney, *The Epistles to the Thessalonians* (London: Hodder & Stoughton, 1892), p. 62 (emphasis added). See also P. T. Forsyth, *The Work of Christ* (Glasgow: Fontana, 1965), p. 86: 'Without a holy God there would be no problem with atonement. It is the holiness of God's love that necessitates the atoning cross.'

[43] G. O. Griffith, as quoted by Leon Morris, *The Apostolic Preaching of the Cross* (London: Tyndale Press, 1955), p. 177.

to be regarded as of little consequence. When Anselm, in his *Cur deus homo*, asks his young interlocutor, 'Tell me then what payment you make God for your sin?' (ch. XX), and Boso attempts to list all the sacrifices that he would and does make, concluding that 'I should suppose that a single repentant feeling on my part would blot out this sin', the saint answers, '*nondum considerasti quanti ponderis sit peccatum* [you have not yet considered what a great burden sin is]' (ch. XXI). It was to rescue humankind from this dire situation that Christ came.[44]

This divine reaction to man's sin has two implications for the doctrine of the atonement in Denney's view. In the first place it shows us that it is not only man's relationship to God that needs to be addressed, but God's reaction towards man. Commenting on Romans 1, Denney writes:

> With ver. 24 the Apostle turns from sin to its punishment. Because of [sin] God gave them up. To lose God is to lose everything: to lose the connection with Him . . . is to sink into an abyss of darkness . . . It is to become fitted for wrath at last under the pressure of wrath all the time . . . παρέδωκεν [*paredōken*, 'give up'] in all three places . . . *expresses the judicial action of God.*[45]

In Romans 1:28 there is a play on the word *dokimazō*, 'to scrutinize before approval':

> As they did not think fit, after trial made . . . , to keep God in their knowledge, God gave them up to a mind which cannot stand trial . . . The one thing answers to the other. Virtually, they pronounced the true God ἀδόκιμος [*adokimos*, 'false', 'spurious'] and would have none of him; and he in turn gave them up to a νουν ἀδόκιμον [*noun adokimon*], a mind which is no mind and cannot discharge the functions of one, a mind in which the divine distinctions of right and wrong are confused and lost, so that God's condemnation cannot but fall on it at last.[46]

Denney says:

> I am not enough of a lawyer to say whether 'forensic' is the proper word to describe this idea . . . but I have no doubt of its truth. I have no doubt of

---

[44] For Denney's assessment of Anselm, see *Reconciliation*, pp. 64–79.

[45] James Denney, *Romans*, Expositor's Greek Testament, vol. 2 (London: Hodder & Stoughton, 1900), p. 593 (emphasis added).

[46] Ibid., p. 594.

the *reality* of God's condemnation of sin ... it is ... as real as spiritual impotence and despair, which are the effects of its paralysing touch. The thing that has to be dealt with, that has to be overcome in the work of reconciliation, is not man's distrust of God, but God's condemnation of man.[47]

The second conclusion is that Christ's work on the cross restored our broken relationship with God by fulfilling the divine requirements for its restoration. In other words, we 'are now justified by his grace as a gift, through the redemption that is in Christ Jesus, whom God put forward as a sacrifice of atonement by his blood, effective through faith' (Rom. 3:24–25). B. G. Worrall says that Denney's discussion of the righteousness of God 'has a more dated air than usual'.[48] This may be true of his idea of righteousness; but it is not true of his idea of propitiation. With varying degrees of persuasion, both Leon Morris[49] and David Hill[50] have demonstrated that Denney's interpretation is closest to the linguistic data. Denney wrote:

The characteristic words of religion cannot be applied in new ways at will. Now the idea of ... propitiation is not an insulated idea ... it is part of a system of ideas, which we have to reconstruct with the means at our disposal. It is related ... to the idea of sin. It is sin ... which creates the necessity for it and which is in some sense the object of it. In other words, sin is the problem with which ἱλασμός [*hilasmos*] deals.[51]

And the reason why sin is the problem with which it deals is because, as Paul says, '[T]he wages of sin is death' (Rom. 6:23, RSV).

In Scripture, death has more than one meaning. It can mean no more than the end of the life of flesh (John 6:49, 58). Here death is merely an event. But death is also a spiritual reality, which we experience while still living in the body (Eph. 2:1, 5). In the account of Lazarus in John 11, these two aspects are not exclusive: physical death is a spiritual reality. The Bible does not distinguish between physical and spiritual death with regard to its cause. Death in all its forms is the consequence of sin and the divine penalty upon it. By his death on

---

[47] Denney, *Studies in Theology*, p. 103. See also his *Reconciliation*, p. 189.

[48] B. G. Worrall, 'Substitutionary Atonement in the Theology of James Denney', *Scottish Journal of Theology*, vol. 28 (1975), p. 346.

[49] Morris, *Apostolic Preaching of the Cross*.

[50] David Hill, *Greek Words and Hebrew Meanings* (Cambridge: Cambridge University Press, 1967), pp. 23–48.

[51] Denney, *Death of Christ*, p. 273.

the cross Christ has gained the victory over sin, which is the 'sting' of death. In the words of P. T. Forsyth, 'He took the sting and pulled out the stinger.'[52] Denney asks what is meant that Christ died for us, died that death of ours which is the wages of sin?

> In His death . . . , God's condemnation of our sin came upon Him; a divine sentence was executed upon the sin of the world. It is all important to observe that it was *God* who made Christ sin . . . God is the subject of the sentence. It is God who is presented dealing in an awful way with the awful reality of sin for its removal; and the way in which He removes it, is to lay it on His son . . . Christ, by God's appointment, dies the sinner's death.[53]

This is also the key to what Denney means when he talks about the 'intelligible relation between the sacrifice which love made and the necessity from which it redeemed'.[54] The necessity was that we were 'dead' through our 'trespasses', 'by nature children of wrath' (Eph. 2:1, 3, RSV), held by the power of sin, and suffering the sting of death. The link between my plight and his work is 'the Cross, *he* bore *our* sins, *he* died *our* death'.[55] Denney summed up his conclusion:

> The Cross is the place at which the sinless One dies the death of the sinful: the place at which God's condemnation is borne by the Innocent, that for those who commit themselves to Him there may be condemnation no more. I cannot read the New Testament in any other sense. I cannot see at the very heart of it anything but this – grace establishing the law, not in a 'forensic' sense, but in a spiritual sense; mercy revealed, not over judgment, but through it; justification disclosing not only the goodness but the severity of God; the Cross inscribed, 'God is love', only because it is inscribed also, 'The wages of sin is death.'[56]

Denney believed that this idea could be supported exegetically in Paul's epistles. In 2 Corinthians 5:14, Paul tells us that 'one has died for all; therefore all have died' (RSV). Now the Greek preposition *hyper* in this passage does not necessarily mean that Christ took our place, just that his death in some way

---

[52] I could not locate this reference. (T. A. N.)
[53] Denney, *Studies in Theology*, p. 112.
[54] Denney, *Death of Christ*, p. 177.
[55] Ibid., p. 178.
[56] Denney, *Studies in Theology*, p. 124.

brings benefit to us all. For the idea of substitution, the preposition *anti* would be required.[57] 'Battles have been fought here', says Denney, 'over the preposition "for," which is ὑπὲρ [*hyper*], on behalf of, not ἀντὶ [*anti*], instead of.'[58] But the important point is not the preposition, but the epexegetic phrase 'therefore all died'. Denney says the phrase

> in one sense . . . is irrelevant and interrupts his argument. He puts it into a hurried parenthesis, then he eagerly resumes what it has suspended . . . Yet it is in this immediate inference – that the death of Christ *for* all involved the death *of* all – that the missing link is found.[59]

'That is to say, His death was as good as theirs. That is *why* His death has an advantage to them; . . . it is *their* death which has been died by *Him*.'[60] This is why the word 'substitution' is valid:

> What the word substitution expresses, in the doctrine of the atonement, is the truth . . . that man is unconditionally and forever dependent for his acceptance with God on something which Christ has done *for* him, and which he could never have done, never needs to do, for himself . . . [W]e are to eternity absolutely indebted to Him. We have no standing in grace but that which He has won for us; nothing but the forfeiting of His free life has freed our forfeited lives. That is what is meant by calling Christ our substitute, and to that use of the word no objection can be taken which does not strike at the root of New Testament teaching.[61]

There is a great deal more to be said, but I want to end with a brief review of Denney's idea of the work of Christ as it is realized in human experience. The question is, 'How does what Christ did for us, especially on the Cross, become a power in our life?'[62] The answer is, of course, by faith:

> If a man with a sense of his sin on him sees what Christ on His Cross means, there is only one thing for him to do . . . to abandon himself to the sin-bearing love which appeals to him in Christ, and to do so unreservedly,

---

[57] This preposition is used in Mark 10:45: δοῦναι τὴν ψυχὴν αὐτοῦ λύτρον ἀντὶ πολλῶν.
[58] Denney, *Studies in Theology*, p. 109.
[59] Denney, *Death of Christ*, p. 141.
[60] Denney, *Studies in Theology*, p. 110.
[61] Ibid., pp. 126–127.
[62] Denney, *Reconciliation*, p. 287.

unconditionally and forever. This is what the New Testament means by faith.[63]

Assuming this faith in Christ, 'in what way will the life of reconciliation manifest itself in men?'[64] Denney answers this in three ways: to begin with, we will be reconciled to God's estimation of sin. It will now be seen in its seriousness in the light of the death of Christ of the Cross: no more excuses; no more pleading extenuating circumstances; no more turning a blind eye to it. 'There is no salvation except in and through the truth, and to take our sin as what it truly is . . . is to enter into the truth through which salvation is realized.'[65] It involves what is called in the book of Leviticus (26:41), making 'amends for their iniquity' (RSV).

There is a second aspect of this reconciliation and that is accepting that love is the law of life. There must be a change in our conduct. Some have shied away from this, not wishing to make it dependent on man's works; but this does not seem to have been a problem in the New Testament:

By faith in him we are really united to him, not metaphysically, but in the passion of love and trust. He brings us into an ethical fellowship with himself, in which the inspiration of his life becomes the inspiration of ours; the love which moved and controlled him, moves and controls us also.[66]

Finally, the life of one who has been reconciled to God through Christ becomes itself a reconciling force in the world:

An evangelist who has himself been reconciled to God through Christ . . . is a far more powerful witness to the reconciliation than any institution or atmosphere can be . . . A reconciled man preaching Christ as the way of reconciliation, and preaching him in the temper and spirit which the experience of reconciliation creates, is the most effective mediator of Christ's reconciling power.[67]

If the word 'evangelical' is taken in its strict sense as referring to that which relates to the evangel, the gospel, then there is no way we can deny that James

---

[63] Ibid., pp. 289–290.
[64] Denney, *Reconciliation*, p. 324.
[65] Ibid., pp. 324–325.
[66] Denney, *Reconciliation*, p. 327.
[67] Ibid., p. 8.

Denney was an evangelical theologian.[68] Not all evangelicals will agree with his understanding of Scripture, but when it comes to the doctrine of the atonement, the touchstone of evangelical faith, his influence has been significant and long-lasting even on some later theologians in this book. And it is not merely a matter of doctrine, but of living faith. Denney's own faith in Christ is clear in the quotation with which James Gordon concludes his intellectual biography: 'And it is not the acceptance of any theology or Christology, however penetrating or profound, which keeps us Christian; we remain loyal to our Lord only because he has apprehended us, and his hand is strong.'[69]

---

[68] This is the second of my added paragraphs. (T. A. N.)
[69] Gordon, *James Denney*, p. 321, quoting Denney, *Jesus and the Gospel*, p. 411.

3

Peter Taylor Forsyth

TREVOR HART

Peter Taylor Forsyth was born in 1848 in Aberdeen, the son of a postman. He studied classical literature at the University of Aberdeen, graduating in 1869 with outstanding honours. So exceptional was his academic accomplishment that he was invited at once to serve as assistant to the university professor of Latin, a post he accepted and held for one academic session and that might have begun a glittering scholarly career in that subject. But it was to ordination within the Congregational tradition rather than academe that Forsyth discerned a call, receiving his theological training in Göttingen and London, and embarking in 1876 upon a quarter of a century as a minister to churches in Bradford, London, Manchester, Leicester and Cambridge. His brilliance as a preacher, speaker and writer (on art, culture, politics and current affairs as well as theology) quickly established him as a bright star in the Congregationalist firmament, and he was duly called (in 1901) to be Principal of Hackney College, London, a position he held until his death in 1921.

Forsyth the man

Forsyth's reputation as a churchman and theologian in his own day was considerable. His total written output amounted to some twenty-four books and hundreds of articles and pamphlets, a striking tally even in an age admittedly more generous to the printed word than our own. The writing and publishing began immediately upon ordination,[1] though Forsyth's most significant theological works were concentrated mostly in the last twenty years of his life, when the role of college principal doubtless laid upon him both the expectation and the opportunity to develop more fully for the benefit of others the insights and

---

[1] For a bibliography of works by and about Forsyth see that compiled by Leslie McCurdy in Trevor Hart (ed.), *Justice the True and Only Mercy: Essays on the Life and Theology of Peter Taylor Forsyth* (Edinburgh: T&T Clark, 1995), pp. 256–330.

convictions gathered over previous decades.[2] Yet it is for the quality, erudition, range and force of his writings rather than their number that Forsyth was acknowledged; and for the range of his reading and thought, engaging, as he did, with key figures and texts in the worlds of painting (Holman Hunt, Rossetti), music (Wagner), literature (Milton, Wordsworth, George Eliot, Hardy), drama (Ibsen), psychology (William James) and philosophy (Hegel, Nietzsche, Schopenhauer), filtering their various contributions through the mesh of his own distinctly Christian theological vision. The result is a rich vein of theological reflection that takes the reader directly to the heart of Christian doctrine and its roots in the biblical gospel without ever leaving behind the shared experiences, complexities and concerns of life as creatures in God's world.

Forsyth's written style has sometimes been criticized for being prolix and difficult. His close contemporary and fellow Congregational minister (and Liberal MP) Silvester Horne notoriously dismissed it as 'fireworks in a fog', and others have complained in similar vein. It is true enough that Forsyth is often less than forgiving to readers craving easy syntax, elementary vocabulary or linear thought. And he could certainly have used a good editor! We should not forget, though, that he was attempting to get to grips with the great truths of the gospel without merely skimming across its surface, and he struggled constantly with the incapacity of language to draw the deepest of truths about anything to the surface in 'simple terms' without at the same time diminishing, distorting and even losing touch with their significance. Like a poet, he is often driven to indirect approaches – metaphor, paradox, epigram – in order to bend language to the task of pointing us (often in more than one way at once) to that which finally eludes or ruptures any straightforward, direct or simple statement of it.[3] This is precisely because he is (in theology and elsewhere) a realist who refuses to suppose that reality submits neatly to, or can be contained exhaustively within, the words and ideas available to us. On the contrary, reality is messy, deep and mysterious, and our responsibility is to bear witness to it as fully and faithfully as we are able with the tools at our disposal. Easy reduction of the complex to the simple and the systematic will not do. Words (and 'the Word'), he repeatedly insisted, were sacramental realities to be used with due reverence rather than clumsily, lightly or in such a way as to elide the distinction between realities lying at and beneath their surfaces.

---

[2] Several of Forsyth's most significant works from this productive period originated in invitations to deliver public lectures.

[3] See e.g. F. C. Bradley, *P. T. Forsyth: The Man and His Work* (London: Independent Press, 1952), p. 66.

In any case, obscurity or unduly literary style is only part of the story, as the following comment from a review by James Denney of 1910's *The Work of Christ* indicates: 'I liked Forsyth more than ever,' he writes, 'not because he was more lucid or consecutive, but because he really strikes sparks from his anvil!'[4] And this is indeed the other characteristic feature of Forsyth's pen. Not only does he typically have striking things to say, but more often than not he says them with passion and power, and litters them with eminently quotable aphorisms. God's gracious self-giving in revelation and redemption, he insists, for example, is interruptive and costly, and 'does not come to grout the gaps in nature'. Well-meaning but misguided talk about the church having a restraining moral and spiritual influence on the forces unleashed in the First World War, meanwhile, was 'meeting the Atlantic with a mop'. And

> So much of our religious teaching betrays no sign that the speaker has descended into hell, been near the everlasting burnings, or been plucked from the awful pit. He has risen with Christ . . . but it is out of a shallow grave, with no deepness of earth, with no huge millstone to roll away.

The voice is identifiably that of the preacher as well as the scholar of theology, and in truth Forsyth understood the difference between the two tasks as being one of register alone.

In Forsyth we have to do with no typical theological product of the nineteenth century, but with one who had weighed its greatest intellectual currents and found them seriously wanting. If the horrors of the 1914–18 war were to give some Liberal Protestant theologians pause for thought, coming as a shock to their enlightened and spiritually developed sensibilities and expectations, to Forsyth, while the thing was no less shattering in personal terms (he was as we shall see a great Germanophile), it was hardly a surprising occurrence in the grand scheme of things. It served, that is to say, rather to confirm than to undermine the basic facts of our humanity as Forsyth took them to be. His complaint over several decades had been directed in large measure against the dominant 'evolutionary' philosophies of Hegel and others and the so-called 'myth of progress' engendered by them – the conviction that with the passage of time (process) things in nature and history alike would and must inevitably advance and improve (progress). His return to this theme in responding to the outbreak of war and its course comes as no surprise. On the contrary, the conflagration comes as the unsolicited and unwelcome validation of forty years

---

[4] Cited in A. M. Hunter, *P. T. Forsyth: Per Crucem ad Lucem* (London: SCM Press, 1974), p. 26.

of authorship in which a note of warning against 'sentimental optimism' or unduly sanguine accounts of human capacity and incapacity had been sounded consistently from his writing desk. In this sense, at least, Forsyth captured much in the spirit of 'twentieth century' theology long before chronology itself caught up with him.

Evangelical theologian

What manner of theologian, then, was P. T. Forsyth in other respects? 'Highly distinctive and not easily categorised' was the judgement of Colin Gunton, one of Forsyth's foremost modern appreciators.[5] Any classification of him must therefore be undertaken with due care. Forsyth would not have sat easily with any form of ecclesial identity politics. His commitment to the gospel was absolute; but his understanding of its truth and authority was cast otherwise than in terms of easy subscription to any list of verbal formulations. And yet, in his characteristic theological instincts, commitments and emphases, Forsyth's theology must be acknowledged as 'evangelical' unless we choose to circumscribe this term's meaning in a manner tantamount to pinning down a definition of 'vacuum cleaner' only to discover (to the incredulity of others if not ourselves) that in doing so we have inadvertently excluded Hoover from consideration.

In a day when published sources were mercifully fewer than in ours, it was possible for intellectual erudition to be broad as well as deep in its portfolio, and Forsyth's reading was impressive in its catholic sweep. As I have already mentioned, he was well versed in a range of different fields of intellectual concern, enabling him to make serious theological contributions to contemporary discourses on the arts, current affairs, politics, social policy, and others, as well as theology's more familiar interlocutors in the academy. It is quite usual, therefore, to find pieces from his pen treating political theory, metaphysics, the direction of current government policy as regards the poor and disadvantaged in society and the Christian doctrines of the Trinity and atonement as though they all belonged on the same page, which in fact he believed they did.[6]

As well as scholarly essays and books, perusal of a list of Forsyth's published works quickly reveals a constant stream of contributions from his pen (articles, reviews, correspondence) to newspapers and other organs reflecting and

---

[5] From his foreword to Hart, *Justice*, p. xiii.
[6] See e.g. essays such as 'Socialism and Christianity in Some of Their Deeper Aspects' (1886) and 'Socialism, the Church and the Poor' (1908).

shaping public awareness on topical issues international, national and local. In all his writing Forsyth is eclectic in his sources and (much to the chagrin of generations of his readers) hardly ever cites them in the manner demanded by present-day academic conventions. He attempts no overall exhaustive 'system' of theology, being in this respect as in numerous others much more the disciple of Luther than of Calvin. His overall corpus does, though, manifest a clear and coherent unity of approach and understanding, presenting a series of contributions to theology on a range of key doctrinal loci (among other things) in which familiar theological landmarks and a consistent orientation can always be discerned, and the probable route of approach to others plotted with reasonable confidence.[7]

There is little doubt that Forsyth's erudition and eclecticism were benefited by an academic term in 1872 sitting at the feet of the great Albrecht Ritschl in Göttingen, a brief sojourn that would leave him a fluent speaker and reader of German as well as a passionate devotee of that nation's great music and literature. When he died, it was found that as much as a third of Forsyth's personal library consisted of works in German, and this in a day when, we ought not to forget, theology in the English home counties was typically imperialistically monoglot, and thus often ignorant even of the most major upheavals of thought occurring across the North Sea.[8] Forsyth's appetite for all things German was voracious and always theologically informed and engaged. Having travelled to Bayreuth to attend a performance of Wagner's *Parsifal*, for instance, he declared it as, apart from Handel's *Messiah*, 'the greatest Redemption music in the world'. Wagner's 'many sided genius' had here finally outstripped the composer's own tortured allegiance to a form of Christian atheism and captured in music, poetry and theatrical action what it is like from the side of the sinful soul ('from below' as we might say) to *experience* deliverance. 'It is the soul singing its own deadly sins, its own mortal agony, and its own regenerate beauty,' he writes; 'Wagner sang one side of the truth, "Work out your own salvation"'; Handel, meanwhile, sang the other, 'from above' perspective on the same event: '"For it is God that worketh in you."'[9] Likewise, while committed to a 'high' view of Scripture's authority in the life of the church and clear about how that ought to be acknowledged, respected and permitted to function, Forsyth could yet

---

[7] See Alan P. F. Sell, 'P. T. Forsyth as Unsystematic Systematician', in Hart, *Justice*, pp. 110–145.

[8] It should be remembered that although his career was spent in England, Forsyth was formed and educated as a Scot. Key texts of German philosophy and theology, in fact, were often made available to English readers in translations made by theologians north of the border, a tradition that continued well into the twentieth century.

[9] P. T. Forsyth, *Religion in Recent Art*, 2nd edn (London: Hodder & Stoughton, 1901 [1st edn 1889]), pp. 253–254.

express huge appreciation rather than any suspicion or anxiety about the development and burgeoning of so-called 'higher criticism' of the biblical text in German universities, even lauding it as the identifiable work and gift of God's Holy Spirit to the church. Again, he was judicious in his application of this judgement – biblical criticism had its proper place in the church, he insisted, but this was merely as the handmaid of the gospel itself, and it had no place whatever in the pulpit – but he was willing and able to make and to defend it (staunchly when required) nonetheless.[10]

If Forsyth remained a Germanophile all his life, he did not remain a thoroughbred Ritschlian for long at all after his return from Göttingen, though Ritschl's theology certainly shaped his early years of ministry as printed sermons from the period reveal quite clearly. One such, delivered from the pulpit of Forsyth's first charge in Shipley, Bradford, in 1877, was entitled 'Mercy the True and Only Justice'. It reads like a manifesto for a soteriology the Protestant roots of which reach back at least as far as Socinus in the sixteenth century but come to their majestic flowering only with the gradual publication of Albrecht Ritschl's magnum opus, *The Christian Doctrine of Justification and Reconciliation* (1870–74).[11] This major theological event coincided conveniently with the arrival of this particular enthusiastic and highly intelligent young Scot determined to make the most of whatever learning there was to be had there. Forsyth, to be sure, learned a great deal from Ritschl that would shape his theology throughout the whole of his preaching, teaching and publishing career. Ritschl's insistence upon a Christ-centred revelation accessed via attention to Scripture as the proper starting point for theology, for instance, his dislike of metaphysics, his foregrounding of the theme of the kingdom of God, and his emphasis on the essentially moral, personal and practical nature of the believer's relationship with God all remained intrinsic to Forsyth's way of thinking to the end. The Ritschlian configuration of the relationship between love, judgement and mercy in the character of God, the aestheticizing of the biblical notion of God's holiness, and the bearing of all this on the theologies of atonement and redemption, though, was something Forsyth not only left behind but began to oppose quite early on in his twenty-five years of pastoral

---

10 See 'The Evangelical Churches and the Higher Criticism', in Marvin W. Anderson (ed.), *The Gospel and Authority: A P. T. Forsyth Reader: Eight Essays Previously Published in Journals* (Minneapolis: Augsburg, 1971), pp. 15–24. The piece was published originally in the *Contemporary Review* 88 (October 1905), pp. 574–599. See also *Positive Preaching and the Modern Mind*, 3rd edn (London: Independent Press, 1949), esp. ch. 1.

11 Albrecht Ritschl, *Die christliche Lehre von der Rechtfertigung und Versöhnung*, 3 vols. (1870, 1874, 1874). The familiar English edition of vol. 3 published under the title referred to above was from the 3rd German edition of 1888, translated under the editorship of H. R. Mackintosh and A. B. Macaulay, and issued by T&T Clark in 1890.

ministry. The need to do so seems to have come to him quite suddenly and as the result of a personal and spiritual crisis shortly after his move in 1881 from Shipley to St Thomas's Square, Hackney, the second of his five ministries. The occasion for the crisis remains appropriately shrouded in the privacy of Forsyth's own relationship with God, but it was clearly urgent and pronounced, and it provoked an intellectual as well as a moral and spiritual paradigm shift. Looking back on the event years later Forsyth himself tells us this much:

> It pleased God . . . by the revelation of his holiness and grace . . . to bring home to me my sin . . . I was turned from a Christian to a believer, from a lover of love to an object of grace.[12]

It was a momentous turning point, and one that was to shape Forsyth's theology profoundly.

Forsyth's *theologia crucis*

In offering an overview of Forsyth's theological contribution I propose to concentrate on those themes most prevalent in his writing. I do so in the hope that readers wishing to know what he also has to say on a range of other subjects (doctrinal and otherwise) may nonetheless in this way be encouraged to go and find out for themselves. It is a venture almost always worth the effort expended.

The moral as the most real

Perhaps the most striking facet of the universe as viewed by one who has discovered that he is an 'object of grace' is its irreducibly moral structure. There is, according to Forsyth, a 'moral order' that is just as surely woven into the fabric of God's creation as that other, physical order investigated by the natural sciences. Indeed, with more than 150 years of the philosophical quest for epistemic certainty in his sights, Forsyth insists that our knowledge of the moral ordering of the cosmos is at once more ultimate and more reliable than whatever knowing we may enjoy of things either physical or intellectual. It is, he avers, in the so-called 'practical' reason and not the 'pure' that real authority is to be had,[13] and it lays hold of us directly through the organ of conscience, unlike the material order that is but an inference from the evidence of our sensory

---

[12] P. T. Forsyth, *Positive Preaching and the Modern Mind*, 3rd edn (London: Independent Press [1st edn 1907]), p. 193.
[13] P. T. Forsyth, 'The Cross as the Final Seat of Authority', in Anderson, *Gospel and Authority*, p. 165.

apparatus.[14] As fundamentally moral beings, in other words, we find ourselves more naturally and immediately engaged with this stratum of reality than with the bodily world of our spatio-temporal existence. Indeed, reality at its deepest and most basic level is moral in nature rather than intellectual or physical,[15] and the most important questions that face us humanly are moral ones. 'That is the final human question,' he writes, 'how to face the eternal moral power. What is it making of us? What is He doing with us? What is He going to do? That is the issue of all issues.'[16]

This conviction that our actions and their consequences can be plotted within a moral and not just a physical framework of cause and effect is a function of Forsyth's supreme emphasis on the *holiness* of God. This holiness, he protests in the face of the term's use by some of his contemporaries, is not the awe-fulness of Romanticism's aesthetic – the sublimity of the raging maritime storm or the mysterious remoteness of a snowy alpine peak[17] – but absolute moral authority and a passionate and unswerving opposition to sin and evil in all its manifestations.[18] It is holiness, Forsyth insists, and not love (at least, love only in the distinct form of *holy* love rather than the sentimental and morally deficient versions that were part of the Ritschlian theological heritage) that is most fundamental to God's own nature. That this same God should invest creation with so direct a reflection of his own being ought not to surprise us unduly. And to say, 'Ultimate reality is moral,' therefore, is finally to say, 'God is holy love.'

All this finds further expression in Forsyth's description – at once both doffing his cap to Hegel and disputing with him – of the cosmic, eschatologically orientated scheme of things as a process in which what is occurring is the 'self-realization' not of *Geist* or 'Spirit' but of the Holy One in history. 'The great object of things,' he writes, 'is not the self-expression of the Eternal in time but His self-effectuation as holy in a Kingdom.'[19] 'Holiness is the eternal moral power which must do, and do, till it sees itself everywhere.'[20] Forsyth's eye here is upon the ancient injunction of the covenant between the Lord and Israel: 'Be holy, for I am holy' (Lev. 11:45, my tr.), a demand that, he insists, far from being

---

14 Forsyth, *Preaching*, pp. 47–48.

15 P. T. Forsyth, 'Christ's Person and His Cross', *Methodist Review* 66 (January 1917), p. 5.

16 P. T. Forsyth, *The Cruciality of the Cross*, 2nd edn (London: Independent Press, 1948 [1st edn 1909]), p. 119.

17 Forsyth, *Preaching*, pp. 207–208.

18 See e.g. P. T. Forsyth, *The Church, the Gospel and Society* (London: Independent Press, 1962) (comprising 'The Holy Church a Moral Guide of Society' [1905] and 'The Grace of the Gospel as the Moral Authority in the Church' [1905]), p. 19.

19 Forsyth, *Preaching*, p. 209.

20 Ibid., p. 240.

arbitrary, is rooted in God's own eternal being and without the satisfactory implementation of which God cannot rest. The effectuation or positive realization of the holy in the world, in a kingdom, in human flesh and blood, in other words, is that which alone could ever 'satisfy' the sort of God he actually is, the Holy One. This insistence and insight duly shapes Forsyth's account of what occurs at the cross and the 'atoning' action of God in the humanity of Christ more widely. In an important sense this 'self-realization' is, for Forsyth as for Hegel, ultimately a matter of the self's finding itself in the other. But Forsyth is not thinking of the kindling into flame of a 'divine' spark latent within the creaturely other, but of a radical act of self-substitution in which God himself *becomes* the other in the kenosis of incarnation, and realizes his own holiness *in* the creature precisely *as* the creature, the eternal Son's offering himself humanly to his Father from first breath to last in a sustained act of holy love and devotion.[21] Atonement – reconciliation with a God who is holiness itself – could be achieved only 'by bringing to practical effect an answering and trusting holiness on a world scale amid the extremest conditions created by human sin';[22] and this could occur only by the redemptive self-substitution of God himself for us, having taken our flesh and been 'made sin' for our sakes. In the act he emptied himself of all but the single divine characteristic, lack of which would compromise his very identity and 'being' as God itself – his eternal holiness;[23] and this he now transposed into the register of our creaturely nature, standing in our place and, in place of our sinful self-absorption and godlessness, 'bringing to practical effect an answering and trusting holiness' to resonate with God's own.[24]

God's nature as the Holy, then, of which the moral ordering of the cosmos and the moral constitution of human beings under its jurisdiction are but pale created reflections or expressions, is the supreme concern that underlies and drives all existence towards its goal, both ours and God's own. It is that with which, as its prime and only perfect exemplar, God himself is and will and must always be chiefly concerned. The text inscribed on the portals of the universe at its creation (and one Forsyth never tires of citing in one context or another) is 'Hallowed be Thy Name',[25] and the question that hangs over human history

---

[21] See 'The Preaching of Jesus and the Gospel of Christ. [VI] The Meaning of a Sinless Christ', *Expositor*, 8th series, vol. 25 (1923), p. 298.

[22] Ibid., p. 299.

[23] Cf. the well-known discussion of the doctrine of kenosis in P. T. Forsyth, *The Person and Place of Jesus Christ* (London: Independent Press, 1961 [1909]), ch. 11.

[24] See n. 22 above.

[25] P. T. Forsyth, *God the Holy Father* (London: Independent Press, 1957) [comprising *The Holy Father and the Living Christ* (1897), *Christian Perfection* (1899) and 'The Taste of Death and the Life of Grace' (1901)], p. 5.

as a whole and each human life in particular is just how it stands here, with regard to this demand that issues not from God's mere choice or preference, but from the very depths of God's being as such. Have we, do we, shall we 'hallow' God's name in what we are and what we do, or shall we be held, as the prophets held Israel, to have desecrated, defiled and denied that name not just in the externals of action, but from within, by the idolatry and lawlessness of our hearts?

When all this is borne in mind, it is unsurprising to find Forsyth insisting at every turn that the liberalism of his theological youth, with what he now held to be its naive, sentimental and optimistic account of the moral relationship between ultimate reality and the human condition, must be abandoned as a dangerous substitute for Christianity of the apostolic sort. Having all but lost sight of (or deliberately misrepresented) the biblical characterization of God's holiness, the previous generation had, he insisted, lost its moral bearings. It had lost sight, above all, of the reality of the human situation as one of guilt, sacrilege and liability to judgement and wrath – terms Forsyth never shies from using, although what he understands by them in proclaiming the gospel of God's grace is more theologically calibrated than their use by enthusiastic systematizers of the 'evangel' among the Protestant orthodoxies of earlier centuries. All have sinned, he insists in Pauline fashion. All have breached that moral order that may not be breached. All have challenged and betrayed the holiness of God rather than being devoted to it. 'Man is not a mere runaway,' Forsyth reminds us, 'but a rebel; not a pitiful coward, but a bold and bitter mutineer.'[26] And all are therefore guilty and stand liable as the objects of God's wrath and holy judgement. That all are simultaneously the objects of God's love – that selfsame love with which in the eternal Godhead the Father loves the Son – is, of course, the very heart of the gospel itself. As rebels and mutineers, though, Forsyth observes, that love necessarily reaches us in the particular form of grace and mercy. The realization of personal and collective guilt and the grateful reception of forgiveness are therefore essential to the full experience of salvation, and not merely one variation upon it (fine for the personally insecure or those with an overdeveloped sense of moral scrupulousness, but needless for those who have discovered that 'God is love'). We are, to be sure, forgiven only because we are loved, Forsyth holds; but no account of God's love that does not begin with, and take its bearings continually from, this peculiar form of it as grace and mercy has yet grasped the truth of it, or properly received and responded to it. This is, he observes, not intended as a test of personal Christianity:

26 See e.g. 'The Taste of Death and the Life of Grace', p. 9.

It is not a *Quicunque vult*. I will only venture to say I never knew my sin so long as I but saw Christ suffering for me – never until I saw Him under its judgment and realized that the chastisement of my peace was upon Him.[27]

But we are in danger of running ahead of ourselves here, and misunderstanding what Forsyth is talking about.

The ends of love and holiness

One of the distinctive notes in Forsyth's account of all this is his utter opposition to the tendency in some atonement theologies to envisage a tension within God's own character between the so-called conflicting 'demands' of justice or holiness and those of love or mercy. The projection of some such dramatic dualism into the eternal nature of God was not uncommon among the traditional accounts of atonement with which Forsyth was familiar. What Forsyth saw was that it was precisely this putative conflict that had led (and would always lead) to dangerous misrepresentations of who God is and the nature of God's involvement in the story of atonement. What was effectively a theological zero-sum game permitted liberal theologians, for instance, to champion the cause of divine 'love' at the expense of any adequate acknowledgement of justice and holiness in God. Meanwhile, those wishing, contrariwise, to maintain a serious place for holy 'wrath' in the scheme of atonement found themselves driven awkwardly to envisage either a settlement hammered out or a marginal victory won in a struggle between two evenly pitched and opposing sets of characteristics and concerns in God, each with its own legitimate claim on the lives of sinful humans.

Forsyth would have none of it! God's love, he insists, is not and never could be at odds with his holiness or held in vulnerable equipoise with it. There can never be any trade-off between God's mercy and God's wrath, nor any eventual overwhelming of one by the other, because love, wrath, mercy, justice are all manifestations and forms of God's holy character (or God's character as the Holy One), distinct from one another only in the artificial abstraction of our thinking and speaking about them, but in themselves and eternally one and the same thing. This is why Forsyth insists on speaking of 'holy love'; for the sort of love that God is and has for his creatures is precisely the love of holiness, and no other, less morally robust, sort. Equally, though, talk of God's 'wrath' or 'anger', his 'justice' or 'holiness', must never be abstracted from this same

---

[27] Forsyth, *Preaching*, p. 253.

singular moral reality and treated as though they were ever anything other than *necessarily* manifestations of the *love* of God, let alone qualities or traits opposed to that love's concerns and its goals. 'Greater love' does not mean less wrath or judgement in God's ways of dealing with sin, therefore, but precisely more, since wrath is always love's wrath, the form love takes in the face of sin and evil, and never has anything other than the realization of love's ends as its purpose.[28] Such things may well be fractured apart and conflicted in our experience of their fallen human approximations, but Forsyth would certainly insist that no serious theological account can begin there.

Theology must begin only with the moral reality of God, revealed to us not in our own experience of ourselves but in the story of Scripture and, supremely and finally, in one man alone – the one in whom God himself has emptied himself and incarnated his own holiness in the creaturely forms of our humanity, despite the fact of its being caught up in the web of sinful historical existence. The conflict between holiness and sin is played out in the whole course of Jesus' life as the human Son of God, but comes to its crisis point in the moment of his death on the cross, where, through his obedience and self-offering, sin is defeated and judged once and for all.[29] This, Forsyth insists, is the moral Armageddon of the human race,[30] the longed-for Day of the Lord, the Last Judgment,[31] which safeguards the moral soul and future of humanity, reconfiguring the structure of the cosmos itself in its moral dimension, and without which the integrity of reality as a whole would be put dangerously at risk.[32] Here a decisive victory is won by God over sin and evil, yet won precisely by God's existing and acting *humanly* in Christ. Here God comes at last to establish *from within* that creaturely holiness that is the answering condition to his own, the necessary correlate to God's own being if God is going to continue to be God with us and God for us; if he is to continue, in fact, to be God at all. Forsyth is adamant that we should not mistake the seriousness of what happens here or the unthinkable consequences of its not having happened or having played out otherwise than it did. In the teeth of the Ritschlian convictions he himself had once championed, his writing from the mid-1880s onwards is emphatic in its assertion of the absolute finality and universality of

---

[28] See e.g. ibid., pp. 253–254.

[29] See e.g. P. T. Forsyth, *The Justification of God: Lectures for War-Time on a Christian Theodicy* (London: Duckworth Press, 1916), p. 136.

[30] P. T. Forsyth, 'The Cross of Christ as the Moral Principle of Society', *Methodist Review* 99 (January 1917), pp. 9–21 (11).

[31] Forsyth, *Justification*, pp. 130, 171; *The Work of Christ* (London: Hodder & Stoughton, 1910), pp. 160–161.

[32] Frederick Godet et al., *The Atonement in Modern Religious Thought: A Theological Symposium* (London: James Clark, 1900), p. 79. Forsyth's eponymous contribution was originally published in *Christian World*, 23 November 1899, pp. 11–12.

the moral ordering of the cosmos and the demands this lays not just on human beings, but on God himself.

God cannot not judge sin

It is not, of course, that Forsyth supposes God to be beholden to any eternal absolute Justice set over against and more ultimate than himself, with the autonomous claims of which he is thus forced to comply. On the contrary, referring back to an analogy to which we have already laid claim, the *moral* order of the cosmos is, like space, time and other transcendental features of its *physical* ordering, part of creation itself, rather than a pre-existing condition with which God's creative labours were obliged to reckon and comply. Put differently, all these things are themselves contingent – the products of God's own sovereign freedom, and features of the sort of world God has *chosen* to summon into being and into relationship with himself. And yet the language of freedom, choice and decision must be handled here, as elsewhere, with great care, lest it conjure up a vision of equal and opposite magnitude in its distortion and falsehood. 'Freedom', Forsyth recognizes, cannot mean mere *caprice* even when we predicate it of God; and 'sovereignty' cannot mean absolute lack of constraint even if, in God's case and in God's case alone, we may have good reason to insist that no *external* constraint (i.e. nothing beyond God's own eternal being and character) can possibly compel God's compliant conformity with its demands. But Forsyth sees that God's freedom is precisely the freedom *to choose and to act in accordance with God's own proper nature*, and not despite it. If the freedom to be true to oneself is properly described as a 'constraint' at all, then we may happily admit that it is one God enjoys and is glad to embrace rather than chafing under its yoke. For the God of whom the Bible speaks, in other words the fact that God may choose and act only in accordance with the sort of God he actually and eternally *is*, is hardly a denial of God's sovereignty. It is rather the expression and realization of it.

How, then, for Forsyth, does this apply to the question of moral order, divine judgement and atonement? We would do well to notice that the aforementioned Ritschlianism of Forsyth's theological juvenilia was in part a well-intended reaction to the first of the two errors described above. That is, it rejected any suggestion that God was or could ever be constrained by a 'justice' or moral order that confronted him with demands he must himself abide by. Surely, the argument ran, since God himself *chose* to create the world with a certain sort of justice built into its fabric from top to bottom, being sovereign over creation he could hardly now be held to account by these same demands. God could, if it suited his purposes, simply waive those demands, 'pulling rank' over them as it were, and finally allowing the concerns of mercy to prevail over those of justice. For, was not mercy the only true 'justice' in any case?

Forsyth's mature response to this latter question was a resounding 'No!' As we have already seen, of course, for him the demands of God's love ('mercy') and those of God's justice (holiness) are not in any case to be placed in apposition, but are in reality one and the same – the implications *ad extra* of God's own nature as Holy Love. Thus, the moral order, he insists, is no mere bylaw arbitrarily imposed and equally arbitrarily suspended;[33] it is an eternal and unchangeable ordinance the demands of which must be met without reserve.[34] Of course it does not stand over against God as an external constraint on his freedom; but nor is God able simply to set it aside at will or allow it to be breached without consequence not for God's human creatures alone, but for God himself too. For the constraint to be considered here is precisely that of God's eternal moral character, and the only freedom compromised is the artificial one of an absolute voluntarism whereby God could choose not to be true to himself. Ritschlianism, in other words, had avoided one theological error only by falling into the arms of another, one equally problematic in its grasp of God's relation to the world and finally of who God himself has shown himself to be *ad intra*. 'The holy law,' Forsyth writes,

> is not the creation of God but His nature, and it cannot be treated as less than inviolable and eternal, it cannot be denied or simply annulled unless He seems false to Himself. If a play on words be permitted in such a connection.

He adds that 'the self-denial of Christ was there because God could not deny Himself'.[35] The morality shot through God's creation, that is to say, is not itself a mere feature of creation as such, but the holy nature of God himself, viewed in relation to and expressed within the fabric of that which he has created. It could not be otherwise without God's himself ceasing to be the sort of God he eternally is.

Atonement, for God's sake

In saying all this, though, we have even yet failed to fathom the true depths of Forsyth's claim that fealty to the moral law is binding upon God as well as God's creatures; that the crisis created by sin is as much a crisis for God as it is for

[33] Forsyth, *Preaching*, p. 243.
[34] Godet et al., *Atonement*, p. 66.
[35] Ibid., p. 79.

human beings; and that the judgement executed in the self-offering of Jesus to his Father on the cross is an adjustment to the entire cosmic order of things and in an important sense one carried out for God's own sake before it is for ours.[36] The cross, as the focus and summit of what Forsyth happily refers to as God's 'self-atonement',[37] is, he insists, crucial for God himself, for what is accomplished in it deals once and for all with that which alone puts God's very being under threat. Forsyth will not shy away from such strong language or radical conclusions. 'Sin', he writes, 'is the death of God.'

> Die sin must or God. Its nature is to go on from indifference to absolute hostility and malignantly to the holy; and one must go down. There is no compromise possible between the holy and the sinful when the issue is seen from the height of heaven to the depth of hell, and followed into the uttermost parts of the soul. And that is the nature of the issue as it is set in the cross of Christ. It is the eternal holiness in conflict for its life. In the Son of God the whole being of God is staked upon this issue. It is a question of a final salvation for man and for God.[38]

Perhaps we should allow for a degree of poetic licence in such statements? Perhaps. But not necessarily, and not much. It is clear that Forsyth sees the reality of sin and evil in the world as the creaturely form taken by something profoundly antithetical to all that God is, something that seeks for ever to deny, contradict and cancel out the rectitude not merely of God's creation but of who God himself is. Far from being mere prodigious rule-breaking or pubescent naughtiness to which a wise and loving father may finally decide to turn a blind eye, sin is here understood as bound up with a powerful and dangerous empire of moral corruption dedicated to nothing less than the eventual undoing of God himself. Or, if we prefer our metaphors less dramatic, something the very presence of which is toxic to God's nature as the Holy One, and with which God cannot simply choose to compromise or coexist but must act finally to destroy in order to protect his own well-being and that of all he has created. That it is God's decision to create that opens the way for the advent and flourishing of evil means, of course, that this is a decision already charged with risk and danger for God, and in full view of the cost to be met in

---

[36] 'The work of Christ', he writes, for example, 'was ethical, final and positive. It was something which had a completeness of its own before human experience, and *apart from it*.' Forsyth, *Church, the Gospel and Society*, p. 12. Italics added.

[37] Forsyth, *Justification*, p. 94.

[38] Ibid., p. 152.

consequence – as much a willing self-limiting, self-emptying and self-risking for the sake of the creature as either a self-expression or self-realization of the eternal in history.

Only when we have taken adequately into account the backdrop of this cosmic drama and the respective roles played by holiness and evil on its stage shall we be able properly to appreciate the force of Forsyth's rejection of 'sentimental' appeals to fatherly love in God, or suggestions that a truly sovereign and good God would always be bound finally to permit the concerns of love to trump or waive those of law. Such notions, Forsyth insists, are both trivial and dangerous in their depiction of the moral realities at stake in the matter of our religion. We are not merely wayward children, but rebels recruited unwittingly as agents of a morally toxic regime. And our humanity, having been transfused with the incurable virus of evil, needs to be not merely enhanced or educated, but put to death and regenerated.[39] And this for God's sake as much as ours. 'Die sin must or God.' That doesn't leave much scope for waiving anything and expecting much good to come of it.

The nature of the atonement

In closing we turn to the question of what the atonement actually amounts to according to Forsyth, and how the death of Jesus on the cross in particular is to be understood in relation to it. It is here, perhaps, that Forsyth's theology lies closest to accounts typically foregrounded within the fold of evangelicalism; but careful reading of him urges thoughtful revisiting of some traditional terms and models with a weather eye to points at which they can go horribly wrong, resulting in versions the theological implications of which are anything but 'good news'.

To begin with, as we have already seen, what occurs in Christ and is sealed by his obedient embrace of the cross is something ontological and cosmic, rather than piecemeal or anthropocentric. It is not a matter of transferring amounts of individual human 'guilt' or 'debt' scrupulously from one column of a Kafkaesque heavenly ledger to another, or adjusting the legal status of sundry criminals so as to grant them filial rights in place of their just deserts. Whatever the place of such language in Scripture or tradition (and Forsyth is far from dismissing pecuniary or forensic imagery as such), we are in danger of missing what really matters and what really occurs in 'atonement' if we do not interpret it in accordance with a much broader and more ultimate perspective, a bigger and deeper reality to which it properly refers us.

---

[39] Ibid., p. 80.

For reasons that we have already rehearsed, according to Forsyth what we call 'atonement' involves an event and an action that occur within the life of God as well as between God and the world (in the relationship between the Holy Father and his 'inhumanized' Son and in the power of the Spirit of Holiness). Here, hidden from human gaze and beyond human grasp, a necessary adjustment is somehow made to the moral order of the entire created cosmos,[40] an adjustment that brings the creation as a whole into a moral condition that complements and corresponds to God's own holy being rather than contradicting it. The adjustment is made by God himself rather than a third party, Forsyth reminds us, and is precisely the *product* of his holy love rather than the condition of it. What it does, he insists, is not change God's 'feelings' about sinful human beings (from 'anger' to 'love'), but enable God to *relate differently* to his morally ordered creation,[41] doing so now without risk either of denying himself or of permitting his own holiness to be fatally compromised. In this atoning action God reasserts his claim to creation as the product of his own holy love, vindicates the judgement of that same holy love on its moral corruption and breaks the hold of the infection of evil that has hitherto poisoned its systems. This change is one that necessarily affects us as sinners. It does so not as individual moral agents, though, but universally as a race, just as we should be affected as a race if a sudden adjustment were made to the physical order, such as gravity being abolished or the molecular structure of oxygen being modified.[42]

The Holiness that God is, Forsyth holds, cannot coexist with evil and cannot rest until 'it sees itself everywhere';[43] until, that is to say, all that exists together with God reflects and shares in God's own moral purity – a holy creation born from above of the Father's holy love, the Holy Spirit's regenerative power, and in union with the holy humanity of the Son – and all that contradicts it ceases to exist. In the face of a world like our own, he writes, God's love

> can only assert itself as holy love; ... as stung and wounded love. But assert itself it must ... by really judging and subjugating once and for all the unholy thing everywhere, killing it in its eye, and replacing Satan's Kingdom by the Kingdom of God.[44]

---

[40] Forsyth, *Holy Father*, pp. 19–20. 'Both Christ and the New Testament', he observes, 'are disappointingly reticent about the cost of grace, the "plan of salvation", the "theory of Atonement", the precise way in which Christ bore our curse before God, and took away the guilt of the world.' Ibid., p. 13.

[41] Ibid., p. 20.

[42] Ibid., p. 8.

[43] Forsyth, *Preaching*, p. 240.

[44] Forsyth, 'Preaching of Jesus', pp. 298–299.

Such judgement, he observes, is no mere matter of inflicting punishment upon sinners in accordance with the calculus of an arbitrary legal code; rather, it is 'the actual final establishment of righteousness on the wreck of sin'.[45] Far from God's holy love finding gratification or 'satisfaction' in the execution of any penalty as such, 'There is only one thing that can satisfy the holiness of God, and that is holiness.'[46] 'The holiness of love's judgment, must be freely, lovingly and practically confessed from the side of the culprit world.'[47] The sworn enemy and servant of evil must die, not because this death is somehow 'pleasing' to God in itself, but because only through being put to death and ceasing to exist can that which is bound up with evil be reborn and restored to its rightful condition as the holy child and true creature of God's heart.

According to Forsyth it is precisely this same perfect confession of God's holiness from within the sinful creation itself that is finally effected in Jesus' life of obedient devotion to his Father, reaching its climax in his submission to that death on the cross to which he was driven by the very Holy Spirit poured out upon him by his Father at his baptism. That Jesus himself committed no sin is, Forsyth insists, less important than the fact that he was 'made sin' for us, and bore our sin in his body on the cross. Again, he thinks more racially and cosmically than individually, 'sin' being the whole polluted condition of social, moral, political, economic and spiritual existence into which the eternal Son plunged himself when he emptied himself and became one of his own creatures. He could not sin, because he could not empty himself of that holiness which God is;[48] but for precisely this reason he could do no other than struggle constantly and terribly under the weight of sin and evil in the world, and his task was, in solidarity with this sinful, godless and unholy world, to seek in all things to hallow God's name rather than to desecrate or defile it, and, finally, from the depths of his human heart and will to concur with God's holy judgement upon it and permit it to be put to death in the self-offering of his own death. In Jesus, God himself became the point in the historical order of space, time and justice where the penalty mandated by his own holy love was at last executed upon a sinful creation. But, vitally, in the incarnate Son it was borne by the creature in an act of voluntary submission which at one and the same time homologated and vindicated it, and that sought its effectuation so that it might die to self and live to God. It is in this aspect of the matter, the death on the cross as a

---

[45] P. T. Forsyth, *Missions in State and Church* (London: Hodder & Stoughton, 1908), p. 52.

[46] Forsyth, *Work of Christ*, p. 126.

[47] Forsyth, *Justification*, p. 172.

[48] Forsyth, *Person and Place*, p. 306.

'decisive moral achievement',[49] the regenerative alignment of the creature with the demands of God's own holy love, that alone satisfies the law of God's being[50] and brings joy to the Father's heart.

Forsyth is thus content to employ all the dark imagery of forensic models of atonement, of Christ's suffering and death as a bearing of the wrath of God, an exhausting of the punishment due to human sin and demanded by God's holiness. Yet he carefully qualifies how this language may and may not legitimately be applied to the unique circumstance, and in doing so avoids the serious theological and moral problems that have led some to relegate or avoid its use altogether to the detriment of any adequate grasp of the divine atonement itself or the crisis that calls for it. So, for instance, Forsyth is quite clear that while Jesus must be said to bear the judgement and the penalty occasioned by the reality of sin, it is a dangerous misrepresentation of things to speak as though he were himself suffering punishment at the hand of God, or becoming even temporarily the object of God's 'anger'. Nothing could be further from the truth than this, as we have seen, since Christ suffers what he suffers gladly and out of love and devotion to his Father. To fail to draw this finely tuned distinction, therefore, would be both to posit an impossible discord in the life of the Trinity and to fail to grasp the character of the satisfaction derived by the Father from the Son's action in offering himself to death. Only a sense of personal guilt, Forsyth avers, can turn the experience of that which is the consequence of human sin into one laden appropriately with the sense of punishment, and Christ, in approaching death, knew no such guilt. Thus, while 'it was the punishment of sin that fell on Him', Jesus cannot have experienced it as a punishment, and his Father must not be misrepresented as having been angry with him as he bore it.[51] Instead, both Father and Son together experience the cross with the same paradoxical mixture of grief, pain and sorrow on the one hand, and joy and delight and love on the other. They are precisely and supremely 'at-one' in this, and it is in this unprecedented fact alone – of the absolute concurrence and concomitance of divine and creaturely holiness in this moment when the moral truth of the cosmos itself is ventured and placed at stake – that 'atonement' is sealed, once and for all.

The purpose and promise of the crucified God

I might do worse than bring this account of Forsyth to a close by quoting a passage from his latest and in many ways his most significant work, *The*

---

49 Forsyth, *Cruciality of the Cross*, p. 181.
50 P. T. Forsyth, *The Old Faith and the New* (Leicester: Midland Educational Company, 1891), p. 14.
51 Godet et al., *Atonement*, pp. 84, 85, 68.

Justification of God (1916), penned as the full horror and scale of suffering of Europe's trench warfare was becoming clear and making itself felt among an appropriately horrified public, raising questions about the adequacy of certain familiar forms of Christian 'belief in God'. Forsyth responded to this, as to all things, by concentrating on the cross and what is done there, and what that tells us about the God whose work it is from first to last. As we shall hear, 'atonement' between God and God's creation is for him no isolated chapter in the history of God's dealings with the world, but a convenient rubric under which to conclude the whole of it, from first to last:

> There is an Eye, a Mind, a Heart, before Whom the whole bloody and tortured stream of evolutionary growth has flowed ... And in the full view of it he has spoken. As it might be thus: 'Do you stumble at the cost? It has cost Me more than you – Me who see and feel it all more than you who feel it but as atoms might . . . Yea, it has cost Me more than if the price paid were all Mankind. For it cost Me My only and beloved Son to justify My name of righteousness, and to realise the destiny of My creature in holy love. And all mankind is not so great and dear as He. Nor is its suffering the enormity in a moral world that His Cross is. I am no spectator of the course of things, and no speculator on the result. I spared not My own Son. We carried the load that crushes you. It bowed Him into the ground. On the third day He rose with a new creation in His hand, and a regenerate world, and all things working together for good to love and the holy purpose in love. And what He did I did. How I did it? How I do it? This you know not now, and could not, but you shall know hereafter. There are things the Father must keep in His own hand. Be still and know that I am God, whose mercy is as His majesty, and His omnipotence is chiefly in forgiving, and redeeming, and settling all souls in worship in the temple of a new heaven and earth full of holiness. In that day the anguish will be forgotten for joy that a New Humanity is born into the world.'[52]

---

[52] Forsyth, *Justification*, pp. 169–170.

4

W. H. Griffith Thomas

ANDREW ATHERSTONE

In autumn 1910, aged 49, Anglican theologian W. H. Griffith Thomas (1861–1924) migrated from the principalship of Wycliffe Hall, Oxford, to a professorship at Wycliffe College, Toronto. For the next fourteen years he conducted a largely peripatetic ministry across North America, transferring to Philadelphia in 1919, which remained his home base until his sudden death from an embolism, aged 63. Thomas was a prominent figure on evangelical platforms at American Bible conferences and Bible institutes, and a prodigious author of theological journalism. At heart a theological educator, one of his last initiatives was planning with American dispensationalist Lewis Sperry Chafer to launch Dallas Theological Seminary, to train pastors committed to premillennialism and scriptural inerrancy.[1]

The pattern of Thomas's career parallels another famous Anglican émigré, James I. Packer, who entered self-imposed exile in Canada in 1979, aged 53, and reinvented himself as a global pan-evangelical theologian. Some assessments of Packer take no account of his previous history, as if he were born fully grown, *ex nihilo*, in Vancouver as a typical North American evangelical.[2] In the same way, modern studies of Thomas have focused predominantly upon the end of his career, especially his connections with the emerging American fundamentalist movement in the 1910s and 1920s.[3] But both Thomas and Packer were first and foremost British theologians, shaped decisively by their formative years and ministry experiences in the Church of England. They were rooted within the distinctive culture of conservative Anglican evangelicalism – the world

---

[1] John D. Hannah, *An Uncommon Union: Dallas Theological Seminary and American Evangelicalism* (Grand Rapids, MI: Zondervan, 2009).

[2] E.g. Timothy George (ed.), *J. I. Packer and the Evangelical Future: The Impact of His Life and Thought* (Grand Rapids, MI: Baker Academic, 2009).

[3] Richard A. Lum, 'W. H. Griffith Thomas and Emergent American Fundamentalism' (PhD thesis, Dallas Theological Seminary, 1994); 'W. H. Griffith Thomas: Anglicanism, Fundamentalism, and Modernity', in William H. Katerberg, *Modernity and the Dilemma of North American Anglican Identities, 1880–1950* (Montreal: McGill-Queen's University Press, 2001), pp. 79–106; Gillis J. Harp and Dwain Waldrep, 'W. H. Griffith Thomas: Anglican Fundamentalist', *Anglican and Episcopal History*, vol. 80 (March 2011), pp. 61–73.

of Oxford, the Established Church, and the historic Reformation tradition of the Book of Common Prayer and the Thirty-Nine Articles of Religion. Those early foundations, which remained their habitat well into middle age, are essential to understanding both men. Both Thomas and Packer were primarily teachers and popularizers, not original theologians. Thomas's main contribution, in Packer's words, was 'collecting, crystallizing and communicating truth and wisdom dug out by others, rather than of breaking fresh ground himself'.[4] Most of his books were compilations of his addresses to congregations, colleges and Bible conventions. Like all teachers, he frequently recycled his material.

Several of Thomas's published works in the USA had British origins. His place in the American fundamentalist pantheon was secured by his participation in the eighth volume of *The Fundamentals: A Testimony to the Truth* (1910–15), published in Chicago and distributed worldwide, but his chapter on 'Old Testament Criticism and New Testament Christianity' was an abridgement of a booklet first published for a British readership by Drummond's Tract Depot in Stirling in 1905.[5] The Moody Bible Institute in Chicago published Thomas's *The Christian Life and How to Live It* (1919), but it first appeared as *Royal and Loyal* (1905), published in London. His lectures to the Montrose Bible Conference, Pennsylvania, in summer 1915 on the nature of Scripture were published by the Bible Institute of Los Angeles (BIOLA) as *Stronghold of Truth* (1915), but a near identical series was delivered the previous year at the Keswick Convention in the English Lake District, and published in London with a slightly longer title, *Strongholds of Truth* (1914). In January 1913, Thomas became the first Anglican to deliver the annual L. P. Stone lectures at the Presbyterian stronghold Princeton Theological Seminary, New Jersey.[6] They were published as *The Holy Spirit of God* (1913), one of his most substantial monographs, dedicated to seven contemporary theologians 'to whom in various ways I owe so much' – only one was American (Princeton's own Benjamin Warfield) and the other six were all British (including James Denney, P. T. Forsyth and James Orr). The British theological world was Thomas's natural home.

Throughout the twentieth century, long after his death, Thomas remained especially popular among evangelicals in the Church of England back in his native land. *The Catholic Faith* (1904), which began as lectures to his

[4] James I. Packer, 'New Lease of Life: A Preface to *The Principles of Theology* by W. H. Griffith Thomas', *Churchman*, vol. 92 (1978), p. 51.
[5] Geoffrey R. Treloar, 'The British Contribution to *The Fundamentals*', in David Bebbington and David Ceri Jones (eds.), *Evangelicalism and Fundamentalism in the United Kingdom During the Twentieth Century* (Oxford: Oxford University Press, 2013), pp. 15–34.
[6] W. H. Griffith Thomas, *The Holy Spirit of God* (London: Longmans, Green, 1913), p. ix.

confirmation class at Portman Chapel in London, went through multiple editions into the 1960s as a handbook of Anglican doctrine and ecclesiology.[7] When it came to dogmatics, Thomas again naturally approached the subject from an Anglican framework. *The Principles of Theology* (1930), his posthumously published exposition of the Thirty-Nine Articles, running to nearly 600 pages, stood in the tradition of Victorian evangelical classics such as E. A. Litton's *Introduction to Dogmatic Theology* (1882) and displayed a thorough schooling in the Reformation Anglican tradition.[8] It became a standard textbook, reaching a sixth edition in 1978 with a new introduction by Packer, who called it Thomas's 'theological Rock of Gibraltar'.[9] It is still being marketed to evangelical ordinands in the 2020s. Another popular volume, Thomas's posthumous *Ministerial Life and Work* (1927), a handbook on evangelical ministry, was published by Moody Bible Institute and used for training young pastors at Dallas Theological Seminary.[10] Yet it began as *The Work of the Ministry* (1911), a series of addresses to his Church of England ordinands at Wycliffe Hall. The American edition was half the length of the original, abridged by his widow, stripped of its Anglican material like the Book of Common Prayer and no longer rooted in the English parish. Thomas may have been recreated as a transatlantic pan-evangelical, but his formative years were deeply embedded in the Church of England.

Although Thomas was described in *Moody Monthly* in 1923 as 'one of America's greatest Bible teachers', he was in fact thoroughly British.[11] He remained closely in touch with his old ministerial circles during his North American sojourn, and his friends petitioned Prime Minister Lloyd George for Thomas to be made a diocesan bishop.[12] His return visits to England were disrupted by the First World War, though he sailed back across the Atlantic in 1912, 1914 and 1922 to address receptive crowds in his old stamping grounds such as the Keswick Convention, the Bible League and the Mundesley Bible Conference. This chapter provides an analysis of Thomas's teaching, especially his theology of the Christian life, with particular focus on his addresses to British audiences.

[7] W. H. Griffith Thomas, *The Catholic Faith: A Manual of Instruction for Members of the Church of England* (London: Hodder & Stoughton, 1904).
[8] W. H. Griffith Thomas, *The Principles of Theology: An Introduction to the Thirty-Nine Articles* (London: Longmans, Green, 1930).
[9] Packer, 'New Lease of Life', p. 48.
[10] Review by Frank Lukens, *Princeton Theological Review*, vol. 26 (January 1928), p. 168.
[11] *Sunday School Times* advertisement, *Moody Bible Institute Monthly*, vol. 24 (October 1923), p. 73.
[12] M. Guthrie Clark, *William Henry Griffith Thomas: Minister, Scholar, Teacher* (London: Church Book Room Press, 1949), p. 25.

The abundant life

Griffith Thomas was born, and 'born again', on the border of Wales, in the market town of Oswestry in Shropshire. He 'found Christ', aged 17, on Sunday 24 March 1878, through the witness of friends in the Young Men's Society at the local parish church. Thomas described it as 'a clear-cut, definite conversion, as clear-cut as anything could be'. In his first few months as a Christian, he enjoyed 'a very blessed, and happy, and glorious time with my Bible', devouring published sermons by prominent preachers such as the English Baptist Charles Haddon Spurgeon and the American Presbyterian Thomas De Witt Talmage. Thomas testified:

> I enjoyed my Bible constantly, and had a good time. But as time went on there was an up and down experience, and I had sometimes joy and was on the mountain-top, and sometimes I had not joy, and was in the valley. I was conscious of a good deal of wandering from God – not into open sin, but I was not satisfied, I felt there was failure.

In this spiritual turmoil, about eighteen months after conversion, he prayed, 'Lord, I cannot stand this any longer; I want to have this settled, and I want to be right.' As he sought God, he was impressed by two words in Scripture, 'yield' and 'abide' – 'Yield yourselves unto God' (Rom. 6:13, AV), 'And now, little children, abide in him' (1 John 2:28, AV). These two words came to dominate Thomas's thinking about the Christian life. He first felt compelled to yield, 'to present myself again to God, as though I had never done it', and next to abide in communion with God. As he did so, he 'entered into a new experience, and realized as I never had before realized, what Christ is in the believer's life.' A few months later Thomas discovered the monthly magazine *The Life of Faith*, which introduced him to the holiness teaching of the Keswick Convention, which chimed with his new experience. He was adamant that he did not come to these new views through Keswick, but independently through prayer and reading the New Testament.[13]

These formative experiences deeply shaped Thomas's theology. He frequently urged the importance of continual growth and progress in the Christian life, rooted in personal intimacy with God. At Keswick in 1906, he suggested there was 'a great deal of danger' in evangelicals being fond of 'a simple gospel'. 'Yes,

---

[13] 'The Leaders' Testimonies: How They Found Victory in Christ', in *The Victorious Life: Messages from the Summer Conferences at Whittier, California (June), Princeton, New Jersey (July), Cedar Lake, Indiana (August)* (Philadelphia: Victorious Life Conference, 1918), pp. 320–321.

I hope we all are,' Thomas declared, 'but do not let that phrase cover your spiritual sluggishness, and prevent you from going on to a Gospel which is at once simple and experienced.' He warned that some Christians never got further than 'justification by faith' in Romans 3, and knew nothing of the spiritual heights of Romans 8. Or they rejoiced in the Protestantism of Galatians, but were ignorant of Christ's headship in Colossians, and thus missed 'some of the most profound experiences of the Gospel'. Or they knew John's Gospel but neglected John's first epistle, which was 'the culminating point of New Testament experience'. Like perpetual children, they were 'always learning and rejoicing in the alphabet, but never get very much further'. Indeed, Thomas believed that the greatest threat facing the church in the early twentieth century was the prevalence of spiritual infancy.[14] Six years later, at Keswick in 1912, he announced that all distinctions between Christians were removed by the gospel, except one – the distinction between immature and mature, between 'elementary' and 'advanced' believers.[15]

Thomas was often drawn to the book of Hebrews with its emphasis on progress in the Christian life, summarized by the apostolic exhortation 'Let us go on unto perfection' (Heb. 6:1, AV). He taught the book to ordinands at Wycliffe Hall in 1905–10, at Moody Bible Institute in 1911, at the Princeton 'Victorious Life' conference in 1916, at Keswick in 1922 and regularly at other Bible institutes and conventions.[16] Because the language of 'perfection' was open to misunderstanding, Thomas was always at pains to explain that in Scripture (or the Authorized Version) it meant spiritual maturity, not sinlessness. It signified the difference between 'the elementary and the ripe Christian'. 'Oh, the sadness, that our churches are often nurseries when they ought to be training camps for soldiers!' Thomas lamented. 'Clergymen have to dandle and coddle the saints like little babies, when they ought to be working in the Lord's vineyard and doing warfare against the Lord's enemies.'[17] For the same reason he was attracted to Colossians with its desire to 'present every man perfect in Christ Jesus' (Col. 1:28, AV) and to 1 John with its recurrent phrase 'love made perfect' (1 John 2:5; 4:12, 17–18, AV). Teaching on 1 John at Keswick in 1912, he defined perfection as 'ripeness, maturity, realising the end, step by step, of our

[14] W. H. Griffith Thomas, 'Spiritual Degeneration and Its Preventives', *Keswick Week* (1906), pp. 68–69.
[15] W. H. Griffith Thomas, 'Andrew, an Ordinary Believer', *Keswick Week* (1912), p. 22.
[16] W. H. Griffith Thomas, *'Let Us Go On': The Secret of Christian Progress in the Epistle to the Hebrews* (London: Morgan & Scott, 1923), pp. v–vi; W. H. Griffith Thomas, 'Continuance in the Life of Victory', 'Christ as Our High Priest', 'Christ's Fourfold Work for Us' and 'Possessing Our Possessions', in *Victory in Christ: A Report of Princeton Conference 1916* (Philadelphia: Managers of Princeton Conference, 1916), pp. 125–164; 'The Christian Life as Revealed in the Epistle to the Hebrews', *Keswick Week* (1922), pp. 192–213.
[17] W. H. Griffith Thomas, 'The Practice of Christian Progress', *Keswick Week* (1922), p. 202.

existence'. Love made perfect was 'the maturity of the Christian life at its highest point', 'the highest possibility of our life here and now'.[18]

Victory over sin was the keynote. In North America, Keswick-style holiness teaching was promoted by the Victorious Life Testimony, a pan-evangelical network founded in 1913. It held summer conferences during the First World War at Princeton, before migrating to other venues such as Cedar Lake in Indiana, Whittier in southern California and Stony Brook on Long Island.[19] Thomas moved seamlessly into these circles, joined the council of the Victorious Life Testimony, and spoke often at its events. Back in England, at the original Keswick, he argued that 'victory' in the Christian life should be a present reality not just an eschatological hope. Taking an illustration from the war, he recalled how shortly before the Armistice some newspapers reported that the Germans and the Allies were both so entrenched that neither side could break through and the result would be permanent stalemate. Thankfully, these gloomy predictions proved false. In the same way, in the war against sin, some Christians seemed to expect 'spiritual stalemate, neither side getting victory over the other'. They wrongly assumed that Romans 7:19 ('the good that I would, I do not: but the evil which I would not, that I do', AV) was the pattern of the normal Christian life. On the contrary, Thomas insisted, Christians should expect to live every day in Romans 8 as 'more than conquerors'.[20]

'Must Christians sin?' Thomas asked boldly. 'The answer is, "No, certainly not."' Christians could live without sinning. In justifying this claim, he drew a careful distinction between principle and practice, between 'sin' and 'sins' or 'the root' and 'the fruit'.[21] Thomas was not suggesting the absence of the sinful instinct, but of sinful behaviour, in the perfected Christian. As evidence for the lifelong persistence of sin in believers, he pointed to scriptural examples such as Abraham who fell into old sins, and to the Church of England formularies which taught that the sinful infection of human nature 'doth remain, yea in them that are regenerated' (Article 9 of the Thirty-Nine Articles).[22] On the one hand, the 'eradication' of sin was clearly contrary to Scripture and human experience. On the other hand, the 'suppression' of sin meant constant struggle

---

[18] W. H. Griffith Thomas, 'The Christian Life (IV): Its Prospects and Possibilities', *Keswick Week* (1912), p. 179.

[19] C. Melvin Loucks, 'The Theological Foundations of the Victorious Life: An Evaluation of the Theology of the Victorious Christian Life in the Light of the Present and Future Aspects of Biblical Sanctification' (PhD thesis, Fuller Theological Seminary, 1984).

[20] W. H. Griffith Thomas, 'The Power of Christ's Salvation', *Keswick Week* (1922), p. 13.

[21] W. H. Griffith Thomas, *Grace and Power: Some Aspects of the Spiritual Life* (New York: Fleming H. Revell, 1916), pp. 131–132.

[22] W. H. Griffith Thomas, *Genesis: A Devotional Commentary*, 3 vols. (London: Religious Tract Society, 1907–8), vol. 1, p. 240.

and inevitable defeat as in Romans 7 and was 'miserably inadequate' to the glories of Romans 8. Therefore, Thomas proposed a third way – the 'counteraction' of sin in the Christian life through the power of the Holy Spirit. He announced:

Do not dream that it is eradicated and do not trouble about suppressing it. Let the Holy Spirit so come into your life, and reign supreme in the throne-room of the will, that there shall be this constant, continuous, blessed, and increasing Counteraction.

For support he turned again to Church of England formularies, this time from the Book of Common Prayer, to demonstrate that the Anglican Reformers 'knew the secret of holiness' 350 years before the Keswick Convention. 'Vouchsafe, O Lord, to keep us this day without sin,' sang the *Te Deum* at Morning Prayer, while the Collect for Grace chimed in, 'grant that this day we fall into no sin'. Likewise, at the Lord's Supper, the Collect for Purity prayed 'that we may perfectly love thee, and worthily magnify thy holy name'. Thomas conscripted these historic liturgical texts for a theology of counteraction. 'So the Christian, while he has the principle of sin in him, need not, and ought not, to express that principle in practice.'[23]

If Romans 7 represented the struggles of the moralist (either converted or unconverted) 'trying to be holy by his own effort', Romans 8 was normal Christian experience, dominated by the Holy Spirit and by grace.[24] It was the vital difference, Thomas told a Victorious Life Testimony conference in 1922, between 'a new leaf and a new life'.[25] Grace was as essential to sanctification as to justification. In another address, Thomas argued strongly against the common Reformed conception of the Christian life as

salvation by grace, but sanctification by our own effort; justification by faith, but sanctification by fighting; salvation by acceptance, but sanctification by struggle. But God does not rescue and redeem from the horrible pit and miry clay, and set our feet upon a rock, and then expect us to go on alone. This way disappointment lies, and often backsliding . . . The grace that saves is the grace that sanctifies.

[23] W. H. Griffith Thomas, 'The Christian Life (I): Its Purpose and Privileges', *Keswick Week* (1912), pp. 58–59.
[24] W. H. Griffith Thomas, 'The Victorious Life (I)', *Bibliotheca Sacra*, vol. 76 (July 1919), p. 276.
[25] W. H. Griffith Thomas, 'Grace', in *The Victorious Christ: Messages from Conferences Held by the Victorious Life Testimony in 1922* (Philadelphia: Sunday School Times Company, 1923), p. 41.

'God's way is all of grace,' he reiterated. 'Grace does not improve the old nature, it overcomes it.'[26] Thomas illustrated this doctrine by Jacob, who wrestled with God at Peniel (Gen. 32). Only when Jacob was brought to the end of his human resources, no longer able to fight, did he realize that blessing from God was obtained by 'passive receptiveness', not by struggle. 'Just as salvation is of God by grace, so is every spiritual blessing derived in the same way.'[27]

The doorway to holiness was therefore 'total surrender' or 'entire consecration', key Keswick emphases. Turning again to Old Testament character studies, Thomas portrayed Lot as representative of 'the Christian who is not fully consecrated', pursuing earthly interests and thus ending in spiritual disaster.[28] To 'put God first' was the 'secret of all real spiritual power and blessing'.[29] 'Unconditional surrender, unquestioning submission, unwavering trust . . . Christ is only truly our Saviour in proportion as He is our Lord.'[30] Thomas spoke often of the perils of worldliness and the need for devoted discipleship. He urged his Wycliffe Hall ordinands that their yielding of everything to God must be 'definite, unreserved, irrevocable'.[31] At Keswick, he outlined the blessings of 'a surrendered will', applied in royalist terms: 'Let the Lord exercise His crown rights over our life.'[32]

This passivist doctrine was encapsulated by the popular motto of the Victorious Life movement, 'Let go and let God'.[33] But it was taught by Thomas long before he emigrated to North America. At Keswick in 1906, he exhorted:

Put yourself in the stream, and allow that stream to take you; put yourself in the wind, and allow the wind to waft you. Open every sail, get every breath of air that is stirring; and then allow that wind to carry you to the haven where you would be. That is what I mean by whole-hearted abandonment, surrender to the Lord Jesus Christ. Thus, you will be carried on unto life's maturity, that full-grown Christianity which glorifies God.[34]

He spoke of abandonment to Christ interchangeably with 'full surrender to the Holy Spirit'.[35] The power of sin was to be overcome not by human effort but

---

26 Thomas, *Grace and Power*, pp. 92–93.
27 Thomas, *Genesis*, vol. 2, pp. 117–118.
28 Ibid., vol. 1, p. 162.
29 Ibid., vol. 2, p. 108.
30 Ibid., vol. 3, p. 219.
31 W. H. Griffith Thomas, *The Work of the Ministry* (London: Hodder & Stoughton, 1911), p. 76.
32 W. H. Griffith Thomas, 'The Power of Peace', *Keswick Week* (1908), pp. 206, 210.
33 Thomas, 'Power of Christ's Salvation', pp. 16–17.
34 Thomas, 'Spiritual Degeneration', p. 70.
35 Thomas, *Genesis*, vol. 1, p. 241.

'through the mighty energy of the Holy Spirit within us'.[36] Sometimes his pneumatology was given free rein, such as at Keswick in 1907, where Thomas divided history into five ages, or 'dispensations' – the first and last were dispensations of God the Father (as creator and king), the second and fourth were dispensations of God the Son (at Christ's first and second advents), but the central age in Thomas's schema, the current period of human existence, was the dispensation 'where the Holy Ghost is supreme'. He asserted that many professing Christians, even some at Keswick, were still living in the two former dispensations and therefore had 'no power, no vitality, no reality' in their spiritual lives. Like the early believers in the book of Acts, they needed to be filled with the Holy Spirit, which was 'God's purpose for all Christians, not a luxury for the few; but an absolute necessity for all'.[37] Nevertheless, Thomas stopped short of Pentecostal manifestations which were beginning to gather momentum in evangelical circles in the early decades of the twentieth century. He upset some at Keswick in 1912 by including the 'Tongues Movement' in his catalogue of anti-Christian modern heresies. Thomas rejected *glossolalia* as a type of 'spiritual materialism – a craving for the visible',[38] and instead emphasized the unseen work of the Holy Spirit in the heart of the believer, sanctifying and overruling the sinful nature.

A miscellany of Thomas's addresses on the Christian life was published in North America as *Grace and Power* (1916), dedicated to Anglican clergymen H. W. Webb-Peploe and Evan H. Hopkins, doyens of the British holiness movement. It attracted the scrutiny of Benjamin Warfield, who included Thomas in his broad demolition of the Victorious Life movement. Focusing especially on Thomas's friend, Charles Trumbull (editor of the *Sunday School Times*), Warfield complained that although the Victorious Life highlighted faith and grace, which gave it a 'specious appearance of Evangelicalism', it was thoroughly unbiblical in its view of sanctification without struggle.[39] In a lengthy riposte, Thomas accused Warfield of misrepresenting the Keswick position. For example, Warfield asserted that its roots lay in the errors of Wesleyan Arminianism, or even in Pelagianism, but Thomas emphasized 'my Anglican Augustinianism' and that he had met several Scottish Presbyterians at Keswick whose ministries were enlivened by its impact. These Scots, 'with their strong, intellectual, Calvinistic Presbyterianism', received at Keswick a 'spiritual glow

---

[36] W. H. Griffith Thomas, *Romans: A Devotional Commentary*, 3 vols. (London: Religious Tract Society, 1911–12), vol. 2, p. 65.

[37] W. H. Griffith Thomas, 'The Three Dispensations', *Keswick Week* (1907), pp. 212–216.

[38] W. H. Griffith Thomas, 'The Christian Life (III): Its Perils and Protection', *Keswick Week* (1912), p. 130.

[39] B. B. Warfield, 'The Victorious Life', *Princeton Theological Review*, vol. 16 (July 1918), pp. 321–373.

and experience which gave force and freshness' to their Reformed doctrines.[40] Thomas further suggested that Warfield's pessimistic alternative offered 'no real Gospel for the saint, but only for the sinner', and would drive Christians to discouragement and despair. What the 'newly-awakened soul' needed to hear was a joyful message that 'sanctification is obtainable in the very same way as justification, through faith', and that, 'in spite of the evil nature within, there should and can be continuous victory'. He lamented that Warfield seemed to approach the subject as a doctrinal theory, without appreciating Keswick's ambition for transformative spiritual experience.[41]

One of Warfield's specific criticisms was that the Victorious Life movement created two classes of Christians, those who had enjoyed a 'second blessing' and those who had not, leading to scorn of 'ordinary' or 'average' believers.[42] Speaking at the annual Winona Lake Bible Conference, Indiana, in August 1923, Thomas defended the language of 'second blessing' to describe 'whole-hearted consecration to God'. However, he emphasized that consecration could be enjoyed from the moment of conversion, without any 'spiritual gap', and that God was ready to bless every Christian not merely a second but a 'second hundredth' time.[43] These redemption blessings were available 'here and now', without waiting for heaven. 'It seems a pity, and often leads to spiritual loss', Thomas advised, 'to project so many of our joys into the future, instead of realising them in the present.'[44] He therefore preferred to speak not merely of the 'victorious life' but the 'abundant life'.[45]

Surrendered to Scripture

Surrender to God was demonstrated by Christian obedience. As Thomas told his Keswick audience, 'If you want to abide, obey.'[46] This was evident not only in sanctified living but in surrender to God's Word in Scripture, another keynote of Keswick spirituality. In his studies in Genesis, Thomas presented Abraham as a model of the 'wholly surrendered' life, someone who believed God's Word 'without hesitation and without questioning'. 'To us also comes the call for absolute trust, the faith that takes God simply at His word, feeling

[40] Thomas, 'Victorious Life (I)', pp. 279, 287.
[41] W. H. Griffith Thomas, 'The Victorious Life (II)', *Bibliotheca Sacra*, vol. 76 (October 1919), pp. 464–466.
[42] Warfield, 'Victorious Life', pp. 330–331.
[43] W. H. Griffith Thomas, 'The Spiritual Life of Jacob', *Winona Echoes: Addresses Delivered at the Winona Bible Conference* (1923), p. 216.
[44] W. H. Griffith Thomas, *Christ Pre-eminent: Studies in the Epistle to the Colossians* (Chicago: Bible Institute Colportage Association, 1923), pp. 34, 44.
[45] Thomas, 'Power of Christ's Salvation', p. 13.
[46] W. H. Griffith Thomas, 'After Keswick – What?', *Keswick Week* (1908), p. 216.

assured that it cannot fail.'[47] 'True faith', he declared, 'is nothing more, as it is nothing less, than this. God speaks: man believes.'[48]

Scripture governed Thomas's outlook. He was a popular speaker at the annual Mildmay Conference in north London, founded in the 1860s by Victorian clergyman William Pennefather and parallel in ethos to Keswick. Addressing the conference in 1899, for example, Thomas ended with a rousing call to honour God's Word 'in the soul, in the home, in the study, in the pulpit, in the congregation, in the college, in the university, in the nation'.[49] Likewise to Keswick, he proclaimed:

> There is no Christianity worthy of the name that is not based upon this Book. There is no spiritual life, at Keswick or anywhere else, that is not found suffused, permeated, dominated, by Holy Scripture ... By this Book we stand; on it we rest; with it we fight; through it we shall conquer, because it is 'the Word of God, which liveth and abideth for ever.'[50]

The Bible should therefore dictate clerical agendas. 'The secret of congregational power', Thomas encouraged his Wycliffe ordinands, 'is the prominence that we give to the Word of God. The source of everything fruitful and mighty in the life of God's people is to be found there.'[51] In line with Reformation Anglicanism, he eschewed the concept of a sacerdotal priesthood and insisted that clergy were ordained instead to the prophetic office as preachers of the Word.[52]

Devotion to the Bible was vital 'for the simple reason that it is through the Word we get to know God'.[53] In *Old Testament Criticism and New Testament Christianity*, Thomas welcomed the Scriptures as an 'infallible' revelation from God. It was impossible to accept Christ and reject the Bible: 'Christ speaks of the Bible. The Bible speaks of Christ. They stand or fall together.'[54] Bible conferences were at the height of their popularity on both sides of the Atlantic in the early twentieth century. Impressed by D. L. Moody's gatherings at Northfield, Massachusetts, George Campbell Morgan (Minister of Westminster Chapel) launched a new summer conference in the village of Mundesley, on the

---

[47] Thomas, *Genesis*, vol. 1, pp. 147, 149–150.

[48] Ibid., p. 264.

[49] W. H. Griffith Thomas, 'Now to Appear in the Presence of God for Us', *The Mildmay Conference, 1899: Report of the Addresses* (London: John F. Shaw, 1899), p. 77.

[50] W. H. Griffith Thomas, 'The Bible as an Authority', *Keswick Week* (1914), p. 231.

[51] Thomas, *Work of the Ministry*, p. 94.

[52] W. H. Griffith Thomas, *Priest or Prophet? A Question for the Day* (London: John F. Shaw, 1899).

[53] Thomas, 'After Keswick', p. 216.

[54] W. H. Griffith Thomas, *Old Testament Criticism and New Testament Christianity* (Stirling: Drummond's Tract Depot, 1905), p. 31.

Norfolk coast, which ran from 1906 until the First World War as a 'British Northfield'.[55] When Thomas spoke there in 1910, he took the inspiration of Scripture as his theme. Cautiously, he acknowledged that it was impossible to know exactly how God had inspired these writings, yet theories of method must be distinguished from 'the blessed reality of the fact'.[56] Likewise at Keswick, he rejected concepts of 'mechanical dictation', while emphasizing that the Holy Spirit inspired the precise words of the biblical text, not just the broad ideas behind it, 'for how can I know God's thoughts if I do not know God's words?'[57]

Towards the end of his career, during the controversies with Modernism, Thomas subscribed to more precise doctrinal formulae. At the World Conference on Christian Fundamentals in Philadelphia in May 1919, the resolutions committee included several leading American conservative theologians such as William Bell Riley (Pastor of First Baptist Church, Minneapolis), James Gray (President of Moody Bible Institute) and Charles A. Blanchard (President of Wheaton College, Illinois), but it was chaired by Thomas. Their nine-point doctrinal statement opened with an affirmation that the Old and New Testaments were 'verbally inspired of God, and inerrant in the original writings', a phrase mirrored by many other conservative bases of faith during the twentieth century.[58] In one of his addresses to the conference, Thomas reiterated the supremacy of Scripture over human reason and the ecclesial magisterium: 'It is our final court of appeal, and contains the last and supreme word on everything connected with the spiritual life.'[59]

The Bible as supernatural revelation was central to Thomas's understanding.[60] To remove the supernatural from Christianity was like 'cutting at the very vitals of faith and godliness'. He therefore lambasted the 'over-weening influence of critical studies which tend to dissolve everything that cannot be vindicated at the bar of reason and physical science'.[61] The philosophical presuppositions of much Old Testament criticism, for instance, he viewed as 'subversive' of belief in divine revelation, such as predictive prophecy.[62] On the same basis, Thomas dismissed modern theories of evolution as unsubstantiated and inherently

---

[55] Jill Morgan, *A Man of the Word: Life of G. Campbell Morgan* (London: Pickering & Inglis, 1951), pp. 169–180.
[56] W. H. Griffith Thomas, 'The Word of God and the Man of God', *Westminster Bible Conference, Mundesley, 1910: Verbatim Report of Sermons and Lectures* (London: Morgan & Scott, 1910), p. 289.
[57] W. H. Griffith Thomas, 'The Bible as a Power', *Keswick Week* (1914), p. 238.
[58] 'Report of Committee on Resolutions', in *God Hath Spoken: Twenty-five Addresses Delivered at the World Conference on Christian Fundamentals* (Philadelphia: Bible Conference Committee, 1919), p. 11.
[59] W. H. Griffith Thomas, 'The Witness of History to the Inspiration of the Word', in *God Hath Spoken*, p. 107.
[60] W. H. Griffith Thomas, 'The Bible as a Revelation', *Keswick Week* (1914), pp. 216–223.
[61] Thomas, *Work of the Ministry*, p. 152.
[62] Thomas, *Old Testament Criticism*, pp. 16, 18.

atheistic.[63] Evolution was incompatible with supernatural Christianity, removing God from the picture and denying the uniqueness of Christ. Put bluntly, 'if the Bible is true, Evolution cannot be true'.[64]

Thomas agreed that, in one sense, the Bible should be studied 'like any other book', echoing Benjamin Jowett's notorious phrase in *Essays and Reviews* (1860).[65] He welcomed biblical criticism, per se, as a legitimate tool for understanding the Bible better, but loudly decried its 'illegitimate, unscientific, and unhistorical' use by contemporary scholars. Most of their conclusions were dubious and short-lived, 'as one hypothesis succeeds another'.[66] At the annual conference of the British Bible League in May 1914, Thomas brushed off the common caricature of evangelicals as ostriches with their heads in the sand, unwilling to face critical ideas. On the contrary, he announced, most of his conservative opinions were formed by the very act of reading critical books, because the more he read the more he saw they were false.[67] The popularity of critical conclusions among university graduates he dismissed as a fad: 'there is a fashion in scholarship as well as in socks' – which the Keswick stenographer unfortunately misheard as 'sex' – 'and as a rule no one likes to be out of fashion in one or the other'. Thomas urged his audience to think independently and refuse to call anyone master, 'whether he is ancient or modern'.[68]

During the First World War, in the context of widespread anti-German sentiment, Thomas launched an assault on the Germanic origins of modern biblical criticism. He traced German bellicosity and immorality (such as the recent Herero genocide in South West Africa) not only to the *Übermensch* philosophy of Friedrich Nietzsche but to German views of Scripture. From David Strauss's notorious *Das Leben Jesu* (1835–6) and the Tübingen School of F. C. Baur, through to the hypotheses of Julius Wellhausen, 'Germany has done more than all other so-called Christian nations put together to destroy faith in the supernatural.' By undermining the authority of Scripture, they had removed the basis for Christian morality. The horrors of the Western Front, Thomas declared, were a clarion call 'to all who love pure, simple, unadulterated, Biblical religion' in Britain and America to break free from German rationalism and proclaim the Scriptures as divine revelation.[69]

---

[63] W. H. Griffith Thomas, *What About Evolution? Some Thoughts on the Relation of Evolution to the Bible and Christianity* (Chicago: Bible Institute Colportage Association, 1918), p. 12.

[64] W. H. Griffith Thomas, 'Evolution and the Supernatural', *Bibliotheca Sacra*, vol. 79 (April 1922), p. 196.

[65] W. H. Griffith Thomas, 'How to Study the Bible', *Keswick Week* (1914), p. 45.

[66] Thomas, *Old Testament Criticism*, pp. 5, 8.

[67] W. H. Griffith Thomas, 'The Weapons of our Warfare', *Bible League Quarterly* no. 54 (July 1914), p. 7.

[68] W. H. Griffith Thomas, *Strongholds of Truth* (London: Morgan & Scott, 1914), p. 87; cf. Thomas, 'Bible as a Power', p. 242.

[69] W. H. Griffith Thomas, 'Germany and the Bible', *Bibliotheca Sacra*, vol. 72 (January 1915), pp. 49–66.

After the Armistice, Thomas extended his analysis with a swingeing attack upon German immorality during the recent hostilities. He accused Prussian militarism of 'many patent violations of civilized ethics' – murdering women and children, torpedoing hospital ships, executing prisoners, poisoning wells, devising cruel booby-traps, disregarding international treaties, using flamethrowers and chemical weapons on the battlefield, and other similar acts of 'fiendish barbarity'. After illustrating this moral degradation in detail, Thomas again diagnosed the root cause as Germany's attitude to Scripture. He lamented that the same critical spirit had infected English-speaking seminaries and pulpits for decades, resulting in 'abundant spiritual powerlessness' in many churches and an absence of conversions or spiritual growth.[70] The fundamental issue at stake, Thomas repeated, was whether or not the Bible was 'a supernatural Book'. He mocked those who bowed down to the supposed superiority of German intellect, observing that 'all the things that are important in ordinary life' – steamships, railroads, electricity, the telegraph, the telephone, aeroplanes, submarines – had been invented outside Germany.[71] The *Bible Champion*, journal of the Bible League of North America, celebrated Thomas's 'virile, vivid truth-telling', and thanked him for reminding the church of 'the shameful sin of pandering to Hun Scholarship'.[72] When Professor Eduard König from the University of Bonn pointed out that there were in fact many orthodox 'defenders of Biblical truth' in Germany, Thomas retorted that if that were really the case, they should find the courage to speak up.[73] Unafraid of controversy, Thomas provoked further uproar in 1921 with an exposé of the alarming spread of Modernism within evangelical missions, after a lecture tour of China with Charles Trumbull. In particular, he warned that higher-critical views of the Bible were destroying the spiritual vitality of the American-funded missions and leading Chinese converts astray.[74]

The highest criticism

Alongside the academic disciplines of 'lower' and 'higher' criticism, Thomas advocated a third approach, which he dubbed 'highest' criticism, represented by the Christian who trembled at God's Word (Isa. 66:2) and invited the Word

---

[70] W. H. Griffith Thomas, 'German Moral Abnormality', *Bibliotheca Sacra*, vol. 76 (January 1919), pp. 84–104.

[71] W. H. Griffith Thomas, 'The German Attitude to the Bible', *Bibliotheca Sacra*, vol. 76 (April 1919), p. 172.

[72] 'For Shame Sake', *Bible Champion*, vol. 25 (December 1919), p. 508.

[73] 'Germany and Biblical Criticism', *Bibliotheca Sacra*, vol. 77 (January 1920), pp. 102–108.

[74] W. H. Griffith Thomas, 'Modernism in China', *Princeton Theological Review*, vol. 19 (October 1921), pp. 630–671.

itself to be the critic (Heb. 4:12). He explained that 'there are humble and earnest souls who know far more than the profoundest scholarship, because they are among the Highest Critics'. He was fond of quoting the aphorism of Scottish Presbyterian James Hamilton, that 'the believer on his knees sees farther than the philosopher on tip-toe'. If the church adopted this attitude, then 'the criticism of the Bible can go on till Doomsday and without any harm'.[75] As Thomas announced on his final visit to Keswick in 1922, 'if we allowed the Word of God to criticise us a little more, we should criticise it a great deal less'.[76]

Therefore, although Thomas was prepared to defend the authority of Scripture when faced by Romanist or Modernist challenges, he was happiest when speaking devotionally to fellow evangelicals. His first book, *Methods of Bible Study* (1902), outlined five stages in scriptural engagement. The first four – textual criticism, literary criticism, biblical exegesis and biblical theology – were accessible to 'anyone with brains', but only people with spiritual discernment could reach the 'summit', receiving the Bible as 'God's personal Word to our own souls'.[77] The study of Scripture was always far more than an intellectual exercise. Expert knowledge in Hebrew philology or archaeology was helpful, but 'spiritual experience' was essential for a proper understanding of the text.[78] The Bible's 'deepest secrets' were revealed only, Thomas reiterated, to those willing to submit to its teaching. He approved of Joseph Agar Beet's observation: 'Access to the inmost sanctuary of Holy Scripture is granted only to those who come to worship.'[79] Among Thomas's many books on Scripture, his fullest expositions on Genesis and Romans were published in the Religious Tract Society's 'devotional commentary' series, focused on the spiritual life and communion with God.

Thomas frequently urged systematic Bible reading as a daily discipline, perhaps using a reading plan from the Bible Prayer Union or the Scripture Union. His own habit since his ordination at St Paul's Cathedral in 1885 was to follow the Church of England's lectionary, reading through the Greek New Testament every year.[80] In the tent at Mundesley he warned that to rely on a diet of sermons from the clergy was to be 'a spoon-fed Christian all your life'. Daily encounter with God's Word was 'the secret of personal power'.[81] Nothing,

[75] Thomas, 'Bible as a Power', pp. 242–243, quoting James Hamilton, *The Lamp and the Lantern: or, Light for the Tent and the Traveller* (London: James Nisbet, 1853), p. 139.

[76] W. H. Griffith Thomas, 'The Possibility of Christian Progress', *Keswick Week* (1922), p. 197.

[77] W. H. Griffith Thomas, *Methods of Bible Study* (London: Marshall, 1902), p. 103.

[78] Thomas, *Old Testament Criticism*, p. 4.

[79] Thomas, *Romans*, vol. 1, p. 19, quoting Joseph Agar Beet, *A Commentary on St Paul's Epistle to the Romans*, new edn (London: Hodder & Stoughton, 1900), p. 27.

[80] Thomas, 'After Keswick', pp. 219–220.

[81] Thomas, 'Word of God', p. 297.

however good, must be allowed to intrude upon this direct engagement with Scripture. It was the fashion for evangelicals to mark their Bibles, underlining and connecting key phrases, and they could often be seen doing so at conferences or during Sunday sermons. Thomas was not averse to the practice, and recommended guides such as Mary Jane Menzies' *How To Mark Your Bible* (1891) and Amos Wells's *The Bible Marksman* (1900).[82] However, he urged that devotional reading should always be from an unmarked Bible, so that instead of feeding on 'old manna' they would receive from Scripture 'something absolutely fresh' and personal.[83]

Among devotional resources, one of the most popular was *Daily Light on the Daily Path*, a selection of very brief daily Scripture readings without commentary, first published in the 1860s and still in wide circulation in the early twentieth century. Yet Canon A. E. Barnes-Lawrence startled some at Keswick in 1908 by criticizing lazy Christians who used *Daily Light* as a Bible substitute.[84] Thomas concurred. He acknowledged the benefit of devotional aids, but insisted that meditation on the Bible must always be first hand. In one of his favourite illustrations, he noted that the surnames of many of Keswick's prominent teachers began with the letter M – George Macgregor, J. Gregory Mantle, F. B. Meyer, E. W. Moore, George Campbell Morgan, Handley Moule, Andrew Murray – but there was a far better M than all of these: '*My* meditation of him shall be sweet' (Ps. 104:34, AV).[85] On another occasion Thomas appealed for the 'total abolition' of devotional books from the evangelical 'quiet time', which should be spent only with the Bible.[86] He advised his American hearers in 1918 to lay aside their Scofield Reference Bibles.[87] Thomas believed that these human aids, if put in the wrong place, became 'dangerous and disastrous, crutches that prevent vigorous exercise, and that will inevitably lead to spiritual senility'.[88]

Daily Bible reading was also a bulwark to holiness and a preventative against 'backsliding'. During a succession of severe storms in Oxford in 1903, 1906 and 1909, a total of eight large elm trees in the Broad Walk at Christ Church Meadow fell with a crash, revealing their internal rottenness.[89] Thomas used this as a visual warning for his Wycliffe ordinands that if they neglected personal Bible

---

82 Thomas, *Methods of Bible Study*, p. 115.
83 Thomas, 'After Keswick', p. 220.
84 A. E. Barnes-Lawrence, 'Christ's Vision and Its Fulfilment', *Keswick Week* (1908), p. 21.
85 Thomas, 'After Keswick', p. 220.
86 Thomas, 'How to Study the Bible', p. 51.
87 W. H. Griffith Thomas, 'The Bible in the Christian Life', in *Victorious Life*, p. 98.
88 Thomas, *Grace and Power*, p. 157.
89 'The Great Gale', *Jackson's Oxford Journal*, 19 September 1903, p. 2; 'Saturday Morning's Gale', *Jackson's Oxford Journal*, 13 January 1906, p. 4; 'Thursday Night's Gale', *Oxford Journal*, 8 December 1909, p. 4.

reading and prayer it would lead to 'spiritual decay', which often resulted in tragic crashes out of ministry through moral failure.[90] The same principle applied to all Christians. 'If you and I do not meditate upon God's Word daily', he warned at Keswick, 'we shall suffer in our spiritual life. In proportion as we neglect it, will be the weakness of our souls.' Conversely, however, 'keep close to the Scriptures, and you will never go wrong'.[91]

Christianity is Christ

In the *Memoir and Remains of Robert Murray M'Cheyne* (1844), a devotional classic, the young Dundee minister counselled his friends, 'For every look at yourself, take ten looks at Christ.'[92] This famous exhortation became popular in Keswick holiness circles. It was frequently referenced by Griffith Thomas, though he thought the balance was wrong. How much better, he rejoiced, to 'take eleven looks at Christ and none at self'.[93] This Christocentrism suffused Thomas's teaching. It was seen, for example, in his early foray into apologetics, *Christianity Is Christ* (1909), with its repeated question 'What think ye of Christ?' A similar emphasis was obvious in one of his last books, *Christ Preeminent* (1923), in which he celebrated that the central theme of Christianity was 'not a theory, not a set of rules, not simply a code of morals, not even a system of truth, but a living Person', Jesus Christ, who must be personally appropriated by faith.[94] Thomas proclaimed at Keswick that the whole message of Scripture, from beginning to end, could be summed up in one word – Christ.[95] He acknowledged that evangelicalism was sometimes misshapen into 'Jesus religion', and that too many evangelical hymns were addressed to Jesus instead of to God the Father, yet a focus on Jesus pervaded his own writings.[96]

Again, supernaturalism was to the fore. Salvation was impossible without the miraculous intervention of Christ. In one of Thomas's first published sermons, *The Power of God* (1891), from his time as a curate at St Aldate's, Oxford, he observed that it was easy to be misled by the many social and cultural improvements of the Victorian age into assuming the fundamental goodness of human nature:

---

[90] Thomas, *Work of the Ministry*, p. 171.

[91] Thomas, 'After Keswick', p. 219.

[92] Andrew A. Bonar, *Memoir and Remains of the Rev. Robert Murray M'Cheyne* (Dundee: William Middleton, 1844), p. 254.

[93] W. H. Griffith Thomas, 'Some Secrets of Ministerial Power', *Westminster Bible Conference, Mundesley 1912: Report of Sermons and Lectures* (London: Morgan & Scott, 1912), p. 150.

[94] Thomas, *Christ Pre-eminent*, p. 60.

[95] W. H. Griffith Thomas, 'The Bible as a Message', *Keswick Week* (1914), p. 232.

[96] Thomas, *Christ Pre-eminent*, p. 32.

But ever and anon there come forth the eruptions of human vice, crime and iniquity, scattering moral destruction everywhere; and at the same time scattering to the winds our ideas of human goodness. We may give man all our nostrums, our education, our social schemes, and they will be useless towards real and permanent reformation. These touch but the symptoms and not the source of the disease . . . Signing the [temperance] pledge does not change the drunkard's heart. Pulling down the rookery and building the model dwelling do not destroy the fascination for crime. No! no! man must be entirely renovated, and receive the power of God into his being.[97]

The Christian gospel, Thomas declared, allowed for the full extent of human depravity and yet provided the perfect remedy. External behaviour must flow from internal transformation. No modern 'ism' was capable of combating 'the inroads of vice, squalor, and degradation'. Only the gospel could 'satisfy the full and deep cravings of the human heart'.[98] In a parallel address, *The Power of Christ* (1894), Thomas stated that despite all the inventions and advantages of Victorian Britain, they were 'powerless to deal with sin. Christ alone can remove its cancer and endow the nature with moral health, purity and power . . . Christ, and Christ alone, is the hope of the world'.[99]

In *Christianity Is Christ*, Thomas again highlighted the impotence of social reforms or modern scientific discoveries to deal with human wickedness. Only Jesus Christ had the answer. The agnosticism of Thomas Huxley and the pessimism of Thomas Hardy were ready illustrations of

the utter powerlessness of philosophy, science, education, culture, progress to deal with the deepest problems of human life. And yet all the while many and many a simple-hearted life is finding in Jesus Christ the secret of deliverance from sin, the guarantee against moral weakness, and the inspiration of an immortal hope.[100]

'If the one thing that man needs is illumination,' Thomas explained, 'then ideas will suffice and no divine incarnation is necessary, but if there is such a thing as sin in the world we must produce a divine sinless Redeemer to deal with it.'[101] Nevertheless, despite his premillennial perspective, he did advocate

---

97 W. H. Griffith Thomas, *The Power of God* (Oxford: J. T. Hall, 1891), p. 7.

98 Ibid., pp. 8, 10–11.

99 W. H. Griffith Thomas, *The Power of Christ* (Oxford: Baxter, 1894), p. 16.

100 W. H. Griffith Thomas, *Christianity Is Christ* (London: Longmans, Green, 1909), p. 95.

101 W. H. Griffith Thomas, 'The Virgin Birth: Reasons for Belief', *Bible Record*, vol. 4 (December 1907), p. 382.

for a distinctively Christian contribution to social reform. He argued that Christian humanitarianism over nineteen centuries had dramatically improved society, in a way no other message or movement could, by raising the status of women and children, abolishing slavery, building hospitals, caring for prisoners and protecting animals. Moreover, the impact of the modern missionary enterprise was 'nothing short of stupendous' in transforming the prospects of far-flung places such as Fiji, Uganda, New Zealand and Tierra del Fuego. 'It is Christianity alone', Thomas declared, 'which gives to the Western world its vast superiority over the Eastern, and its irresistible impulse to progress.'[102] At Keswick in 1906 he rejected the accusation that evangelicals were disinterested in the social ills facing modern Britain, such as unemployment, poverty, the alcohol trade, gambling, sexual immorality and desecration of the Lord's Day. On the contrary, Thomas believed there was no better way to tackle these problems than with 'the old-fashioned Evangelical verities of the New Testament' as taught at Keswick.[103]

Central to Christ's supernatural intervention was the atonement. The cross, Thomas celebrated, was 'the heart of Christianity'.[104] 'The Cross is the core of the gospel', he wrote in another essay, and therefore the church must proclaim it 'without any hesitation or qualification, as the means of Divine redemption'.[105] Often his interpretations emphasized its penal and propitiatory aspects. The death of Christ was not a martyrdom, nor merely an example to imitate, but a 'sacrifice for sin'.[106] This remained Thomas's consistent position throughout his ministry. At the World Conference on Christian Fundamentals, for example, he proclaimed the cross as 'vicarious sacrifice'.[107] Nonetheless, in other contexts he drew out wider dimensions. Addressing the Mildmay Conference in 1903, Thomas emphasized that Christ's death was 'first and foremost an atoning sacrifice, and as such is absolutely unique', yet it was also 'a revelation of Unutterable Love' and a model of loving service that Christians should emulate.[108] At Keswick he spoke of the cross of Christ as encompassing three ideas – substitution ('he died instead of me'), representation ('he died on behalf of me') and identification ('I died when he died').[109] Therefore, although penal substitution remained

---

[102] Thomas, *Christianity Is Christ*, pp. 91–93.
[103] W. H. Griffith Thomas, 'Knowledge, Action, Blessedness', *Keswick Week* (1906), p. 206.
[104] W. H. Griffith Thomas, 'A Study in the Atonement', *Biblical Review*, vol. 3 (January 1918), p. 39.
[105] Thomas, 'Germany and the Bible', pp. 65–66.
[106] Thomas, *Christianity Is Christ*, pp. 50–52.
[107] W. H. Griffith Thomas, 'Atonement by Blood', in *God Hath Spoken*, pp. 249–261.
[108] W. H. Griffith Thomas, *'Ich Dien, I Serve': A Call for the New Year* (Stirling: Drummond's Tract Depot, 1904), p. 9.
[109] W. H. Griffith Thomas, 'What Keswick Stands For', *Keswick Week* (1914), p. 38.

primary, 'The true idea of the atonement is wide and inclusive, and danger lies in limiting it to one explanation.'[110]

All religious movements and philosophies were to be judged by these criteria. Thomas was alarmed that several 'anti-Christian' sects were gathering momentum in the early twentieth century. At Keswick in 1912 he named specifically Christian Science ('which is neither Christian nor scientific'), Millennial Dawn (which Thomas dubbed 'Millennial Darkness'), Spiritualism ('one of the most terrible corrosives of spirituality') and Theosophy as all guilty of denying the deity of Christ and the cross as an atoning sacrifice for sin.[111] Elsewhere he added Unitarianism, Socialism and Occultism to his catalogue of heresies that failed the same two doctrinal tests.[112]

As always in Thomas's teaching, biblical truth was to be embraced experientially, not just cerebrally. He warned against 'any mere intellectual orthodoxy which stops short of personal experience'.[113] On the opening Sunday of the Keswick Convention in July 1907 he instructed the attendees to seek Christ directly and personally that week, not mediated by Keswick preachers. 'We must hear the voice of *His* mouth, we must have contact with Christ through His Word, we must come face to face with Christ direct, and hear the voice of God speaking by the Holy Spirit.' This might happen in the main tent, or their own rooms, or while walking by the local hills and lakes. 'But wherever we are, Keswick will fail for us if we do not hear the voice of His mouth.' Direct knowledge was essential: 'Everything will count for nothing except so far as all our life is permeated with the glow of a personal experience.' To his fellow theological writers, Thomas urged specifically, 'Our pens must be dipped in our personal experience.' Much modern Christian literature was 'dry, dull, unprofitable, and unconvincing' because it lacked 'personal testimony' when teaching truth.[114]

Conclusion: abiding in Christ

In July 1907, amidst great fanfare, the London Electrobus Company launched a new technological wonder upon the capital – a fleet of six buses to carry passengers between Victoria Station and Liverpool Street, powered by electric battery. This new green form of transport looked certain to rival not only the

---

110 Thomas, 'A Study in the Atonement', p. 53.
111 Thomas, 'Christian Life (III)', pp. 129–130; Thomas, 'Christian Life (IV)', pp. 173–174.
112 Thomas, *Christ Pre-eminent*, p. 13.
113 Thomas, *Holy Spirit of God*, p. 236.
114 W. H. Griffith Thomas, 'Knowing and Showing', *Keswick Week* (1907), pp. 11–12.

ubiquitous horse-drawn buses but also the growing number of petrol buses that were beginning to choke London with their noise and fumes.[115] The electric bus operated on the storage principle, running down its battery until it was recharged at the depot. Thomas observed that many Christians lived by the same rule – they aimed to survive from week to week, or year to year, by being spiritually recharged via a Sunday sermon or a Bible convention, returning home from Keswick with full notebooks and hoping their spiritual batteries would last until the next summer. A much better model, he suggested, was the older technology of the electric tram (such as those opened at Brighton and Blackpool in the 1880s) which operated on the contact principle, kept moving by an electric rail and losing all power if the connection was broken. The tram-car itself had no power but was brought alive by an extrinsic source. This became one of Thomas's favourite illustrations for 'abiding in Christ', or 'keeping in touch with Christ'. Only by constant spiritual connection with Christ would there be power in the Christian life.[116] By 1910 the fraudulent London Electrobus Company had collapsed, mired in financial scandal, and its fleet was retired, so Thomas updated his image to the petrol motor car, but his point remained the same. As he told the Mundesley Bible Conference in 1912, the Christian life was not complex or difficult, but 'blessedly easy'. It could be summed up in one fundamental idea: 'full and constant contact with the Lord Jesus Christ'.[117]

Griffith Thomas's theology of the Christian life was encapsulated in this single illustration. Wherever he taught, whether sitting among a small group of students in the Wycliffe Hall library or standing before several thousand on the Keswick platform, communion with Jesus Christ was his grand theme. Since his own teenage experiences of spiritual 'failure' as a young convert, he had eschewed the language of struggling and striving, in favour of resting and abiding in Christ. He called his hearers to yield everything to God, in total surrender, and then to progress to full maturity or 'perfection' in the grace-filled, Spirit-empowered life, enjoying victory over sin. Thomas's habitual emphasis was upon abundant spiritual blessings in the present, not delayed until heaven, and the need for Christians to live up to that reality by 'possessing our possessions'. Communion with Christ, as his comparison of electric buses and trams emphasized, was to be 'full and constant', dwelling daily in the

---

[115] Mick Hamer, *A Most Deliberate Swindle: How Edwardian Fraudsters Pulled the Plug on the Electric Bus and Left Our Cities Gasping for Breath* (Haywards Heath: Red Door, 2017).

[116] W. H. Griffith Thomas, 'Faith and Sanctification', *Keswick Week* (1907), pp. 140–141.

[117] W. H. Griffith Thomas, 'In Touch with God', *Westminster Bible Conference, Mundesley 1912*, pp. 256, 261–262.

Scriptures and listening to Christ's voice direct and unmediated. This attractive portrayal of the Christian life was criticized by Reformed theologians such as Benjamin Warfield as unbiblical and unrealistic, but it won Griffith Thomas an enthusiastic following on both sides of the Atlantic among those who had known many defeats in the valleys of Christian experience and longed instead for joyful triumphs on the mountaintops.

5

H. R. Mackintosh

DAVID L. RAINEY

Hugh Ross Mackintosh was born in Paisley in 1870, the son of a minister in the Free Church of Scotland. As a divinity student at New College, then the college of the Free Church in Edinburgh, he won a fellowship in 1896 enabling him to take summer sessions at Freiburg, Halle and Marburg. He was licensed in the Free Church in 1896 and served as a parish minister in Tayport, moving to Beechgrove, Aberdeen, in 1901 in what was now the United Free Church. In 1904 he was appointed to New College as Professor of Divinity, becoming a professor of the University of Edinburgh when New College united with the Divinity Faculty in 1929 at the union of the established Church of Scotland and the United Free Church. He was Moderator of the General Assembly of the newly united Church of Scotland in 1932, and died in 1936. Although a prolific writer, Mackintosh's two most significant contributions to evangelical theology were *The Doctrine of the Person of Jesus Christ*[1] and *The Christian Experience of Forgiveness*.[2] These two books are foundational in analysing the contours of his critical constructive theology. Despite his innumerable writings, there are very few assessments of H. R. Mackintosh's contribution to evangelical theology, but Alan Sell wrote, 'Many regarded Mackintosh as the greatest British theologian of his generation.'[3]

T. F. Torrance, a student of Mackintosh, wrote an evaluation of his major work on Christology in his introduction to some conference addresses given by Mackintosh in 1911 and edited by Torrance for publication in 2000. He regarded *The Doctrine of the Person of Jesus Christ* as

> one of the really great works in Christian Dogmatics in which Mackintosh sought to put into historical and lucid conceptual form the truth of the

---

[1] *The Doctrine of the Person of Jesus Christ* (Edinburgh: T&T Clark, 1912). References will be abbreviated to *DPJC*.

[2] *The Christian Experience of Forgiveness* (London: Nisbet, 1927). References will be abbreviated to *CEF*.

[3] A. P. F. Sell, 'Mackintosh, Hugh Ross', in *Dictionary of Scottish Church History and Theology*, ed. Nigel de M. Cameron (Edinburgh: T&T Clark, 1993), p. 525.

biblical and doctrinal teaching about the Lord Jesus Christ as incarnate Son of God and Saviour of the world.[4]

It is with this major study that we will begin our analysis of Mackintosh's contribution to theology.

A brief historical overview

According to Mackintosh, the early history of the development of Christian doctrine was typified by a certain latitude in topics such as the atonement and eschatology as long as a theologian adhered to the historic ecumenical Creeds and was orthodox on the Person of Christ. By medieval times there was less tolerance of divergent proposals. After the Reformation both Protestant and Roman Catholic authorities began to assert theological conformity and this resulted in theological stagnation. Mackintosh wrote that 'by the seventeenth century both Roman and Protestant writers had become pretty closely tied up by the details of their creeds',[5] and for him, this resulted in a sterile departure from living constructive theology. But from the beginning of the nineteenth century, theologians had worked on 'fresh interpretations': 'The result', Mackintosh wrote, 'has in some good ways been to quicken interest and banish stagnation.'[6] But the attempt to negate stagnation created another problem. None of the major theologians of the nineteenth century, according to Mackintosh, would have survived 'Presbyterian discipline'! Creative innovative theology had begun, but Mackintosh was not a supporter of many of the contributions. In an interesting footnote he added, 'One defect of the German academic theology as a whole has been its lack of vital contact with the life of the worshipping Church.'[7]

In an additional comment Mackintosh added, 'In the seventeenth century began the ascendency of what is known as Protestant scholasticism . . . It was an age of vast condescending patronage as ignorant as it is absurd.'[8] The exception, according to Mackintosh, was the interlude in the later seventeenth century, when German Pietism made a contribution. Against the dry scholastic style, he added, 'It was largely owing to Pietism that when the tides of negation

---

[4] H. R. Mackintosh, *The Person of Jesus Christ*, ed. T. F. Torrance (Edinburgh: T&T Clark, 2000), p. vii. These lectures, originally given by Mackintosh in 1911 and edited for publication by T. F. Torrance in 2000, should not be confused with the book that expanded on them, *The Doctrine of the Person of Jesus Christ*.

[5] H. R. Mackintosh, *Types of Modern Theology* (London: Nisbet, 1937), p. 1.

[6] Ibid., p. 1.

[7] Ibid., p. 3.

[8] Ibid., p. 8.

flowed in later, submerging Christian belief and self-sacrifice, so much of vital religion outlasted the deluge.'[9] To add further difficulties for theology, and partly as a product of Protestant scholasticism, the subsequent development of the Enlightenment established the consistent denial of the necessity of a Mediator between God and humanity so that the Bible and the theology of the Reformation were negated. The strength of the Enlightenment was the sufficient Self and later, in Hegel, the process of the becoming of the divine. When theological discourse took this direction, the biblical and early creative credal doctrine of God and Reformation theology lost their influence. It was against the background of that understanding of trends in modern theology that Mackintosh saw the central significance of Christology.

The Person of Christ

Interpreting the incarnation

According to Mackintosh, Christ is at the centre of all Christian thought and without Christ Christianity would wither into an ineffective religious system.[10] How the church defined Christ became central to the church's effectiveness and thus there was a reason to publish a critical study of Christology. According to Mackintosh, the church had begun to see its influence wane at the beginning of the twentieth century, and, in line with the decline of the church as a social influence in society, there was a decline in the influence of Scripture in identifying who Christ is and what he accomplished. Three key theological points made Christ central for the believer. First, Christ reigns because of the resurrection: this indicated his victory over sin. Second, Christ is perfect in his humanity: this supplied the requirement for an effective doctrine of atonement. Third, Christ is inherently divine: this described God's personal participation in the redemption of humanity.[11]

The basis for interpreting the incarnation was God's love, holiness and redeeming power.[12] This, then, gave the interpretation for the cross of Christ. He stated, 'It is an act of love for the salvation of the world . . . it is to the Cross we owe that profound and poignant interest which alone makes it worthwhile to have a Christology at all.'[13] Christology and salvation are to embrace the

---

[9] Ibid., p. 13.
[10] *DPJC*, p. 283.
[11] Ibid., p. 427.
[12] Ibid., p. 431.
[13] Ibid., p. 440.

whole world. God's love is infinite and measureless, so the work of Christ is organically related to the Person of Christ. Through this infinite love God became what we are that we might become what he is.[14] Themes like this from the second-century theologian Irenaeus pervade the whole of his theology.[15]

Mackintosh wrote that Christ's atonement and the way it was expressed defined evangelical theology. On this he gained support from his Glasgow colleague James Denney.[16] Further, the way in which the atonement is interpreted will shape the doctrine of the Person of Christ.[17] In evangelical theology, our solidarity with Christ meant that in Christ's death we also died, in his grave we also were buried, and in his resurrection we were raised to new life. In all of this Christ is our representative, on behalf of us; otherwise the evangelical understanding of atonement becomes ineffective.[18] The key, then, in understanding Christianity is Jesus, the object of faith. We are not called to believe like Jesus; we are called to believe *in* Jesus.[19] Salvation, then, is by grace not by our own procurement of holiness.

Theology was never a final system and hence Mackintosh's massive Christological tome was written in response to the current thought and prevailing theology at the beginning of the twentieth century.[20] The context was the academic world of continental Europe and Great Britain. Within the evangelical tradition all theology is a direct response to Scripture, so H. R. Mackintosh became a strong advocate of Scripture by starting his Christology from it. Scripture gave the foundation for theology and the task of theology was to gain direction from Scripture. Theology should be designed to use Scripture to address current questions and yet it is clear that he avoided philosophical presuppositions in his biblical hermeneutic.

Mackintosh took seriously the diversity of Christological expression in the New Testament. He identified six main types of apostolic doctrine: in the Synoptics, 'the primitive' (including 1 Peter), Paul, Hebrews, the Apocalypse and John.[21] Yet the unity was grounded in the experience of Jesus, mediated to his disciples, that God is personally involved in the salvation of the whole world.

---

[14] Ibid., p. 146.

[15] Mackintosh was not in disagreement with the early creeds of Christendom but it appears that he tended to understand them as static and entrenched with philosophic influence, so at no point did he work from the Christology of the first four ecumenical Christological creeds. Later in the twentieth century his student T. F. Torrance established an alternative interpretation of the early church fathers and the creeds.

[16] *DPJC*, p. 329.

[17] Ibid., p. 321.

[18] Ibid., p. 335.

[19] Ibid., p. 345.

[20] Ibid., preface, p. vii.

[21] Ibid., p. 1; see also p. 48, n. 1.

Again, this meant that the Person of Christ was also the work of Christ. Importantly, Mackintosh attempted no mechanical harmony of the Gospels or the rest of the New Testament. To attempt a rigid mechanical harmony was opposed to the fluidity of the New Testament.

The humanity of Christ

A constant thread woven through Mackintosh's Christology dealt with the humanity of Jesus. For him, an inadequate doctrine of the humanity of Christ created an inadequate atonement doctrine. Mackintosh proposed three important considerations. First, Jesus is the human being par excellence and this is vital for redemption. Second, Jesus possessed a humanity visible to eyewitnesses (rejecting Docetism) and, third, Jesus had a human nature common to all humanity.[22] The result is that the saving power of Christ is contained in the full humanity of Christ. Importantly, Mackintosh cautioned against a Christology either of a merely particular human individual or of merely common human nature. Christ was both 'Man' (i.e. the one who represented the whole of humanity) and 'a man' (i.e. a particular human being).[23] Still, to have a true humanity Jesus had to be limited according to the time in which he lived and by his country and location.[24] He was truly tempted but it was owing to the close relationship to the Father through the Holy Spirit (a trinitarian perspective) and to his own holiness that he was free from sinful actions.[25]

Mackintosh included a brief but important discussion of the controversial Christology of Edward Irving, who had been deposed from the ministry of the Church of Scotland following a dispute from 1828 to 1830. Irving had held to the position that though the divine Person of Christ was sinless, he inherited a sinful human nature. Mackintosh opposed this Christology knowing that it also had an independent pedigree in German theology.[26] But as in all his criticisms of any Christology that he rejected, he gave the other side a fair hearing.

Mackintosh saw the problem with Irving as his insistence that Christ inherited a 'fallen' human nature, yet that by the power of the Holy Spirit in Jesus and his divine nature, sin was never actualized in Jesus' life. Irving's point was to advance the unity of Christ with all humanity since Christ not only

---

[22] Ibid., pp. 383–386.
[23] Ibid., p. 385. The word 'man' was of course universally understood as gender inclusive.
[24] Ibid., p. 397.
[25] Ibid., p. 404.
[26] The discussion is contained in *DPJC*, pp. 276–278.

endured the penalty of sin for us, but could give hope and strength to the tempted Christian through his sinless life. Mackintosh was bothered by the idea that Christ lived with a 'germ of evil' that was inconsistent with his perfect righteousness. The unity of Christ's human and divine Person now lay in peril. Mackintosh proposed that although Christ was liable to death and decay, that did not require a fallen human nature. Barth probably became acquainted with Edward Irving by reading Mackintosh, but added a list of German theologians who followed a similar pathway. He too developed his Christology from this position and so was in disagreement with Mackintosh.[27]

Mackintosh further elaborated on Jesus' earthly ministry and life. Not only was Jesus a localized person and limited in power, but he was thwarted in his ministry by consistent unbelief of the people and his knowledge was under-developed through lack of experience. His moral awareness was also developed in time and by experience. He was exposed to lifelong temptations and his personal piety demonstrated his dependence on his Father.[28] Mackintosh believed that traditional Christology had often lost sight of the humanity of Jesus and that whenever this is done, Jesus is no longer seen to belong to the human order.[29] The epistle to the Hebrews asserted that the historic Jesus passed through every stage of a human learning and obedience and that no aspect of Jesus' humanity escaped the assault of evil. As a result, Jesus became a merciful and faithful High Priest.[30] In Jesus' human condition his consciousness of his divine essence developed over time. Mackintosh offered no event when Jesus consciously recognized his divinity but the fact that there was no specific event did not invalidate the point that there was a process in which Jesus became aware of his divine nature.[31]

The concern of Mackintosh was to retain the authentic deity defined by the incarnation and still preserve the humanity of Christ. Like P. T. Forsyth he asserted that infinite power took effect in self-limitation.[32] He believed that this type of kenotic Christology was woven throughout the New Testament and should not be relegated to particular texts. In becoming incarnate, God had to relate to time, which he had created, and doing so required 'a great act of self-abnegation'. So, prior to the historic incarnation, there had to be a self-adjustment

---

[27] *Church Dogmatics*, I.2 (Edinburgh: T&T Clark, 1956), p. 155: 'He exists in the place where we are, in all the remoteness, not merely of the creature from the Creator, but of the sinful creature from the Holy Creator. Otherwise His action would not be a revealing, a reconciling action. He would always be for us an alien word.'

[28] *DPJC*, p. 419.

[29] Ibid., p. 467.

[30] Ibid., p. 79.

[31] Ibid., p. 44.

[32] Ibid., p. 465.

in God.[33] Omnipotence had to be morally conditioned by God's love in relation to creation.[34]

The divinity of Christ

We can follow on from this with a few comments on Jesus' divinity based on the New Testament records. According to Mackintosh there were three revelations of Christ's divine essence. One is in Jesus' sinlessness, the second is in Jesus' relationship of unique sonship and the third is Jesus' resurrection from the grave.[35] Resurrection is distinct from being raised back to life. The first implies no more death, while the second implies another death is still to come. With God's essential presence in Jesus, salvation belongs properly to God, who is the doer, and this constituted Jesus' sinless behaviour.[36] While Jesus' sonship is unique, his sonship is a sonship of subordination to the Father while his Person is still divine. Here Mackintosh referred to a functional subordination without implying an essential subordination.[37] Mackintosh recognized that the word 'God' was not used with any frequency in relation to Jesus in the New Testament. But the word lacked any useful meaning in first-century Graeco-Roman culture since 'gods' were self-proclaimed men who used the title 'divine' as an appellation and many gods were acknowledged in culture. The New Testament, therefore, specialized in other language and images of description to identify divine essence.[38]

A summative statement of Mackintosh's Christology can be made. Mackintosh insisted that the Logos had a divine existence prior to the descent into human life and Jesus' earthly ministry. This expressed God's deep love for humanity in God's experience as the Son of God entered human life and assumed full human existence.[39] While insisting on the full deity of Christ and union with God the Father, there was an incipient earthly subordination in Christ's union with the Father.[40] Mackintosh rejected any tendency to rigidity in Christological doctrine and, because the task was an ongoing enterprise, Christology is to be conceived in fluid, moral and ethically responsive language. This will create a lively understanding of the Person and work of Christ.

---

[33] Ibid., p. 470.
[34] Ibid., p. 478.
[35] Ibid., pp. 412–418.
[36] Ibid., p. 413.
[37] Ibid., p. 415.
[38] Ibid., p. 419.
[39] Ibid., p. 67.
[40] Ibid., pp. 71–74.

Further theological implications

Mackintosh understood that from Christology it is possible to construct pneumatology and a doctrine of the Trinity and both these doctrines appear in initial form in his study on Christology. He believed that the New Testament had an underdeveloped doctrine of the Trinity apparently owing to an impoverished language barrier. It was not possible, at this early stage in the first century, to construct the language required for a developed trinitarian doctrine.[41] But there was also a decline in trinitarian theology at the beginning of the twentieth century due to the continuing influence of Friedrich Schleier-macher: this was not because of a language barrier but because of a theological barrier. Mackintosh set the stage for the later twentieth-century development by Karl Barth. He affirmed James Denney's conclusion from Ephesians 2:18, 'The Father, the Son, and the Spirit in their unity constitute the God whom we know as the God of our salvation.' Mackintosh expressed the point in a statement that can be seen to point the way for later twentieth-century theologians: 'So the Father disclosed in the Son is imparted in the Spirit.'[42]

It is important to emphasize that Mackintosh was familiar with nineteenth-century and early twentieth-century German liberalism. He had studied in Germany and had become a friend of Wilhelm Herrmann. He took the time to bring German liberal theology into the awareness of the English-speaking world by translating Friedrich Schleiermacher and Albrecht Ritschl. Robert Redman gave this assessment of his contribution: 'He skilfully translated Ritschl's *Justification and Reconciliation* and Schleiermacher's *The Christian Faith.*' But he added, 'He cared for the way in which doctrine lays the foundation for the pulpit ministry.'[43] Redman's point was that in reading theology in its various models, Mackintosh asserted that theology lays the foundation for preaching.

As we have seen, one of the hallmarks of H. R. Mackintosh's theology was his view of kenosis, the self-limitation of God. But rather than attempting to diminish the nature of God as in nineteenth-century German kenotic Christ-ology, Mackintosh proposed the kenosis model of fellow-Scot P. T. Forsyth. Forsyth had previously written that kenosis more fully recognizes the full divinity of Christ, and thus the divine nature of God can be conceived without essential limitation. Against late twentieth-century panentheism and Open

---

[41] Ibid., p. 514.

[42] Ibid., pp. 508–509.

[43] Robert R. Redman Jr, 'H. R. Mackintosh's Contribution to Christology and Soteriology in the Twentieth Century', *Scottish Journal of Theology* 4.4 (1988), p. 517.

Theism, we can think of Mackintosh as making his own pre-emptive move. In his dogmatics it was not necessary to put limits on God in order to affirm God's supremacy. God acted in love through self-limitation but not according to essential limitation. This more powerful God, understood within a Christological framework, had more clearly the power to descend.[44]

In a striking conclusion to his Christology, Mackintosh included a short piece on the virgin birth. Positively stated, the virgin birth asserted an overshadowing of the presence of the Holy Spirit throughout Jesus' earthly ministry. It cannot be proved historically but there is no genuine parallel in pagan myths. Nor is it an explanation of, or a basis for, the deity or the sinlessness of Christ. But he concludes that 'strong grounds can be asserted for accepting this belief as in complete harmony with the Christian thought of Jesus as dove-tailing naturally and simply'.[45] As later with Barth, it was its dogmatic appropriateness that commended its acceptance.

Forgiveness

The key to the incarnation

From an analysis of the Christology of H. R. Mackintosh we can turn to his formative work on forgiveness. *The Christian Experience of Forgiveness* was written as an integral part of a series that intended to re-examine the foundation of Christianity. The series' introduction made the claim that the discipline of apologetics had come to an end and that now the question of authority was the paramount question.[46] This was combined with the accompanying emphasis on the value and validity of religious experience and yet all experience had to be critiqued and interpreted.[47]

Mackintosh began by insisting that one cannot call oneself a Christian without experiencing the forgiveness of God.[48] Forgiveness is the key to evangelical theology, and yet it is not without its problems.[49] A common problem to be addressed is the criticism that we do not require forgiveness. As Mackintosh would state, guilt is a reality, but the morbid use of guilt is abusive.[50] Still, people are appalled at human inability to modify or create a remedy to

---

[44] *DPJC*, p. 474.
[45] Ibid., p. 532.
[46] *CEF*, p. vii.
[47] Ibid., pp. viii–ix.
[48] Ibid., p. 2.
[49] Ibid., p. 6.
[50] Ibid., p. 7.

inequality and iniquity. At the same time forgiveness is contrary to the nature of the world.[51] According to the ethical standards of society, forgiveness is a type of immorality. Even the apostle Paul is accused of an immoral system by offering forgiveness. Alternatively, for Mackintosh, theology should be transforming so that it carries with it a positive, creative understanding.[52] Forgiveness is so renovating that the Old Testament prophets imagined creation singing in response to God's forgiveness.[53] Forgiveness is received by faith and that makes us one with Christ through God's holy love. God does not accept us because we are good but we become good through God's forgiveness and we should be careful that forgiveness can be twisted into an antinomianism.[54] According to H. R. Mackintosh the evangelical doctrine of pardon will answer the objections to forgiveness when properly constructed. The entire book is a defence against the objections to forgiveness from a moral or ethical viewpoint.[55]

Christianity triumphed over other religious views because Jesus was known as a friend of sinners and publicans.[56] Christianity triumphed because God was present in Christ, who received sinners. When this message is lost, the gospel loses its impact. God's intense holiness did not distinguish between pure and impure, since all are in the same situation in the eyes of God.[57] The identity of evangelical theology therefore includes a behavioural aspect. But experience in this theological formation must be placed in its proper order. The evangelical understanding of faith and grace makes merit and the attempt to earn God's favour a repulsive theology. The word 'evangelical' refers to the experience of God's grace, mercy and love freely given to all humanity. It carries no political weight or political theory. Once again, according to Mackintosh forgiveness has a Christological reference. There is an improper forgiveness that requires no transformation: on the other hand, true forgiveness includes reconciliation. Later he developed the idea that suffering is close to reconciliation. Forgiveness by God is greater than that expressed by humanity: it involves God's suffering.[58] Christianity is defined by the reception of sinners by grace. From his definitions of grace and forgiveness, H. R. Mackintosh avoided the rigidity of a static Christian life by seeing spirituality as daily renewal.[59]

---

[51] Ibid., p. 9.
[52] Ibid., p. 11.
[53] Ibid., p. 12.
[54] Ibid., p. 14. Antinomianism is the view that Christians do not have to obey the law of God.
[55] Ibid., p. 16.
[56] Ibid., p. 17.
[57] Ibid., p. 21.
[58] Ibid., p. 30.
[59] Ibid., p. 36.

Jesus and Paul on forgiveness

In his constructive Christology, Mackintosh began from an assumption of the historical reliability of the Synoptic Gospels and the certainty of the apostle Paul's interpretation of Christ in line with the historic Gospel records. In other words, Paul did not corrupt the gospel of Christ. In line with this, two aspects of Jesus' life were revealed during his ministry. One was that his personality was laden with grace towards the sinful and the other that there was a believing response evoked in those who encountered him.[60] Biblical scholarship at the time tended to state that Paul corrupted Jesus' message of salvation. But according to Mackintosh, while the language and terms were not the same, there was a common identity in the meaning, which he clarified. This formed the heart of evangelicalism, or, as Mackintosh stated it, the contrast was between 'legalism, which rests on and revolves around merit and reward, and evangelicalism, adoring the free grace that calls us sons'.[61] A lengthy quotation will summarize his point:

> St. Paul, that is to say, by his paradox about God justifying the ungodly is carrying on the message (known by Jesus to be true because of His fellowship with the Father, known by St. Paul to be true because of his contact with the living Christ) that the unworthy are received not for the reason that the account of precept and performance has been squared, but out of the Father's mercy. Both trace everything up to the free act of a gracious God.[62]

There was another way to say this:

> Men are not employees, laying before God a bill of wages: they are blessed with good, most of all they are blessed with pardon because God has love and they have faith. This is the gospel, pledged to sinful men in Christ, which St. Paul sets forth in intellectual form of his own.[63]

Paul used old language but adapted it with new meaning based on his experience and contact with Christ. As Mackintosh stated, 'St. Paul repeats the gospel brought by Jesus to the sinful.'[64]

---

[60] *DPJC*, p. 7.
[61] *CEF*, p. 108.
[62] Ibid., p. 109.
[63] Ibid., p. 110.
[64] Ibid., pp. 112–113.

This analysis by Mackintosh set up his presentation on Jesus: he was asserting that in the Christian context forgiveness is possible and credible. The encounter with Jesus means that forgiveness is given. God's true character is in Christ's forgiveness and it transforms our way of thinking. What is determinative is the experience described in the New Testament.[65] Jesus' healing and forgiveness of sin are on the basis that forgiveness is in the hands of God. In his self-consciousness, Jesus knew himself to be the Bearer of God's salvation and people saw this in the encounters they had with him.[66]

Mackintosh promoted the idea that Paul's concept of forgiveness was grounded in repentance and Christ's forgiving love.[67] Here repentance cannot be understood as a work that we do since repentance is a gift from God. Justification by faith, in Paul's perspective, is based on the Old Testament. Mackintosh was out of step with much of the current biblical scholarship, which believed that Paul had corrupted Jesus' teaching, or that the Old Testament was to be dismissed as a legalistic document. Yet Mackintosh claimed that he gained support for his interpretation of the Old Testament from James Denney.[68] These evangelicals anticipated the later development of Pauline studies that located Paul's thought on salvation within ancient Jewish literature. Mackintosh also critiqued the then biblical scholarship that tried to remove justification by faith from the kernel of Paul's thought. Justification, when understood properly in Paul, 'is St. Paul's evangelical message not in part but as a living whole'.[69] Justification was not a sterile concept but a living activity. In writing in this manner by connecting Paul to Jesus, and, with an alteration in language yet communicating a common message, Mackintosh interpreted justification by faith in Paul's language and meaning as the salvation described by Jesus.[70]

The problem of sin

Mackintosh devoted a chapter to the analysis of sin and guilt. This was required because forgiveness assumes sin. According to Mackintosh, to deny the requirement of forgiveness is to deny the reality of sin and God's holy love.[71] Humanity's purpose, which sets it apart, is a reference to the image of God. Happiness lies in obedience to God yet we find humanity divided against itself,

---

[65] Ibid., pp. 82–83.
[66] Ibid., p. 92.
[67] Ibid., p. 101.
[68] Ibid., pp. 102, 111.
[69] Ibid., p. 104.
[70] Ibid., p. 116.
[71] Ibid., p. 50.

neighbour and God: our will is evil.[72] The paradox of humanity, as stated by Mackintosh, is, 'Nothing that can be said, and said truly of the good that is in a man, can change the fact that this evil, so fierce and guilty, is also there.'[73] In the three pages prior to this sentence Mackintosh painted a dire picture of the plight of humanity. We live in a created moral order and sin and its consequences are found throughout creation. This means that sin is a social and relational concept. His point was to demonstrate that as great and terrifying as sin is, the forgiveness of God has the greater power to change humanity from the tendency to perpetuate sin.

Choosing to do evil does not necessarily mean that we want to disrupt our relationship with God permanently. Yet sin is an act against God: it is more than ignorance since it includes the chains of evil habits.[74] There are, then, innumerable ways to describe sin. It is opposition to the will of God; it is lack of faith and love; it is godlessness, that is, life without God.[75] The power of sin leaves deep scars that cannot be obliterated.[76] There are sins we commit with no idea of the outcome and no power to counteract the result. The ethical dilemma is that God forgives to the uttermost both inadvertent and deliberate sins, and while no one is unpardonable there are those who refuse to accept pardon. Sin has to be defined distinctively in relation to Christ. Colloquially, 'sin' is a common term but technically it is a religious term to be understood in relation to God. Mackintosh makes sin appear as wilful and does not include mistakes or oversights. There is a difference between motive and the concept of mere acts: one is moral and the other is not.[77]

Sin is unintelligible; it comes from within but we are still responsible.[78] Sin deals with the self, what we are, not just what we do. Evil is inconceivable and its existence is beyond logic; it is absurd, yet humanity has sunk into the horror of its darkness.[79] He compared sin to a civil war within humanity. In the imagery of war, we are like a beleaguered garrison torn apart from within.[80] And while sin has its own self-inflicted punishment that centres round isolation from God and fellow human beings, it disrupts any healthy relationship so deeply that humanity is at a loss to overcome its devastation. But there is still good within humanity and this goodness is from God's love and

[72] Ibid., pp. 51–52.
[73] Ibid., p. 231.
[74] Ibid., pp. 57–58.
[75] Ibid., pp. 59–60.
[76] Ibid., p. 26.
[77] Ibid., pp. 53–56.
[78] Ibid., p. 60.
[79] Ibid., pp. 158–159.
[80] Ibid., p. 256.

presence.[81] Forgiveness implies and includes this concept of guilt and reveals sin's power. But God is at work even in guilt. Guilt, then, makes us aware of hope since we are not totally lost.[82] Sin is so grave a corruption of ourselves that only divine intervention will be equal to the task of healing its annihilating consequences. Indispensable presuppositions in clarifying humanity's relation to God and sin are clarified by Mackintosh. One is our unworthiness, a second is our perpetual debt in our sinfulness and a third is the conviction that Christ mediates between God and humanity.[83] Ultimately, God will judge sin, but God bears the judgement in sacrificial love for the perpetrator and victim, and then God freely forgives.[84]

Mackintosh identified Schleiermacher and Ritschl with the tendency to diminish the terrifying effect of sin and, in contrast to them, he emphasized sin's destructive power. Because of this he was also able to intensify the power of forgiveness. But within this world of sin and forgiveness he did not shy away from the wrath of God against sin. He made the claim that Ritschl perpetuated the misunderstanding of God's wrath by consigning it to caprice and wilful passion, but this, he claimed, was not the New Testament idea. When properly conceived, the wrath of God does not create an unresolvable problem. God's anger against sin must always end in forgiveness and reconciliation.[85] As Mackintosh expressed it, 'It is because God loves that anger in him is conceivable and credible; the behaviour of Jesus in the Gospels and our own highest experience indicate as much. It is love alone that makes wrath pure, sublime, redemptive.'[86] With this understanding, one of the cornerstones of evangelical theology is the condemnation of sin. The cross of Christ reveals sin's true identity of rebellion, horror, sheer evil, and yet it is overcome in God's grace and mercy found in Christ. God forgives: God can also exercise vengeance.[87] But Mackintosh never developed God's vengeance in any detail.

Forgiveness as travail

Mackintosh proposed that the Old Testament prophets set the stage for a new interpretation of the God of forgiveness but that it was developed further in the New Testament's depiction of Christ. The Old Testament included the view that

[81] Ibid., p. 63.
[82] Ibid., p. 66.
[83] Ibid., p. 192.
[84] Ibid., p. 271.
[85] Ibid., p. 164.
[86] Ibid., p. 210.
[87] Ibid., p. 28.

God might be present in pain and suffering,[88] and in Jesus' understanding pain and suffering were later interpreted from Isaiah 53. But his pain would be vicarious, not just as a passive victim or a martyr, but by his deliberate decision as a divine-human Person who 'took the responsibility of our evil upon himself'.[89]

With this in mind, Robert Redman attempted to bring clarity to Mackintosh's version of penal substitution. He began by stating first, 'Although Mackintosh rejected the penal substitution theory in its cruder forms, he insisted that room must be made for the older theology's understanding of the relationship of the cross and punishment of sin.'[90] In this sense, rather than positing a firm position, Mackintosh offered a flexible way forward. An important and essential aspect of the suffering and death of Jesus is his identity with humanity. According to Mackintosh, sin and the pain of condemnation go together.[91] In other words, according to Redman, 'Christ's suffering can only have the same origin as ours – human sin – and not a special decree from God that Jesus suffer in a qualitatively different way for us.'[92] The second point, as Redman explained, is grounded in the vicarious suffering based on Isaiah 53. Working from *The Christian Experience of Forgiveness*,[93] Redman concludes that for Mackintosh, God the Father and the Son were directly involved in the suffering on the cross and thus God's passion for us is a revelation of self-sacrifice.

In Jesus' teaching and ministry, the kingdom of God is built on forgiveness. It is not a mechanical activity and, since it is built within human experience, it is a creative act from God.[94] For this reason Mackintosh criticized rigid predestination; that is, the idea of a fixed number of saved persons in the mysterious will of God as depicted in the Synod of Dort. For Mackintosh such an erroneous idea led to doubt about the assurance of salvation. Assurance of salvation lies in the spirituality of life in the risen Christ: it is a Christocentric assurance.[95] Assurance is to be lived out: it is giving outside ourselves through our spirituality. This is coupled with the rejection of the changeless God of philosophy. God shares our grief and shame.[96]

Mackintosh agreed with James Denney that forgiveness is neither painless nor easy. God's anguish is greatest at the point of forgiveness and remitting sin:

[88] Ibid., p. 172.
[89] Ibid., pp. 204–205.
[90] Redman, 'H. R. Mackintosh's Contribution', p. 530.
[91] *CEF*, p. 203.
[92] Redman, 'H. R. Mackintosh's Contribution', p. 530.
[93] *CEF*, pp. 204–206.
[94] Ibid., p. 213.
[95] Ibid., pp. 247–249.
[96] Ibid., p. 186.

there is evident travail at the cross.[97] Since God enters 'voyages of anguish' it will be similar for us. Mackintosh wrote:

> To enter by passionate imagination and self-projection into another's conflict, to hold by intercession his faltering hand, to weep with his sorrow, actually to think self still at the other's side in the misery and loneliness of guilt – all this is requisite; and how true it is that in heart and mind the forgiver must set out on 'voyages of anguish'! It is an experience of sacrificial pain, of vicarious suffering.[98]

Then he added:

> Let the man be found who has undergone the shattering experience of pardoning, nobly and tenderly, some awful wrong to himself, still more to one beloved by him, and he will understand the meaning of Calvary better than all the theologians in the world.[99]

He had already written, 'Here experience is clarified; God is personal and the doer of miracles. Forgiveness is a miracle. It is God reconciling the world to himself and it comes at a cost to God.'[100]

Forgiveness and the life of sanctification

Salvation is a 'trustful communion with God ... and with men as a brother among brethren'.[101] Pardon and forgiveness are synonyms. Forgiveness as a remission of a penalty is inadequate since that is purely an external act and this limited function does not comprehend the whole extent of forgiveness. Forgiveness is God's self-communication and communion with sinful people and, for the disciple of Jesus, the life of habitual, repetitive sin is therefore inconceivable. Mackintosh was not hesitant to propose an active antagonism to the sinful life.[102] Grace evokes faith that works in a person with the result that regeneration and renewal become evident. In the light of this, evangelical theology has ethical outcomes.[103] Forgiveness is to produce change in the understanding of

[97] Ibid., pp. 87, 190.
[98] Ibid., p. 188.
[99] Ibid., p. 191.
[100] Ibid., p. 185.
[101] Ibid., p. 23.
[102] Ibid., p. 27.
[103] Ibid., pp. 144–145.

our relationship with God and fellow human beings.[104] One way to describe this experience of forgiveness is that it enters into a person's life, and with the evidence of God's presence new attitudes develop in which we stand beside God.[105] Forgiveness of this type is supernatural and this is a norm in evangelical theology.[106]

Mackintosh insisted that forgiveness, properly understood, creates renewal in the human mind and reconciliation in relationships. This is an inseparable part of the life of sanctification. It is combined with the destruction of social wrong that is the outcome of forgiveness.[107] In this understanding, faith is active. Sanctification is a process always lived in tension with the prevailing influence of sin, but Mackintosh could talk of harmony and reconciliation as the Christian lifestyle. He wrote:

> It scarcely needs saying that this harmony, born of reconciliation, is far from being fully actualised from the outset, and is given at first only in principle ... the conditions which led to its first bestowal in order to secure that it shall steadily gain predominance over our inward life.[108]

He continued to affirm that

> the man who has known the joy of being received to God's mercy despite his sin has thereby awakened to a new ideal for his own life, since he personally is bound to exhibit to others the loving mercy shown to himself, and, that this vision of a new and lofty ideal is itself an immensely moral event.

The word 'ideal' requires clarification. It was not a reference to a philosophical ideal but a Christ-centred ideal the Christian is perpetually striving to emulate. It is renewal in the light of the cross.[109] The emphasis on transformation revealed how little we forgive in relation to God's forgiveness; how little we have loved in relation to God's self-sacrificial love; how little we have given ourselves in self-sacrifice in relation to God's self-sacrifice. Consequently, we understand so little of God's all-consuming love for humanity, but, 'Only as the forgiveness

104 Ibid., p. 177.
105 Ibid., p. 181.
106 Ibid., p. 184.
107 Ibid., p. 253.
108 Ibid., pp. 256–257.
109 Ibid., p. 258.

of the cross transforms our minds as well as our lives will we begin to understand the cross theologically.'[110]

Forgiveness and the church

Mackintosh did not develop the larger picture of social ethics in the light of forgiveness. The closest he came was in developing forgiveness in the life of the church. He described the situation in Europe at the beginning of the twentieth century: the confession 'I believe in the Holy Catholic Church' no longer gripped people's attention. Evidently, the church had fallen out of favour in society. Yet Mackintosh put forward the proposition that since Christianity is a historic faith, it is passed on to the next generation and, apart from the church, forgiveness is devoid of meaning.[111]

Previously the church took precedence over the person but now the person takes precedence over the church and sometimes the Christian moves against the church.[112] Yet Mackintosh concluded that the church is to be understood as the forgiven life of the people. In the light of this, evangelism is contained within the life of the church as well as in the preaching of the gospel.[113] Mackintosh had already put forward the idea that forgiveness is not easy and can be a reality only within the work of God lived out in the life of the church. Practising the life of forgiveness is crucial in maintaining the distinctive life of the church. If the church becomes ineffective, in some sense, it has not made visible the life of forgiveness. An important statement was made by Mackintosh with implications beyond the church into social ethics:

> It is just because the Church is a forgiven community, rejoicing in fellowship with the Father of men and suffused with the spirit of forbearing love, that to-day she is called as never before to play alike in international difficulties and industrial disputes, the part of a Society of Reconciliation for the world.[114]

This had implications for Mackintosh in understanding the Lord's Supper. Since he understood that Christ's love was for all people and the direction of Christ's love was in reconciliation, then all are welcome at the Lord's Table. No condition was to be applied for anyone receiving the bread and cup.

---

[110] Ibid., p. 533.
[111] Ibid., pp. 270–271.
[112] Ibid., p. 272.
[113] Ibid., pp. 275–277.
[114] Ibid., p. 285.

Conclusion

H. R. Mackintosh wrote in a very lively, fluid style. The two books used in this chapter are like a scriptural compendium of critical, constructive, evangelical theology built with a biblical hermeneutic. Mackintosh began in Christology, which led to pneumatology and trinitarian doctrine in a way of thinking comparable to that of fellow Scottish theologians James Denney and P. T. Forsyth. The love of God for all humanity revealed in Christ gave the foundation in understanding God's forgiveness to all humanity. Forgiveness, even for God, was costly, sacrificial and painful, and a full understanding of forgiveness within the human condition will be similar. This means that forgiveness is not natural to humanity: it is a gift from God. All of this formed a foundation for a lively, critical, evangelical theology.

H. R. Mackintosh can be located in the academic tradition of British evangelical theology. He did not set out to create a new school of thought, but he influenced pastors, missionaries and academics with a presentation of theology closely related to Christian experience. Robert Redman concluded:

> For the church to live and flourish, it must ever proclaim the good news of Christ who came to live with people, who died that their sins might be forgiven, and who rose and ascended that they might have life in a living relationship with him. Mackintosh gave his best thought and work to that glorious task.[115]

A final word can be given by Thomas F. Torrance, who offered a significant insight.[116] He addresses the stereotype that academics who work in the doctrinal discipline are far removed from the spiritual disciplines, and in Torrance's evaluation, Mackintosh denied the stereotype. For the most part, Torrance's evaluation dealt with Mackintosh's final year in the classroom as his teacher in 1935–6. At that point there was no indication that Mackintosh would not return for the autumn term of 1936, but Mackintosh died on 8 June of that year. Torrance reflected on his spirituality:

> In New College, I was more than ever drawn to his deeply evangelical and missionary outlook in theology, and to his presentation of Christ and the

---

[115] Redman, 'H. R. Mackintosh's Contribution', p. 534.

[116] These comments were originally published in T. F. Torrance, 'Hugh Ross Mackintosh: Theologian of the Cross', *Scottish Bulletin of Evangelical Theology* (1987), pp. 160–173; then republished as an 'Appreciation' in Torrance's edited version of lectures given by Mackintosh in 1911, published as *The Person of Jesus Christ* (Edinburgh: T&T Clark, 2000), pp. 71–94. These quotations come from the edited version of 2000.

gospel of salvation through the cross in ways that struck home so simply and directly to the conscience of sinners.[117]

Torrance commented, 'He was above all a man of God, full of the Holy Spirit and of faith.'[118] Then he added an interesting observation: 'Many a would-be theological student was converted in his classes, although some, as I well remember, used to get very angry for they found themselves questioned down to the bottom of their being.'[119] Torrance highlights the way in which Mackintosh exemplified the integration of doctrinal theology, spirituality and mission in a truly evangelical theology:

> Along with his shrewd epistemological questions, he put to them the searching questions with which he was wont to test every theology. How far is it rooted in God's self-revelation in Jesus Christ? Can it be preached to sinful people in need of forgiveness? How effective will it be in the mission field? The message that does not evangelize, the Christianity that does not convert, abroad or at home, cannot be true.[120]

© David L. Rainey, 2022

---

[117] Torrance, 'Hugh Ross Mackintosh', p. 71.
[118] Ibid., p. 72.
[119] Ibid., p. 75.
[120] Ibid., p. 89.

6

W. E. Sangster

ANDREW J. CHEATLE

William Edwin Robert Sangster (1900–60)[1] is known almost exclusively as a Methodist preacher of some stature, still appearing in lists of the twentieth century's greatest preachers. During his lifetime, most within the evangelical fold were familiar with his large collection of written sermons and his extensive writings on homiletics.[2] His recorded sermons, some of which can now be found on the Internet, exemplify crafted examples of scholarly preaching and oratory skill, which any devotee of preaching or student of homiletics would benefit from.[3] Sangster's preaching won him national and international recognition. His 1953 New Year sermon entitled 'A Sermon for Britain' hit national headlines and detailed what a revival of the Christian religion would do for Britain, occasioning a revival tour sponsored by the *Daily Express*. Dr Billy Graham introduced Sangster to a camp meeting at Junaluska, North Carolina, as 'a preacher without peer in the world'.[4] David Larsen asserted:

> Sangster was unquestionably part of the royalty of the pulpit in the last century; and though long silenced, we would profit by reading him. [He] may well be, more than we realize, something of a man for our times as well.[5]

Life and influence

As with John Wesley, two central themes or motivating concerns dominated Sangster's ministry: evangelism and holiness. For Sangster 'going out into all

---

[1] Leslie Weatherhead, 'The New President of Conference', *Methodist Recorder*, 13 July 1950, p. 9.

[2] For a full and critical discussion of W. E. Sangster's understanding of holiness, see Andrew J. Cheatle, *W. E. Sangster: Herald of Holiness* (Milton Keynes: Paternoster Press, 2011). A volume of previously unpublished sermons was released in 2018, Andrew J. Cheatle, *Sermons in America* (Eugene, OR: Wipf & Stock, 2018).

[3] An online audio archive is being developed at Liverpool Hope University that will make a number of the better-quality recordings available for research purposes.

[4] Paul Sangster, *Doctor Sangster* (London: Epworth Press, 1962), p. 265.

[5] David L. Larsen, 'Past Masters: William E. Sangster: In the Wake of the Wesleys', *Leadership*, 3 May 2008.

the world making disciples' (Matt. 28:19, my paraphrase) was inseparable from the need for the church to exemplify the life of Christ in holy living. The interconnectedness and importance of these two aspects of the Christian life were reiterated numerous times in books, newspapers, magazines, pamphlets and sermons. For Sangster, a church that does not live a life 'higher than the world' cannot truly witness to the world. Conversely, a church full of people exuding the life and love of Christ is a powerful witness. This explains Sangster's dual approach during his year as President of the Methodist Conference, 1950–51: evangelism and holiness. His messages were designed to establish the pattern for the year: the importance of holiness to the clergy and the need for evangelism to the representative session.

Within mid-twentieth-century British Methodism he was a giant, emulated by young ministers, respected and revered even by his contemporaries. His literary output was huge, spanning multiple volumes of sermons, books on homiletics, critical volumes on Christian holiness and hundreds of articles in the field of evangelism.

William Sangster's life spanned the troubled first sixty years of the twentieth century, an era that encompassed the rise of the Labour movement, two world wars, economic and industrial depression, the Holocaust, the forming of the welfare state, the decline of the British Empire, the advent of the nuclear age and the gradual effect of secularization on the church. The intellectual world of 1960 when he died was very different from the Edwardian era in which he grew up. Major developments within science and the intellectual environment, scarred by the carnage of war, challenged Christian thinkers and consequently led to traditional theological ideas coming under scrutiny. It is only within this context that Sangster's life and thought can be truly understood: within the context of the changing face of world and British history and the ideological, theological and ecclesiological influences of the era.

Most of Sangster's childhood was spent around City Road near Bunhill Fields, the Nonconformist burial ground.[6] As a young boy he began to attend the local Methodist mission on Radnor Street, adopting and thriving on the principles and practices of this more rigorous form of Methodism.[7] By the time of his conversion on 19 October 1913[8] he had adopted a puritan

---

[6] Sangster, *Doctor Sangster*, pp. 17–20.
[7] A flavour of the mission, its life and of the neighbourhood can be gained from Westerdale's enlightening history, Thomas E. Westerdale, *Centenary of the Radnor Street Day, Sunday, Ragged Schools and Mission, in the Parish of St. Luke's, London E. C. 1798–1898* (London: Hazell, Watson and Viney, 1899).
[8] See Cheatle, *Herald of Holiness*, p. 3.

otherworldliness that would follow him for the rest of his life.[9] Just over three years later, in February 1917, he preached his first sermon and by his seventeenth birthday was a regular preacher, preaching his trial sermon as a local preacher at the historic Wesley's Chapel, aged 17.[10]

By the time of enlisting in the army on his eighteenth birthday a simple foundation of belief had been laid of the nineteenth-century evangelical type. He had experienced a personal conversion, he preached the gospel in order to let others know of salvation, and saw this life primarily as a preparation for eternity.[11] Although it cannot be substantiated without question, he had probably adopted a high reverence for the text of the Scriptures typical of the lay-led Methodist missions of the era. The Bible was understood literally, though always with salvation as the goal.[12] The Scriptures were also the ethical codebook, and ethical sermons abounded. Much was therefore also made of children attending Sunday school to learn the stories of the Bible and to be confronted at an early age with the need to 'decide' for Christ. This belief in the need for conversion never left Sangster, and as his later work bore witness, as Secretary of Home Missions in 1955–8 and his involvement in the many ecumenical evangelistic campaigns in the 1950s, he was constantly seeking ways to bring the claims of the gospel before unbelievers with a view to conversion.[13] When later reflecting on the many positive influences of the mission upon his own life, however, Sangster criticized aspects of the religion of the missions as being, at times, coarse and somewhat vulgar.[14]

After being demobbed, Sangster embarked on his Methodist ministerial training, first at Handsworth College in Birmingham, but the bulk of his studies were at Richmond College, a college under the auspices of the University of London, where he excelled in philosophy, eventually gaining BA and MA degrees. His pastoral charges saw him minister in Littlehampton, North Wales (Conwy and Rhos-on-sea), Liverpool, Scarborough, Leeds, before ending at

---

[9] Cf. W. E. Sangster, 'The Peril of Expediency', in *Why Jesus Never Wrote a Book* (London: Hodder & Stoughton, 1932), pp. 46–54.

[10] Sangster, *Doctor Sangster*, p. 33.

[11] R. Ensor, *England 1870–1914* (Oxford: Clarendon Press, 1985), pp. 137–139.

[12] The missions were not, by this time, affected by the growing impact of the liberal theology of the late Victorian and pre-Great War era. Indeed, the missions were typical of the type of evangelicalism of the nineteenth century. This pattern of religious faith expressed itself generally by setting great store on external observance. Although characterized by a lower view of the sacraments, the missions placed great stress on the pulpit ministry. Indeed, theologically speaking, preaching was 'the sacrament'. Every service would contain some sort of scriptural exhortation, and young people who showed any sort of calling or gifting were encouraged to preach.

[13] W. E. Sangster, 'God Enjoys Forgiving', *Sunday Times*, 15 June 1958, p. 18.

[14] W. E. Sangster, 'Those Back Street Missions', *Methodist Recorder*, 12 May 1960, p. 11. Though he never clearly states what he means, arguably it was that the missions did not take seriously enough the importance of dealing with genuine intellectual barriers during evangelism.

Westminster Central Hall. His first writings from the early 1930s, written to earn extra money during the depressed times of the era, give evidence that he was drawing from the principles and methods of psychology as a means of aiding people spiritually.[15] He avoided at this stage applying scientific categories to Christian doctrine except when he referred to human sinfulness.[16]

The human condition and the grace of God

Repeated throughout all Sangster's writings is his belief in the utter sinfulness of humanity and the inviolability of the human will. Humanity needs to be saved and can be saved only by the intervention of God, but each and every person is able to respond and is responsible to the promptings of grace, though God never violates the human will.[17] Sangster defined the limits of God's influence upon the will: 'Never does He violate the personality that He has made. With infinite patience, He seeks to win the wayward and the wicked by all the dear inducements of love.'[18] Sangster emphasizes the work of God's loving grace yet sets limits to God's influence upon the individual: 'Mighty as the Spirit of God is to work swift revolutionary changes, no method which God uses, and which respects our personal freedom, can bring the Kingdom to the hearts of men overnight.'[19] Throughout all his authorship he maintained the view that humankind must have true freedom towards God and be able to refuse the offer of God's grace.[20] Here Sangster is certainly reflecting his Arminian roots, seeking to maintain human freedom and not making concessions to notions of irresistible grace and predestination. In the *Christian Advocate*, Sangster addressed those who ultimately choose to reject the offer of salvation:

> Far be it from me to put any limit to the resource of the love of God, but honesty compels me to declare that God always respects our freedom. He will not force salvation on anyone. He will not save us against our will. The awful responsibility of being alive is just – that our freedom in

---

[15] Sangster, *Why Jesus Never Wrote a Book*, pp. 28, 29, 41, 132. W. E. Sangster, *God Does Guide Us?* (London: Hodder & Stoughton, 1934), p. 93.

[16] W. E. Sangster, 'Does It Pay to Be a Rogue?', in *Why Jesus Never Wrote a Book*, p. 34.

[17] Sangster follows closely the synergistic scheme that (it has been argued) John Wesley inherited from the Eastern church fathers.

[18] W. E. Sangster, 'When Hope Is Dead – Hope On!', *These Things Abide* (London: Hodder & Stoughton, 1934), p. 70.

[19] W. E. Sangster, 'Security', *Ten Statesmen and Jesus Christ* (London: Hodder & Stoughton, 1941), p. 63.

[20] W. E. Sangster, *The Path to Perfection* (London: Hodder & Stoughton, 1943), pp. 122–123; *The Pure in Heart* (London: Epworth Press, 1954), p. 235; *Give God a Chance* (London: Epworth Press, 1959), p. 75.

its measure is real and inviolable. Within a tiny orbit we can withstand God.[21]

His understanding of the internal ministry of God's grace drawing humanity towards himself and creating a desire for goodness certainly carries many of the attributes of John Wesley's understanding of prevenient grace.[22]

It should not be surprising that 1939 marks a point of transition in Sangster's sermons and writings. The start of the Second World War, the second major war within a generation, and the possibilities of immediate and widescale death and destruction triggered difficult theological and pastoral reflections on the faith. From this point forwards the tone and content of Sangster's theology changes. Modern philosophical and theological thought becomes explicit in his thinking as he attempts to restate Christian concepts for the modern era in these new circumstances. Of particular note is his clear appeal to evolutionary understandings of human beginnings and the idea of life and the earth being far more ancient than commonly accepted, which many felt opposed traditional interpretations of the Genesis creation and fall narratives.

One sermon in particular illustrates the shift in emphasis and content, namely 'And After Death – What?' (1939). This war sermon explores the contentious idea of progress after death. Sangster asserts that moral transform-ation continues after death:

> I believe that in heaven we shall develop. No static life will be ours. God entertains the highest purposes for His children. He aims to bring us to perfection, to the 'measure of development which belongs to the fullness of Christ' – and this task is not a task for earth alone. Busy in His royal service for others, by which alone selfishness and pride of our nature is subjugated, He fosters our growth in all things good.[23]

Sangster refers to John 14:2, where Jesus tells his disciples that his Father's house contains many dwellings; the Greek word used 'normally referred to stations on a journey, places of comfortable accommodation for a night. Two ideas are implicit in it – rest and *progress*.'[24] Sangster suggests that believers are not perfected at death:

---

[21] W. E. Sangster, 'A Question God Can't Answer', *Christian Advocate*, 6 March 1952, p. 7.
[22] For comparison, see John Wesley, 'On Working out Our Own Salvation', in *Works*, vol. 3 (Nashville: Abingdon Press, 1986), pp. 199–209 (esp. 202–203).
[23] Sangster, *These Things Abide*, p. 188.
[24] Ibid., p. 189.

Devout souls are not made perfect in the instant of death by some stroke of power. Perfection can never be given: it can only be co-operatively attained. But that is God's ambition for us all, and the end He will pursue through all eternity.[25]

This issue of the afterlife re-emerges at the start of his first major treatise on holiness, *The Path to Perfection*. According to Sangster, the common view of the eighteenth century, when Wesley ministered, was 'that everyone must be entirely sanctified in the article of death' and this was a major barrier to the modern mind. How could this even be envisaged in the context of a world in which bombs were falling from the sky, cities were burning and young and old were sent into eternity with little or no preparation? Sangster attempted to solve the relationship of sin to the afterlife by projecting God's prevenient grace into the afterlife, allowing for continual cooperative progress. He then raises the question of an intermediate state without unambiguously committing himself to the views expressed:

> but it is now generally allowed that something precious was lost to Protestantism when all idea of progress was eliminated from the life after death. Dr. A.E. Garvie pleads for this idea of eternal progress . . . He even cherishes the hope that God will pursue with His grace even those who die impenitent . . . So something of the concept of purgatory has worked itself back into Protestant thought. Not the name, and certainly not the seven sharply divided ledges of Dante's mountain *Purgatorio*, but the idea of discipline, of grace vouchsafed, of enrichment, and of progress.[26]

Sangster admitted that such a view which allows progress after death for the impenitent was far from the thought of Methodism's founder and would have been considered 'rank heresy' in the eighteenth century.[27] His suggested pastoral solution to the needs of the day led Maynard James, one the leaders of the British holiness movement, who saw Wesley's doctrine of 'perfection *in this* life' under threat, to condemn what he saw as Sangster's capitulation to popish ideas.[28] It is certainly understandable that a thinker such as Sangster was looking for theological solutions to the great pastoral issues occasioned by the war, and it is no coincidence that the high point of Sangster's views on these

---

[25] Ibid., p. 185.
[26] Sangster, *Path to Perfection*, p. 69.
[27] Ibid., p. 70.
[28] Maynard James, 'Dr. Sangster's New Book', *The Flame*, May–June (1943), p. 27.

matters was written during the Blitz of London. After the war, in seeking to understand the eternal plight of those who pass through this life and never hear the gospel, he explored again this area of the afterlife and adopted a position that I have called 'tempered universalism'. He reasons:

> Millions die never having heard of Him. Millions more have heard of Him, but He is little more than a name to them; they have never felt the unconscious impact of His love, nor traced some of the loveliest things in the world to His influence. Even in countries classified as 'Christian', thousands of children grow up in homes from which Christ is virtually excluded, and hear His name only in blasphemy. It is unthinkable that the God whom Christ came to reveal could allow these multitudes to miss their highest bliss because of the accident or misfortune of their birth. A God of love is compelled by His nature to pursue with the offer of salvation all creatures made in His own image.[29]

Sangster never committed fully to a universalist stance, for his unswerving commitment to the inviolability of the human will leaves the door open to any person's decision ultimately to refuse the offer of God's grace. The different context of twentieth-century history, with its devastating wars, posed questions and demanded pastoral answers that traditional theology struggled to find. Sangster's view of God's grace was rooted in the cross, not in an implicit antinomian stance, for his belief in the absolute authority and unchangeableness of God's law remained constant.[30] The historical context is key in understanding Sangster at this point. In contrast to the late Victorian period and Edwardian era, the lives of the people of George VI's reign were again dominated by the threat of death. His two books of sermons from the war period,[31] more than any other of Sangster's publications, reveal the ever-present expectation of death. Compared to previous eras, the media coverage of the events of war, with its casualties and sorrows, brought grief and fear into the living room of the average person. Sangster's sermons of the era aimed, therefore, to address these issues and events and the resultant anxieties. The closeness of death seemed very real to many people and after years of declining mortality rates and longer life spans, in which the church had tailored its message to the idea

---

[29] Sangster, *Give God a Chance*, p. 54.
[30] W. E. Sangster, 'God's Law Is Not on Approval', *Westminster Sermons* (London: Epworth Press, 1960), vol. 1, pp. 58–67.
[31] These were *These Things Abide* and *Ten Statesmen and Jesus Christ*, although the latter was not strictly speaking 'Sunday sermons', but addresses from the air-raid shelter.

of Christian living rather than dying, the church was confronted again with carnage and the reality of untimely death.

The progression in Sangster's thinking regarding the afterlife and hell is, therefore, significant for it illustrates a departure from an important tenet of conservative evangelicalism and, it could be suggested, from mainstream evangelicalism.[32] His decision to preach and publish such views about the afterlife, which also included the ideas of growth, employment and progress,[33] was brave, for Westminster was the heart of Methodism and was publicly known to be, after all, the foremost pulpit in British Methodism, with a powerful recent history of strong conservative evangelicalism. Towards the end of his life, when engaged in the task of evangelism as Secretary of Home Missions, Sangster appears, however, to trawl back on this issue. In the light of his late sermons in which he speaks of hell, 'the outer darkness' and eternity, it appears that Sangster maintained his optimistic view of God's grace, which pursues lost souls for all eternity, while admitting more forcefully the stark possibility that people can refuse God, and ultimately thwart his grace. In a little-known pamphlet Sangster muses on death, hell and judgement:

What is hell like? Certain passages in the Bible describe it as a place of fire and eternal torment. Not many Christians believe in literal flames, and the merciful character of God has led some to doubt whether his striving with human souls ends at death. The idea that people should be shut out of the presence of God, who have never heard of him is repugnant to any sensitive conscience. Even among those who *have* heard of him, only God can know those who have resolutely rejected him. But there is no authority in the Bible for the view that all will be saved at the last . . . The enormous importance of this life emerges again. Character solidifies. Our taste becomes part of ourselves. To lose taste for the things of God heads us in another direction. Heaven would be hell to an irreligious man. The shortest definitions of both heaven and hell are these: Heaven is to be with Him: Hell is to shut yourself out.[34]

---

[32] Evangelicalism continues to this day to emphasize the necessity of conversion and salvation in this life alone. It could be argued from an evangelical position that Sangster's view ultimately undermines the necessity of the atonement. But one can also compare another development in this area, the doctrine of 'conditional immortality', in evangelicals such as John Wenham and even John Stott's refusal to rule it out as a possible interpretation of Scripture. See John Wenham, *Facing Hell: An Autobiography 1913–1996* (Carlisle: Paternoster Press, 1998), and Timothy Dudley-Smith, *John Stott: A Global Ministry* (Leicester: Inter-Varsity Press, 2001), pp. 348–355.

[33] Sangster, *These Things Abide*, p. 188.

[34] W. E. Sangster, 'The Probation of Life', in *The Great Mystery of Life Hereafter* (London: Hodder & Stoughton, 1957), pp. 103–104.

Even at this later point in his ministry and in the changed pastoral context we find Sangster stressing the inviolability of the human will, the continued striving of God's grace, but here the sobering realization that a person can close God out for ever.

Sin and the need for salvation

From 1939 onwards there is strong evidence to suggest that Sangster held to a view of created reality informed primarily by modern science, accepting in particular that humankind originated in the most primitive forms of life and evolved through millions of years into what it has become. In a sermon published under the title 'Gold From Dross' Sangster sees God's method of creation as being one of transformation:

> All creation is transformation. We begin with a speck of protoplasm and, aided by our biologists, we watch the vast transforming process through the ages that have gone. We study the origin and differentiation of species. We see form transformed to form. The diplodocus, and the brontosaurus, and pelycosaur have all disappeared, but more wonderful forms take their place and man who once, in half-brutish fashion, crawled out of the primeval slime, now turns his telescope to the stars and measures the miles to the moon.[35]

This obvious reliance upon the theory of evolution to describe humankind's derivation was common to the liberal theology of the era but not to most evangelicals. This positive assessment of evolution was by no means universal in the Christian church at the time, for from its very beginning in the mid-nineteenth century many Christians of all persuasions objected to its implications for Christian thought and the Bible.

Within British Methodism, by the late 1930s, a number of viewpoints concerning the theory of evolution were prevalent. On the whole Methodist scholarship accepted the scientific value of the theory but concluded that the history of humankind necessitated a rejection of the ideas of moral evolution and continual human progress. The First World War and its brutality and carnage was of major significance. The Christian faith was seen as necessary for the moral dimension of humanity's being, although, by this time, many of Methodism's scholars felt that the science of evolution coupled with biblical

---

[35] Sangster, *These Things Abide*, p. 42.

criticism necessitated a re-evaluation and restatement of Christian views of sin and the fall. Among the more conservative Methodists a tension existed between accepting the science of evolution and the perceived problems the theory presented to the validity of the biblical story of the fall, especially the anchoring of human sinfulness in the Bible, and its evangelical consequence: the need for salvation. The necessity of upholding and promoting the need for the real Christian experience of forgiveness, while leaving theological speculation to others, was perceived as a genuine Methodist way forwards, a method claiming some support from John Wesley.

A much more conservative position was taken by many within the holiness movement of Methodism, who, on the whole, attempted to support a more literal interpretation of the Scriptures and would, therefore, reject Darwin's theory primarily on biblical grounds. Some came to oppose vehemently the evolutionary theory, however, because of its view of humankind and the belief that the theory roundly contradicted the doctrine of original sin, a particular formulation of which was seen to be essential to the Methodist holiness movement's doctrine of entire sanctification.

The evidence of Sangster's writings from 1939 onwards places him in harmony with a more liberal position on this matter, therefore aligning with the majority of British Methodism's scholars. While accepting the science of the evolutionary theory, Sangster rejected, however, in the strongest terms any talk of inevitable human progress; that is, moral evolution. At the start of the Second World War, shortly before the onset of hostilities, Sangster wrote, 'All this talk of "inevitable progress" is seen for the patter that it is, for we are watching now for the wings of enemy planes.'[36] Two years later, following the Blitz, Sangster set out his own programme for progress, rejecting in no uncertain terms the idea of inevitable moral evolution, while asserting a Christian alternative:

And the first step … is the abandonment of the idea that men *must* improve: that there is something automatic in 'progress': that just as planes get faster, men get better: that it is certain as sunrise and as inevitable as the tides. The widespread dissemination of that false idea was much older than Darwin, but took new impetus from men's interest in evolution. So sure were they that form evolved from form in some ascending spiral of perfection that they carried the idea over into the realm of freedom and asserted it with the same confidence there. Herschel

---

[36] Ibid., p. 19.

committed himself to the statement: 'Man's progress towards a higher state need never fear a check,' and Herbert Spencer was 'certain that man must become perfect.'

Of course, it is *not* certain. If men are free, they are free to choose evil. *If* there is a mechanical development in things, there can never be a mechanical development in persons. The evil in the world will not just *come* right: it has got to be *put* right. There is no escalator to perfection on which the untoiling race can rise by steady degrees to spiritual distinction: only by redemption, grace, discipline, and effort will the height be made.[37]

It could be argued that such a pessimistic position regarding humankind's innate possibilities was inevitable during the conflict of war and more mellow positions would naturally develop as life returned to normal in the years of peace. Sangster's view, however, remained unchanged. In 1951, as President of the Methodist Conference, Sangster looked back at two wars of 'unprecedented scale', saying, 'The facile optimism of the later nineteenth century has given place to a realistic mood which forbids complacency.'[38] In debate with a democratic humanist a few years later, Sangster dismisses again the idea of inevitable human progress:

He seemed to think that, despite the ups and downs, our race was steadily improving. He appeared to believe that it *had* to. This inner necessity had no relation to religion in his mind. It seemed semi-mechanical. As planes get faster men get better. I reminded him of Dachau and Belsen, and our stockpiling of hydrogen bombs. I told him again that if he could believe in this kind of perfection he could believe in anything.[39]

For Sangster the history of humankind argues against any claims to inevitable progress, with the two world wars as the ultimate proof. His writings post-1945 assert the Christian belief in the sinfulness of humankind, believing firmly that recent history supported his view. In the late 1950s, Sangster wrote:

In the middle years of the last century there was a sharp controversy between the philosophers and the theologians of the Western world over man's perfectibility. The philosophers were saying that man *must* become

---

[37] Sangster, *Ten Statesmen and Jesus Christ*, pp. 113–114, 142.
[38] W. E. Sangster, 'Message to the Methodists of the World', *Methodist Recorder*, 3 May 1951, p. 4.
[39] W. E. Sangster, *Sunday Times*, 31 March 1957, p. 14.

perfect; perfect on his own. They thought there was some kind of ethical revolution at work in our race, unrelated to any particular religion. 'Man must become perfect', Herbert Spencer said. The theologians (who were having the worst of the argument then) were quoting the Scriptures and saying that man was 'carnal, sold under sin'. That was nearly a hundred years ago, and now most people are willing to concede that the theologians were right. There is no escalator to perfection. There is no mechanical progress. In this century we have had two world wars, and live in the shadow of a third. Man by himself cannot become perfect. Some of the philosophers themselves are saying now that, maybe, the theologians were right! Man is carnal, sold under sin.[40]

In his latest published sermons Sangster's position remains unchanged, dismissing the futility of human optimism and reasserting that humankind is lost in sin, needing salvation. Apart from its modern allusions the text could have been taken from John Wesley, who insisted on the utter hopelessness of natural man.[41] Sangster writes:

It was nice to be told that there was no truth in the old doctrine of original sin; in fact there was no sin at all – just a bit of selfishness which time would correct; that the Golden Age was inevitable and that, by gradual steps, man would move unaided to perfection. I say it flattered the egotism in us. It made redemption unnecessary. It emptied the cross of meaning . . . And then we woke up! First in 1914 and then again in 1939, we found ourselves in hellish war. The mid-years of the century find us still unsure of peace. This, then, is the perfect world we had been promised by the men who sneered at original sin; a world of atomic submarines, air-raid shelters, gas-masks for babies, guided missiles, and hydrogen bombs. A world of television, plastics, possible trips to the moon – but also the possibility of radiation poisoning, and mass death! The incredible folly of it; the ignorant conceit; the puffed-up egotism.[42]

Sangster, therefore, although accepting the science of evolution, wholly rejects any notion of humankind's inherent goodness or innate ability to progress towards moral or societal perfection. He thereby affirms belief in a

---

[40] W. E. Sangster, *Westminster Sermons*, 2 vols. (London: Epworth Press, 1960), vol. 1, p. 81.

[41] See e.g. Wesley's sermon 'The Deceitfulness of the Human Heart', *Works*, vol. 4 (Nashville: Abingdon Press, 1987), pp. 149–160, esp. 152–153.

[42] W. E. Sangster, *Westminster Sermons*, 2 vols. (London: Epworth Press, 1961), vol. 2, p. 3.

pessimistic evaluation of the human condition, a starting point consistent with historic Christianity and at the heart of evangelical concerns about the necessity of the gospel. When Sangster set about restating John Wesley's doctrine of sanctification for the modern era between 1940 and 1950, he based it on modern premises rooted in evolutionary theory and on a reinterpretation of the doctrine of original sin. In doing so, Sangster was taking on the task deemed necessary by the scholars of British Methodism: to marry a modern view of humanity's derivation with a biblical view and experiential of human sinfulness. Sangster's formulation would of necessity represent a radical departure from John Wesley, for Wesley was totally pre-modern, accepting the biblical account of human origins as factual.

But the radical sinfulness of humanity, according to Sangster, demands a radical cure. This could only come from God, and though the Bible testifies to the continual loving and salvific purposes of God, even in the Old Testament, it was in the event of Jesus Christ that, according to Sangster, salvation is rooted.[43]

The cross

A number of Sangster's sermons from *He Is Able* contain characteristic emphases of the Fellowship of the Kingdom of which he had become a member in the 1920s.[44] Visible are allusions to Abelardian or Moral Influence theories of the atonement,[45] which characterized the Christology of the Fellowship. During his many evangelistic crusades Sangster was not afraid to 'paint a picture' of the crucified Christ on the cross, arms outstretched in love, again picking up the notes of the Moral Influence theory.[46] At no point, however, in all of Sangster's writings does he ever subscribe to one theory of the atonement. Though Sangster finds the solution to most of humankind's deepest needs in the cross of Christ, he states, 'The New Testament has no theories of the Atonement. It has the Atonement – but no explanation.'[47] Increasingly through his life Sangster roots the cross in the historical event of Christ's incarnation and

---

[43] W. E. Sangster, 'God Without God?', in *These Things Abide* (London: Hodder & Stoughton, 1939), pp. 87–95 (89).

[44] For an excellent discussion of The Fellowship of the Kingdom, see Ian M. Randall, *Evangelical Experiences* (Carlisle: Paternoster Press, 1999), ch. 5.

[45] W. E. Sangster, *He Is Able* (London: Hodder & Stoughton, 1936), pp. 18, 34, 59, 60, 82, 104, 116, 163, 238.

[46] 'What It Is to Be a Christian', a recording from Evangelical Records, 1961. It is likely that this recording was originally made for the 'For Such a Time As This' campaign in 1951.

[47] W. E. Sangster, *Westminster Sermons* (London: Epworth Press, 1962), vol. 2, p. 70.

within the eternal pattern of the incarnational sacrificial God; that sacrifice, death and resurrection is written into the very fabric of the universe:

> You can take me to Golgotha and say: 'There is a Cross up there.' I point to the earth and say: 'There is a Cross down here.' The Cross is inherent in life. It is life's foundation. It is not an incongruity. Your Saviour is focusing in a moment of time a fact that is timeless, and on Good Friday the Lamb slain before the foundation of the world is *seen* slain . . . The Cross is in all of life.[48]

Humans access the reality and power of the cross through conversion, but this is just one moment, though significant, and the weight is placed, by Sangster, on continual moral transformation through the mystical concept of 'union with Christ':

> in the midst of our human dilemma, which the passing ages revealed – our utter failure to reach a height that was utterly necessary – God sent His only begotten Son, and grace was thrown like a bridge across the abyss, and the path to the highest was made possible by union with Christ.[49]

Elsewhere and in similar tones Sangster sees the core of the gospel as being anchored in the indwelling Christ, citing Paul's constant use of 'in Christ'.[50] Salvation is essentially a relationship with the crucified Lord. He shows particular fondness for Henry Scougal's classic book *The Life of God in the Soul of Man* (1677).

This type of Methodist theological approach that does not subscribe to particular theories of the atonement has led to accusations that Methodism lacks theological substance. On this point D. Martyn Lloyd-Jones said, 'Arminianism, ultimately, is non-theological.'[51] Iain Murray further emphasized the point, for according to him, John Wesley 'was a great evangelist but no theologian'.[52] Murray boldly goes so far as to argue that the decline of Methodism in Britain in the twentieth century was because it inherited its lack of theology from its founder, though evidence for his contention is left wanting.[53] The evidence of Sangster's sermons, however, closely follows his strong contention that preaching

---

[48] Ibid., p. 67.
[49] Sangster, 'God Without God', p. 89.
[50] W. E. Sangster, 'The Doctrine of the Indwelling Christ', in Cheatle, *Sermons in America*, p. 31.
[51] D. Martyn Lloyd-Jones, *Preaching and Preachers* (Hodder & Stoughton, 1971), p. 101.
[52] Iain Murray, *Wesley and the Men Who Followed* (Edinburgh: Banner of Truth, 2003), pp. 249–263.
[53] Ibid.

must be anchored in sound Christian doctrine, framed within an overall concern for the truth and reality of the incarnate God. Correspondingly, he was adamant about the importance of doctrinal preaching.[54] 'Christianity is not vague sentiment or an amiable feeling.'[55] Typical of Sangster's more vivid use of language is his comment 'It is not "being kind to grandmother and the cat".'[56] According to Sangster the Christian faith is a hard, dogmatic core of doctrine that centres on a living Person, built on certain historical facts concerning Christ with a number of, what he calls, 'immense affirmations regarding God, man and the universe'.[57] Horton Davies in his classic text *The Varieties of English Preaching 1900–1960* confirmed Sangster's commitment to sound theological content in his preaching, 'Dr W. E. Sangster excelled in doctrinal preaching.'[58]

Sangster and the Bible

Years ago I played a recording of one of Sangster's unpublished sermons entitled 'I Know My Redeemer Liveth' to an audience at a theological college. It had been recorded live at an evangelistic campaign in September 1951. Sangster was using philosophical argument against objections to the existence of God with a view to breaking down intellectual barriers to belief. When the question time came at the end, I was astounded that the first comment was that the sermon was not 'biblical', obviously implying that it was of lesser or little value. So was Sangster biblical, for it is evident that he rarely delivered expository sermons or reeled off biblical texts?

In a recent excellent study, the war sermons of Martyn Lloyd-Jones and W. E. Sangster were compared with a view to identifying, in layperson's terms, which of them were more biblical. Most people would presume that Lloyd-Jones' sermons would be much more biblical. Using a form of 'Corpus Analysis' the results of it were very interesting, with Lloyd-Jones only marginally referencing or alluding to the Bible more than Sangster. The real differences appeared in the use of language, with Lloyd-Jones referencing 'God' and terms such as 'Lord' and 'sovereignty' much more than Sangster, and conversely, Sangster referencing 'Jesus' and 'Christ' and 'salvation' much more than Lloyd-Jones. Indeed, one of the not wholly unsurprising conclusions from the analysis was that Lloyd-Jones' sermons repeated and utilized concepts from Calvinism,

---

[54] W. E. Sangster, *Doctrinal Preaching: Its Neglect and Recovery* (Birmingham: Berean Press, 1953), pp. 4–5.
[55] Ibid., p. 5.
[56] Ibid., p. 7.
[57] W. E. Sangster, *Power in Preaching* (London: Epworth Press, 1958), pp. 34–35.
[58] Horton Davies, *The Varieties of English Preaching 1900–1960* (London: SCM Press, 1963), p. 197.

whereas Sangster utilized a Wesleyan soteriological framework. The major differences could not be ascribed to use of the Bible but to theological points of view.[59]

When analysing Sangster's use of Scripture we quickly become aware of Methodism's overriding agendas of evangelism and holiness: issues concerning salvation. This approach speaks particularly to the function or purpose of the Bible. Sangster's theological education, being under the auspices of the University of London, would certainly have contained up-to-date scholarship and obvious familiarity with the historical criticism of its time but for him the function of the Bible was revelation.[60]

By the time of his main ministry and influence Sangster had accepted the methods of biblical criticism as a given. All Sangster's writings prior to his arrival at Westminster in 1939 were of a more conservative evangelical ethos, and avoided the contentious debates with biblical criticism, so it is highly unlikely that his arrival caused any consternation among the more austere evangelicals. Even his comments in support of historical criticism, published sixteen months prior to his arrival in London, were couched in a robust criticism of the arrogance and insensitivity of some of its proponents, whom he further blamed for some of the decline in Methodism:

The pulpit grew unsure of the Book of God. At one time only four epistles of Paul were felt to be authenticated, and the number of sayings of Jesus that could be 'relied' upon were absurdly few. It was considered smart at one period to employ the precious moments in the pulpit to tell people what *not* to believe, and 'having a smack' at obscurantism became a homiletical fashion. The bill came in for that. For those scholars whose reverent researches have made the Bible a new volume to this generation, we have nothing but gratitude, but we share the conviction that some responsibility for the decay of faith is to be laid at the door of those who lost the positive note in preaching, did their thinking aloud, and thought it laid upon them to give currency to the latest extravagances of German criticism. Recent vagaries of 'Form Critics' do not encourage the hope that this period is quite past.[61]

[59] Emma Swai, 'How Did Lloyd-Jones and Sangster Use Scripture in Their Sermon Response to the Outbreak of World War 2? Trialling Methods to Discover a Corpus-Based Analytical Approach to the Homiletical Use of Scripture' (unpublished MA Dissertation, Liverpool Hope University, October 2018).
[60] Of particular influence in Sangster's education in this area was Ryder Smith.
[61] W. E. Sangster, *Methodism Can Be Born Again* (London: Hodder & Stoughton, 1938), pp. 21–22.

It appears that Sangster saw the benefit of biblical criticism, and certainly used it in his own sermon preparation, but felt that its place should be confined to the study, not propagated from the pulpit. Sangster says:

> Get the background of the epistle, and understand the historical setting of the minor prophet. You need not burden your people with all you know. What you say at any time will be but a tithe of your knowledge. Parading scholarship is an unpleasant vanity in the pulpit. To help people is your ruling aim.[62]

Just a fleeting glance at the biblical scholarship used by Sangster in *The Path to Perfection* (1942) demonstrates that while he supported the methods of biblical criticism, his selection of commentaries had a tendency to offer more conservative conclusions. Five commentaries in the Moffatt New Testament Commentary are present, and one commentary by James Moffatt himself, out of a total of eleven.[63] Although today the need to understand the historical background and literary agenda of the original authors of the Scriptures would be normative for most conservative evangelicals, Moffatt proved too liberal for some evangelicals at the time, on both sides of the Atlantic.[64] To his own mind Sangster was evangelical, a fact supported by David Bebbington's well-known scheme. His life and work clearly held as central the need for salvation, a stress on activism, a devotion to the Bible and the centrality of the cross.[65] In his manifesto for Central Hall, published before his first Sunday in Westminster (which incidentally was 3 September 1939), Sangster promised, among other things, 'to maintain at the heart of the Empire an expression of the Christian religion which shall be . . . intellectually honest and satisfying . . . a witness that shall be earnestly evangelical'.[66]

While Sangster regarded the Christian Scriptures as authoritative, he denied any theory of verbal inspiration, a phrase he equated with a notion of mechanical

---

[62] W. E. Sangster, *The Craft of the Sermon* (London: Epworth Press, 1954), p. 153.

[63] W. E. Sangster, *The Path to Perfection* (London: Hodder & Stoughton, 1943), pp. 203–204.

[64] James D. Douglas (ed.), *The New International Dictionary of the Christian Church* (Exeter: Paternoster Press, 1978), p. 669.

[65] D. W. Bebbington, *Evangelicalism in Modern Britain* (London: Unwin Hyman, 1989), pp. 1–19. Although Bebbington's categories are useful, the range of difference between proponents perhaps demands a more thorough categorization. A typical example of the problems of definition also must include the fact that in the USA there is a tendency towards a more literal understanding of the Bible as being an essential characteristic of evangelicalism. See Randall Balmer (ed.), *Encyclopedia of Evangelicalism* (Louisville, KY: Westminster John Knox Press, 2002), pp. 196–197. For a British approach that takes issue with Bebbington's definition, see John Stott, *Evangelical Truth* (Leicester: Inter-Varsity Press, 1999). Also see the good discussion of these issues in the introduction to this volume.

[66] W. E. Sangster, 'What I Intend to Do at Westminster', *The Christian Herald and Signs of Our Times*, no. 31, August 1939, p. 195.

dictation. Sangster saw the authority of the Bible as lying in the message of the gospel itself, not in any theory of inspiration, as evidenced in his article 'On Certainty by Authority':

> *The Bible is still authoritative,* not (for most of us) because of any theories of verbal inspiration, as though God dictated His divine word to the sacred writers as a business man dictates to a stenographer, but because herein we have found the word of the living God, and on all major questions of our life it speaks clear, God: His Being and Nature, Jesus: His Deity, atoning Death, Resurrection and Ascension, The Holy Spirit: Inspirer, Guide, and Comforter, Man: his nature, need, and destiny, Eternal life: The consummation of all things.[67]

Sangster remained constantly against biblical literalism, reiterating his views in April and May 1955,[68] June and July 1957,[69] and 1959.[70] Sangster clearly saw his position as being at the middle ground between the liberal and conservative evangelical poles within Methodism. Indeed from 1955 until 1957 he set about attempting to mould a consensus between the two evangelical poles for the sake of cooperation in evangelism. As a consequence, he published in 1955 'A Simple Statement of Common Belief', as an attempt to find common ground concerning the Bible:

> We take the whole Bible seriously – as God's own appointed channel of communication with men; as the record of man's predicament (sin) and God's remedy (salvation); as the sufficient rule for Christian faith and practice.
>
> We affirm that the Scriptures owe their existence to an activity of the Holy Spirit, whose illuminating power is essential for their under-standing.
>
> We believe the Bible to be true; consistent with this, we allow variation between passages in respect of:

---

[67] W. E. Sangster, 'On Certainty by Authority', *Methodist Recorder*, 12 April 1951, p. 3.

[68] W. E. Sangster, 'Bible Basis of All That We Believe', *Methodist Recorder*, 28 April 1955, p. 3. This was followed by a reply two weeks later to two letters challenging his views, *Methodist Recorder*, 12 May 1955, p. 7.

[69] W. E. Sangster, 'Hindrances to Revival', *Joyful News*, 13 June 1957, p. 2; '"Moral Tone-up of Nation": First Consequence of Return to God', *Methodist Recorder*, 18 July 1957, p. 5.

[70] W. E. Sangster, *Give God a Chance* (London: Wyvern Books, 1959), pp. 21, 58. Although Sangster seems to apply critical methods to his study of the Bible only from 1939 onwards, as early as 1934 he repudiates a hard literalist interpretation of the Scriptures: *God Does Guide Us* (London: Hodder & Stoughton, 1934), p. 91.

(1) The fullness of revelation. God's self-manifestation is partial and veiled in the Old Testament; full and final in the New. Further while all parts are of value, we rely most upon those scriptures which bear witness to the Person and Work of Christ.

(2) The channel of revelation. God's truth comes to us in different forms – poetical, historical, allegorical. No one approach unlocks the meaning of the whole.

(3) The interpretation of revelation. Men are not infallible: hence their expositions are not always identical. Therefore, we will endeavour to let Scripture speak for itself, by refusing to let presupposition blind us to its message.

We find the fundamental truths of our faith to be clear to those who read with reverence and devotion; and the Bible's guidance in these matters to be utterly reliable. Such fundamentals we judge to be:

GOD – the Creator; the final Judge; the present Redeemer. JESUS CHRIST – His only Son; our only Saviour; the only Lord. HOLY SPIRIT – regenerating; sanctifying; glorifying. SALVATION – from sin; for all; by grace; through faith; with assurance; to holiness. CHURCH – people of God; body of Christ; temple of Holy Spirit.[71]

A high respect for the Bible is evident, as is the stress on the major tenets of evangelicalism, more particularly a Protestant and Methodist understanding of salvation. Of note is the lack of defining words such as 'infallibility' and 'inerrancy'. Also evident is a commitment to an openness of interpretation, the centrality of literary genre and the fallibility of human interpreters, yet the action of the Holy Spirit.

Sangster's personal faith and his preaching presupposed, therefore, a high view of the Bible. This did not, however, imply any sort of obscure fundamentalist view of literalism or even claims to inerrancy. The Bible was, for Sangster, the primary witness to the revelation of Jesus Christ and therein was its authority and not an authority intrinsic to itself. He firmly believed that the Bible is the Word of God with a timeless and always relevant message – Christ. Sangster believed in the usefulness and relevance of biblical criticism and felt that its methods had saved the Bible for many in the modern era. One could say Sangster subscribed to a form of theological interpretation of Scripture, even a form of canonical interpretation, for the message at the heart of the Bible and

---

[71] From W. E. Sangster, 'A Bible Basis for All that We Believe', *Methodist Recorder*, 28 April 1955, p. 3.

its very purpose was *salvation*, the elements of which correspond closely to the content of the historic creeds of Christianity, interpreted through the grid of Protestant and Methodist theology.[72]

Conclusion

W. E. Sangster was a Methodist evangelical who had the aim of restating the Christian faith for his historical and intellectual context. He utilized philosophical and psychological categories in expressing his theology. One could say that this agenda was rooted in theological liberalism's quest to make the Christian faith comprehensible to modern people; however, he would have seen it as the task of every minister of God to communicate in meaningful terms to the people of that minister's day. Perhaps the most contentious issue was his reinterpretation of the biblical narratives of creation and fall and the consequent necessity of reinterpreting the doctrine of sin. His flirting with 'universalism' can be ascribed to the particular context of his ministry, with over 500,000 passing through the air-raid shelter for which he had charge, and the daily loss and carnage of war. Humankind was radically sinful and needed the cross of Christ. Conversion and union with Christ through his Spirit were the essence of salvation, with sanctification playing a large role, as it should for a true Methodist. The Bible is the book that contains the story of God's dealings with humankind and through which we can know of God and meet Jesus Christ, which is its true purpose; therein lies its inspiration and authority.

So, on all the points, the cross, the Bible, evangelism/conversion, Sangster evidences not only true theological engagement with the core of Christian belief but also a commitment to the key tenets of evangelical faith.

© Andrew J. Cheatle, 2022

---

[72] On this point Sangster comes close to the position of John Stott in *Evangelical Truth*.

7

Martyn Lloyd-Jones

DAVID CERI JONES

In his closing address to the Puritan Conference in 1968, Martyn Lloyd-Jones chose as his subject William Williams and Welsh Calvinistic Methodism, marking the 250th anniversary of Williams's birth in 1717. Delivered just after his ministry at Westminster Chapel had drawn to a close, Lloyd-Jones's lecture was a tour de force. In a characteristic blend of historical analysis and theological reflection, Lloyd-Jones argued that eighteenth-century Calvinistic Methodism, especially in its Welsh form, was nothing less than '1st-century Christianity', and that 'the first Christians were the most typical Calvinistic Methodists of all!'[1] 'Methodism', he maintained, was 'essentially experimental or experiential religion, and a way of life.'[2] When married to Calvinistic theology, he argued, Methodism restrained Reformed theology from its natural tendency towards 'intellectualism and scholasticism'. 'Calvinism', Lloyd-Jones asserted,

> not only does justice to the objective side of our faith ... it does equal justice to the subjective ... Calvinism of necessity leads to an emphasis upon the action and the activity of God the Holy Spirit.[3]

For Lloyd-Jones, Calvinism and Methodism dovetailed perfectly – each was essential to keep the other in check. And where doctrine and experience were both present, a harmonious evangelical faith was invariably the result.

Nurtured in the cradle of Welsh Calvinistic Methodism, Lloyd-Jones grew up under the shadow of the statue of Daniel Rowland at Llangeitho, the village that had witnessed Rowland's remarkable ministry in mid-eighteenth-century Cardiganshire.[4] Lloyd-Jones remained a Welsh Calvinistic Methodist

---

[1] D. M. Lloyd-Jones, 'William Williams and Welsh Calvinistic Methodism' (1968), in D. M. Lloyd-Jones, *The Puritans: Their Origins and Successors* (Edinburgh: Banner of Truth, 1987), p. 213.

[2] Ibid., p. 195.

[3] Ibid., p. 210.

[4] For an introduction to Calvinistic Methodism, see David Ceri Jones, Boyd Stanley Schlenther and Eryn Mant White, *The Elect Methodists: Calvinistic Methodism in England and Wales, 1735–1811* (Cardiff: University of Wales Press, 2012).

throughout his life. When he commended Calvinistic Methodism in such extravagant terms, he was describing his own theological vision, the fusion of convictions that had both shaped his Christian formation and continued to inform every aspect of his ministry. This chapter introduces some of the distinguishing features of Lloyd-Jones's theology, and argues that only by appreciating the importance of his Calvinistic Methodist hinterland can he be adequately understood.

From physician to preacher

In the middle decades of the twentieth century, British evangelicalism was dominated by the figure of Martyn Lloyd-Jones. As a Nonconformist, for thirty years he occupied one of the most influential pulpits in Britain, Westminster Chapel, just a stone's throw from Buckingham Palace in central London. He had entered the ministry after a glittering medical career that saw him rise to become the assistant to George V's chief physician in the early 1920s. Returning to Wales in 1927, 'the Doctor', as he came affectionately to be known, took pastoral charge of a run-down Forward Movement mission in the industrial town of Port Talbot, experiencing something close to revival during the industrial depression of the early 1930s. After just over a decade in South Wales he returned to London and Westminster Chapel just before the outbreak of the Second World War, and quickly gained a reputation as a preacher of considerable renown. From his Westminster pulpit he inspired a resurgence in both expository preaching and Reformed evangelicalism. Inevitably, his influence quickly began to be felt beyond Westminster Chapel. In the student world, he became one of the first presidents of the Inter-Varsity Fellowship, and was the founding president of the International Fellowship of Evangelical Students in 1947. Through the Evangelical Library and the Banner of Truth Trust he encouraged a revival of interest in Puritan and historic evangelical Christianity, something given tangible expression through the annual Puritan (later Westminster) Conference that he co-led with James Packer from 1950. Through his involvement with London Bible College and Tyndale House he encouraged evangelical intellectual endeavour, and through the Westminster Fellowship and Evangelical Movement of Wales he influenced generations of Christians with his experiential Calvinism. There were few new evangelical agencies in mid-twentieth-century Britain in which Lloyd-Jones was not critically involved, and that did not bear his stamp.

The watershed moment of Lloyd-Jones's ministry remains the public disagreement that took place between him and John Stott in 1966 when, against the backdrop of the gathering ecumenical pace, Lloyd-Jones issued a challenge to evangelicals to leave their doctrinally mixed denominations and come together in a new ecclesiastical relationship untainted by theological compromise. The evangelical movement he had done so much to shape was polarized between those who seceded and aligned themselves with doctrinally untainted evangelical networks such as the British Evangelical Council, and those who chose to remain in their traditional denominations. Following retirement from Westminster Chapel, Lloyd-Jones devoted the last decade or so of his life to itinerant preaching and to preparing for publication his sermons on Paul's letters to Ephesians and Romans, his two longest Westminster expository sermon series. The eight volumes of *Ephesians* and fourteen volumes of *Romans* began to appear in the early 1970s, and they remain his chief posthumous legacy. Lloyd-Jones died, appropriately enough for such a passionate Welshman, on St David's Day aged 81.[5]

Lloyd-Jones was not a formally trained theologian; he never attended a theological college or received any ministerial preparation, and never sat down to write a book. The whole of his published output consists of lightly edited transcripts of his sermons; apart from the very earliest years of his ministry, Lloyd-Jones did not write out sermons in full before preaching. One of the compelling features of the published sermons as a result is that they read very much as they were originally delivered, and the rhythm and cadences of Lloyd-Jones's voice can be heard clearly. Only a handful of Lloyd-Jones's sermons appeared in book form during his lifetime, although one of his Sunday sermons did appear in the in-house Westminster Chapel magazine, *The Westminster Record*, every week. But since his death, in addition to the completion of the publication of his two major expository series, a vast number of books containing collections of Lloyd-Jones's sermons on various books of the Bible have appeared in print. His sermons are also freely available to listen to in their entirety online.[6] Few figures in the history of the church have had so many of their spoken words appear in print. They represent a remarkable body of theological and devotional literature, and a lavish resource for contemporary evangelicals. This chapter makes use of a selection of these sermons to tease out some of the distinctive themes of Lloyd-Jones's theology. It does so in five broad

---

[5] For accounts of his life, see Iain H. Murray, *David Martyn Lloyd Jones: The First Forty Years* and *The Fight of Faith* (Edinburgh: Banner of Truth, 1982, 1990). The two volumes have been abridged as *The Life of Martyn Lloyd-Jones, 1899–1981* (Edinburgh: Banner of Truth, 2013). For more analytical studies, see John Brencher, *Martyn Lloyd-Jones (1899–1981) and Twentieth-Century Evangelicalism* (Carlisle: Paternoster Press, 2002), and Andrew Atherstone and David Ceri Jones (eds.), *Engaging with Martyn Lloyd-Jones: The Life and Legacy of 'the Doctor'* (Nottingham: Apollos, 2011).

[6] See the Martyn Lloyd-Jones Trust: <www.mljtrust.org>.

areas: his passion for robust biblical conviction, his revival of Calvinism, his commitment to Spirit-anointed preaching, his quest for evangelical unity and his encouragement of Spirit-empowered revival. The roots of each of these convictions and concerns stemmed directly from his Welsh Calvinistic Methodism.

Biblical conviction

The Calvinistic dimension of Lloyd-Jones's Calvinistic Methodism manifested itself in his efforts to encourage a resurgence of robust biblical conviction within the evangelical movement. Despite his reputation as an expositor, Lloyd-Jones saw himself first and foremost as an evangelist. Indeed, his wife once commented that her husband was 'first of all a man of prayer and then an evangelist'.[7] While his sermons on the major Pauline letters overshadow the rest of his published output, in reality they represent just a fraction of the sermons he preached. At Westminster Chapel his customary practice was to assume that he was addressing Christians on a Sunday morning, while on Sunday evenings he preached evangelistically. On Friday evenings he preached what he called 'instructional' sermons, where the priority was on teaching; his mammoth series on Romans was of this kind.[8] During the week he engaged in an itinerant ministry and might be found preaching in any part of the British Isles on a Tuesday or Wednesday evening. These sermons were almost always evangelistic in nature.

Lloyd-Jones's approach to evangelistic preaching owed much to his medical training: the problem of the human condition was diagnosed, the false remedies were shown to be wholly ineffective and the only cure was revealed and applied. Lloyd-Jones thought that effective gospel preaching, like all preaching, had to be addressed first of all to the mind. 'It is not sufficient to tell a man that he is a sinner – you must prove it to him – give him examples and make him think.'[9] To do so he invariably began his evangelistic sermons by speaking about some of the problems facing the world at the time he was speaking, before showing the futility of life without God, often drawing on contemporary evidence from prominent figures of the day to reveal to his listeners the bankruptcy of their true spiritual condition. A sermon on 1 Corinthians 6:9–11, part of a series on the kingdom of God, preached at the climax of the Profumo scandal in 1963, is typical of his approach.

---

[7] Quoted in Murray, *Fight of Faith*, back cover.
[8] Martyn Lloyd-Jones, *Preaching and Preachers* (1971) (London: Hodder & Stoughton, 1998), p. 63.
[9] Murray, *Life of Martyn Lloyd-Jones*, p. 58.

At a time of national scandal and moral panic, Lloyd-Jones began by addressing the 'ridiculous charge' that the Bible was an out-of-date book. 'It is always contemporary,' he said, 'always up to date, and always has the exact word to say at any particular juncture.'[10] 'The Bible', he continued, 'is a book that looks you in the face, examines you in the depths and tells you the truth about yourself – unvarnished – it exposes it all.'[11] For Lloyd-Jones, the Bible's explanation for why society had gone so badly awry was that the human race 'has been deceived by the devil'. He suggested five ways in which this deception was manifesting itself in the early 1960s: the devil's masterstroke, he asserted, was that he had been so successful in preventing people from reading the Bible. More specifically he argued that moral relativism was the cause of the 'present muddle', and the idea that you can keep the Christian ethic while dispensing with Christian doctrine had 'landed us in the present moral morass'. People had been deceived into thinking that death was the end of human consciousness, and the idea that God was just a being of love and that there was no final judgement had inoculated them against the reality of their true spiritual condition. The answer to all of these developments, he said, 'is that God *is*', and he condemned 'dignitaries in the Church' for presenting people with a false and distorted picture of God. 'I hold them, too, responsible for the present moral collapse,' he alleged.[12]

From detailed diagnosis he moved on to the remedy: there could be no excuse for human ignorance, he claimed, because God had revealed himself fully in the Bible. Beginning in the garden of Eden, Lloyd-Jones argued that men and women had the law of God written on their hearts, that God's moral standards were plain, and that there would certainly be a final judgement. When he came to the gospel itself, he went to great pains to clear away false perceptions. The gospel was not a 'mere message of denunciation of sin and of the sinner', nor was it an encouragement for greater moral effort, nor a demand for more education, moral or otherwise, nor merely an appeal for men and women 'to believe in Christ and to say "Lord Lord!", and then say that everything is all right'. All of these remedies, he said, did not cure the real disease. In the days to come, he prophesied, 'we shall have some kind of moral cleansing; and people will attend services and will be told in the Press that Cabinet Ministers are attending services and people are showing an interest in religion'. But if they hear a gospel that does not hold out the possibility of a radical change

[10] D. Martyn Lloyd-Jones, *The Kingdom of God* (Cambridge: Crossway Books, 1992), p. 137.
[11] Ibid., p. 139.
[12] Ibid., pp. 140–144.

of heart, 'it is a lie, it is deceit again!'[13] As he reached the climax of the sermon, Lloyd-Jones turned to the real message of the gospel. 'We do not denounce sinners, we save them,' he said.

> It is a message of hope, a message of salvation . . . it tells them that God will take hold of them . . . that they can be converted, that they can be saved, that they can be renewed.

For Lloyd-Jones, the Christian message was one of regeneration, rebirth, 'that a new man or woman can rise out of the ashes of the failure and walk as a saint before God'.[14]

Lloyd-Jones never ended his evangelistic sermons with a call to make a decision, still less an appeal to make a public declaration of faith, preferring to trust wholly to the sovereign work of the Holy Spirit to bring about redemption and new birth. Indeed, he once said that 'the term "decide" has always seemed to me to be quite wrong . . . A sinner does not "decide" for Christ; the sinner "flies" to Christ in utter helplessness and despair.'[15] Throughout his evangelistic sermons Lloyd-Jones deployed reason and argument, he called upon his hearers to think, and having demonstrated the futility of contemporary life without God, he left people with no choice but to embrace the gospel and 'know the moral, spiritual cleansing that the Son of God alone can give, and the new walk and the new life which the Holy Spirit of God alone can enable one to walk'.[16] It was this sort of evangelistic preaching that led to something close to revival in South Wales during the 1930s, and that made Westminster Chapel a 'soul trap', much as Spurgeon's Metropolitan Tabernacle had been a few generations earlier.[17]

Lloyd-Jones's evangelistic preaching was based on his unshakable confidence in the Bible as God's authoritative Word. It was precisely here, he argued, that the contemporary church had catastrophically lost its nerve. In three addresses given at a conference of the International Fellowship of Evangelical Students in Canada in 1957 he insisted that 'the question of authority is one of the most important problems confronting us . . . [T]hings are as they are in the Christian church throughout the world today because we have lost our authority'.[18] The contemporary decline of the church, he argued, was because of its rejection of

---

[13] Ibid., pp. 149–150.
[14] Ibid., pp. 150–151.
[15] Lloyd-Jones, *Preaching and Preachers*, p. 279.
[16] Lloyd-Jones, *Kingdom of God*, p. 154.
[17] See Bethan Lloyd-Jones, *Memories of Sandfields* (Edinburgh: Banner of Truth, 1983).
[18] D. M. Lloyd-Jones, *Authority* (1958) (Edinburgh: Banner of Truth, 1992), p. 7.

the authority of the Bible, and the distortion of the biblical gospel. His three addresses focused in turn on the authority of Christ, the authority of the Bible itself and the authority of the Holy Spirit, as he challenged evangelicals that we 'either accept this authority or else we accept the authority of "modern knowledge", modern science, human understanding, human ability'.[19] In the first address he laid down the importance of revelation itself:

> use your reason, use your intellect; do so honestly, and you will come to the conclusion that there is a limit to reason . . . It is at this point that God in His infinite grace and kindness meets us in revelation.[20]

The culmination of that revelation was the person of Jesus Christ himself, something that led Lloyd-Jones to stress that our knowledge of Christ has to be built upon a trustworthy and authoritative Bible.

For Lloyd-Jones the main challenge facing those who believed in the authority of the Bible at mid-century came not from biblical criticism as such, but from those who argued 'that we must accept and believe in the message, but that we can ride very loosely to the facts' of the Bible, and those who said that it was only 'when something in the Bible speaks to your condition it is the Word of God'.[21] This may have been an allusion to the teaching of Karl Barth, popular in some evangelical circles in the 1950s, but by way of answer Lloyd-Jones adduced various arguments for the authority of the Scriptures, though he stopped short of discussing theories of biblical inspiration, and made no reference to the concept of inerrancy. However, this is not to say that he did not believe in the plenary inspiration of Scripture. Elsewhere, in a series of addresses on great biblical doctrines given earlier in the 1950s, he had affirmed that '[i]t is not merely that the thoughts are inspired, not merely the ideas, but the actual record, down to the particular words. It is not merely that the statements are correct, but that every word is divinely inspired.'[22]

While he encouraged students to study theology at an advanced level, and was one of the founders of Tyndale House in Cambridge, a research institute aimed at stimulating evangelical biblical research,[23] the final authority of the Bible, he stressed, was primarily 'a matter of faith and not of argument'. He

---

[19] Ibid., p. 60.
[20] Ibid., p. 13.
[21] Ibid., pp. 34–35.
[22] D. M. Lloyd-Jones, *Great Doctrines Series*, vol. 1: *God the Father, God the Son* (London: Hodder & Stoughton, 1996), p. 24.
[23] T. A. Noble, *Tyndale House and Fellowship: The First Sixty Years* (Leicester: Inter-Varsity Press, 1996), p. 32.

warned his fellow conservative evangelicals not to fall into the trap of 'a form of rationalism'. Ultimately, he said, 'it is only as the result of the work, and the illumination, of the Holy Spirit within us that we can finally have this assurance about the authority of the Scriptures'.[24]

On the basis of an authoritative Bible, Lloyd-Jones held that there were certain fundamental truths in Scripture over which there could be no debate or question. In his series on the great doctrines of the Bible he said, 'There must be no disputing about the person of Christ, about the miraculous and the super-natural, about the substitutionary death upon the cross, and about the literal, physical resurrection . . . This is final; this is absolute.'[25]

He drew a distinction between those doctrines essential for salvation, over which there could be no question or debate, and those not essential, such as baptism, Calvinism or Arminianism and the doctrine of the last things, over which there had always been considerable divergence of opinion among evangelicals. But on the fundamentals of the faith he was unequivocal. To take just one example: on the atonement he argued that substitution was the 'essential Protestant' interpretation of the sacrifice of Christ, because it was the only theory that adequately emphasized the 'penal elements of the atonement'.[26] Only the substitutionary view of the atonement, he said, 'clarifies the whole thing where nothing else can' because 'it magnifies the cross and the love of God in a way that all these other theories, which have been put forward in order to safeguard the love of God, completely fail to do'.[27] Through his pulpit ministry and deep commitment to agencies such as the Inter-Varsity Fellowship, Lloyd-Jones's preaching fortified successive generations of evangelicals with a renewed confidence in the Bible, the cross and the need for conversion.

Calvinism revived

Lloyd-Jones's theological development was shaped by two historical strands: the seventeenth-century Puritans and the evangelical revivals of the eighteenth century. He received a set of the works of John Owen as a wedding present,[28] though it was stumbling across a set of the works of Jonathan Edwards in a second-hand bookshop in Cardiff in 1929 that, he claimed, 'helped me more than anything else'.[29] Occasional influences from more recent theologians

---

24 Lloyd-Jones, *Authority*, pp. 38–39.
25 Lloyd-Jones, *Great Doctrines Series*, vol. 1, p. 46.
26 Ibid., p. 328.
27 Ibid., p. 316.
28 Murray, *First Forty Years*, pp. 155–156.
29 Ibid., pp. 253–254.

included the works of R. W. Dale, James Denney and P. T. Forsyth on the atonement, while on his first visit to North America in 1932 he discovered the writings of the Princeton Reformed theologian B. B. Warfield: 'no theological writings are so intellectually satisfying and so strengthening to faith', he later confessed.[30] As important as each of these influences was, though, his theological lodestar remained the Welsh Calvinistic Methodists. 'My reading of the Calvinistic Methodist revival of the eighteenth-century', he once admitted, 'governed me and when anything presented itself to me, if it did not fit into that framework, I had no difficulty over my duty.'[31] His Calvinism bore an eighteenth-century stamp.

As much as he saw himself as a Calvinistic Methodist, he could be reluctant to use the word 'Calvinism', and rarely dealt with the subject directly. One of the exceptions was a series of three addresses on the sovereignty of God that he gave at the third Welsh Inter-Varsity Fellowship (IVF) conference in 1951, an event that proved critical in the resurgence of Calvinistic theology among evangelicals in Wales.[32] A full text of these addresses has unfortunately not survived and they were never published,[33] but it is possible to piece together what he might have said from other sources in which he specifically addressed Calvinistic principles. In a radio address on John Calvin for BBC Wales in 1944, he said, 'The great central and all-important truth was the sovereignty of God and God's glory.' Human beings, he went on, are 'totally unable to save' themselves 'and to reunite with God. Everyone would be lost if God had not elected some for salvation, and that unconditionally.' Nobody would be saved 'if God through His irresistible grace in the Holy Spirit had not opened their eyes and persuaded them (not forced them) to accept the offer'. God 'sustains . . . and keeps' us 'from falling . . . salvation, therefore, is sure, because it depends, not on' us and our abilities, 'but on God's grace'.[34] This sort of summary of Calvinist theology remained uncommon in Lloyd-Jones's preaching: Calvinist principles were usually dealt with more obliquely, as they arose naturally in his exposition of the Scriptures. Indeed, he repeatedly warned that Calvinism as a theological system had a dangerous tendency to replace the Bible with man-made Confessions of Faith as 'the primary and supreme standard'.[35]

[30] Martyn Lloyd-Jones, 'Introduction', in B. B. Warfield, *Biblical Foundations* (Eerdmans: London, 1958), pp. 8–9.
[31] Quoted in Murray, *First Forty Years*, p. 195.
[32] Geraint D. Fielder, *'Excuse Me, Mr Davies – Hallelujah!' Evangelical Student Witness in Wales, 1923–83* (Bridgend: Evangelical Press of Wales, 1983), pp. 155–159.
[33] For an unattributed summary of their content, see Murray, *Fight of Faith*, pp. 238–245.
[34] D. M. Lloyd-Jones, 'John Calvin' (1944), in *Knowing the Times: Addresses Delivered on Various Occasions, 1942–1977* (Edinburgh: Banner of Truth, 1989), pp. 35–36.
[35] Lloyd-Jones, 'William Williams', p. 209.

Nevertheless, Lloyd-Jones invested considerable energy into the recovery of Reformed views. His own preaching was, of course, one of the initial impetuses for the mid-twentieth-century Reformed reawakening, but a number of institutions also championed the cause. The Evangelical Library that opened in 1945 made Reformed books readily available to ministers all over the country, while from 1950 the Puritan Conference drew together many of those same ministers every December to listen to historical lectures that extolled the virtues of the theological perspectives of the Protestant past. The highlight of the conference was invariably Lloyd-Jones's own closing lecture, occasions when he drew upon the insights of the past to shed light on the issues confronting the contemporary evangelical church.[36] However, it was the Banner of Truth Trust, a publishing agency formed in 1957, that proved to be the most important single factor in propagating Reformed theology. Inexpensive, attractively produced and sometimes lightly modernized versions of classic Calvinist works were widely disseminated throughout the evangelical world. The Banner was to become Lloyd-Jones's publisher of choice for his major biblical expositions.

By the time Lloyd-Jones delivered his lecture on William Williams at the Puritan Conference in 1968 he had become deeply concerned at some of the tendencies he had witnessed among those who had embraced Reformed theology with such vigour under his tutelage. It was this that led him to stress with renewed determination the importance of religious experience – Methodism alongside Calvinism. As well as the dangers of intellectualism, and the elevation of Confessions of Faith above the Bible, he argued that Calvinism without its Methodist corrective had a tendency to 'discourage prayer', and produce 'a joyless, hard, not to say a harsh and cold type of religion'. He warned, 'If your Calvinism appears to be dead it is not Calvinism, it is a philosophy, it is a philosophy using Calvinistic terms, it is an intellectualism, and it is not real Calvinism.' Genuine Calvinism, he argued, always 'leads to experiences, and to a great emphasis on experience', and the greatest experience of all was a visitation of God himself in revival.[37] It was no accident that an emphasis on the work of the Holy Spirit in revival became increasingly prominent during the second half of his ministry, especially among those who championed the recovery of the doctrines of grace with most zeal.

---

[36] John Coffey, 'Lloyd-Jones and the Protestant Past', in Atherstone and Jones, *Engaging with Martyn Lloyd-Jones*, pp. 293–325.

[37] Lloyd-Jones, 'William Williams', pp. 210–211.

Spirit-anointed preaching

If Lloyd-Jones was committed to the recovery of robust theological conviction, he was no less concerned with the means by which those convictions were communicated. Pre-eminently a preacher, Lloyd-Jones thought much about the nature of preaching and had strong opinions on what made for good preaching. The 'most urgent need in the Christian church today', he never tired of saying, 'is true preaching',[38] and the blame for the ineffectiveness of the contemporary church he laid squarely at the door of the demise of preaching.[39] In a much-quoted phrase, he defined preaching as 'logic on fire'.[40] Here, as with almost every other aspect of his theological vision, was his Calvinistic Methodism. Indeed, he argued that where the two elements were present, robust theology and a genuine experience of the Holy Spirit, 'great preaching' would inevitably result.[41] His most extended treatment of what he regarded as true preaching was the lectures he delivered at Westminster Theological Seminary in Philadelphia in 1969, shortly after his retirement from Westminster Chapel. The lectures, published as *Preaching and Preachers* (1971), remains one of his most widely read books.

Much has been written about Lloyd-Jones's theology of preaching, not least by those who regard him as a champion of expository preaching. While he certainly thought that all preaching had to be expository, and that preaching consecutively through books of the Bible was essential if congregations were to be exposed to the full range of scriptural teaching, what he meant by expository preaching was distinctive. While a sermon must be based on biblical exposition, he warned, it should not be 'a running commentary on, or a mere exposition of, the meaning of a verse or a passage or a paragraph'.[42] Preachers who approached their task in this way 'have only preached the introduction to a sermon'.[43] Rather, he thought that preaching should go well beyond the mere exposition of the text. It is possible, he said, 'to miss the wood for the trees and lose the glory of the gospel' by over-concentrating on the minutiae of textual analysis.[44] According to Lloyd-Jones, it was the preacher's role to identify the overarching message of the text or passage, draw out the message from a text,

---

[38] Lloyd-Jones, *Preaching and Preachers*, p. 9.

[39] Ben Baillie, 'Lloyd-Jones and the Demise of Preaching', in Atherstone and Jones, *Engaging with Martyn Lloyd-Jones*, pp. 156–175.

[40] Lloyd-Jones, *Preaching and Preachers*, p. 97.

[41] Lloyd-Jones, 'William Williams', p. 202.

[42] Lloyd-Jones, *Preaching and Preachers*, p. 72.

[43] Ibid.

[44] Iain H. Murray, *Lloyd-Jones: Messenger of Grace* (Edinburgh: Banner of Truth, 2008), p. 103.

work out its 'relevance ... to the people who are listening to you',[45] and then apply it directly to their particular circumstances. The message of the Bible, he held, always came back to the twin themes of reconciliation and regeneration, and the role of the preacher was to proclaim that human beings are 'rebel[s] against God and consequently under the wrath of God', and need 'to be told the truth about [themselves], and to be told of the only way in which this can be dealt with'.[46] This was the logic element in his definition of true preaching. As the message was applied, he said, a mere sermon was transformed into true preaching. God was acting: 'it is not just a man uttering words: it is God using him ... He is under the influence of the Holy Spirit.'[47]

Yet Lloyd-Jones also argued that logic on its own was insufficient; the logic had to catch fire. It was here, perhaps, that Lloyd-Jones's teaching on the nature of preaching was most distinct. For Lloyd-Jones the purpose of preaching was unlike anything else: 'the first and primary object of preaching', he said, 'is not only to give information. It is ... to produce an impression. It is the impression at the time that matters, even more than what you can remember subsequently.'[48] What he meant was that it was the role and purpose of the preacher to 'give men and women a sense of God and his presence'.[49] That could happen only if the theology being preached came 'through a man who is on fire',[50] and that fire, he stressed, was 'the result of the unction and the anointing of the Holy Spirit'.[51]

The last of his sixteen lectures was devoted to just this – 'the greatest essential in connection with preaching'.[52] The first fifteen lectures had dealt largely with the mechanics of preaching, but in the final chapter Lloyd-Jones dealt with the subject of power, the element that made preaching effective. The preacher, he said, should always be looking for and seeking the Holy Spirit's anointing on his preaching.[53] When it came, the efforts of the preacher would be transformed:

It is the Holy Spirit falling upon the preacher in a special manner. It is an access of power. It is God giving power, and enabling, through the Spirit, to the preacher in order that he may do this work in a manner that lifts it

---

[45] Lloyd-Jones, *Preaching and Preachers*, p. 76.
[46] Ibid., pp. 27–28.
[47] Ibid., p. 95.
[48] Martyn Lloyd-Jones, 'Jonathan Edwards and the Crucial Importance of Revival' (1976), in Lloyd-Jones, *Puritans*, p. 360.
[49] Lloyd-Jones, *Preaching and Preachers*, p. 97.
[50] Ibid.
[51] Ibid., p. 304.
[52] Ibid.
[53] For a more detailed exploration of his views, see Tony Sargent, *The Sacred Anointing: The Preaching of Dr Martyn Lloyd-Jones* (London: Hodder & Stoughton, 1994).

up beyond the efforts and endeavours of man to a position in which the preacher is being used by the Spirit and becomes the channel through whom the Spirit works.[54]

Lloyd-Jones rooted his understanding of this anointing of the Spirit in the experience of the apostles in the book of Acts. While the disciples had received the Holy Spirit at conversion, he argued, on the day of Pentecost and multiple times thereafter they experienced a further 'baptism of power, or a baptism of fire, a baptism to enable one to witness'. As it was experienced repeatedly by the apostles, so he argued, 'this "effusion of power" upon Christian preachers is not something "once for all"; it can be repeated, and repeated many many times'.[55] To reinforce his point he turned to church history, piling up instance upon instance of these effusions of the Spirit on preachers from the Puritan era right through to the end of the nineteenth century. Welsh Calvinistic Methodist examples from the eighteenth century to the 1859 revival unsurprisingly featured prominently. For Lloyd-Jones the recovery of robust theological conviction, something in which he had been instrumental in the middle decades of the twentieth century, had to be married to Spirit-anointed preaching. Logic and fire were both essential. Only 'a return of this power of the Spirit on our preaching is going to avail us anything . . . it is the greatest need of all today – never more so'.[56] It was this sort of preaching, he argued, that was at the heart of all religious revivals.

Lloyd-Jones rarely talked about his own preaching, confessing once that he thought he had 'only really preached twice in my life, and on both occasions I was dreaming'.[57] But for many he was the epitome of the sort of preaching he so often idealized. James Packer once described Lloyd-Jones's preaching as 'the passionate, compassionate outflow of a man with a message from God that he knew his hearers needed'.[58] Yet Lloyd-Jones's own preaching defied simple explanation and categorization: he championed the place of theology, yet at the same time argued that theology alone was not enough. He was simultaneously expositional and ecstatic. Among his admirers, some heard only the former emphasis, while others only the latter. Both, he said, were of the essence of true preaching: logic without fire or fire without logic was wholly ineffective.

---

[54] Lloyd-Jones, *Preaching and Preachers*, p. 305.
[55] Ibid., p. 308.
[56] Ibid., p. 325.
[57] D. M. Lloyd-Jones, 'What Is Preaching?', in Lloyd-Jones, *Knowing the Times*, p. 263.
[58] J. I. Packer, 'Foreword', in D. Martyn Lloyd-Jones, *The Heart of the Gospel: Who Jesus Is and Why He Came*, ed. Christopher Catherwood (Eastbourne: Crossway Books, 1991), p. 8.

Evangelical unity

The evening of 18 October 1966 has gone down in evangelical mythology as the defining moment in the development of British evangelicalism in the twentieth century. It was certainly a critical moment in Lloyd-Jones's life and ministry and has to a great extent shaped subsequent views and interpretations of him. The occasion was the second National Assembly of Evangelicals (NAE) at Westminster Central Hall. Lloyd-Jones had been invited to speak by the Evangelical Alliance on the subject of church unity, at precisely the moment when the rate of ecumenical advance seemed to be gathering considerable momentum. By the mid-1960s Lloyd-Jones had come to believe that evangelicals were confronted by a situation as great and as challenging as the sixteenth-century Protestant Reformation itself. The World Council of Churches, established in 1948, had as its aim the formation of a single Christian church, and in Britain the date of Easter Day 1980 had been pencilled in as the deadline for the reunification of the British churches. Frantic efforts were underway to reach some form of understanding between the various Christian denominations, and it seemed, not least following the first meeting between an Archbishop of Canterbury and the Pope since the Reformation in 1960 (and then again in 1966), that many of the old divisions were finally breaking down.

For Lloyd-Jones these developments represented an opportunity for a fundamental rethinking of evangelical identity. Evangelicals tended to be drawn from across the whole spectrum of denominations, Free Church and Anglican, and rubbed shoulders on a regular basis with those who held radically different views from them, only coming together and expressing their evangelical unity in para-church conferences and organizations such as the Keswick Convention or the IVF Christian Unions. For much of the 1960s, in addition to his regular pulpit ministry at Westminster, Lloyd-Jones devoted considerable energy to speaking about church unity, challenging evangelicals to face up to both the inconsistent position in which they found themselves, and the potential opportunity contemporary developments afforded them.

His most extended treatment of the subject, which anticipated what he said in his famous address in 1966, was two addresses he delivered to the Westminster Minsters' Fraternal in 1962, published by Inter-Varsity Press shortly afterwards. 'It is a tragedy', he confessed, 'that division ever entered into the life of the church,' but it was vital that evangelicals began with the teaching of the New Testament on the subject of unity before they thought about practical or institutional ways to give it expression. Basing his consideration of the subject on John 17 – Christ's high priestly prayer – and Paul's discussion of the church as the body of Christ in Ephesians 4, Lloyd-Jones argued that before talking about unity, evangelicals had to be clear about what it meant to be a Christian and what they meant by the church. Unity, he said,

> can obtain only among those who are regenerate or born again . . . It is a matter of blood and essence . . . It is something which is inevitable because it is the result of being born into a given family.[59]

But more than that, there had to be agreement on the fundamental doctrines of the faith for there to be genuine unity:

> there is an absolute foundation, an irreducible minimum, without which the term 'Christian' is meaningless, and without subscribing to which a man is not a Christian . . . apart from that there is no such thing as fellowship, no basis of unity at all.[60]

Those who questioned the 'cardinal truths that have been accepted through the centuries', he argued, 'do not belong to the church, and to regard them as brethren is to betray the truth'.[61] The logic of his position was inevitable: evangelicals had no business associating in their churches and denominations with those whose message was diametrically opposed to their own. In such circumstances no spiritual unity existed, or indeed could possibly ever exist.

By the time of his NAE address four years later, Lloyd-Jones's views were well known, and had been aired frequently. All the same, hearing Lloyd-Jones effectively preach, rather than lecture, on these themes seemed to inject a new urgency into his case. Our position as evangelicals was 'a pathetic one', he argued. We have neglected the issue of unity.[62] He challenged his hearers: were they prepared to be 'just an evangelical wing in this comprehensive national, territorial church', and coexist with those who denied the very essentials of the faith?[63] His address built to what he himself referred to as an appeal:

> You and I are evangelicals. We are agreed about these essentials of the faith, and yet we are divided from one another . . . we spend most of our time apart from one another, and joined to and united with people who deny and are opposed to these essential matters of salvation . . . Let me

---

[59] D. Martyn Lloyd-Jones, *The Basis of Christian Unity: An Exposition of John 17 and Ephesians 4* (London: Inter-Varsity Fellowship, 1962), p. 14.

[60] Ibid., p. 45.

[61] Ibid., p. 62.

[62] D. M. Lloyd-Jones, 'Evangelical Unity: An Appeal', in Lloyd-Jones, *Knowing the Times*, p. 249.

[63] Ibid., p. 251.

therefore make an appeal to you evangelical people . . . What reasons have we for not coming together? . . . Do you not feel the call to come together, not occasionally, but always? . . . I am a believer in ecumenicity, evangelical ecumenicity. To me the tragedy is that we are divided.[64]

There has been no little confusion over exactly what Lloyd-Jones had in mind by this appeal. He certainly did not envisage forming a new united evangelical church. The closest he came to spelling out his alternative vision was the closing statement of his address:

And who knows but that the ecumenical movement may be something for which, in years to come, we shall thank God because it has made us face our problems on the church level instead of on the level of movements, and really brought us together as a fellowship, or an association, of evangelical churches.[65]

However, what turned Lloyd-Jones's address into a dramatic flashpoint was not so much what he said as the response of the chairman, after he had finished and sat down. The Anglican John Stott rose, suggested that both Scripture and history were against what they had just heard, and urged people not to 'make a precipitate decision after this moving address'.[66] It proved to be a polarizing moment, immediately dividing evangelicals into followers of the Nonconformist Lloyd-Jones or the Anglican Stott. The division only widened further the following year, when at the National Evangelical Anglican Congress at Keele, evangelical Anglicans turned decisively away from any talk of secession and committed themselves afresh to full engagement with the life of the Church of England.[67] Lloyd-Jones's position seemed to harden in the months immediately afterwards, and in an address to mark the 450th anniversary of Luther's nailing of ninety-five theses to the church door in Wittenberg in 1517, he suggested that those who stayed within a territorial church, whether an existing one or any future ecclesiastical configuration, in the hope of reforming it along evangelical lines, raised 'the question of guilt by association'.[68] It was a painful accusation, and suggested that a point of no return had been reached.

---

[64] Ibid., p. 254.

[65] Ibid., pp. 255–257.

[66] Timothy Dudley-Smith, *John Stott: A Global Ministry* (Leicester: Inter-Varsity Press, 2001), p. 68.

[67] Andrew Atherstone, 'The Keele Congress of 1967: A Paradigm Shift in Anglican Evangelical Attitudes', *Journal of Anglican Studies*, vol. 9 (November 2011), pp. 175–197.

[68] D. M. Lloyd-Jones, 'Luther and His Message for Today' (1967), in Hywel Rees Jones (ed.), *Unity in Truth* (Darlington: Evangelical Press, 1991), p. 41.

Lloyd-Jones turned to the British Evangelical Council (BEC) as the agency best placed to unite those churches that chose to secede from their denominations. Only a few Anglicans took the plunge,[69] but the number of Nonconformist churches that seceded grew steadily throughout the 1970s. Larger networks of churches, such as the Fellowship of Independent Evangelical Churches and the Evangelical Movement of Wales, as well as evangelical denominations such as the Free Church of Scotland, threw their weight behind the BEC. Yet there were also casualties: many long-standing friendships and collaborations were lost in these months, none more damaging to the fortunes of the British evangelical movement perhaps than the partnership that had existed between Lloyd-Jones and Packer in the revival of Puritan theology.[70] There were others who wished to draw the boundary lines ever tighter, but attempts to make loyalty to Calvinism integral to this new realignment were fiercely resisted by Lloyd-Jones.[71]

Lloyd-Jones's vision was for an association of evangelical churches in which differences over secondary matters could be set aside in an effort to proclaim the gospel without the taint of compromise. His concern was never ecclesiastical politics, but always the clarity and success of evangelical witness in the nation at large. Unfortunately, its aftermath was characterized by division and recrimination, and to some extent the further hardening of the Anglican–Nonconformist divide, the very opposite of what Lloyd-Jones had intended. Yet a very real realignment did take place: with the exception of the Church of England, many denominations lost their largest and most vibrant congregations to evangelical independency, while towns and cities up and down the land acquired self-styled evangelical churches. It represented a major reshuffling of the evangelical pack, though the experience of evangelical independence did not necessarily usher in the bright new dawn some had anticipated. Lloyd-Jones's vision for a major evangelical realignment nonetheless fundamentally reshaped the nature and character of British evangelicalism.

Spirit-empowered revival

Such has been the dominance of Lloyd-Jones's plea for evangelical unity in the popular memory that it can sometimes crowd out other aspects of his

---

[69] Andrew Atherstone, 'Lloyd-Jones and the Anglican Secession Crisis', in Atherstone and Jones, *Engaging with Martyn Lloyd-Jones*, pp. 261–292.

[70] Alister McGrath, *To Know and Serve God: A Biography of James I. Packer* (London: Hodder & Stoughton, 1997), pp. 49–54.

[71] Iain H. Murray, 'Forty Years On: 1962–2002', *Banner of Truth*, vols. 467–468 (August–September 2002), pp. 12–15, 20–22.

ministry and teaching. Concurrent with the debates over evangelicalism and ecumenism, the late 1960s saw the emergence of the charismatic movement in Britain as elsewhere; the prominent place Lloyd-Jones gave to the ministry of the Holy Spirit meant that those who thought they had experienced a new move of the Spirit inevitably looked to him for advice. Lloyd-Jones preached frequently on the role of the Holy Spirit in the Christian life, and few of his sermons did not contain at least some reference to the need for revival. Here, once again, the influence of his Welsh Calvinistic Methodism was crucial. In his lecture on William Williams he said, 'The thing that characterised Methodism was the pneumatic element. Over and above what they believed, there was this desire to feel and to experience the power of the Spirit in their lives.'[72]

Indeed, it could be argued that this was the dominant motif of Lloyd-Jones's whole ministry. His teaching on the Spirit focused on two main areas: baptism with the Holy Spirit, and revival. Both were intimately related to one another, and proved highly controversial, not least among some of those who were closest to Lloyd-Jones in the recovery of Calvinistic belief.[73]

In a series of twenty-four sermons from the first chapter of John's Gospel, part of his final expository series at Westminster Chapel in 1964–5, Lloyd-Jones gave his most in-depth teaching on the baptism of the Spirit. Published after his death, initially in two parts as *Joy Unspeakable* (1984) and *Prove all Things* (1985), Lloyd-Jones argued from Scripture and church history that 'there is a distinction between believing and being baptised in the Holy Spirit', and that it was possible for the Christian to 'be regenerate without being baptised with the Holy Spirit'.[74] In doing so he was consciously departing from the traditional Reformed view on the subject, a position he had himself articulated in an earlier address at an IVF conference on 'Christ our Sanctification' in 1939, when he had stated that the baptism with the Spirit was synonymous with conversion.[75] Lloyd-Jones's change of opinion seems to have arisen from his increasing conviction that 'we are living, let us remind ourselves, in an age hopelessly below the New Testament – content with a neat little religion'. The missing dimension, the factor that accounted for the power, vibrancy and joy that

[72] Lloyd-Jones, 'William Williams', p. 200.
[73] See Andrew Atherstone, David Ceri Jones and William K. Kay, 'Lloyd-Jones and the Charismatic Controversy', in Atherstone and Jones, *Engaging with Martyn Lloyd-Jones*, pp. 114–155.
[74] D. Martyn Lloyd-Jones, *Joy Unspeakable: The Baptism and Gifts of the Holy Spirit* (Eastbourne: Kingsway, 1995), pp. 32–33.
[75] D. M. Lloyd-Jones, 'Christ Our Sanctification', in *Christ Our Freedom: The Message of the Fourth International Conference of Evangelical Students, Cambridge 1939* (London: Inter-Varsity Fellowship, 1940), pp. 54–78.

characterized the faith of the apostles and the early Christians, he held, was the baptism with the Spirit.[76]

The New Testament, he argued, used different terms for Spirit baptism, each describing essentially the same experience.[77] In sermons on the witness of the Spirit in Romans 8:16 he said that the witness was the 'direct operation' of the Holy Spirit 'on our minds and hearts and spirits' by which we receive 'an absolute certainty and assurance of our sonship'.[78] Similarly, in sermons on the sealing of the Spirit from Ephesians 1:13 he argued that the sealing was 'something subsequent to believing, something additional to believing', the 'direct assurance which the Holy Spirit gives us of our relationship to God in Jesus Christ'.[79] But while assurance was at the heart of the baptism of the Holy Spirit, it was not of its essence. The primary function of Spirit baptism, he argued, was 'to enable us to be witnesses to the Lord Jesus Christ and to his great salvation . . . This is primarily a matter of witness.'[80] The Holy Spirit 'makes us witnesses because of our assurance'.[81] This he tied to the experience of the apostles themselves, who had been told by Jesus to wait at Jerusalem until they received the empowerment of the Spirit at Pentecost (Luke 24:49). After they did so they were able to witness with stunning success. This 'repetition of Pentecost', Lloyd-Jones asserted, 'is a kind of pattern or standard or norm of what we should expect individually and in the case of the Christian church'.[82]

Where Lloyd-Jones differed from the Pentecostal tradition and the emerging charismatic movement was in his view on the place and role of the gifts of the Spirit, especially speaking with tongues. While he was not a cessationist in the Reformed mould, regarding that view as similar to the attitude of 'higher criticism . . . which sits in judgement on the Scriptures',[83] neither did he accept that glossolalia was the sign or evidence of the baptism with the Holy Spirit. He argued, '[Y]ou may have a baptism with the Spirit, and a mighty baptism with the Spirit at that, with none of the gifts of tongues, miracles, or various other gifts.'[84]

---

[76] Lloyd-Jones, *Joy Unspeakable*, p. 89.

[77] Ian M. Randall, 'Lloyd-Jones and Revival', in Atherstone and Jones, *Engaging with Martyn Lloyd-Jones*, pp. 91–113.

[78] D. M. Lloyd-Jones, *Romans: Exposition of Chapter 8: 5–17: The Sons of God* (London: Banner of Truth, 1974), p. 301.

[79] D. M. Lloyd-Jones, *God's Ultimate Purpose: An Exposition of Ephesians One* (Edinburgh: Banner of Truth, 1978), pp. 250, 274.

[80] Lloyd-Jones, *Joy Unspeakable*, p. 89.

[81] Ibid., p. 98.

[82] Ibid., p. 38.

[83] Ibid., p. 170.

[84] Ibid., p. 180.

However, the greatest danger in relation to the baptism with the Spirit was not overenthusiasm, but the possibility of quenching the activity of the Spirit by those who argued that the baptism of the Spirit occurred at conversion. In one of his most compelling warnings from a pair of sermons on quenching the Spirit in his treatment of the Christian's warfare in Ephesians 6, he pleaded:

> There is nothing, I am convinced, that so 'quenches' the Spirit as the teaching which identifies the baptism of the Holy Ghost with regeneration. But it is a very commonly held teaching today, indeed it has been the popular view for many years. It is said that the baptism of the Holy Spirit is 'non-experimental', that it happens to every one at regeneration. So we say, 'Ah well, I am already baptized with the Spirit; it happened when I was born again, at my conversion; there is nothing for me to seek, I have got it all'. Got it all? Well, if you have 'got it all', I simply ask in the Name of God, why are you as you are? If you have 'got it all', why are you so unlike the Apostles, why are you so unlike the New Testament Christians?[85]

Lloyd-Jones's focus on the baptism with the Spirit as a mean of empowerment for witness was tied closely to the need for revival. The only difference between Spirit baptism and revival, he argued, was degree; a revival was 'a large number, a group of people, being baptised by the Holy Spirit at the same time'.[86] In a series of sermons preached to commemorate the centenary of the 1859 revival, Lloyd-Jones brought together his teaching on the baptism of the Spirit and the unction of the Spirit as he spoke about the need for a repeat of what had occurred in 1859. According to Lloyd-Jones, revival happened when

> the Holy Spirit comes down upon a number of people together, upon a whole church, upon a number of churches, districts, or perhaps a whole country. That is what is meant by revival. It is, if you like, a visitation of the Holy Spirit, or another term that has often been used is this – an outpouring of the Holy Spirit.[87]

Revival, for Lloyd-Jones, was the overriding need of the contemporary church, the only thing that could arrest the decline of the church and the marginalization of religion in the nation as a whole. He argued that the history

---

[85] D. M. Lloyd-Jones, *The Christian Warfare: An Exposition of Ephesians 6:10 to 13* (Edinburgh: Banner of Truth, 1976), p. 280.

[86] Lloyd-Jones, *Joy Unspeakable*, p. 55.

[87] D. M. Lloyd-Jones, *Revival: Can We Make It Happen?* (London: Marshall Pickering, 1992), p. 100.

of the church had not been one of uninterrupted progress and improvement, but a continuous series of peaks and troughs: periods of success and advance had often been preceded by periods of decline and declension. As Britain entered the 1960s, he thought, the church found itself marooned at the bottom of one of those troughs. What was needed, Lloyd-Jones argued, was

> some mighty demonstration of the power of God, some enactment of the Almighty, that will compel people to pay attention and to look, and to listen . . . when God acts, he can do more in a minute than man with his organising can do in fifty years.[88]

The historical examples he drew upon more than any other in support of his convictions about Holy Spirit baptism and revival, apart from the Scriptures themselves, were from his native Wales. From the early eighteenth century until the early years of the twentieth century, Wales had been especially 'favoured with frequent revivals',[89] and in his closing lecture to the Puritan Conference in 1973 Lloyd-Jones turned to the example of Howell Harris, one of the twin founders of Welsh Calvinistic Methodism in the 1730s, to 'help us come to an understanding of the true nature of revival'.[90] The insignificant and unknown Harris, he argued, was a perfect illustration of the sovereignty of God in revival. Harris's experience showed revival to be 'an outpouring of the Spirit of God . . . a kind of repetition of Pentecost',[91] while the power of his preaching and his 'compassion for the lost' was 'the most prominent and chief characteristic' of his experience of the baptism of the Holy Spirit.[92] Harris, Lloyd-Jones said, 'lived in the realm of the Spirit . . . and was sensitive to the Holy Spirit's influences'.[93] Turning to the contemporary situation in the 1970s in his concluding peroration, he asked, 'Is not the great sin among evangelical people today that of "quenching the Spirit"?'

> Does our doctrine of the Holy Spirit, and His work, leave any room for revival either in the individual or in the church . . . Does our doctrine allow for an outpouring of the Spirit – the 'gale' of the Spirit coming upon us individually and collectively?[94]

---

[88] Ibid., pp. 121–122.

[89] D. Geraint Jones, *Favoured with Frequent Revivals: Revivals in Wales, 1762–1862* (Cardiff: Heath Christian Trust, 2001).

[90] D. M. Lloyd-Jones, 'Howell Harris and Revival', in Lloyd-Jones, *Puritans*, p. 283.

[91] Ibid., p. 289.

[92] Ibid., pp. 292–293.

[93] Ibid., p. 293.

[94] Ibid., p. 302.

Lloyd-Jones's longing for revival permeated every aspect of his ministry. As he toured Britain in his final decade the need for a fresh outpouring of the Spirit was a constant theme.

Conclusion

Martyn Lloyd-Jones was a major influence on the shaping of twentieth-century British evangelicalism. His commitment to the recovery of a robust evangelical theology did much to inject new confidence into a beleaguered movement, while his Calvinism led to a resurgence of Reformed theology through such agencies as the Banner of Truth Trust and the Puritan Conference. Yet that commitment sometimes brought him into conflict with other evangelicals, not least under the pressure of ecumenical change. While his plea for genuine evangelical unity led to a major realignment within British evangelicalism, his vision was not uniformly welcomed. Yet it was as a preacher that Lloyd-Jones was most admired, indeed lionized. His abilities to present the gospel of Christ to the modern age had a prophetic quality, and his forensic exposition of the message of the Scriptures was life transformative for many, and through his numerous recorded and published sermons continues to be so. His constant stress on the exceptional work of the Holy Spirit in revival and renewal was formative for many within the early charismatic movement, although he never publicly associated with that renewal as it developed. Lloyd-Jones remained, above all else, an unreconstructed Welsh Calvinistic Methodist who harmoniously combined the twin emphases of Calvinist theology and profound Spirit-led religious experience. As such he has much still to say to the contemporary evangelical cause, divided in its preference for either one emphasis or the other.

© David Ceri Jones, 2022

8

John R. W. Stott

IAN M. RANDALL

In his *A History of the Church of England, 1945–1980*, Paul Welsby wrote about the situation of evangelicals in the Church of England in the years before and immediately after the Second World War. He described them as 'a depressed minority', regarding themselves as 'almost a Church within a Church'. Welsby spoke of a gradual change taking place in the 1950s, which was 'largely due to the status and influence of one man', John Stott. He described Stott as 'a person of wide vision and deep understanding, and very persuasive'.[1] Ranging beyond the Church of England, David Edwards in *Essentials: A Liberal–Evangelical Dialogue* saw Stott as 'a loved and trusted leader, teacher and spokesman of the world-wide Evangelical movement', and also – apart from William Temple – 'the most influential clergyman in the Church of England in the twentieth century'.[2] Adrian Hastings, in similar vein, in a discussion of Stott in his *A History of English Christianity, 1920–2000*, called him 'the recognized senior theologian and thinker of world evangelicalism'.[3] In this chapter I attempt to examine some of the main contours of Stott's theology. James Packer, reviewing Stott's *The Cross of Christ* (1986), remarked that Stott had been heard to insist that he was not a theologian but that this book refuted any such idea. Packer also spoke of Stott's passion to proclaim truth that changes lives.[4]

The making of a theologian

Timothy Dudley-Smith, in his comprehensive two-volume biography of Stott, called the first volume 'The Making of a Leader'. Here the main focus is on the

---

[1] Paul Welsby, *A History of the Church of England, 1945–1980* (Oxford: Oxford University Press, 1984), p. 212.

[2] David L. Edwards and John Stott, *Essentials: A Liberal–Evangelical Dialogue* (London: Hodder & Stoughton, 1988), p. 1.

[3] Adrian Hastings, *A History of English Christianity, 1920–2000* (London: SCM Press, 2001), pp. 615–616.

[4] J. I. Packer, 'A Milestone for Stott', *Christianity Today*, 4 September 1987, pp. 35–36. My first personal encounter with John Stott came in the late 1960s when I was an undergraduate at Aberdeen University and on the University Chapel Committee. I was able to secure Stott to preach at a chapel service, despite the hesitations of the chaplain. Stott delivered a splendid message.

making or formation of a Christian thinker. John Stott was born in London, in 1921, to Sir Arnold and Lady Lily Stott. His father was a distinguished physician, with consulting rooms in Harley Street. There were two daughters (a third had died, aged 3) and a son, John. He was evidently spirited: Sir Arnold once received a letter from the Clerk of the Park Square Gardens, adjoining Regent's Park, London, that passed on complaints about the 'unruly behaviour' of his son (John was then aged 8) and requested 'disciplinary action'.[5] John Stott recognized the role of family, writing much later, 'The most formative influence on each of us has been our parentage and our home.'[6] Although his privileged background would mark him, in his spiritual journey the evangelical convictions he embraced were determinative. His father had no Christian faith, but his mother took the children to the local parish church, All Souls, Langham Place, which at that time had a 'liberal evangelical' ministry.[7] It was in 1938, when at the prestigious Rugby School, where he became head boy, that John Stott made a personal commitment to Christ after a talk to the school's Christian Union by Eric Nash (widely known as 'Bash'). What brought him to Christ, he said, was a 'sense of defeat and of estrangement, and the astonishing news that the historic Christ offered to meet the very needs of which I was conscious'.[8] His conversion shaped his future, issuing in a highly disciplined spiritual life and in prodigious activity in the service of Christ.[9]

From Rugby, Stott went to Trinity College, Cambridge, in 1940, where he began studying French and German, before switching to theology for his third and fourth years. He gained a double-first-class honours and was elected a senior scholar by Trinity. A major involvement became the Cambridge Inter-Collegiate Christian Union (CICCU), which his father had advised him not to join, describing members as 'anaemic wets'. Although he never became a formal member, by his final year he was composing position papers for CICCU. Alister Chapman speaks of CICCU as being, for Stott, a 'perfect bridge' between what was undoubtedly the narrowness of the approach of Nash, who distrusted

---

[5] Timothy Dudley-Smith, *John Stott: The Making of a Leader* (Leicester: Inter-Varsity Press, 1999), p. 22. See also, Roger Steer, *Inside Story: The Life of John Stott* (Nottingham: Inter-Varsity Press, 2009). And for memories by friends, Christopher Wright (ed.), *John Stott: A Portrait by His Friends* (Nottingham: Inter-Varsity Press, 2011).

[6] John Stott, *Guard the Gospel: The Message of 2 Timothy* (London: Inter-Varsity Press, 1973), p. 27. The way in which Stott's name is shown in various books he has authored varies. I have chosen to use 'John Stott'.

[7] For the liberal evangelicals, see Ian Randall, *Evangelical Experiences: A Study in the Spirituality of English Evangelicalism, 1918–1939* (Carlisle: Paternoster Press, 1999), pp. 46–76.

[8] Dudley-Smith, *John Stott*, p. 89.

[9] David Bebbington's now classic definition of evangelicalism as conversionist, biblicist, crucicentric and activist in his *Evangelicalism in Modern Britain: A History from the 1730s to the 1980s* (London: Routledge, 1995), pp. 2–17, applies perfectly to Stott.

academic endeavour, and 'a slightly more open style of evangelicalism'. Chapman explores Stott's position at this stage, noting that in the university's Faculty of Divinity, Stott appreciated only one of the lecturers, the Congregationalist J. S. Whale, who in 1942 produced his influential book *Christian Doctrine*, based on lectures he delivered in the university. Even C. F. D. Moule, an evangelical scholar of deep devotion, was too liberal for Stott.[10] The description of CICCU as 'slightly more open' is appropriate: it was wary of cooperation with any Christian body that was not explicitly conservative evangelical.[11]

In his theological studies, Stott immersed himself deeply in Scripture. Charles Raven, the university's Regius Professor of Divinity, once said in a conversation that Stott had 'the record for accurately quoting verses from the Bible in the Tripos examination'.[12] In 1944, Stott moved from Trinity College to Ridley Hall, which had been founded in 1881, with the eminent evangelical leader Handley Moule as the first principal. Stott chose Ridley, which was then a 'liberal evangelical' college, and encouraged others to study there. He found the vice-principal (and later principal), Cyril Bowles, a supportive figure.[13] With the assistance of Bowles, Stott pursued his own course of reading. In his final year he did not attend any lectures. He wrote later about how his engagement with theology in this period meant he 'wrestled painfully with the challenges of liberalism'.[14] Oliver Barclay, a close friend of Stott's at Cambridge, who was CICCU President and subsequently General Secretary of the Inter-Varsity Fellowship, recalled that Stott 'struggled quite acutely at times'.[15] He was helped by attending meetings at the newly formed Tyndale House, which had emerged out of a concern, as expressed by F. F. Bruce, to roll away English evangelicalism's 'reproach of anti-intellectualism, if not outright obscurantism'.[16]

In December 1945, Stott was ordained in St Paul's Cathedral and began as assistant curate at All Souls, Langham Place. Harold Earnshaw Smith, who was now Rector, was an ideal person for Stott at this point. He had worked for Inter-Varsity Fellowship, had been a missionary in Nigeria and was a speaker at the Keswick Convention, an annual holiness gathering that attracted several

---

[10] Alister Chapman, *Godly Ambition: John Stott and the Evangelical Movement* (Oxford: Oxford University Press, 2012), pp. 26, 29.

[11] David Goodhew, 'The Rise of the Cambridge Inter-Collegiate Christian Union, 1910–1971', *Journal of Ecclesiastical History*, vol. 54, no. 1 (January 2003), p. 73.

[12] John Collins to Timothy Dudley-Smith, 31 March 1994, cited in Dudley-Smith, *John Stott*, p. 194.

[13] Michael Botting, *Fanning the Flame: The Story of Ridley Hall*, vol. 3 (Cambridge: Ridley Hall, 2006), pp. 48, 55–56.

[14] Tim Chester, *Stott on the Christian Life* (Wheaton, IL: Crossway Books, 2020), p. 21; Edwards and Stott, *Essentials*, p. 35.

[15] Oliver Barclay, *Evangelicalism in Britain, 1935–1995* (Leicester: Inter-Varsity Press, 1997), p. 57.

[16] Chester, *Stott on the Christian Life*, p. 21; F. F. Bruce, *In Retrospect: Remembrance of Things Past* (London: Pickering & Inglis, 1980), p. 122.

thousand evangelicals. His ministry, as Chapman puts it, 'was a textbook case of evangelical Anglican parish life'.[17] But Stott was not sanguine about the Church of England. His assessment at the time of his ordination was that the 'few evangelical clergy' within it 'fought bravely, but had their backs to the wall'.[18] This was probably too gloomy an assessment. If there had been so few Anglican evangelicals, Keswick would not have been able to call on the speakers it did, since the majority were Anglican.[19] At All Souls, Stott gave himself to the work of the parish, and in 1950 became Rector. This followed the death of Earnshaw Smith, who had previously suffered a heart attack. With responsibility for a congregation of 450, Stott turned to Acts 2:42 and set out a model to imitate: study of Scripture, Christian fellowship, worship, prayer and evangelism.[20] Stott was also heavily involved in university missions and was beginning to shape wider evangelical thinking through his writings. His first book, in 1954, was *Men with a Message: An Introduction to the New Testament and Its Writers*.[21] In the midst of demanding ministries, part of Stott's enormous contribution was through his over forty books. His output was evidence not only of his own ability but also the outstanding efficiency and dedication, over the course of a remarkable fifty-five years, of his personal assistant, Frances Whitehead.[22]

An ecclesial theologian

John Stott was pre-eminently a theologian for the Christian community, someone deeply committed to the health of local churches and the wider church. His concern was not primarily the academic world, although he was passionate about encouraging evangelical theological education. In 1947 he was invited to join the teaching staff at London Bible College (LBC), but chose to remain a curate.[23] Out of five books Stott wrote in the 1950s, two were directly

---

[17] Chapman, *Godly Ambition*, p. 54.

[18] Dudley-Smith, *John Stott*, p. 217.

[19] For Keswick, see Charles Price and Ian Randall, *Transforming Keswick* (Carlisle: Paternoster Press, 2000).

[20] Dudley-Smith, *John Stott*, p. 251. All Souls' congregation was to grow substantially. Stott was Rector until 1975, although from 1970 Michael Baughen took on the church's leadership.

[21] John Stott, *Men with a Message: An Introduction to the New Testament and Its Writers* (London: Longmans Green, 1954).

[22] See Julia Cameron, *John Stott's Right Hand: The Untold Story of Frances Whitehead* (Eugene, OR: Wipf & Stock, 2018).

[23] Stott was later invited to consider the LBC principalship. He received a Brunel University DD through London Bible College when Derek Tidball was the principal. See Ian Randall, *Educating Evangelicalism: The Origins, Development and Impact of London Bible College* (Carlisle: Paternoster Press, 2000), p. 279. Stott was to be approached about a variety of academic and episcopal posts, all of which he declined.

concerned with the church: *Your Confirmation* and *What Christ Thinks of the Church*, on Revelation 1 – 3, both published in 1958.[24] In 1964 he wrote *Confess Your Sins: The Way of Reconciliation*, looking at confession in Christian spirituality.[25] After presenting the place of confession, Stott outlined three types: in secret to God, in private when hurt has been caused to another person, and in public in a Christian congregation. Stott also made critical comments about the Catholic/Anglo-Catholic practice of confessing to a priest. Writing in 1967, in one of his key books of that period, *Our Guilty Silence*, Stott set out a twofold calling for churches: 'to be occupied with God and with the world'. Although that did not entirely do justice to churches as centres of fellowship, these twin foci were crucial for Stott: 'God has constituted his church', he argued, 'to be a worshipping and witnessing community.'[26] In 1979, in *The Message of Ephesians*, Stott wrote more broadly about the evangelical tendency to overlook the central importance of the church, and offered a description of 'a single new humanity, a model of human community, a family of reconciled brothers and sisters'.[27]

In his ecclesiology, Stott was firmly Anglican. As Chapman puts it, the Church of England was the church of his birth, his school, his college and his ordination. An All Souls 'Rector's Letter' in 1954 gave an insight: for Stott the Church of England was 'beloved'.[28] One of his initiatives was the reinvented Eclectic Society: the original society was formed in the eighteenth century by evangelicals seeking to renew the Church of England. An important member at that time was Charles Simeon, Vicar of Holy Trinity Church, Cambridge. Tim Chester, in *Stott on the Christian Life*, describes Stott as in many ways 'a twentieth-century mirror of Simeon'.[29] Through the Eclectics, Stott aimed to encourage young evangelical Anglican clergy. From a founding membership of 22, it grew to over 1,000 members by the mid-1960s. Out of this and other initiatives came the National Evangelical Anglican Congress at Keele in 1967, with 1,000 delegates, which Stott chaired. Keele affirmed, 'We are deeply committed to the present and future of the Church of England.'[30] A year before,

---

[24] John Stott, *Your Confirmation* (London: Hodder & Stoughton, 1958); *What Christ Thinks of the Church: Expository Addresses on the First Three Chapters of the Book of Revelation* (London: Lutterworth Press, 1958).

[25] John Stott, *Confess Your Sins: The Way of Reconciliation* (London: Hodder & Stoughton, 1964).

[26] John Stott, *Our Guilty Silence* (London: Hodder & Stoughton, 1967), p. 59. '"To Be Occupied with God": John Stott on Worship', *Anvil*, vol. 23, no. 4 (2006), pp. 247–257.

[27] John Stott, *The Message of Ephesians* (Leicester: Inter-Varsity Press, 1979), pp. 111–112.

[28] John Stott, 'The Rector's Letter', *All Souls*, July 1954, p. 11, cited by Chapman, *Godly Ambition*, p. 79.

[29] Chester, *Stott on the Christian Life*, p. 67. The full and helpful comparison is on pp. 67–78. Marcus Loane, former Archbishop of Sydney, said that 'John Stott was for our generation all that Charles Simeon had been for his generation': Marcus Loane, in Wright, *John Stott*, p. 91.

[30] 'The Congress Statement', in Philip Crowe (ed.), *The National Evangelical Anglican Congress Statement* (London: Falcon Books, 1967), p. 38.

at a momentous Evangelical Alliance gathering, Stott had publicly opposed what he saw as a secessionist call by Martyn Lloyd-Jones, Minister of Westminster Chapel, London.[31] Yet Stott reached far beyond Anglicanism. In the 1960s and 1970s, for example, he delivered keynote expositions on six occasions at the Urbana Convention in the USA, which drew over 12,000 predominantly young people from over seventy countries.[32] Nonetheless, Stott's desire to contribute to Anglican life, especially globally, was strong. He was behind the formation of the Church of England Evangelical Council (CEEC) and the Evangelical Fellowship in the Anglican Communion (EFAC). At a significant EFAC consultation in 1993 on 'Understanding and Applying Scripture Today', Stott spoke of how classical Anglicanism 'constantly affirms both the supremacy and the sufficiency of Scripture'.[33]

Stott was not entirely content with the traditional designation 'word and sacrament' when applied to worship, since for him a sacrament was 'a word'. He spoke instead of the building up of the church taking place by means of 'the ministry of God's word as it comes to us through Scripture and Sacrament (that is the right coupling), audibly and visibly, in declaration and drama'.[34] It was 'declaration' to which Stott gave by far the greatest attention. In *The Bible: Book for Today* (1982), he spoke of the need for the church constantly to be hearing the Word of God. 'Preaching', Stott averred, 'is not an intrusion into it [worship] but rather indispensable to it.'[35] In other Christian traditions, including major strands within Anglicanism, the Eucharist has been at the heart of worship, but it is perhaps significant that Tim Chester, with his focus on Stott on the Christian life, does not cover the 'drama' of the Lord's Supper. This is not to say that Stott neglected the Lord's Supper. In *The Cross of Christ*, his most important theological work, his chapter on 'The community of celebration' gives considerable attention to the Lord's Supper, engaging in careful historico-theological analysis.[36] What he wished to do was align himself with what he saw as the heritage of the Church of England in the Protestant Reformation. In a foreword to Marcus Loane's *Masters of the English Reformation*, Stott argued that Reformers such as Cranmer, Ridley and Latimer were consistent, 'as we should be', in expressing their position: that 'the

---

[31] For this public dispute and its aftermath, see Ian Randall and David Hilborn, *One Body in Christ: The History and Significance of the Evangelical Alliance* (Carlisle: Paternoster Press, 2001), pp. 246–256.

[32] See e.g. John Stott, *Christ the Liberator* (London: Hodder & Stoughton, 1972).

[33] John Stott et al., *The Anglican Communion and Scripture* (Oxford: Regnum Books, 1996), pp. 13–49. See Chapman, *Godly Ambition*, pp. 82–84, for penetrating comments on the CEEC and EFAC.

[34] John Stott, *The Message of Acts* (Leicester: Inter-Varsity Press, 1990), p. 321.

[35] John Stott, *The Bible: Book for Today* (Leicester: Inter-Varsity Press, 1982), p. 57.

[36] John Stott, *The Cross of Christ* (Leicester: Inter-Varsity Press, 1986), ch. 10, pp. 255–273.

presbyter is a minister serving a sacramental supper from a table, not a priest offering a sacrifice on an altar'.[37] Stott did not use the term 'priest' for pastors, since he believed strongly in the priesthood of all believers, and warned against 'too much autocracy' in Christian leaders and preachers. 'Too many', he continued, 'behave as if they believed not in the priesthood of all believers but in the papacy of all pastors.'[38]

It was in 1982 that Stott's definitive book on preaching, *I Believe in Preaching*, was published. The title of the American edition was *Between Two Worlds*, which emphasized preaching as 'bridge-building', the bridge being between Scripture and the hearers.[39] This was closely associated with Stott's understanding of 'double listening' – to the Word and the world.[40] Michael Quicke, in *360-Degree Preaching*, has suggested that the 'two poles' model does not do justice to 'the activity of our Triune God' in the preaching event.[41] In reality Stott himself operated with more than two worlds: he traced preaching as it took place in the 'worlds' across the centuries. From the early church, for example, he quoted Tertullian, a North African theologian, who spoke of Christians assembling 'to read our sacred writings . . . With the sacred words we nourish our faith, we animate our hope, we make our confidence more steadfast.'[42] Not surprisingly, Stott affirmed Protestant leaders and referred to probably the most famous sermon by the English Reformer Hugh Latimer, 'The Sermon of the Plough' (1548). Here Latimer spoke of the seed of God's Word, asserted that 'the preacher is the sower', and even depicted the devil's sowing of evil to spur preachers to fuller application to their task.[43] Stott's twentieth-century survey of preachers ranged widely, including Karl Barth and Dietrich Bonhoeffer. Within Anglicanism, he spoke of Archbishop of Canterbury Donald Coggan's testifying to having been for half a century 'under the joyful tyranny of being a minister of the Word'. In Free Church life, Stott highlighted Lloyd-Jones, for whom preaching was 'the highest and the greatest and the most glorious calling'.[44] Stott's purpose was to show that the Christian consensus had

---

[37] John Stott, 'Foreword', M. L. Loane, *Masters of the English Reformation*, 2nd edn (London: Hodder & Stoughton, 1983), p. xiv.

[38] John Stott, *Basic Christian Leadership: Biblical Models of Church, Gospel, and Ministry* (Downers Grove, IL: InterVarsity Press, 2002), p. 113.

[39] John Stott, *I Believe in Preaching* (London: Hodder & Stoughton, 1982); *Between Two Worlds: The Art of Preaching in the Twentieth Century* (Grand Rapids, MI: Eerdmans, 1982).

[40] For more see Chester, *Stott on the Christian Life*, pp. 52–56, 81–82.

[41] Michael Quicke, *360-Degree Preaching: Hearing, Speaking, and Living the Word* (Grand Rapids, MI: Baker Academic, 2003), pp. 45, 48. My thanks to my friend and colleague Michael Quicke for his help.

[42] Tertullian, ch. 39, *Ante-Nicene Fathers*, vol. 3, p. 46, cited in Stott, *I Believe in Preaching*, p. 19.

[43] *Works of Hugh Latimer*, vol. 1, pp. 59–78, cited in Stott, *I Believe in Preaching*, pp. 26–28.

[44] Stott, *I Believe in Preaching*, pp. 45–56. Stott quotes from D. M. Lloyd-Jones, *Preaching and Preachers* (London: Hodder & Stoughton, 1971), p. 297, that preaching is 'the greatest work in the world'.

been 'to magnify the importance of preaching'. It was, for him, an inspirational 'common testimony'.[45]

In subsequent chapters of *I Believe in Preaching* Stott covered contemporary objections to preaching; theological foundations; preaching as bridge-building; study and preparation; sincerity and earnestness; and courage and humility. He argued at considerably greater length than he had done in previous books that 'Word and worship belong indissolubly to each other'. All of the church's worship was, as he characteristically expressed it, an 'intelligent and loving response to the revelation of God'. The need for an 'intelligent' approach conveys much about Stott's theological thinking. He considered that true Christian preaching, by which he said he meant 'biblical' or 'expository' preaching, was 'extremely rare in today's Church', the reason being lack of conviction about its importance.[46] There was also a conviction about spirituality, which Stott expressed in this way: 'It seems to me that one might well single out fresh-ness of spiritual experience as the first indispensable quality of the effective preacher.'[47] The theology that undergirded Stott's view of preaching included conviction about God, Scripture and the church. 'A deaf church', that is one not listening to God's Word, he wrote trenchantly, 'is a dead church.' He was convinced that 'God feeds, inspires and guides his people by his Word'. The pastors of a church, often seen as those involved in care of the flock, were for him 'fundamentally teachers'.[48] He later explored in *The Contemporary Christian* (1992) the quest in wider society for 'transcendence'. Employing his own principle of 'double listening', he suggested that evangelical worship often lacked the 'sense of the numinous', or in biblical language 'the fear of God'.[49]

A biblical theologian

There has been a long tradition of theologians producing works of 'systematic theology'. Within Reformed evangelicalism the influence of Calvin's approach, in his *Institutes of the Christian Religion*, has been massive. James Packer, who identified himself with the Calvinist tradition, wrote that Stott was

a first-class biblical theologian with an unusually systematic mind, great power of analysis, great clarity of expression, a superb command of his

---

[45] Stott, *I Believe in Preaching*, p. 47.

[46] Ibid., p. 82.

[47] John Stott, 'Charles Simeon: A Personal Appreciation', in James M. Houston (ed.), *Evangelical Preaching: An Anthology of Sermons by Charles Simeon* (Portland, OR: Multnomah Press, 1986), p. xxix.

[48] Stott, *I Believe in Preaching*, pp. 113, 120.

[49] J. R. W. Stott, *The Contemporary Christian* (Leicester: Inter-Varsity Press, 1992), p. 227.

material, and a preacher's passion to proclaim truth that will change lives.[50]

This sums up well Stott's approach. He never wrote a 'systematic theology'. Here again, Simeon's influence on Stott was significant. Simeon was opposed to 'systematizers in theology' and for Stott 'biblical antinomies', in which there were contradictions that could not logically be resolved, should be left to stand. Stott adduced, as Simeon had done, the example of the Calvinist–Arminian controversy, highlighting differing views of God's sovereignty and human freedom. Stott wrote, 'Simeon (like Calvin himself) was convinced that we do not have to choose between these, since Scripture teaches both.'[51] Chester seeks to use the phrase 'like Calvin himself' to argue that while Stott might have avoided the term 'Calvinist' there is every reason to suppose that 'his thought was consistent with that of the Reformed tradition'.[52] In a broad sense this was the case, but Chapman is on firmer ground in stating that by contrast with Packer and Lloyd-Jones, Stott refused to sign up to 'the Calvinist theology of the Puritans'.[53]

Just as Stott did not take the label 'Calvinist', so he repudiated the description 'fundamentalist'. During the Billy Graham crusades in Britain in the mid-1950s, H. K. Luce, Headmaster of Durham School, writing in *The Times* in August 1955, referred to the forthcoming CICCU-sponsored mission in the University of Cambridge with Graham as the main speaker and called on religious leaders to make plain that fundamentalism would cause 'disillusionment and disaster for educated men and women in this twentieth-century world'.[54] Stott, who entered the debate in *The Times*, distanced himself from what he saw as the characteristics of fundamentalism: 'bigoted rejection of all Biblical criticism, a mechanical view of inspiration and an excessively rigid interpretation of Scripture'.[55] In November 1955, in the widely read *Crusade* magazine, Stott criticized the 'extravagances' of fundamentalism, particularly found, he said, in the USA, while also arguing for a 'more traditional and conservative' approach to Scripture.[56] Aspects of his thinking appeared in 1959 in

---

[50] Packer, 'Milestone for Stott', pp. 35–36.

[51] Stott, 'Charles Simeon: A Personal Appreciation', in Houston, *Evangelical Preaching*, pp. xxiii–xxiv.

[52] Chester, *Stott on the Christian Life*, p. 59.

[53] Chapman, *Godly Ambition*, p. 86.

[54] H. K. Luce, *The Times*, 15 August 1955, p. 7.

[55] John Stott, *The Times*, 25 August 1955, p. 14. The correspondence was later published as *Fundamentalism: A Religious Problem: Letters to the Editor of The Times and a Leading Article* (London: The Times Publishing Company, 1955).

[56] John Stott, 'Fundamentalism', *Crusade*, November 1955, pp. 10–11.

Fundamentalism and Evangelism.[57] His position was consistent over time. In his dialogue with David Edwards he stated that for thirty-five years he had repudiated the label 'fundamentalist' and he outlined eight tendencies of the fundamentalist 'mind-set' with which he disagreed. He drew attention especially to the danger of a 'dictation theory' of biblical inspiration, which denied the human, cultural element in Scripture and the need for 'biblical criticism' and 'careful hermeneutics'.[58] Again, in *Evangelical Truth: A Personal Plea for Unity*, in 1999, he contended that evangelicals differed from fundamentalists over the nature of the Bible, biblical inspiration and biblical interpretation.[59]

The theme of biblical meditation as true wisdom was of interest to Stott.[60] However, his main focus was on grasping the meaning of Scripture and making appropriate application. His approach, one that had been honed over time, was admirably outlined in *The Contemporary Christian*, in which he offered thorough treatment of the topics of the gospel, the disciple, the Bible, the church and the world. On the Bible he asked, 'What is Scripture that it should occupy such an important place in our lives?' His answer – spelled out in some detail – was that Scripture was able to instruct readers for salvation; Scripture was 'God-breathed' and Scripture was useful. Stott concluded this part of his study with the words, 'Thank God for the Bible!' In typical fashion, however, he then went on to speak of the importance of 'intellectual integrity' and the problems inherent in approaching the Bible without a recognition of everyone's 'cultural imprisonment' and the Bible's own 'cultural conditioning'. There was a requirement for 'cultural transposition', for example in relation to the role of women.[61] Having grappled with these issues, he returned in *Contemporary Christian* to the topic of communicating God's Word. He painted a picture of those trying to do this but with 'no Scripture to expound'. By contrast, there were those who 'enter the pulpit' – Stott's picture was still of a traditional pulpit setting – with the confidence that God had spoken and they had an inspired text – 'ah!', Stott exclaimed, 'then our heads begin to swim, our hearts to beat, our blood to flow, our eyes to sparkle with the sheer glory of having God's Word in our hands and on our lips'.[62]

[57] John Stott, *Fundamentalism and Evangelism* (Grand Rapids, MI: Eerdmans, 1959).
[58] Edwards and Stott, *Essentials*, pp. 89–91.
[59] John Stott, *Evangelical Truth: A Personal Plea for Unity* (Leicester: Inter-Varsity Press, 1999), pp. 17–22.
[60] See e.g. John Stott's two contributions on 'Biblical Meditation' in M. A. Noll and D. F. Wells (eds.), *Christian Faith and Practice in the Modern World* (Grand Rapids, MI: Eerdmans, 1988).
[61] Stott, *Contemporary Christian*, pp. 166–170, 189–206. In a letter in 1993 Stott wrote that he did not agree with the dogmatic statements that had been made about the ordination of women; namely, that it was 'plainly contrary to Scripture'. He was convinced that it was 'nothing of the kind'. It involved the whole area of 'cultural transposition'. Timothy Dudley-Smith, *John Stott: A Global Ministry* (Leicester: Inter-Varsity Press, 2001), p. 414. Dudley-Smith refers to a letter of Stott's of 1 July 1993.
[62] Stott, *Contemporary Christian*, p. 210.

Such a perspective – the heart beating – needs to be given proper weight, since Stott can be seen as someone whose main concern was intellectual understanding. One of his influential books in the 1970s was *Your Mind Matters*,[63] and the theme is taken up by Chester in his first thematic chapter, 'A Christian Mind'.[64] The question could be raised whether Stott gave insufficient attention to the situation of those who could not engage in that way, for example those with learning disabilities. However, in his exposition of Pauline theological writing, for example in *The Message of Romans*, Stott's call for serious theological thinking was balanced by an emphasis on the fact that there should be 'no theology without doxology'. Indeed, he went so far as to say that there was 'something fundamentally flawed about a purely academic interest in God'. He categorically rejected the idea that the Bible could be studied in a 'cool, critical, detached' way.[65] Yet in debates about the role of the Holy Spirit, precipitated by the charismatic movement, Stott seemed to be 'cool' rather than 'warm'. He wrote in his work on this subject, 'The fullness of the Spirit leads to restrained and rational moral behaviour.'[66] It is not readily apparent that the word 'restrained' applies to all that happened in the book of Acts. Despite his desire to be true to Scripture, in his exposition of 1 Corinthians 14, where Paul says that those who speak in tongues edify themselves and that he wishes all spoke in tongues, Stott tried hard to avoid the force of this, even seeing in it 'a note of irony, if not of sarcasm'.[67] More convincingly, in *The Message of Acts* (1990), he wrote of the Spirit in the church and the need for Christians to humble themselves before the Spirit's sovereign authority and allow him freedom.[68]

While Stott was cautious in the area of pneumatology, seeing the Holy Spirit as 'reticent', when it came to Christology he was confident. There was a compelling Christological element in Stott's approach to Scripture. He always wished to do justice to the broad range of biblical material, but it is noteworthy that his sermons on the All Souls website show that only 14 per cent were on Old Testament passages.[69] He was New Testament editor of The Bible Speaks Today series, with his own commentaries on New Testament books – and his

---

[63] John Stott, *Your Mind Matters* (London: Inter-Varsity Press, 1972).

[64] Chester, *Stott on the Christian Life*, ch. 2, pp. 37–63.

[65] John Stott, *The Message of Romans* (Leicester: Inter-Varsity Press, 1994), p. 311.

[66] John Stott, *Baptism and Fullness: The Work of the Holy Spirit Today*, 3rd edn (Downers Grove, IL: InterVarsity Press, 2006), p. 74.

[67] Stott, *Baptism and Fullness*, pp. 147–149. See the discussion in Chester, *Stott on the Christian Life*, pp. 135–153. Chester comments that when Stott speaks about Paul's not being able to 'contemplate Christian prayer and praise in which the mind is not actively engaged', Stott is offering a portrait of himself. It may be possible to go further and ask if in that instance Stott was constructing a Paul in his own image.

[68] Stott, *Message of Acts*, p. 87.

[69] Chester, *Stott on the Christian Life*, p. 79.

outstanding *Christian Counter-Culture* on the Sermon on the Mount – coming out of his preaching.[70] In his book *The Authentic Jesus* (1985) Stott spoke of Christianity as trinitarian, but 'above all our testimony is directed to Jesus Christ'. He made the somewhat unusual statement – for him – that what mattered was 'not whether our tongue can subscribe to an orthodox formulation of the person of Jesus, but whether our knee has bowed before his majesty'.[71] His *The Incomparable Christ* (2001) was based on fascinating lectures he gave for the London Institute for Contemporary Christianity (LICC). Stott had founded the LICC in 1982 to 'offer courses in the inter-relations between faith, life and mission to thinking Christian lay people'. It was a major venture by Stott, who was its first director.[72] In his 2002 lectures he dealt with the 'Original Jesus' found in the New Testament, the 'Ecclesiastical Jesus' as interpreted by twelve Christian thinkers through history, the 'Influential Jesus', which looked at twelve people he inspired, and the 'Eternal Jesus'.[73] Although Stott would have wanted to identify himself with the 'Original Jesus', he was also part of the story of Christian interpreters and of those whom Christ inspired.

A crucicentric theology

This stress on Christ brings us to Stott's concern to present the cross of Christ in a way that could be understood and accepted. This was a constant theme and focus. Stott wrote in 1958, 'The cross is blazing fire at which the flame of our love is kindled, but we have to get near enough for its sparks to fall on us.'[74] Three years later he wrote:

> There is wonderful power in the cross of Christ. It has power to wake the dullest conscience and melt the hardest heart; to cleanse the unclean . . . to transform our wayward characters into the image of Christ; and finally make us fit to stand in white robes before the throne of God.[75]

In his commentaries, Stott made much of the theology of the cross. *The Message of Galatians* (1968) contains a typical example. Writing on Christ's becoming 'a curse' for us, Stott spoke of how

---

[70] Stott wrote eight of The Bible Speaks Today commentaries.
[71] John Stott, *The Authentic Jesus* (London: Marshalls, 1985), pp. 9, 24.
[72] Chapman, *Godly Ambition*, p. 113. Stott became the LICC president in 1986.
[73] John Stott, *The Incomparable Christ* (Leicester: Inter-Varsity Press, 2001).
[74] Stott, *What Christ Thinks*, p. 27.
[75] John Stott, *The Preacher's Portrait* (London: Tyndale Press, 1961), p. 102.

the cross tells us some very unpalatable truths about ourselves; namely that we are sinners under the righteous curse of God's law, and we cannot save ourselves. Christ bore our sin and curse precisely because we could gain release from them in no other way.

He continued by picturing Christ's seeming to say from the cross, 'I came here because of you. It is your sin I am bearing, your curse I am suffering, your debt I am paying, your death I am dying.'[76] Again, in his *The Message of Ephesians* (1979), he spoke about ancient commentators picturing the cross: 'its upright pole reached down into the earth and pointed up to heaven, while its crossbar carried the arms of Jesus, stretched out as if to invite and welcome the whole world'.[77]

Other sources could be cited, and together they show that it was not only in Stott's *The Cross of Christ* that he dealt with the doctrine of the atonement; although it is here that we have what can be termed a classic exposition, to take its place alongside books such as James Denney's *The Death of Christ* (1902) or P. T. Forsyth's *The Work of Christ* (1910), sources to which he referred throughout his own book. Writing *The Cross of Christ* was for Stott a deeply personal experience. 'More of my own heart and mind went into it', he said, 'than into anything else I have written.'[78] As he probed the meaning of the cross in a chapter 'Looking below the surface', Stott wrote that the cross 'enforces three truths'. The first is that

> our sin must be extremely horrible. Nothing reveals the gravity of sin like the cross . . . For if there was no way by which the righteous God could righteously forgive our unrighteousness, except that he should bear it himself in Christ, it must be serious indeed.

His second affirmation was that

> God's love must be wonderful beyond comprehension . . . He pursued us even to the desolate anguish of the cross, where he bore our sin, guilt, judgement and death. It takes a hard and stony heart to remain unmoved by love like that.

---

[76] John Stott, *The Message of Galatians* (Leicester: Inter-Varsity Press, 1968), p. 179.

[77] John Stott, *The Message of Ephesians* (Leicester: Inter-Varsity Press, 1979), p. 137.

[78] Cited in Steer, *Inside Story*, p. 216.

Third, Stott stated that Christ's salvation 'must be a free gift'. He 'purchased' it for us, Stott continued, 'at the high price of his own life-blood. So what is there left for us to pay? Nothing!'[79]

Stott was fully aware of what he saw as legitimate criticisms of crass theories of the atonement. He wished to convey classic crucicentrism, although he did depart from the doctrine of divine impassibility, positing 'a conflict of emotions, a strife of attributes, within God', in relation to his love and justice.[80] Later in the book, in his important chapter 'The self-substitution of God', Stott insisted that the focus must be God in Christ on the cross. He quoted P. T. Forsyth's affirmation of the phrase 'God dying for man'. Forsyth wrote simply in *The Work of Christ*: 'I am not afraid of that phrase; I cannot do without it.' Karl Barth's words in *Church Dogmatics* II.1 were also quoted by Stott: 'God's own heart suffered on the cross.'[81] Stott was adamant that atonement did not take place because an innocent third party, Jesus, came between an angry God and sinners. He wrote with considerable feeling, 'Any notion of penal substitution in which three independent actors play a role – the guilty party, the punitive judge and the innocent victim – is to be repudiated with the utmost vehemence.' What was to be seen in the drama of the cross, he argued, was

> not three actors but two, ourselves on the one hand and God on the other . . . it is the Judge himself who in holy love assumed the role of the innocent victim, for in and through the person of his Son he himself bore the penalty.[82]

Another writer Stott drew from was R. W. Dale, like Forsyth a Congregational minister and theologian, in his 'great book' *The Atonement* (1894). Stott quoted with approval Dale's statement that 'the mysterious unity of the Father and the Son rendered it possible for God at once to endure and to inflict penal suffering'.[83]

The cross was the means of salvation from sin, which included not only conversion but also the living of the Christian life. Stott opposed the traditional teaching of the Keswick Convention that holiness came through claiming the

---

[79] Stott, *Cross of Christ*, p. 83.
[80] Ibid., pp. 129–130. Here, unusually, Stott parted company with P. T. Forsyth. Noting that in *The Work of Christ* (Hodder & Stoughton, 1910, p. 118) Forsyth had said that there was nothing in the Bible about 'a strife of attributes', Stott suggested, citing Hos. 11:8–9, that Forsyth was incorrect.
[81] Stott, *Cross of Christ*, p. 153.
[82] Ibid., pp. 158–159.
[83] Ibid., p. 159; cf. R. W. Dale, *The Atonement* (London: Congregational Union of England & Wales, 1897 edn), p. 393.

power of the cross to counteract sin in the believer. In 1965 addresses Stott gave at Keswick, on Romans 5 – 8, he made a case for 'death to sin' (Rom. 6:1–14) being understood as the Christian's having borne sin's penalty in the vicarious work of Christ and in union with him. In this, someone enters 'a life that is altogether new'.[84] Stott considered that in portraying Paul's teaching as being about the objective nature of Christ's work, rather than the subjective 'dying to sin' that had frequently been taught at Keswick, he was issuing a challenge for the Convention.[85] He was by no means the first to criticize Keswick. A decade before his addresses, Packer had referred to Keswick as 'Pelagian through and through' and characterized Pelagianism as 'the natural heresy of zealous Christians who are not interested in theology'.[86] However, statements by Packer, Stott and others about the Convention's history suggest that they failed to engage at any depth with the wide range of Keswick speakers or with the different strands of holiness teaching. For instance, 'eradication' of sin was a position Keswick never espoused, and thus it is a misunderstanding to see Stott as wanting to warn against 'slipping back into the old Keswick holiness mind-set, thinking the danger of sin has been eradicated'.[87] The new life, for Stott, was marked by ongoing 'ruthless repudiation' of sin and 'unconditional surrender' to the Spirit.[88] Both of those emphases, rather than being new, had been present in the Keswick tradition of spirituality.

In the Christian life the death of Christ was also an example. Stott made it clear to David Edwards, 'I do not find that your story of Christ crucified offers me a radical enough remedy for my needs. I need more than an example, a revelation, a martyr.'[89] In *The Incomparable Christ*, Stott took as his example of someone presenting 'Christ the ethical exemplar' Thomas à Kempis, in *The Imitation of Christ*, which Stott said was 'universally recommended'. While admiring aspects of it, Stott raised queries, such as whether Thomas à Kempis had grasped the gospel invitation 'to put our trust in Christ crucified as our Saviour', or the way of holiness 'through union with Christ'.[90] Nonetheless, in *The Cross of Christ*, dealing with Christian conduct, Stott drew from Paul in

---

[84] John Stott, *Men Made New* (London: Inter-Varsity Press, 1966), pp. 45–47.

[85] See Price and Randall, *Transforming Keswick*, pp. 234–244.

[86] J. I. Packer, '"Keswick" and the Reformed Doctrine of Sanctification', *Evangelical Quarterly*, vol. 27, no. 3 (1955), pp. 153–167.

[87] Chester, *Stott on the Christian Life*, p. 124. In Chester's chapter on Stott and Keswick (ch. 5, pp. 113–134) he rightly refers to this area as one of Stott's more neglected contributions. Although Chester seems to associate 'eradication of sin' with Keswick and also sees a closer relationship between Stott and Puritan spirituality than Stott himself acknowledged, the chapter covers the issues with care.

[88] Stott, *Contemporary Christian*, pp. 154–155.

[89] Edwards and Stott, *Essentials*, p. 168.

[90] Stott, *Incomparable Christ*, pp. 94–96.

Romans 12 and 13, showing that these passages echoed the Sermon on the Mount. At the cross, Stott continued, Jesus perfectly exemplified his own teaching, for 'when they hurled their insults at him, he did not retaliate; when he suffered, he made no threats' (1 Peter 2:23). In the new community of Jesus, 'curses are to be replaced by blessings, malice by prayer, and revenge by service'. The opposite way to the way of the cross is 'repaying evil for evil', which serves to '*increase* the world's tally of evil'. Stott quoted Martin Luther King Junior's phrase 'the chain reaction of evil', seen as hate multiplies hate in 'a descending spiral of destruction'. For Stott, the cross is 'the only alchemy which turns evil into good'. It is our 'supreme example'.[91]

A missional theologian

John Stott's early evangelistic experience was to a large extent with students. He led around fifty university missions between 1952 and 1977 in Britain, North America, Australia, New Zealand, Africa and Asia. He was also Vice-President of the International Fellowship of Evangelical Students from 1995 to 2003. As an example of his evangelistic influence, his *Basic Christianity*, first published in 1958, sold over 2.5 million copies and was translated into over fifty languages. In line with his priorities, Stott began his evangelistic book with the person of Christ: 'Take Christ from Christianity, and you disembowel it; there is practically nothing left.'[92] Stott was one of the speakers at a World Congress on Evangelism held in Berlin in 1966, jointly organized by the Billy Graham Evangelistic Association and *Christianity Today*. It was an occasion when he encountered at first hand more of the world church. Of the 200 speakers, 57 came from the non-Western world.[93] Stott's three Bible Readings on 'The Great Commission' made a profound impression. He argued, taking a stance he would later amend, that 'the primary task of the members of Christ's Church is to be Gospel heralds, not social reformers'.[94] It was in the 1970s that his thinking about this began to change. In *Christian Mission in the Modern World* (1975), he wrote that 'social responsibility becomes an aspect not of Christian mission only, but also of Christian

[91] Stott, *Cross of Christ*, pp. 299–302, citing Martin Luther King Jr, *Strength to Love* (Hodder & Stoughton, 1964), p. 51.
[92] John Stott, *Basic Christianity*, rev. edn (Leicester: Inter-Varsity Press, 1971), p. 21.
[93] Brian Stanley, *The Global Diffusion of Evangelicalism* (Nottingham: Inter-Varsity Press, 2013), pp. 69–70.
[94] John Stott, 'The Great Commissions', in Carl Henry and Stanley Mooneyham (eds.), *One Race, One Gospel, One Task: World Congress on Evangelism, Berlin, 1966* (Minneapolis: World Wide Publications, 1967), vol. 1, pp. 50–51.

conversion. It is impossible to be truly converted to God . . . without being thereby converted to our neighbour.'[95]

Stott's *Christian Mission* was part of his contribution to the 1974 International Congress on World Evangelization held at Lausanne, Switzerland. Much of the finance for Lausanne came from the Billy Graham Evangelistic Association, but it was far from being a Western event. Of the approximately 2,500 participants from 150 countries, over 1,000 were from the non-Western world.[96] Three Latin American speakers, René Padilla, Samuel Escobar and Orlando Costas, issued powerful calls for evangelical social concern. For Padilla there was no place for statistics about 'how many souls die without Christ every minute' if they did not 'take account of how many of those who die are victims of hunger'.[97] Stott wrote in the *International Review of Mission* (*IRM*) for an ecumenical audience that Lausanne considered socio-political-economic liberation and salvation were distinct works of God.[98] Stott's *Christian Mission* was reviewed in *IRM* by the Orthodox Metropolitan Mar Osthathios from India, who saw it as 'a laudable attempt' by 'one of the liberal spokesmen for the evangelicals' to solve evangelical–ecumenical tensions in thinking about mission. Although critical of what he saw as Stott's selective use of Scripture (he noted the book of James was not cited by Stott), he recommended Stott's work 'to all those who have a deep desire to communicate the redeeming Gospel of Christ to the whole world'.[99]

While Stott had little contact with the Orthodox, he conceived and co-chaired with Monsignor Basil Meeking, of the Vatican's Secretariat for Promoting Christian Unity, the Evangelical–Roman Catholic Dialogue on Mission. The report on the seven-year Dialogue was first published in the *International Bulletin of Missionary Research* in 1986 and hailed by the editor as a landmark 'that will have lasting influence on our understanding and action in Christian mission'.[100] In 2016 Meeking wrote to Graham Kings, Mission Theologian in the Anglican Communion, recalling the Dialogue. Meeking emphasized that in no way did Stott 'act or speak as though divergences in belief did not matter'.

---

[95] John Stott, *Christian Mission in the Modern World* (London: Falcon Books, 1975), p. 53.

[96] John Stott (ed.), *Making Christ Known: Historic Mission Documents from the Lausanne Movement, 1974–1989* (Carlisle: Paternoster Press, 1996).

[97] René Padilla, 'Evangelism and the World', in J. D. Douglas (ed.), *Let the Earth Hear His Voice* (Minneapolis: World Wide Publications, 1975), pp. 125–132.

[98] John Stott, 'The Significance of Lausanne', *IRM*, vol. 64 (July 1975), pp. 288–294.

[99] Geevarghese Mar Osthathios, Review of *Christian Mission in the Modern World*, *IRM*, vol. 66 (January 1977), pp. 81–82.

[100] See editorial and 'The Evangelical–Roman Catholic Dialogue on Mission, 1877–1984: A Report', *International Bulletin of Missionary Research*, vol. 10, no. 1 (January 1986), pp. 1, 2–21. Subsequently published as Basil Meeking and John Stott (eds.), *The Evangelical–Roman Catholic Dialogue on Mission, 1977–1984: A Report* (Grand Rapids, MI: Eerdmans, 1986).

For Meeking, Stott's *The Cross of Christ* showed that clearly. However, from his Anglican perspective Stott saw that 'important Christian doctrines are in fact held by Roman Catholics and many Evangelical Christians of various denominations and that these undergird the Christian mission as understood by Evangelicals and Catholics'. It was, Meeking said, Stott's 'genius and his holiness that enabled him to help all of us in the dialogue meetings to see that we hold certain common understandings in faith that require us to engage in mission'. Kings quoted these reflections in a detailed analysis he gave at the Pontifical Urban University, Rome, in October 2016, on the significance of the Dialogue. He noted in his lecture that its pioneering work led on to World Evangelical Alliance and Roman Catholic dialogues.[101]

In his treatment of what he calls a 'radical departure' by Stott in the 1970s – embracing the social dimensions of mission – Chapman links it with political change. He states, 'Stott started to drift left.'[102] It is difficult to imagine Stott drifting anywhere, but he acknowledged his own reappraisal. He wrote in *Walk in His Shoes* (1975), 'Our evangelical neglect of social concern until recent years, and the whole argument about evangelism and social action, had been as unseemly as it has been unnecessary.' While affirming evangelical rejection of any 'social gospel' substituting a message of social amelioration for the good news of salvation, Stott asked from the story of the 'Good Samaritan', 'Who is my neighbour, whom I am to love?' He answered:

> He is neither a bodyless soul, nor a soulless body, nor a private individual divorced from a social environment . . . My neighbour is a body-soul-in-community. I cannot claim to love my neighbour if I'm really concerned for only one aspect of him, whether his soul or his body or his community.[103]

For Stott, this was integrally related to the cross. In *The Cross of Christ* he described the cross as 'a revelation of God's justice as well as of his love'. He continued:

> That is why the community of the cross should concern itself with social justice as well as with loving philanthropy. It is never enough to have pity on the victims of injustice, if we do nothing to change the unjust situation

---

[101] Lecture by Graham Kings, 'Evangelical–Roman Catholic Dialogue on Mission: Insights and Significance', 7 October 2016, Pontifical Urban University.

[102] Chapman, *Godly Ambition*, pp. 117–120, 121.

[103] John Stott, *Walk in His Shoes* (London: Inter-Varsity Press, 1975), p. 16.

itself. Good Samaritans will always be needed to succour those who are assaulted and robbed; yet it would be even better to rid the Jerusalem–Jericho road of brigands.[104]

In the later 1980s and into the 1990s the concern for global issues, which had been present in Stott's missional vision in earlier decades, became more apparent. His *Issues Facing Christians Today* (1984) was revised and reissued in 1990 and again in 1999 as *New Issues*. Working with ten specialist consultants, he addressed the topics of war, the environment, economic inequality, human rights, work and unemployment, industrial relations, race, poverty and wealth in relation to simplicity, women and men, marriage and divorce, abortion and euthanasia, and same-sex relationships.[105] A number of these issues had been of continuing concern for him. In his early Christian life Stott was a pacifist and although he later resigned from the Anglican Pacifist Fellowship he retained a strong conscience about war.[106] Environmental matters and care for creation were also of long-term importance for Stott, as seen in his support for A Rocha, *Christians in Conservation*,[107] his book *The Birds Our Teachers*, which came out of his lifelong love of bird-watching,[108] and his belief in his last book, *The Radical Disciple*, that climate change was 'the most serious' of all 'the global threats which face our planet'.[109] Global themes were also present in Stott's *People My Teachers* (2002). As Stott reflected on different places and people he had come to know over eighty years, he described sixteen 'Teachers'. Several were part of the evangelical story, but others, such as Gandhi and Charles Darwin, were not.[110]

Stott's concerns and interests were broad, and they broadened over time, but it should not be thought that his core theological convictions became less important to him. He was keen to strengthen links between evangelical theologians in Europe and made a key contribution to the founding of the Fellowship of European Evangelical Theologians, and in the post-communist era Stott travelled and encouraged development in Eastern Europe.[111] The substantial royalties from Stott's books – which amounted to millions of copies – went

---

[104] Stott, *Cross of Christ*, p. 292.

[105] John Stott, *New Issues Facing Christians Today* (London: HarperCollins, 1999).

[106] John Stott, 'Introduction', D. Mills-Powell (ed.), *Decide for Peace* (London: Marshall Pickering, 1986), p. xi.

[107] Dudley-Smith, *Global Ministry*, p. 319.

[108] John Stott, *The Birds Our Teachers* (London: Candle Books, 1999).

[109] John Stott, *The Radical Disciple: Wholehearted Christian Living* (Nottingham: Inter-Varsity Press, 2010), p. 62.

[110] John Stott, *People My Teachers* (London: Candle Books, 2002).

[111] Dudley-Smith, *Global Ministry*, pp. 319, 386.

largely to two other bodies he founded: the Evangelical Literature Trust, which provided evangelical books for pastors in poorer countries, and the Langham Trust, which funded young evangelicals from the majority world studying for doctorates. Chapman rightly speaks of what became Langham Partnership, with Chris Wright its International Ministries Director, as 'Built to Last' and comments, 'The rationale was simple. Stott saw the growing strength of Christianity in the non-Western world first hand and wanted to see it flourish even more.' Scholarship provision was crucial, and books and preaching seminars were added as part of this work.[112] When a Festschrift was produced in 1991 for Stott's seventieth birthday, only two of the ten contributors were Westerners. It was part of the intention to bring together authors who 'represent and belong to a network of evangelical mission theologians from the Two-Thirds World'.[113] The fact that the production of a volume like this was possible owed a great deal to Stott himself.

Conclusion

In his *The Radical Disciple*, Stott said that where his mind had come to rest was in seeing Christlikeness as God's will for the people of God and that Christlikeness could be achieved only through dependence on and understanding of the Word of God. He wrote of the Bible that it 'could be described as the Father's portrait of the Son painted by the Holy Spirit'.[114] This was not a new discovery. He had experienced Christ in a personal way while at school and had given himself to working out the implications of this more fully while at Cambridge University and Ridley Hall. Moving to All Souls was a move to a teaching ministry offered to the people of God. Stott was an ecclesial theologian. However, what was at the heart of the church's life, in his view, was a message: the message of the Bible. Within Scripture, there was a revelation pointing to Christ and supremely to the cross. As Stott put it in *Evangelical Truth*, 'If the

---

[112] Chapman, *Godly Ambition*, pp. 150–153. See Ian Shaw, 'John Stott and the Langham Scholarship Programme', in Stephen Bevans, Teresa Chai, J. Nelson Jennings, Knud Jorgensen and Dietrich Werner (eds.), *Reflecting on and Equipping for Christian Mission* (Oxford: Regnum Books International, 2015), pp. 308–326.

[113] Vinay Samuel and Chris Sugden (eds.), *AD 2000 and Beyond: A Mission Agenda* (Oxford: Regnum Books International, 1991), p. x.

[114] Stott, *Radical Disciple*, p. 45. In 2005 I had conversations with John Stott about an idea that had been put to me by Darton, Longman and Todd that I write a book on John Stott's approach to spiritual disciplines. I sketched out a book and wrote a sample chapter and DLT and John Stott were happy with my ideas. John Stott made a number of encouraging and helpful comments in a letter in November 2005. He did ask if I could refer to him as much as possible as John Stott. He said, 'I hate being referred to as "Stott".' As I moved back to Prague, I was unable to write the book but his own book was a vastly preferable outcome. Here I have followed the academic custom, with 'Stott'.

first essential of evangelical Christianity is the revelation of God in the Bible, the second is the cross of Christ, together with all the glorious benefits he achieved by it.'[115] These benefits were far-reaching and Stott himself wanted to explore all the dimensions of evangelical faith. Stott was not only cruci-centric; he was also passionately missional in his theology. Indeed, the two were integrally related. Gospel preaching was a proclamation, and what was proclaimed was Christ crucified. Speaking of Paul's aim when he spoke to those who did not yet believe in Christ, Stott insisted that his purpose was 'to persuade them to come and put their trust in him as their crucified Saviour'.[116] John Stott was a theologian with a passion to proclaim truth that would change lives.

---

[115] Stott, *Evangelical Truth*, p. 79.
[116] Stott, *Cross of Christ*, pp. 343–344.

9

James I. Packer

DON J. PAYNE

No treatment of British evangelical theologians would be complete without attention to one, much of whose notoriety was attained outside Great Britain. Few theologians have embodied a more fertile and influential coefficient of theological rigour, sensitivity to the Christian experience and widespread appeal than James Innell Packer (1926–2020). Frequently, queries of thoughtful American evangelicals about the most significant influences in their faith journey have yielded reference to Packer's most widely recognized and read book *Knowing God* (1973), which *Christianity Today* estimates to have sold 1.5 million copies.[1] Leland Ryken notes that in *Christianity Today*'s 2006 survey of 'The Top 50 Books That Have Shaped Evangelicals', *Knowing God* was fifth.[2] The accolades and analysis of Packer and his ministry reflect not only the scope but also the unique character of his theological work.[3]

For those without deep familiarity with Packer, his work must be understood and appreciated in the context of his life. He seems to have been generally underappreciated within the established British theological scene of his time, largely due to two factors: first, his having intentionally focused the bulk of his scholarship and writing towards wider (though not always 'popular'), non-academic audiences and, second, for never having published a full-length systematic theology – a magnum opus.[4] Yet, as Ryken reflects in his posthumous

---

[1] Leland Ryken, 'J. I. Packer, "Knowing God" Author, Dies at 93', *ChristianityToday.com/news* (17 July, 2020) <www.christianitytoday.com/news/2020/july/j-i-packer-died-evangelical-theologian-knowing-god.html>. Accessed 15 January 2021.

[2] Ibid.

[3] Extensive coverage of Packer's life and thought can be found in Donald Lewis and Alister McGrath (eds.), *Doing Theology for the People of God: Studies in Honor of J. I. Packer* (Downers Grove, IL: InterVarsity Press, 1996); Alister McGrath, *To Know and Serve God: A Biography of James I. Packer* (London: Hodder & Stoughton, 1997); Mark A. Noll, 'The Last Puritan', *Christianity Today*, 16 September 1996, p. 513; Don J. Payne, *The Theology of the Christian Life in J. I. Packer's Thought: Theological Anthropology, Theological Method, and the Doctrine of Sanctification* (Carlisle: Paternoster Press, 2006); Sam Storms, *Packer on the Christian Life: Knowing God in Christ, Walking by the Spirit* (Wheaton, IL: Crossway Books, 2015); and Wendy Murray Zoba, 'Knowing Packer', *Christianity Today*, 6 April 1998, pp. 30–40.

[4] The closest Packer ever came to a systematic work, though of different intent and far short of the scale reflected in many systematic works, is his *Concise Theology: A Guide to Historic Christian Beliefs* (Wheaton, IL: Tyndale House, 1993).

tribute, 'Packer's writings show what mattered most to him, and what he also thought the church must value most.'[5]

The range of topics Packer chose to address over the course of his writing career is rather breathtaking, encompassing ecclesiological and ecclesiastical concerns within the Church of England, evangelism, fundamentalism, the role of women in ministry, ministerial training, historical theology, tributes, ecumenical concerns and a wide array of matters related to practical Christian living.[6] Among his most recurring themes, however, were the doctrines of Scripture (particularly inerrancy), soteriology, sanctification and pneumatology.

After completing his Oxford DPhil thesis on Richard Baxter's theology of redemption,[7] his profile began to rise on the British theological scene with two publications. In the first of these pieces, '"Keswick" and the Reformed Doctrine of Sanctification',[8] Packer challenged the widely popular and deeply introspective Keswick spirituality in which his own faith had been nurtured in the Oxford Inter-Collegiate Christian Union. This model of the Christian life had frustrated him deeply until he came across a Reformed understanding of the Christian life in the works of John Owen, which he found liberatingly realistic.[9] In the second piece, *'Fundamentalism' and the Word of God*,[10] he entered the fray about the relationship of higher criticism to the Biblical Theology movement of the time.[11] Whether or not Packer accurately assessed the debate, it vaulted him into conversations about the nature and authority of Scripture that were to carry on through much of his career.

Packer relocated to Vancouver, British Columbia, in 1979 at the invitation of James Houston to join the faculty of Regent College. Though by that time he had already achieved considerable fame through writings such as *Knowing God*, the North American scene provided a context ripe for his particular theological

---

[5] Ryken, 'J. I. Packer'.

[6] Packer wrote multiple pieces on each of these and other topics, both practical and theological, and for both scholarly and lay audiences. For a more complete list of his works up to the early 2000s, see the bibliography in Don J. Payne, *The Theology of the Christian Life in J. I. Packer's Thought: Theological Anthropology, Theological Method, and the Doctrine of Sanctification* (Carlisle: Paternoster Press, 2006).

[7] J. I. Packer, 'The Redemption and Restoration of Man in the Thought of Richard Baxter' (DPhil thesis, University of Oxford, 1954).

[8] J. I. Packer, '"Keswick" and the Reformed Doctrine of Sanctification', *Evangelical Quarterly* 27 (1955), pp. 153–167.

[9] There can be little doubt that Packer's personal spiritual experience profoundly influenced his theology of sanctification from this point throughout the rest of his life. While not intended to minimize or invalidate his understanding of the doctrine of sanctification, it does serve as an illustration of how experience factors into one's theological method; a point that Packer seemed increasingly to acknowledge, even if at times he sent mixed signals about its role. See Payne, *Theology of the Christian Life*, pp. 53–54, 232–240.

[10] J. I. Packer, *'Fundamentalism' and the Word of God: Some Evangelical Principles* (London: Inter-Varsity Press, 1958).

[11] Payne, *Theology of the Christian Life*, pp. 65–67.

contributions. His own English context had become increasingly frustrating to him, while his theological interests were moving in directions that connected with issues and controversies of increasing interest on the North American continent, particularly in the USA.

In his biography of Packer, Alister McGrath notes a number of factors that disheartened him in England and prompted his transition to Regent College.[12]

First, since his early encounter with John Owen's writings Packer had steadily committed himself to a Reformed, Puritan theological perspective. John Wenham observes that Packer 'had made a name for himself not only by his *"Fundamentalism"* book, but also by his association with Martyn Lloyd-Jones in the promotion of Puritan and Reformed studies'. Furthermore, Wenham states, along with Lloyd-Jones 'Packer thought that a revival of Puritan theology and pastoral practice was the key to true renewal in the church'.[13] On the whole, however, evangelical Anglicanism and particularly younger Anglicans were not falling in line behind Packer's neo-Puritanism.

Second, Packer was ostracized by his mentor, D. Martyn Lloyd-Jones, in 1966. Lloyd-Jones, a Welsh Calvinistic Methodist, was a prominent leader among free church evangelicals in Britain. Packer and Lloyd-Jones had enjoyed considerable ministry together, bonded by their mutual affection for Reformed Puritanism. Yet,

> in 1966 Lloyd-Jones urged evangelicals to leave the Anglican Church, following the view that the church must be pure, i.e., composed only of those who could offer evidence of spiritual regeneration. Packer followed the lead of George Whitefield, Charles Simeon and J.C. Ryle in choosing to stay with the Anglican Church for the sake of facilitating reform. Lloyd-Jones found this choice intolerable.[14]

Though ecclesiology was not a doctrine to which Packer gave as much attention as other doctrines, his ecclesiological views and practice were pivotal in the most influential phases of his career.

Third, Packer had become increasingly suspicious of the growing interest in hermeneutics. Over subsequent years he became far more open and wrote constructively on the matter, equating hermeneutics with the process of doing

---

[12] Alister McGrath, *To Know and Serve God: A Biography of James I. Packer* (London: Hodder & Stoughton, 1997), pp. 217–219, 221, 226.

[13] John Wenham, *Facing Hell: The Story of a Nobody* (Carlisle: Paternoster Press, 1998), p. 173.

[14] Payne, *Theology of the Christian Life*, p. 70.

theology[15] and portraying it, within the parameters of evangelical commitments, as part of 'the discipline of Christian discipleship'.[16] Yet, in the earlier stages of his theological work he saw hermeneutics as a deconstructive effort that relativizes the biblical text.[17] As the British theological scene moved ahead with attention to hermeneutics, the American evangelical theological scene tended to prioritize the straightforward approaches to the biblical text fostered by the philosophical tradition of Common Sense Realism as utilized by theologians such as B. B. Warfield, whose 'Old Princeton' theology so profoundly shaped American evangelical bibliology in the twentieth century.[18]

Packer's influence in North America

Packer's influence on the North American church and theological scene can be analysed from numerous angles, including the reasons his work connected with the concerns of the church in North America when it did not seem to do so on his home continent. As mentioned above, his own theological priorities had moved in a direction not widely shared by many younger Anglican evangelicals. On the other side of that equation was a North American ecclesiastical and theological scene that was ripe for those emphases.

Though Packer's Reformed soteriology did not connect with all North American evangelicals, his emphases on Scripture – especially inerrancy – and the Christian life found eager, receptive audiences. Since the late nineteenth century the 'battle for the Bible'[19] had continued to rage, particularly in the USA. In the early twentieth century, B. B. Warfield prominently carried the torch for biblical inerrancy, providing a welcome scholarly resource for fundamentalists who were reeling from the effects of German higher criticism on confidence in the integrity of Scripture and who, on the whole, lacked the academic background to engage in that conversation on an equal footing. Warfield, a Presbyterian, provided a theological rallying point on this issue for those both inside and outside Reformed circles – curiously, even for dispensationalists.

Packer's 'Fundamentalism' and the Word of God set the stage for him later to become a key resource for evangelicals on that issue in the second half of the

[15] J. I. Packer, 'Infallible Scripture and the Role of Hermeneutics', in J. D. Woodbridge and D. A. Carson (eds.), *Scripture and Truth* (Grand Rapids, MI: Zondervan, 1983), p. 334.

[16] J. I. Packer, 'Understanding the Bible: Evangelical Hermeneutics', in M. Tinker (ed.), *Restoring the Vision* (Eastbourne: MARC, 1990), p. 159.

[17] Payne, *Theology of the Christian Life*, pp. 234–235.

[18] Ibid., pp. 41–44, 63.

[19] No pun intended, though my use of the phrase warrants acknowledgement of Harold Lindsell's widely popular and influential volume *The Battle for the Bible* (Grand Rapids, MI: Zondervan, 1976).

twentieth century. In 1980 he attempted to update and clarify the conversation with his *Beyond the Battle for the Bible*.[20] His attention to bibliology was so significant in his corpus that his most salient, shorter contributions on that locus were assembled at the end of that century into one of the four volumes of his collected works.[21] To many American evangelicals, Packer became an adopted champion for the cause of biblical inerrancy.

A second point of connection for Packer on the North American continent was his emphasis on the Christian life. Renowned academic theologians often devote attention to some aspect of practical Christian living. Yet it is not the norm for that theme to occupy as much space in a corpus as Packer gave it. His rationale is found in his pursuit of seamless integration between theology and Christian living. 'I want to arrange a marriage. I want our systematic theology to be practised as an element in our spirituality, and I want our spirituality to be viewed as an implicate and expression of our systematic theology.'[22] The Puritans receive credit for this understanding of the relationship between theology and spirituality. Packer states:

> It seems to me in retrospect that by virtue of this Puritan influence on me all my theological utterances from the start, on whatever theme, have really been spirituality (i.e., teaching for Christian living), and that I cannot now speak or write any other way.[23]

Thus, Packer's writings in this arena reflected, perhaps more than in any other theological domain, his commitment to develop the theological underpinnings of the Christian life and his insistence that Christian experience is intrinsically a theological act, for good or ill.

When dealing with the theological root system of the Christian life, Packer's favourite topic seems to have been the doctrine of sanctification. Though he acknowledged that the Bible's teachings on the subject include an accomplished or 'relational' aspect,[24] he followed the conventional Reformed emphasis by devoting primary attention to the 'progressive' nature of sanctification, which in this approach defines the theological character of Christian growth into

---

[20] J. I. Packer, *Beyond the Battle for the Bible* (Westchester, IL: Cornerstone, 1980).

[21] J. I. Packer, *The Collected Shorter Writings of J. I. Packer: Honouring the Written Word of God*, vol. 3 (Carlisle: Paternoster Press, 1999).

[22] J. I. Packer, 'An Introduction to Systematic Spirituality', *Crux* 11 (March 1990), p. 7.

[23] J. I. Packer, *Among God's Giants: The Puritan Vision of the Christian Life* (Eastbourne: Kingsway, 1991), p. 16; first published in the USA as *A Quest for Godliness: The Puritan Vision of the Christian Life* (Wheaton, IL: Crossway Books, 1990).

[24] J. I. Packer, *Concise Theology: A Guide to Historic Christian Beliefs* (Carol Stream, IL: Tyndale House, 1993), p. 169.

Christlikeness. 'Sanctification', he states, 'is an ongoing transformation within a maintained consecration, and it engenders real righteousness within the frame of relational holiness.'[25] For Packer, 'Sanctification is growth.'[26] This must be appreciated against the backdrop of Packer's early Christian experience, as mentioned above, and the defining transition that occurred in his own theology and experience when he abandoned the Keswick emphasis on the normative Christian experience as passive, faith-driven and punctiliar for the Reformed emphasis on the normative Christian experience as synergistic between God's grace and human effort, embattled, and steadily progressive even if marked by a jagged trajectory. Nowhere was Packer's approach to the doctrine of sanctification and Christian living in general more theologically developed than in his treatment of Romans 7 and the theme of indwelling sin. On this subject he remained a convinced Augustinian.[27]

From within this Reformed, Puritan framework for the doctrine of sanctification, Packer sought to bolster the process of discipleship with a dose of Spirit-empowered realism – sober yet hopeful, dependent on God along with full and aggressive engagement. He frequently offered short pieces on a variety of concerns to a range of publications and periodicals. His concerns included pain, suffering and death;[28] faith and doubt;[29] conscience, ethics and decision-making;[30] vocation and the will of God;[31] prayer;[32] and the impact of culture, comfort and affluence on the character of discipleship.[33]

---

[25] Ibid., p. 69.

[26] Ibid., p. 170.

[27] J. I. Packer, 'The "Wretched Man" Revisited: Another Look at Romans 7:14–25', in S. K. Soderlund and N. T. Wright (eds.), *Romans and the People of God: Essays in Honor of Gordon D. Fee on the Occasion of His 65th Birthday* (Grand Rapids, MI: Eerdmans, 1999), pp. 70–81; J. I. Packer and O. Johnston, introduction to M. Luther, *The Bondage of the Will* (London: James Clarke, 1957), repr. (Grand Rapids, MI: Revell, 1999).

[28] J. I. Packer, 'Are Pain and Suffering Direct Results of Evil?', in F. Colquhoun (ed.), *Moral Questions* (London: Church Pastoral Aid Society, 1977), pp. 26–29; 'Death: Life's One and Only Certainty', *Eternity* (March 1965), pp. 22–26; 'Dying Well Is the Final Test', *Eternity* (April 1987), p. 46; *A Grief Sanctified: Passing Through Grief to Peace and Joy* (Ann Arbor, MI: Servant, 1997); 'Poor Health May Be the Best Remedy: But if You've Got a Headache, Thank God for Aspirin', *Christianity Today*, 21 May 1982, pp. 14–16; 'Seeing God in the Dark', *Discipleship Journal* (May 1992), pp. 10–12.

[29] J. I. Packer, 'Crises of Faith Are Yardsticks for Growth', *Eternity* (January 1989), p. 45; 'Faith', in E. F. Harrison (ed.), *Baker's Dictionary of Theology* (Grand Rapids, MI: Baker, 1978), pp. 208–211.

[30] J. I. Packer, 'Conscience, Choice and Character', in B. Kaye and G. Wenham (eds.), *Law, Morality and the Bible* (Downers Grove, IL: InterVarsity Press, 1978), pp. 168–192; 'The Puritan Conscience', in *Faith and a Good Conscience* (London: The Puritan and Reformed Studies Conference, 1962), pp. 18–31; 'Situations and Principles', in B. Kaye and G. Wenham (eds.), *Law, Morality and the Bible* (Downers Grove, IL: InterVarsity Press, 1978), pp. 151–167; 'True Guidance', *Eternity* (June 1986), pp. 36–39.

[31] J. I. Packer, *God's Plans for You* (Wheaton, IL: Crossway Books, 2001).

[32] J. I. Packer, 'Prayer 101: Talking to God', *HIS* (November 1985), pp. 28–29.

[33] J. I. Packer, *Hot Tub Religion* (Wheaton, IL: Tyndale House, 1987); 'Leisure and Life-Style: Leisure, Pleasure, and Treasure', in D. A. Carson and J. D. Woodbridge (eds.), *God and Culture: Essays in Honor of Carl F. H. Henry* (Grand Rapids, MI: Eerdmans, 1993), pp. 356–368.

Packer on pneumatology

Reformed theologians have not always been famous for having developed robust pneumatology. Yet, Packer's overall theological programme would be impossible to apprehend apart from his pneumatology. He would claim that his attention to and understanding of the Holy Spirit's work falls clearly in line with the best of the Reformed tradition, critiquing Augustine to some extent while heartily continuing the pneumatological lineage of Calvin, the English Puritans and Jonathan Edwards.[34]

For Packer, these historic, Reformed pneumatological drumbeats were decidedly shaped by his encounters with and reactions to the pneumatological emphases of other theological traditions, especially as they shaped the theology of the Christian life in those traditions. Just as his bibliology took shape early, prompted by his encounter with the Biblical Theology movement and his 1958 publication of *'Fundamentalism' and the Word of God*, his pneumatology rose to theological prominence in his thought even earlier through his encounter with the particular pneumatology at work in the Keswick movement and his 1955 publication of '"Keswick" and the Reformed Doctrine of Sanctification'.

Against the backdrop of his even earlier personal engagement with and subsequent rejection of Keswick spirituality as an undergraduate student, Packer highlighted what he considered a salient and problematic feature of that movement. In his estimation Keswick spirituality erred by making the Holy Spirit the object of conscious attention with the expectation that, through proper attention to the Spirit and submission to the Spirit on the believer's part, the Spirit would provide direct and immediate guidance in the believer's life and deliver the believer from the vicissitudes of struggle against sin and temptation. Packer had found this inconsistent with his personal experience and with his reading of the biblical portrayal of the Spirit as diverting attention away from the Spirit's own Person and towards the Person of Christ.

The notion of the Holy Spirit as the 'shy sovereign' captured much of Packer's pneumatology. He states:

> [I]t is the Spirit's way to keep out of direct view, like a shy child hiding behind the door. So Christians never know the Spirit in the way they know the Son, and we can be led astray by questioning that suggests we do.[35]

---

[34] J. I. Packer, 'The Holy Spirit and His Work', in *The Collected Shorter Writings of J. I. Packer*, vol. 1, *Celebrating the Saving Work of God* (Carlisle: Paternoster Press, 1998), p. 213.

[35] J. I. Packer, 'Shy Sovereign', in *Shorter Writings*, vol. 1, p. 203.

The Spirit's work, to Packer, is intensely and dominantly Christocentric. The Spirit's ministry, as begun at Pentecost, was eightfold:

> [T]he Spirit 1. *reveals* Jesus' reality and the truth about him . . . 2. *unites* believers to Christ in regenerative, life-giving co-resurrection . . . 3. *assures* believers that they are children and heirs of God . . . 4. *mediates fellowship* with the Father and the Son of a kind that is already heaven's life begun . . . 5. *transforms* believers progressively through prayer and conflict with sin into Christ's moral and spiritual likeness . . . 6. *gives gifts* – that is, witnessing and serving abilities – for expressing Christ in the believing community that is his body . . . 7. *prays effectively* . . . in and for believers in Christ who feel unable to pray properly for themselves . . . 8. *prompts missionary action* to make Christ known . . . and *pastoral decision* for consolidating Christ's church.[36]

As mentioned above, the Holy Spirit was central to sanctification for Packer, and was so in a particular manner. The Spirit's activity generally operates at the unconscious level for the believer – behind the scenes, in a sense – prompting loving worship and service of God by actualizing the life of Christ in the believer.

In later years Packer developed his pneumatology further as he interacted with Pentecostalism and its unique pneumatological emphases and expectations for the Christian life. He sought to offer a balanced and practical understanding of the Spirit's role, while acknowledging and respecting Pentecostalism's desire for the Christian experience to include the affective domain. His 1984 book *Keep in Step with the Spirit* captured and culminated much of his thinking in this area, criticizing what he saw as theological imbalances in the charismatic movement while attempting to offer an empowered pneumatological model for the Christian life within the framework of Reformed theology.[37] Typical of Packer, he went beyond critique to attempt

---

[36] J. I. Packer, 'Holy Spirit', in S. B. Ferguson, D. F. Wright and J. I. Packer (eds.), *New Dictionary of Theology* (Leicester: Inter-Varsity Press, 1988), p. 317.

[37] J. I. Packer, *Keep in Step with the Spirit* (Old Tappan, NJ: Revell, 1984). He also offered smaller contributions leading up to and following that publication. See 'Charismatic Renewal: Pointing to a Person and a Power', *Christianity Today*, 7 March 1980, pp. 16–20; 'The Empowered Christian Life', in G. S. Grieg and K. N. Springer (eds.), *The Kingdom and the Power: Are Healing and the Spiritual Gifts Used by Jesus and the Early Church Meant for the Church Today?: A Biblical Look at How to Bring the Gospel to the World Today* (Ventura, CA: Regal, 1993), pp. 207–215; 'The Holy Spirit and His Work', *Crux* 23 (June 1987), pp. 2–17; *Life in the Spirit: A 30-Day Devotional* (Wheaton, IL: Crossway Books, 1996); 'On Being Serious About the Holy Spirit', in D. Wells (ed.), *God the Evangelist: How the Holy Spirit Works to Bring Men and Women to Faith* (Grand Rapids, MI: Eerdmans, 1987), pp. xii–xvii; 'Shy Sovereign', *Tabletalk* (June 1988), p. 4; 'Theological Reflections on the Charismatic Movement', *Churchman*, vol. 94, no. 1 (1980), pp. 7–25; no. 2 (1980), pp. 108–125.

and often retrieve constructive presentations of the Holy Spirit's role in the life of the church and personal faith,[38] on one occasion even co-authoring on the subject with a Pentecostal scholar.[39]

Packer on soteriology

Perhaps predictably for a Reformed theologian, no theme has been more prominent in Packer's writings than the doctrine of salvation. The subordinate themes of sanctification and holiness – primary focal points for Packer – were integrally related to his soteriology even though those are often shifted to and treated under the domain of spiritual formation and Christian living.

The most notable feature of Packer's soteriology was his thoroughgoing embrace of Calvinism with an unhesitating affirmation of all five of the Synod of Dort's landmark responses to the Arminian Remonstrance. Yet he was not uncritical of what he considered hyper-Calvinism, particularly when it compromised other important biblical motifs such as evangelism and human responsibility. Interestingly, insight into the nuances and character of Packer's Calvinism can be gained through his writings that work out implications of that framework for faith and ministry. In *Evangelism and the Sovereignty of God* he offered a salient example of these nuances by arguing that, contrary to popular perception, the doctrines of predestination and election provide the greatest motivation for sharing the gospel rather than eliminating the need for evangelism.[40]

Though certainly affirming the Heidelberg Catechism, Packer's Calvinism ran most prominently on the theological tracks laid by the Westminster Confession of Faith. This Confession, through both its 'Larger' and 'Shorter' catechisms, represented a subsequent generation of Calvinism that reflected the work of John Calvin's protégé Theodore Beza in the way its method shaped the work's content and ethos. Packer was neither unaware nor uncritical of those theological developments and their consequences. Most notably, he drew attention to a methodological shift in how Beza treated the doctrines of predestination and election:

> [Beza] removed predestination back from where Calvin put it in his final (1559) revision of the *Institutes* – in book III, after the gospel and the

---

[38] J. I. Packer, 'The Witness of the Spirit: The Puritan Teaching', in *The Wisdom of Our Fathers* (London: The Puritan and Reformed Studies Conference, 1956), pp. 11–19.

[39] J. I. Packer and R. Spittler, 'The Holy Spirit: God at Work', *Christianity Today*, 19 March 1990, pp. 27–35.

[40] J. I. Packer, *Evangelism and the Sovereignty of God* (Downers Grove, IL: InterVarsity Press, 1961).

Christian life, so that it appears as undergirding a known salvation, as in Romans 8:29–38 – and subsumed it once more under the doctrine of God and providence, as the medievals had done: which was an invitation to study the gospel promises in the light of predestination, rather than vice versa (an invitation also given – regrettably, it may be thought – by the Westminster Confession).[41]

The way you [Calvin] dealt with predestination, in particular, strikes me as an all-time brilliancy. Like Paul in Romans, you separated it from the doctrine of providence and postponed it till you had spelled out the gospel, with its *bona-fide*, whosoever-will promises; then you brought in the truth of election and reprobation, just as in Romans 8 and 9, not to frighten anyone, but to give believers reassurance, hope, and strength.[42]

This indicates that at least in some respects Packer attempted to make his Calvinism accountable more to Calvin himself than to later expressions of Calvinism, regardless of how much he appreciated and drew upon those later versions.

Post-Calvin Calvinism has often been known (perhaps caricatured) predominantly for its particularist emphasis on divine sovereignty as exercised directly and deterministically through predestination and election. Packer, however, loved to place the theological accent marks of Calvinism where he felt Calvin himself placed them – on soteriology. The prominence of soteriological concerns is illustrated in Packer's thought nowhere more saliently than in his extensive (over 400,000 words – prior to word limits being placed on theses!) Oxford DPhil thesis on Richard Baxter's soteriology, in which he critiqued Baxter's governmental view of the atonement.[43]

However directly or indirectly related to his overall Calvinistic approach to theology, Packer frequently championed the penal, substitutionary nature of Christ's atonement as the definitive biblical atonement motif. Though

---

[41] J. I. Packer, 'Arminianisms', in *The Collected Shorter Writings of J. I. Packer*, vol. 4: *Honouring the People of God* (Carlisle: Paternoster Press, 1999), p. 305.

[42] J. I. Packer, 'Fan Mail to Calvin', *Christianity Today*, 14 January 1999, p. 11.

[43] J. I. Packer, 'The Redemption and Restoration of Man in the Thought of Richard Baxter', DPhil thesis (University of Oxford, 1954). See also Payne, *Theology of the Christian Life*, p. 98, n. 81: 'Baxter, Packer contends, held a view of the atonement different from Calvin's view inasmuch as he held a different view of God's law. Calvin interpreted God's law as a reflection of God's inner character. Hence, it was impossible for God to change the law without denying God's own being. Baxter held to a view of God's law that reflected the notion found in human legal systems. God's law was external to God's self and could be changed.'

acknowledging the existence and contribution of other motifs such as *Christus Victor*,[44] Packer insisted that those motifs displayed and elaborated on the effects of Christ's atoning work while depending on penal substitution as the core of what the atonement accomplished.[45]

The doctrines of original and indwelling sin also resided in the heart of Packer's soteriology and constituted a bridge to his view of the Christian life as expressed in his theology of sanctification/holiness. While he avoided hypothesizing about the method of sin's universal transmission, he was clear about its nature.

> Original sin is a mystery. That means there is more in it than our minds can grasp, or more than God has told us, or maybe both. Certainly, the folly, discontent, ingratitude, thoughtlessness, irreverence, credulity, and arrogance of the first human sin, as narrated in Genesis 3, defy rational explanation. When Paul affirms everyone's solidarity with Adam in condemnation and subjection to sin and death . . . he does not enlarge on how this is so. We have to say of original sin, therefore, that it is a perversion in us all that none of us fully understand.[46]

His views on sin were deeply Augustinian and integrated with his other Calvinistic commitments, though his definition of the nature of sin seemed to resemble Augustine somewhat more than Calvin.[47]

> Augustine analyzed 'original sin' as pride (*superbia*), the passion to be 'top person', independent, self-sufficient, big, strong and, thus, secure. And surely he was right. No profounder analysis is possible, for this is the very heart – the heart of the heart, we might say – of the 'play-God,

---

[44] Gustaf Aulén, *Christus Victor: An Historical Study of the Three Main Types of the Idea of Atonement*, tr. A. G. Herbert (London: SPCK, 1931).

[45] J. I. Packer, 'What Did the Cross Achieve? The Logic of Penal Substitution', *Tyndale Bulletin* 25 (1974), pp. 1–43. See also 'Sacrifice and Satisfaction', in J. M. Boice (ed.), *Our Savior God* (Grand Rapids, MI: Baker, 1981), pp. 125–137.

[46] J. I. Packer, 'Doing It My Way – Are We Born Rebels?', in J. N. Akers, J. H. Armstrong and J. D. Woodbridge (eds.), *This We Believe: The Good News of Jesus Christ for the World* (Grand Rapids, MI: Zondervan, 2000), p. 45.

[47] Payne, *Theology of the Christian Life*, p. 110, n. 116. 'Calvin agrees with Augustine's declaration that sin is essentially pride but develops his definition more fully in light of the temptation that precipitated Adam's sin. Calvin claims, "Unfaithfulness, then, was the root of the Fall. But thereafter ambition and pride, together with ungratefulness, arose, because Adam by seeking more than was granted him shamefully spurned God's great bounty, which had been lavished upon him." [*Institutes*, 2.1.4]' (J. Calvin, *Institutes of the Christian Religion*, vol. 2, ed. J. T. McNeill and tr. F. L. Battles [Louisville, KY: Westminster Press, 1960], p. 245). Interestingly, he demurred from Augustine on the 'how' of sin's transmission and followed Calvin more in stopping short of speculation on that question.

fight-God, kill-God' syndrome that infected our race in Eden and rules the unregenerate still.[48]

This relentless proclivity to defy God is put to death in principle by Christ's atoning work on behalf of the believer but continues throughout the believer's life as a battle that must be engaged in with full vigour, dependent on God's grace in the power of the Spirit. Thus, the extension of the power of original sin as an indwelling and existential reality provided a key foundation stone for Packer's view of the Christian life.

Packer on the Christian life

Literature on spiritual formation, discipleship and Christian living in general is not always connected to a particular theological tradition such that the assumptions and approaches reflected in that literature are overtly linked to the distinctive theological emphases of the tradition. Packer's writings on the Christian life provide a noteworthy exception to that pattern. Not only did he heartily depict his views on Christian living as formed by and reflecting the Puritans – primarily, though not exclusively, the seventeenth-century, English Puritans – his own bibliology, pneumatology and soteriology clearly influenced his approach to the Christian life throughout his writings in this area.[49]

D. Bruce Hindmarsh refers admiringly to Packer's work with the chapter title 'Retrieval and Renewal: A Model for Evangelical Spiritual Vitality'.[50] Hindmarsh states:

> Since his first encounter with the Puritans at Oxford as librarian for the OICCU . . . through his doctoral dissertation on Richard Baxter and his part in founding the Puritan Studies Conferences, Packer has drawn deeply from this particular well of historical theology, this fount of 'experimental Protestantism.' . . . So, in his role as Robin Hood for some half a century, J. I. Packer has raided chiefly the theologically wealthy castles of the seventeenth-century Puritans and redistributed these stolen

---

[48] J. I. Packer, 'The Christian and God's World', in *The Collected Shorter Writings of J. I. Packer*, vol. 2: *Serving the People of God* (Carlisle: Paternoster Press, 1998), p. 278.

[49] Packer's admission and development of the linkages he makes between theology and spirituality are evident even in the title of his article 'An Introduction to Systematic Spirituality', *Crux* 11 (March 1990).

[50] D. Bruce Hindmarsh, 'Retrieval and Renewal: A Model for Evangelical Spiritual Vitality', in Timothy George (ed.), *J. I. Packer and the Evangelical Future: The Impact of His Life and Thought* (Grand Rapids, MI: Baker Academic, 2009), p. 99.

riches to the theologically impoverished masses of a whole generation of evangelicals. He has even had to deal here and there with antagonists who did not like his project, theological Sheriffs of Nottingham of one sort or another.[51]

How, though, and in what ways did Packer develop his 'Puritanesque' approach to the Christian life: bibliologically, pneumatologically and soteriologically?

In his work that most closely approximates a systematic theology, Packer treated the Christian life under the doctrinal heading of sanctification, followed by treatment of three legally oriented themes: liberty, legalism and antinomianism. These align with his primarily forensic understanding of the atonement.[52] These forensic motifs are followed by three more existentially oriented themes: love, hope and enterprise – reflecting his intentional priority on the objective aspects of God's saving work and subordination of the subjective aspects in a dependent fashion.[53] Significantly, 'These soteriological aspects cohere by means of the doctrines of predestination and election.'[54] He states, 'Predestination . . . gives force to what the Bible says about sanctification in the Christian life.'[55]

Within a covenantal soteriological framework,[56] Packer's development of the doctrine of sanctification/holiness included being both set apart and morally conformed to Jesus Christ through God's moral law:

> *Holy* in both biblical languages means separated and set apart for God, consecrated and made over to him. In its application to people, God's 'holy ones' or 'saints', the word implies both devotion and assimilation: devotion, in the sense of living a life of service to God; assimilation, in the sense of imitating, conforming to, and becoming like the God one serves. For Christians, this means taking God's moral law as our rule and God's incarnate Son as our model.[57]

In unpublished lecture notes at Regent College, he extended this theological definition of sanctification/holiness into a broader definition of 'biblical spirituality' as,

---

[51] Ibid., p. 103.

[52] Payne, *Theology of the Christian Life*, p. 78.

[53] Ibid.

[54] Ibid.

[55] J. I. Packer, 'Predestination and Sanctification', in *Shorter Writings*, vol. 2, p. 317.

[56] J. I. Packer, 'On Covenant Theology', in *Shorter Writings*, vol. 1, pp. 11, 14–15.

[57] J. I. Packer, *A Passion for Holiness* (Nottingham: Crossway Books, 1992), p. 19.

recognition of and response to the reality and power of God through Jesus Christ in the covenant of grace; and the first rule for practising biblical spirituality is: know the new world of which you are now part (i.e. the old world, made new by your new covenant relationship with God), know yourself as part of it, and learn to live in it according to your knowledge . . . The second definition of spirituality is . . . living out the new life which God has wrought in you and constantly sustains in you; and the second rule for practising biblical spirituality is: know your own newness in Christ, and be natural in espressing [*sic*] it and in negating all that is now unnatural to you.[58]

Biblical spirituality involves knowledge of God's will as expressed through God's law, and the intentional, embattled, Spirit-empowered pursuit of conformity to God's will as seen in Jesus Christ. More must be said, however, about the nature of God's law and how Scripture functions to convey it.

He urges:

Keep two truths in view. First, God's law **expresses his character**. It reflects his own behaviour; it alerts us to what he will love and hate to see in us. It is a recipe for holiness, consecrated conformity to God, which is (this is the second truth) God's law **fits human nature**.[59]

The Ten Commandments bring together the character of God's law in trans-cultural and transhistorical fashion. The New Testament authoritatively expresses this law as the rules and expectations of God's kingdom.[60]

As I have observed elsewhere:

Packer points out that the thread of divine authority extends through the law and into the New Testament writings. This sets the stage for his understanding of the nature of Scripture as the communicative medium for God's law. Furthermore, it offers perspective on his insistence that biblical inerrancy is a logical necessity for the Christian life. The law demands a medium of communication that is adequate to the divine nature that it reflects and the human holiness that is its goal. To Packer,

---

[58] J. I. Packer, unpublished lecture notes, 'Systematic Theology B, Man, Sin and Grace', section on 'The Reality of Salvation', p. 6.

[59] J. I. Packer, *The Ten Commandments* (Basingstoke: Chandos; Abingdon: Marcham, 1977), no page (emphases original).

[60] Payne, *Theology of the Christian Life*, pp. 87–89.

God's written communication to humanity must exist in perfect form . . .
and must, at least theoretically, be comprehensible in a manner com-
mensurate with its character.[61]

What about pneumatology in the Christian life? As mentioned above,
Packer's theology of the Holy Spirit in the Christian life was formed substantially by his own early Christian experience; especially how that experience later
served as a diagnostic and critical lens through which he viewed the role of the
Spirit as articulated in the Keswick movement. Herein lies perhaps the most
significant feature of his pneumatology as it relates to the Christian life: that
the believer's attention is not primarily to be directed towards the Spirit, but
towards Jesus Christ through the Spirit.[62] This emphasis on the Spirit's ministry
featured heavily into Packer's repeated critiques of what he thought the Spirit's
role is *not*, as he perceived pneumatological aberrations in the Wesleyan tradition and the charismatic movement.

More constructively, Packer drew upon the Calvinism he saw in many
Puritans[63] to emphasize the following salient pneumatological themes in
relation to the Christian life. First, the Holy Spirit is the experiential link to
the forensic nature of the atonement, which mitigates the otherwise sterile
character of a legally oriented atonement and makes an existential impact.[64]
Second, the Spirit provides assurance of salvation by grounding the believer's
faith on the objectivity of Jesus Christ and his saving work and by providing
subjective conviction of the truthfulness of salvation's objective basis.[65] Third,
the Spirit transforms the believer into the character and image of Jesus Christ.
Uncomfortable with the accusation of synergism, Packer situated the believer's
effort in the transformation process as the 'second cause' in response to the
Spirit as the 'first cause'.[66]

Echoing perhaps his primary overall theological mentor, John Calvin, whom
he referred to as '*the* theologian of the Holy Spirit in the post-apostolic Christian
church',[67] Packer sought to develop a robust and experiential theology of the

---

[61] Ibid., p. 89.

[62] Packer, '"Keswick" and the Reformed Doctrine', pp. 160–161.

[63] Packer departs from Puritans such as Thomas Goodwin and Thomas Brooks in their assertion of a
gap in time between faith and the sealing of the Spirit as described in Eph. 1:13. See Packer, 'The Holy Spirit',
in S. B. Ferguson, D. F. Wright and J. I. Packer (eds.), *New Dictionary of Theology* (Leicester: Inter-Varsity
Press, 1988), pp. 317–318.

[64] J. I. Packer and A. M. Stibbs, *The Spirit Within You: The Church's Neglected Possession*, Christian
Foundations series (London: Hodder & Stoughton, 1967), vol. 18, p. 16.

[65] J. I. Packer, 'Assurance', in J. D. Douglas (ed.), *New Bible Dictionary* (London: Inter-Varsity Press,
1961), p. 100.

[66] J. I. Packer, 'Sanctification – Puritan Teaching', *Christian Graduate* (December 1952), p. 126.

[67] Packer, 'The Holy Spirit and His Work', *Shorter Writings*, vol. 1, p. 213.

Holy Spirit in the Christian life. Reformed theology has often been accused of having a deficient pneumatology, at least functionally. His Reformed pneumatology, however, emerged from both what he found in Calvin and the Puritans who he felt had long been overlooked and as a response to what he considered the spiritually damaging effects of pneumatological imbalances in traditions and movements that claim the pneumatological high ground in their appeal to believers' hunger for the subjective aspects of their Christian faith.

Packer's theological method

Discussions of theological method are often considered prolegomena, yet sometimes make more sense of a theologian's approach when treated as post-legomena.[68] Although theological method was not among the formal theological subjects Packer treated most frequently, he certainly attended to it. In a few places he addressed it directly. In far more instances he addressed it indirectly under other headings and with respect to hermeneutics. Of equal significance, however, the theological method he modelled helps account for the type and extent of his theological influence.

Until recent years theological method received far more attention in Roman Catholic and some other Protestant circles than it has in evangelical circles. The corpus of literature on the subject is in some cases dizzyingly philosophical and can range across so many concerns and approaches as to be disorienting. At its core, theological method includes such factors as

> the organizational paradigms of our theological systems and why we construct our paradigms as we do, how various doctrines relate to other doctrines in our systems and which ones have controlling influence over others, and the epistemological assumptions that shape what we mean by 'knowing God' (to admiringly borrow Packer's words).[69]

As Packer's theological work developed over the decades, developments in his theological method can be traced. When studying theological method in general, it is illuminating to see how theologians' work reflects the struggles and questions of their personal spiritual journeys as well as the struggles and

[68] My theological mentor and the editor of this volume, Tom Noble, recounted to me anecdotally that in his student days at the University of Edinburgh, T. F. Torrance used to say that you can't really explain how to do something until after you have done it.

[69] Donald J. Payne, 'J. I. Packer's Theological Method', in Timothy George (ed.), *J. I. Packer and the Evangelical Future: The Impact of His Life and Thought* (Grand Rapids, MI: Baker Academic, 2009), p. 56.

questions of their historical, cultural and theological contexts. Packer is no exception. In his case those theologically formative struggles and questions include his own early personal struggles with Keswick piety and his turn to Reformed theology by way of the Puritans, his engagement in early battles about Scripture and his attempt to find a balanced pneumatology that allowed for the life of the affect without making it normative.

In one of the few places where he overtly addressed the subject of theological method, Packer referred to it as the procedures by which theology is done and the justification for those procedures.[70] Clearly and unapologetically, Packer anchored his own theological method in his priority on the text of the Bible as 'the revealed Word of God' that functions authoritatively to provide guidance for life and can be progressively comprehended through both research and the Holy Spirit's illumination.[71]

The field of hermeneutics constitutes an area where Packer's methodological thinking shifted or progressed over time. When Anthony Thiselton addressed the National Evangelical Anglican Congress in 1977, Packer expressed disappointment that Thiselton's treatment of hermeneutics seemed to raise further questions rather than provide biblical answers to contemporary questions.[72] Alister McGrath records, 'Packer never discounted the importance of hermeneutical questions; however, he felt that the approach adopted by Thiselton risked generating a relativistic mindset, which could pervade every aspect of theology.'[73] Yet, since the time that he expressed his misgivings about Thiselton's approach, he

> authored numerous monographs that reflect a broadened, if selective, appreciation for various contributions made by Hans-Georg Gadamer, Anthony Thiselton, and a host of thinkers outside evangelicalism. His later writings give evidence that he has grown to value the challenges and the necessity of hermeneutics, offering critical analysis on a wide range of theological questions.[74]

Among the methodological factors most indicative of Packer's overall theological commitments was an epistemology based on an analogical relationship between divine and human rationality, as reflected in the *imago Dei*. He states,

---

[70] J. I. Packer, 'Method, Theological', in Sinclair B. Ferguson, David F. Wright and J. I. Packer (eds.), *New Dictionary of Theology* (Leicester: Inter-Varsity Press, 1988), p. 425.

[71] Ibid.

[72] McGrath, *To Know and Serve God*, pp. 213–218.

[73] Ibid., p. 218.

[74] Payne, 'J. I. Packer's Theological Method', p. 56.

'God is rational and unchanging, and all men in every generation, being made in God's image, are capable of being addressed by him.'[75] However, for Packer this universal rational capacity, analogical to God's rationality, does not provide for a detached or neutral epistemic access to the knowledge of God:

> Packer holds to what could be called an *epistemology of engagement*; that is, he makes *commitment to* and *experience of* the object of one's knowledge prerequisite to the possibility of genuinely knowing that object. He argues that this approach preserves the integrity of the relationship between theology and its object.[76]

He pointed out a tension between

> the educational demand that method be unprejudiced, open-minded and scientific – in a word, *rational* – and the churchly requirement that method be faithful and obedient, confessional and doxological – in a word, *religious*.[77]

Thus, Packer's insistence on human rationality as both divinely derived and epistemologically essential went hand in hand with the way he emphasized discipleship in the overall experience of knowing God.

Packer's epistemological commitment to the analogical relationship between divine and human rationality extended into the linkage he posited with the inerrancy of Scripture.[78] Inerrancy was central and crucial to his theological method because he saw inerrancy, including the demonstrable unity of Scripture,[79] as guaranteeing that the mind and will of the rational God can be made known effectively to the mind of human persons and as necessary to activate the human will in obedient response to God.[80] Thus, for Packer, inerrancy is coextensive with biblical authority, though it does not function apart from the hermeneutical task.[81] The logic of this combination of epistemological, anthropological and biblical commitments makes inerrancy crucial for faithful discipleship in Packer's theology.

---

[75] J. I. Packer, 'The Adequacy of Human Language', in Norman Geisler (ed.), *Inerrancy* (Grand Rapids, MI: Zondervan, 1980), p. 201.

[76] Payne, 'J. I. Packer's Theological Method', p. 57.

[77] Packer, 'Method, Theological', pp. 424–425.

[78] At times Packer used the words 'inerrancy' and 'infallibility' interchangeably, though he preferred the term 'inerrancy' as clearer and more forceful. See Packer, 'Infallible Scripture', pp. 349–350, and 'Encountering Present-Day Views of Scripture', *Shorter Writings*, vol. 3, pp. 21–22.

[79] J. I. Packer, 'Upholding the Unity of Scripture Today', *Shorter Writings*, vol. 3, p. 141.

[80] Packer, 'Infallible Scripture', pp. 351–352.

[81] Packer, *'Fundamentalism' and the Word of God*, p. 96.

Five other features deserve brief mention as marks of Packer's overall theological method. First, this profile includes the manner in which he extended his commitment to inerrancy to posit the 'analogy of Scripture' and the 'analogy of faith' as corresponding in rational harmony.[82] Second, it includes the covenantal framework that provides both rails and trajectory for the work of hermeneutics.[83] Third, the canonical character of Scripture (in the Protestant canon) reflects God's coherent revelation to humanity over the ages and enables both a systematic approach to theology and the applicational component of hermeneutics as it makes the internal coherence of Scripture clear and relevant to the times.[84]

Fourth, the aforementioned features culminate in Jesus Christ as the central principle of Scripture's internal coherence. The hypostatic union of divine and human natures in the incarnation provided Packer with a means of affirming Scripture as inerrant while still being a fully human product. He 'emphasizes Jesus Christ as the focal point and interpretive criterion for Scripture'.[85] Though Packer clearly insisted that divine revelation through the incarnation is personal, the incarnation just as clearly provides 'the supreme expression of God's verbal or propositional revelation. Jesus's teaching constitutes the ultimate form of God's self-revelation.'[86]

Fifth, and not least, Packer's pneumatology shaped his theological method in a particular and significant manner. He adopted a conventional, Western distinction and sequence between the interpretation and the application of Scripture.[87] Though he insisted that these steps go together, he erected a sort of partition between them by making interpretation possible through the work of grammatico-historical exegesis – a rational and scientific exercise – and by making application dependent on the Holy Spirit.[88] This move reflected a narrow definition of 'interpretation' and 'meaning' in regard to the biblical text, and the assumption that those concepts refer strictly to what can be discerned about formal assertions as conveyed through linguistic apparatus.

---

[82] J. I. Packer, *Truth and Power: The Place of Scripture in the Christian Life* (Wheaton, IL: Harold Shaw, 1996), p. 103; 'Infallible Scripture', p. 350.

[83] Packer, 'On Covenant Theology', vol. 1, pp. 9, 12, 13, 15.

[84] J. I. Packer, 'Understanding the Differences', in Alvera Mickelsen (ed.), *Women, Authority and the Bible* (Downers Grove, IL: InterVarsity Press, 1986), p. 296; 'In Quest of Canonical Interpretation', in R. K. Johnston (ed.), *The Use of the Bible in Theology: Evangelical Options* (Atlanta: John Knox, 1985), p. 223.

[85] Payne, 'J. I. Packer's Theological Method', p. 61.

[86] Ibid.

[87] Harvie Conn shows the uniquely Western character of this hermeneutical assumption. See H. M. Conn, *Eternal Word and Changing Worlds: Theology, Anthropology, and Mission in Trialogue* (Grand Rapids, MI: Zondervan, 1984).

[88] Packer, *Truth and Power*, p. 149.

Packer's theological method displayed numerous other features of note, not least the way in which an Augustinian anthropology forms a taxonomy of process for the impact of Holy Scripture on the human person[89] and the impressive range of theologians and theological traditions he either acknowledged, interacted with or drew upon while maintaining a consistent commitment to the principles of Reformed orthodoxy in the tradition of the Westminster Confession.

Perhaps most notably and impressively, Packer's theological method was oriented towards preaching and faithful Christian living. He credited D. Martyn Lloyd-Jones with having profound influence on his understanding of preaching as a theological act,[90] the character of which is reflected in Packer's approach to the comprehensive hermeneutical process and its culmination in practical response to God.[91] He states, 'The purpose of knowledge is that we might apply it to life. This is nowhere truer than in Christianity, where true knowledge (knowledge of the true God) is precisely knowledge about God – applied.'[92]

Conclusion

Among British evangelical theologians J. I. Packer occupies a place of prominence owing to the unusual scope of his influence, particularly outside his home country of England. Some were disappointed that he never produced the type of scholarship traditionally recognized and celebrated within the academic guild. Others questioned his scholarly rigour for that same reason. Yet, he seemed unperturbed by those criticisms, content to use his gifts in ways that would provide the broader spectrum of God's people with theologically practical resources while not playing to populist themes.

Interestingly, Packer's wide impact did not depend upon or reflect theological minimalism. He remained a thoroughgoing Calvinist and did so within the wide ecclesiastical berth of Anglicanism. So, what accounts for the fact that Christians from such a wide spectrum resonated with Packer so deeply, even if at times they found certain of his writings or stances disagreeable?

The answer(s) to that question could involve considerable further research and yield beneficial insight into the theological sociology of twentieth-century

---

[89] Ibid., pp. 168–169.
[90] Ibid., p. 161.
[91] Packer, *Among God's Giants*, p. 84.
[92] J. I. Packer, *Growing in Christ* (Wheaton, IL: Crossway Books, 1994), p. 18. See also *Knowing God*, pp. 17–18.

North American evangelicalism in particular. One possibility is that from a sociological vantage point Packer was able to connect with an American evangelical scene whose ethos still bore the marks of the adventurous pioneer, with pragmatic and experiential concerns often overshadowing more abstract considerations. That does not necessarily imply a lack of interest in theology. Rather, it reflects an interest in viewing theological matters through the lenses of practical needs in the Christian life. This allowed Packer's theological priorities, if not always his Reformed perspectives, to connect with Christians far beyond the boundaries of his Calvinism and Anglicanism.

As theologically consistent and straightforward as Packer strove to be, he was also something of an enigma. From a methodological standpoint he seasoned an approach marked in many ways by Enlightenment rationalism and a rationalistically oriented anthropology with hints of a more holistic and experiential epistemology found in theologians such as Karl Barth and T. F. Torrance. Though he expressed reserve and sometimes disagreement with theological trajectories such as Barth's and Torrance's, he tacitly reflected some of their emphases. Arguably, these echoes allowed him to connect at a deeply experiential level with readers who would otherwise never embrace his Reformed commitments.

In these senses J. I. Packer served as a timely bridge figure. Throughout his Christian life and ministry he offered an increasingly seamless combination of impressive intellect and credentials, clear communication skills, love for people, personal integrity and fidelity to the triune God. As countless colleagues, friends and students attested, his life pulsed with the theological themes that preoccupied him. All this allowed him to touch the lives of countless individuals around the globe and, thankfully, in many instances gave the work of theology a better name outside the academy.

10

Thomas F. Torrance

ROBERT T. WALKER

If asked to sign something formally, in place of his normal signature Thomas Forsyth Torrance (1913–2007) would simply write, 'T. F. Torrance, minister of the gospel'. That was the way he thought of himself and his preferred way of characterizing himself. To him, preaching the gospel and evangelism were his primary calling. It is therefore rather ironic that he could be styled as 'a theologian's theologian' for the depth and complexity of some of his writings. Growing up in Chengdu, China, where his Scottish Presbyterian father and Anglican mother were missionaries, he had a boyhood dream of studying at Edinburgh University, and then returning to China to be a missionary himself. As a student at New College, however, he was persuaded by Hugh Ross Mackintosh, his revered teacher in the chair of dogmatics, that he could best fulfil his lifelong ambition by giving students of theology a thorough grounding in the gospel. Mackintosh had clearly realized Torrance's ability and importance in helping to equip ministers with the evangel they were to preach. Not confined to students, this lifelong evangelical calling remained with Torrance throughout his career, whoever he was addressing. He took part in missions as a student, and as a professor was involved in the invitation of Billy Graham to Scotland, sharing the platform with him at one of his major rallies. In his lectures, he sought to lead students to a deeper understanding and regularly prayed for them, in his little study just outside the lecture room, before and after each lecture. He also did not hesitate to tell people in class on occasion that they needed to be converted and students did indeed find themselves being brought to faith through him.

Life and career

Torrance's career may be divided roughly into four decades followed by a further two very creative decades after retirement.[1] After graduation at New

---

[1] See Alister E. McGrath, *Thomas F. Torrance: An Intellectual Biography* (Edinburgh: T&T Clark, 1999).

College in dogmatics, and a DTheol under Karl Barth in Basel, he served a decade in parish ministry (1941–50) that included a spell as a frontline padre during the war.[2] In the Italian campaign, he insisted on being with the troops in the front line, narrowly escaping death on several occasions and ministering to the dying. All of this he valued as preparation for the ensuing decade (1950–60) of university lectures and involvement in ecumenical discussions. Appointed Professor of Church History at New College in 1950, he transferred in 1952 to the Chair of Christian Dogmatics.[3] As a student he had been identified as a theological star on the horizon, and quickly became known as a leading Scottish theologian, in no small measure for his input[4] as Church of Scotland delegate to the World Council of Churches' ecumenical dialogues of the 1950s and for his painstaking work as Convener of the Church of Scotland's Special Committee on Baptism with its annual reports.[5] During this decade he continued as editor of the *Scottish Journal of Theology*, which he had launched in 1948 while still a parish minister, and undertook the major task of editing the English translation of Barth's *Church Dogmatics* along with Geoffrey Bromiley.

Torrance spent the third decade (1960–70) of his career in intensive research on the relation between theology and science, culminating in his groundbreaking *Theological Science* in 1969 for which he received the Templeton Prize.[6] During this decade he also co-edited a new translation of Calvin's *Commentaries* with his brother, David W. Torrance. The fourth decade (1970–80) saw him publishing widely on theology and science, including an important collection of essays on theological method, *God and Rationality*.[7] He also

---

[2] British army chaplains were popularly called 'padres'.

[3] New College, Edinburgh (with its sister colleges in St Andrews, Aberdeen and Glasgow), embodied the Scottish tradition of holding together church and academy by being at once Church of Scotland training colleges for ordinands and full university divinity faculties.

[4] Subsequently published as *Conflict and Agreement in the Church*, vols. 1, 2 (London: Lutterworth Press, 1959, 1960).

[5] Presented to the General Assembly of the Church of Scotland and printed in its Annual Year Book (May 1955 – May 1962).

[6] Thomas F. Torrance, *Theological Science* (London: Oxford University Press, 1969; new edn, 1996).

[7] T. F. Torrance, *God and Rationality* (London: Oxford University Press, 1971). See also the later publications *Christian Theology and Scientific Culture* (Belfast: Christian Journals; New York: Oxford University Press, 1980); *The Ground and Grammar of Theology: Consonance Between Theology and Science* (Charlottesville, VA: The University of Virginia Press; Belfast: Christian Journals, 1980); *Divine and Contingent Order* (Oxford: Oxford University Press, 1981); *Reality and Scientific Theology* (Edinburgh: Scottish Academic Press, 1985). Part of the stimulus behind Torrance's string of publications on theology and science lay in his realizing the parallels between the epistemological insights of Einstein, John Macmurray and Michael Polanyi and the ontological basis for faith he had found in a full incarnational-trinitarian account of knowledge of God. Torrance was able to utilize to fruitful effect some of their key concepts in articulating his own theological epistemology. In so doing, he was able to enhance greatly the depth and power of his account of the relation between knowledge of God in theology and knowledge of the natural world in science, to the benefit of both disciplines. See Colin Weightman, *Theology in a Polanyian Universe: The Theology of Thomas Torrance* (New York: Peter Lang, 1994).

developed relationships with the Eastern Orthodox churches, inspired by his developing work on the theology of the Eastern church father Athanasius. In his work at New College T. F. Torrance was ably aided by his brother James B. Torrance,[8] who taught alongside him in the New College dogmatics department for several years before moving to his own chair in Aberdeen. Sharing the same theology, 'JB' was able to develop a terminology and find ways of expressing it that complemented his brother's approach, highlighting in different ways concerns directly related to pastoral ministry and preaching and helping to make theology accessible to many.[9]

Taking early retirement in 1979, T. F. Torrance devoted his last two decades mainly to writing his two great monographs on the doctrine of God, *The Trinitarian Faith* and *The Christian Doctrine of God*.[10] The first of these was a study of 'the Evangelical Theology of the Ancient Catholic Church', published to mark the sixteen hundredth anniversary of the Nicene Creed as reformulated at the Council of Constantinople (381). During these last two decades, Torrance also led the delegation from the World Alliance of Reformed Churches in the consultation with the Eastern Orthodox churches, reaching a consensus on the doctrine of the Trinity.[11] His many honorary degrees, his membership and presidency of prestigious international academies (the Académie Internationale de Philosophie des Sciences and the Académie Internationale des Sciences Religieuses, of which he was President 1972–81), along with his fellowships, are all testament to the width and depth of his academic achievements.[12] Yet students often remembered him most not for academic brilliance but for his openness and pastoral concern for them.

---

[8] See Alexandra S. Radcliff, *The Claim of Humanity in Christ: Salvation and Sanctification in the Theology of T. F. and J. B. Torrance* (Eugene, OR: Pickwick, 2016). Beautifully written, Radcliff's book is an excellent account of the Torrances' shared theology and can be read as a good introduction to them.

[9] J. B. Torrance was able to do this even more in his own department at Aberdeen, where he had a tremendous influence on inspiring a whole generation of students, who established the Thomas F. Torrance Theological Fellowship with its online journal *Participatio*. For an excellent Festschrift written in honour of James B. Torrance, see Todd Speidell (ed.), *Trinity and Transformation: J. B. Torrance's Vision of Worship, Mission, and Society* (Eugene, OR: Wipf & Stock, 2016).

[10] T. F. Torrance, *The Trinitarian Faith: The Evangelical Theology of the Ancient Catholic Church* (Edinburgh: T&T Clark, 1988); *The Christian Doctrine of God: One Being Three Persons* (Edinburgh: T&T Clark, 1996).

[11] See Thomas F. Torrance (ed.), *Theological Dialogue Between Orthodox and Reformed Churches*, vols. 1, 2 (Edinburgh: Scottish Academic Press, 1985, 1993); also Thomas F. Torrance, *Trinitarian Perspectives: Toward Doctrinal Agreement* (Edinburgh: T&T Clark, 1994); see also Jason Robert Radcliff, *Thomas F. Torrance and the Orthodox–Reformed Theological Dialogue* (Eugene, OR: Pickwick, 2018).

[12] Leading academics are elected by their peers to be Fellows of the Royal Society of Edinburgh or Fellows of the British Academy.

The meaning of 'Christian dogmatics'

The centrality of Christ

The abiding interest of Torrance's career was 'Christian dogmatics'. He understood Christian dogmatics as the theological discipline that sees the whole of Scripture as pointing to and focused on Christ. 'Dogmatics' in its original meaning refers to disciplines that have an objective subject matter and therefore basic principles and norms of understanding and it was in this sense that physics could be understood as a 'dogmatic science' in the early modern period.[13] Dogmatic disciplines are open to the reality they investigate, guided by it, continually open to further discovery of it and the reshaping of their understanding by it.

Because Christian dogmatics is focused on Christ, the terminal point of its thought, it is not a system in itself, or one that holds the truth in itself, but one that points beyond itself to him. In the nature of the case, however, it is systematic in two senses; first that it sees all Scripture as referring to Christ the living truth, and second, that it sees all Christian doctrine as being related to every other Christian doctrine. All Scripture and doctrine find their full meaning only in Christ, through the conjoint meaning they find in him. This means that each element of Scripture or doctrine can be fully understood only in relation to the meaning found in Christ through the witness of Scripture and doctrine as a whole to him. To neglect any particular element of Scripture or doctrine is therefore to weaken the meaning of the whole. The systematic nature of dogmatics simply derives from the need to understand all Scripture and doctrine in their systematic relation to the rest of Scripture and doctrine.

The biblical foundation

Torrance's dogmatics thus emerges out of a profoundly biblical foundation. Steeped in the Bible from an early age and proficient in Hebrew and Greek (particularly the latter, and in Latin also) his dogmatics lectures abounded in scriptural allusions, often implicit and unreferenced but immediately recognizable to anyone familiar with the King James Version. Torrance's familiarity with the biblical text and its thought forms, in translation or the original, is a dimension of his thought that is insufficiently recognized but provides the basis of all his theology.

---

[13] See Torrance, *Theological Science*, pp. 337–347, and the opening chapters of T. F. Torrance, *Theology in Reconstruction* (London: SCM Press, 1965).

Dogmatics, mission and the reality of the triune God

Three further features of Torrance's dogmatics deserve the closest attention. First, he draws a clear distinction between statements about God and the reality of God. While God makes himself known through the Bible, the Bible is not the reality of God nor the word of God in the same way that Jesus is the Word of God. Similarly, statements of dogmatics, important as they are in providing understanding of the gospel, have no meaning in themselves except as they succeed in pointing to a reality beyond themselves.

Second, there is an inherent connection between dogmatics and mission, or between systematic theology and theological evangelism. The primary aim of mission should not be thought of merely as one of conversion, but of accessibly conveying the content of the gospel in the belief that only so can it be truly assessed and lead to solid conversion. The supreme aim of dogmatics accordingly is to unfold, as accurately and accessibly as possible, the content and meaning of the gospel of Christ and of the Christian doctrine he informs. The outgoing nature of dogmatics was vividly seen in Torrance's lifelong commitment to the church at every level and his willingness to preach, teach and talk about the faith whenever time and opportunity arose, even to small groups. His own dogmatics lectures were a patient, sustained unfolding in considerable depth, without rhetorical flourish, of the whole of Christian doctrine on its biblical basis, and his published lectures read like a profound commentary on the Bible.

For Torrance, dogmatics has a crucial role to play in guiding the church and helping it to a grasp of the gospel that can not only inform its life and thinking but have a profound effect on society by its coherence and power. From a boyhood ambition to be a missionary in China, Torrance was persuaded that the best way to fulfil his lifelong calling would be to train others and equip them with a thorough understanding of the gospel. For Torrance therefore, dogmatics and theology were never simply for their own sake, however important and fascinating, but outward looking and evangelical in the best sense of the word. It is noteworthy, for example, that his immense efforts at exploring the relations between reason, belief and faith, and theology and science, were aimed at helping 'to evangelise the foundations, so to speak of scientific culture, so that a dogmatics can take root in that kind of structure'.[14]

Third, as inherently Christocentric, Christian dogmatics must also be inherently and inescapably trinitarian, for Christ cannot be truly known except

---

[14] Michael Bauman, *Roundtable: Conversations with European Theologians* (Grand Rapids, MI: Baker, 1990), 'Interview with T. F. Torrance', p. 114.

ontologically, as he is in his eternal being, the Son of the Father in the triune unity of God. An integral part of Torrance's dogmatics therefore is his sustained examination, in the two great monographs already mentioned on the Christian doctrine of God.

Original, ecumenical and constructive

Three other features of Torrance's theology should be noted. First, he brought to his dogmatics an encyclopaedic knowledge, prodigious memory and indefatigable energy, rigorous scholarship and an ecumenical, pastoral outlook, a formidable intellect always able to see the whole and the keen originality of being able to make new connections and see far-reaching implications. All this allowed him not only to make connections, for example between elements of Christian doctrine, between reason and faith, or science and theology and their respective methodologies, but to see their ground-breaking implications.

Second, Torrance was also comfortable straddling and harnessing the best elements in different traditions, as in his prolonged engagement with Anglicans and others in ecumenical discussions, while his lifelong fascination and profound knowledge of the church fathers led to historic agreement with Orthodox theologians on trinitarian doctrine. Such was the esteem in which he was held by them that he was given the signal honour of being consecrated proto-presbyter of the Orthodox Church.

Third, the result of all this is that Torrance's dogmatics is a historic integration of classical Christian theology, rooted in the ecumenical Councils of Nicaea (AD 325) and Chalcedon (AD 451) but harnessing key elements from medieval, Reformation and modern theology. The single most distinctive feature behind Torrance's work is the way he has attempted to think everything out from a Christocentric (and therefore trinitarian) perspective, 'the Christological correction of all doctrine' as he and his brother James used to call it. This supplies the basic unity, fertility and originality of his theology. It may be argued that no one else has attempted to see the implications of a Nicene-Chalcedonian Christology so thoroughly and so consistently applied them to the same extent. Throughout the process of constructing his own dogmatics,[15] Torrance's approach to theology was one of critical engagement with the past and retrieval as well as constructive development and fresh theological articulation.

---

[15] For more on dogmatics and its place in the church, see T. F. Torrance, *Theology in Reconstruction*, ch. 8, and the editor's introduction to Thomas F. Torrance, *Incarnation: The Person and Life of Christ*, ed. Robert T. Walker (Milton Keynes: Paternoster Press; Downers Grove, IL: InterVarsity Press, 2008), pp. xxii–xxix.

Christ-centred trinitarian theology[16]

Here I can give only a severely abridged summary of Torrance's theology, drawing mainly from his published lectures and concentrating on key themes and having to bypass much that is essential.[17]

Knowing the triune God through the mediator

Torrance understands the knowledge of God in the Old Testament, given to Israel as his covenant people, as his careful preparation – in their language, laws, worship and the institutions of priest, king and prophet – for the coming of Christ. These were to be the conceptual tools appropriate to understanding Christ when he came. In the Old Testament, God is always known by his word, which *does* what it *says*. In the New Testament, it becomes apparent that Christ is himself the word of God and as the eternal Word and Son of God the mediator of all knowledge of God as he is.

In the order of our knowing, therefore, it is to Christ that we look for knowledge of God and through him that we come to know God as his Father, and the Spirit as his Spirit. For Torrance, we come to know Christ at the 'evangelical and doxological' level of faith, but as we grow in theological understanding we find God revealed as Father, Son and Holy Spirit in being and are led to see that the very being, person and work of Christ is grounded in the Trinity. Here faith finds itself deepened in understanding that all that Christ is and does is the work of Father, Son and Spirit together. It is deepened to understand that our faith does not just rest on Christ alone but on the whole triune God and that in all his acts, God works as Father, Son and Spirit. Known in this way as the Evangelical Trinity, God becomes a triple joy and the triple guarantee of salvation. The best way to grasp this is to read and reread all Jesus says in the Gospel of John about the Father and the Spirit. We can then begin to sense the mutuality among Father, Son and Spirit and understand how all that Christ is and does is grounded in, and points to, all the Father is and does in him. Likewise, what Christ is and does is done in the power of the Spirit and points to the work of the Spirit in bringing us to faith and uniting us to him.

---

[16] See Paul D. Molnar and Myk Habets (eds.), *T&T Clark Handbook of Thomas F. Torrance* (London: T&T Clark, 2020), a major resource on Torrance, with eighteen contributors on topics central to his theology.

[17] Torrance, *Incarnation*; Thomas F. Torrance, *Atonement: The Person and Work of Christ*, ed. Robert T. Walker (Milton Keynes: Paternoster Press; Downers Grove, IL: InterVarsity Press, 2009).

One whole Christ: the risen Jesus in his person, word and work

For Torrance, there is a unity of person and work in Jesus Christ. He is not simply who he is, Son of God and son of man in one person. Jesus Christ is who he is *and* all he has done in time and history, person and work in one indissoluble whole. This is a point that can hardly be overstressed and it springs from the very nature of what he is and has done. He is the eternal God acting in time, taking our humanity and reconstructing it *from within* in a lifelong action that does not disappear into past time since the resurrection of Jesus in our humanity is for all time. It is the same Jesus who lived on earth, but the same Jesus now enthroned in the heaven, clothed with our humanity made perfect in him. He is 'Christ clothed with his gospel' as Calvin put it,[18] Christ in the unity of his person, word and work.[19]

Jesus Christ is the gospel

The unity of Christ in his person and work means the gospel is not just *about* Christ. It *is* Christ. Jesus Christ himself *is* his own gospel. He is the gospel in all he has done as God *and* man. He is the gospel because he has achieved our salvation, but he has achieved it precisely because of who he is, God *and* man.[20] If he were not God, he could not have done so, because only God can undo and annul the power of sin and evil and redeem us. But equally, if he were not man he could not have done so either, for it is humankind that needs to be saved, come to know God, be forgiven and brought to repentance. He has done all this for us in becoming truly human and, without any sin of his own, being baptized into our baptism, taking our judgement on himself and making atonement for us. For Torrance, as for Calvin, the cross is the great completion of our salvation, but the incarnation is its beginning.[21]

The significance of the incarnation

From the very outset of his career, Torrance had realized the critical significance of the incarnation. If creation out of nothing, the bringing into being of a vast creaturely reality to exist in relation to God, was astounding, the event whereby God himself became a creature was even more so. The critical significance of the incarnation was in the person of Christ, for in him God remained God and

---

[18] John Calvin, *Institutes of the Christian Religion* (1659), 3.2.6.
[19] Torrance, *Incarnation*, pp. 107–109.
[20] Throughout Torrance's life, the word 'man' was understood (as it always had been) as gender inclusive.
[21] Cf. Calvin, *Institutes*, 2.16.5: 'From the moment when he [Christ] assumed the form of a servant, he began, in order to redeem us, to pay the price of deliverance.'

man remained man (indeed, became real man), but the two were united in his person. This was an event, 'new even for God', in which at this one point, this one person in space and time and nowhere else, God became man. In Jesus Christ, there was no confusion between God and man, nor any change of one into the other, yet in him they were united and inseparable. In his one person the risen Jesus Christ is thus the living bond of God and man, 'the linchpin of our salvation' for all time.

Seen in its fullness, as Torrance sees it, the incarnation is a dynamic event, forged at Bethlehem, but worked out in the whole life of Jesus and then held firm in the agony of judgement and atonement on the cross to its fulfilment in the victory of resurrection, ascension and the sending of the Spirit. The significance of the incarnation is therefore not just the astonishing reality of Christ in his person, but that it was a real event worked out, step by step, 'with strong crying and tears' in time. In Jesus, we have *God* in time and his resurrection *as man*, a conjunction which means that the incarnation was not just a fleeting event but permanent. God *as man* was working out *our* salvation. Here we have Torrance's seminal concept of 'vicarious humanity'.

The 'vicarious humanity' of Jesus

The word 'vicarious' refers to someone acting for another by standing in their place. 'Vicarious humanity' is thus the phrase used to sum up the meaning of what Christ is for us in his humanity, not simply in his taking our sin and judgement on himself, but in his whole life of positive obedience for us. Torrance has seen and consistently worked out the radical implications of the integrity of the humanity of Christ in his one person, the full significance of his 'vicarious humanity', and therefore the full substitutional-representational significance of his faith, his worship, his priesthood and his knowledge of God in our humanity, as the ontological basis of ours. The fact that Torrance has wrongly been taken to belittle the importance of our human faith and response shows the extent to which his insights into the meaning of Christ's 'vicarious humanity' have yet to be fully grasped. There is pressing work to be done here in finding ways of communicating Christology, soteriology and pneumatology to people starved of knowing the riches of Christ for us.[22]

Critical stages and elements in Christ's life and work

For Torrance, the life and work of Christ as man is one of struggle with entrenched powers of evil and the sinful hostility of the human heart. In his

---

[22] Cf. ibid., 2.16.19.

lectures he spoke of various stages of Jesus' growth and struggle and drew attention to the Greek of Luke 2, which he translated as 'battled his way forward in blows'.[23] He also pointed to Jesus' statement in Luke 12, 'I have a baptism to be baptized with; and how I am constrained until it is accomplished!'[24] Jesus clearly saw his baptism in the Jordan as a lifelong undertaking only completed on the cross. In his lectures Torrance also drew attention to the significance of Matthew 8:17,[25] where Matthew understands Jesus' healing miracles in the context of Isaiah 53 and therefore sees him as healing us by taking our sicknesses and sins on himself. The passages above, taken together with several other passages from Scripture such as the instances when power went out of Jesus or he groaned in healing, are all indicators that his whole life was one of saving significance and struggle, an aspect Torrance brings out strongly in the last chapter of *Incarnation*, 'The Kingdom of Christ and Evil'. Throughout, Torrance sees the whole life of Christ, particularly from his baptism onwards, as one of 'increasing solidarity with sinners'.[26]

Critical elements are the contrasting but related types of action or movement in the life and work of Jesus and it is important to see that throughout his life the contrasting elements went side by side, never one without the other. First, there is *active and passive obedience*. Christ's 'active obedience' is the term used to refer to Jesus' active fulfilment of the will and law of God and his life of positive human obedience. Second, there is *revelation and reconciliation*. A seminal feature of Torrance's theology is his emphasis on the importance and inseparability in soteriology (the doctrine of salvation) of revelation and reconciliation. It is only through knowledge of God *as he is* that we can be reconciled, but at the same time it is only through reconciliation that we can come to know God, for we cannot know God without atonement and cleansing from sin. Torrance is therefore very strong on the nature of knowledge of God and for him, theology is not theology without real personal knowledge of God.

Third, there is *descent and ascent*. Jesus came down from heaven that he might lift us up to heaven. He humbles himself to share our lowly state, but in so doing (though not manifest as such yet), his very presence with us is actually the beginning of his lifting us up. He descends to die our death and rises to give us eternal life. In the incarnation, he is the meeting of God and man in man's place, and in the ascension, the meeting of God and man in God's place. Fourth,

---

[23] Luke 2:52.

[24] Luke 12:50, RSV.

[25] Matt 8:14–17, esp. 17, 'This was to fulfil what was spoken through the prophet Isaiah: "He took up our infirmities and carried our diseases"' (NIV); see Isa. 53:4, 'Surely he took up our pain / and bore our suffering' (NIV).

[26] Torrance, *Incarnation*, pp. 62, 106, 112, 137–138, 153.

there is *the bearing of sin and the cleansing from sin*. Jesus bears our sin and, in so doing, bears it away and cleanses us. He takes our fallen humanity on himself, *but* in the very act of doing so sanctifies it by his purity. He who had no sin was 'made to be sin' on the cross 'that in him we might become the righteousness of God'. In this astonishing verse in 2 Corinthians 5:21, we have the essence of Torrance's understanding of Christ's mediatorial work and of incarnation and atonement.

What is important however, and repeatedly stressed by Torrance, is the oneness of Christ, the unity of his person and work and of God and man in his one person. Everything Christ does, he does in his one indivisible person and therefore we cannot separate out the work of God and the work of man in him. All his mediatorial and saving acts are the work of the one whole Jesus Christ.

Incarnation and atonement[27]

The heart of Torrance's understanding of the gospel is the logic of Hebrews 2:14, that since death holds us as creatures of flesh and blood in its grip, Christ became exactly what we are that by dying himself he might destroy the power of death. It is the same logic as the verse in 2 Corinthians 5:21, where Christ became what we are, 'was made sin for us', that he might make us what he is, righteous. But what is sin (not 'sins'), sin as a living state of being? It is not something apart from a doer but an active, integral part of the life and being of the doer. To take on sin sinlessly, therefore, is somehow to take on oneself the being and nature of the sinner without being sinful or sinning oneself. This would seem to be a complete contradiction and impossible, just as it would be for the holy God 'to be made sin'! Here we have one of the most distinctive and controversial points of Torrance's teaching: that in the incarnation Christ assumed fallen humanity, not the unfallen humanity of Adam before the fall. In doing so he is following Gregory Nazianzen's famous maxim, 'The unassumed is the unredeemed', that any part of being human not assumed by Christ remained unredeemed.[28] This means that in order to redeem us, Christ had to take on himself all we are in our state of being sinful in body, mind and soul. He does so of course *without sin or sinning himself*. Torrance emphasizes that in the very act of taking our fallen nature on himself *Christ sanctifies it*. He sees the life of Christ, from birth to death, as one of 'increasing solidarity with sinners', in

---

[27] See *Participatio* (vol. 3), the free online journal of the Thomas F. Torrance Theological Fellowship. Vol. 3 of *Participatio* is devoted to 'Incarnation and Atonement' (accessible via <www.tftorrance.org>). See also Thomas A. Noble, 'Incarnation and Atonement', ch. 12 in Molnar and Habets, *Handbook*, pp. 173–188.

[28] Strictly, 'the unassumed is the unhealed': see Gregory Nazianzen, Epistle 101, To Cledonius, 5, *Nicene and Post-Nicene Fathers*, 2nd series (Grand Rapids, MI: Eerdmans, 1891; repr. 1974), vol. 7, p. 440.

which at each stage Christ wrestles with our recalcitrant humanity and bends it back into obedience and love to God.[29]

The mystery of atonement

Torrance writes:

> The innermost mystery of atonement and intercession remains mystery: it cannot be spelled out, and it cannot be spied out. That is the ultimate mystery of the blood of Christ, the blood of God incarnate, a holy and infinite mystery which is more to be adored than expressed. Here we tread the holy ground of Gethsemane and Calvary and here we must clap our hand upon our mouth again and again for we have no words adequate to match the infinitely holy import of atonement.[30]

It is in the fearful mystery and judgement of the cross that Jesus completes the course of his baptism in two great acts of passive and active obedience. He shrinks from the cup he has to drink but willingly accepts it; he takes the judgement of God and our cry of God-forsakenness on his own lips, but holding steadfastly on to God in faith converts it to 'Father, into your hands I commit my spirit.' He had completed his course. 'It is finished,' he said and died in peace.

The heart of atonement

It is Christ's intercessory prayer to the Father, the 'work of mediation and intercession in his person', the oneness of mind between Father and Son, that for Torrance must be seen as the heart of atonement. '*It is that oneness which constitutes the inner heart of atonement.*'[31] This is a matter of *radical substitution*, Christ's assumption and sanctification in himself of fallen humanity. Torrance sees the life of Christ as a lifelong dynamic act in which he becomes what we are, in order not only to stand alongside us, but to take our fallen humanity on himself that he might reconstruct it, cleanse it of sin, guilt and corruption and

---

[29] See Bruce Ritchie, *T. F. Torrance in Recollection and Reappraisal* (Eugene, OR: Pickwick, 2021), for a careful consideration of 'made sin for us' and the work of Christ as assuming and sanctifying fallen humanity.

[30] Torrance, *Atonement*, p. 2.

[31] Ibid., p. 75 (emphasis original): 'In the mediation on the cross, that oneness between God and man already wrought out in the incarnation and in the complete oneness between the incarnate Son and the heavenly Father, is fully consummated, and the union between the person of Christ the Son and his work in our flesh is likewise consummated and fulfilled. *It is that oneness which constitutes the inner heart of atonement*' (emphasis original).

make it perfect in himself. Wearing our humanity, he sanctifies it to make it his perfect humanity, his yet ours, our new humanity reconstructed in him. This is radical substitution in which he so stands in for us that in his active and passive obedience he not only takes on himself all the negative consequences of our sin, but positively fulfils and offers up to God for us the perfect repentance, faith, trust, worship, prayer, love, faithfulness and righteousness that should have been ours but that we were unable to offer.[32]

The meaning of grace

Far from this meaning we are not called to faith, prayer and all the fruits of the Spirit, the mystery and miracle of grace is that Christ has so stood in our place that everything he has done and offered up is ours and ours as a free gift. When the eyes of our hearts are opened by the Spirit to know that in faith, we are freed from thinking we have to offer up autonomously to God something Christ has already offered for us. Knowing that what is Christ's is ours, we find ourselves united to him and participating in all he is and has for us. Our faith, our prayer, our worship is ours and something we genuinely and freely do, but it is a gift of grace, given and not achieved. What we come to understand is that our life and our faith are actually a resting and a participation in Christ's faith: 'the life which I now live in the flesh I live by the *faith of the Son of God*'.[33]

Cross and resurrection

The cross and the resurrection go inextricably together and each is unthinkable without the other. The resurrection is the completion of the cross but it is also the revelation of the victory of the cross, its undoing of sin and victory over death. By itself the cross is nothing, but the resurrection can happen only on the basis of the cross: 'he [Jesus our Lord] who was put to death for our trespasses and raised for our justification'.[34] In the Bible sin and death are linked. To undo sin is to undo death, and therefore the bodily resurrection of Jesus is not simply the confirmation of forgiveness, it *is* our forgiveness. Likewise, forgiveness is not just something Jesus gives us, for in his person he *is* the resurrection and *is* our

---

[32] For Torrance's most accessible and extensive account of Jesus Christ and human response see Thomas F. Torrance, *The Mediation of Christ*, rev. edn (Edinburgh: T&T Clark, 1992), foreword, xii–xiv, and ch. 4, 'The Mediation of Christ in Our Human Response', pp. 73–98. This book, together with his considerably larger *Incarnation* and *Atonement*, makes the best introduction to Torrance's biblical-dogmatic theology.

[33] Gal. 2:20, AV, where the Greek is 'the faith *of* the Son of God', not 'faith *in* the Son of God'. See Torrance, *Incarnation*, p. 28, extended n. 40, for references to Torrance's early advocacy of this point in lectures and publications and the debate of the issue in modern scholarship. See also ch. 13, esp. pp. 204–206, in Molnar and Habets, *Handbook*.

[34] Rom. 4:25, RSV.

forgiveness,[35] yet the church has so often emphasized the cross to the detriment of the resurrection and failed to see the resurrection's full significance.

Cosmic implications

Christ is one man but he is the Word of God through whom the universe was created, who upholds it by his power, in whom all things hold together and who in the loving purpose of God has become human to gather all things up under him as their head.[36] He has so made himself one with us as our substitute and representative, that when he died we died and when he rose we rose, in him and with him to be seated with him in heaven.[37] The cosmic significance of the cross and resurrection comes out strongly in the New Testament, particularly in the letters of Paul.[38] It means that when Christ died all creation died in him, and when he rose that was the beginning of the new creation. The 'old creation' has not yet died in itself, but it has died in Christ and with him and to the eye of faith has passed away. The 'new creation' has already dawned and faith is already participant in it.

This leads to the intense eschatological joy of the resurrection and new creation. Such is the New Testament understanding of the magnitude of the resurrection (Eph. 1:19–22) that it is shot through with the sheer joy of what has happened in Jesus. The kingdom has come, the new creation has dawned (2 Cor. 5:17), our sins are forgiven, death has been conquered, we are here on earth but risen with Christ, reconciled to God, seated with him in heaven (Eph. 2:6) and already tasting the joy of the new creation and of the world to come (Heb. 6:4–5).

Ascension: Christ's reception of the Spirit

This brings us to the significance of the ascension and Christ's reception of the Spirit. The ascension of Jesus into heaven, wearing our humanity, is not to be interpreted as leaving us behind but as taking us with him into the very presence of God. He has so bound us to himself as our kingly-priestly head that where he is, there we are and will be. 'Here am I, and the children God has given me,'[39] says Athanasius of Christ's words of entry into heaven! But then the astonishing insight of Peter in his Pentecostal sermon tells us, 'Being therefore exalted at the right hand of God, and having received from the Father the promise of the

---

[35] See Torrance, *Atonement*, p. 217.
[36] John 1:3; Heb. 1:3; Col. 1:15–17; Eph. 1:10.
[37] 2 Cor. 5:14; Col. 2:13; 3:1–4; Eph. 2:4–6. Cf. Rom. 6:4, 8.
[38] See Torrance, *Atonement*, pp. 196, 428.
[39] Heb. 2:13.

Holy Spirit, he [Jesus] has poured out this which you see and hear.'[40] Jesus was born of the Spirit, at his baptism anointed with the Spirit for his messianic mission and now has received the Spirit in his risen humanity. This could only be because he has completed the work of atonement, taken our now purified humanity into heaven, received for us the promise of the Spirit and can therefore pour the Spirit out on us.

Revelation completed through the Spirit

Everything Christ did as man on earth he did through the Father in the power of the Spirit, but it was not till he had completed his great work of atonement and reconciliation that he could complete his revelation and self-disclosure to the disciples through the Spirit. The peculiar role of the Spirit is to witness to Christ, to remind the disciples of all he had said and to bring them to full understanding.[41] So close is the relation between Christ and the Spirit that Torrance calls the Spirit Christ's 'other self'.[42] Jesus had known full well the disciples' incapacity to comprehend his coming death until his resurrection and the coming of the Spirit. In sending his Spirit now to open the disciples to understand and participate in all he was and had accomplished for them, it is the same Jesus Christ still working, just as it is the same Father working, but through the Spirit the sphere of that work is now extended to the disciples, the church and all flesh. Torrance emphasizes that the coming of the Spirit does not add anything to Christ's objective work of atonement and reconciliation. It was simply that until it had been completed and Christ had opened the way to heaven, the way was not open for God to pour out his Spirit and complete Christ's revelation in the apostolic mind.[43]

The New Testament: Christ's word in apostolic word

As the Old Testament is the inspired word of God looking forward to Christ's coming, so the New Testament is the inspired word of God that witnesses to his coming. A chapter in *Atonement*[44] gives us an outline here of Torrance's thinking on the biblical witness to Christ and the coming of the Spirit, the creation of the apostolic witness and tradition, and the doctrine of Scripture. In his earthly mission, Christ was his own witness in person, word and deed. In sending the Spirit, Christ opened his disciples' hearts and minds to so

---

[40] Acts 2:33, RSV.
[41] John 14:26; 15:26; 16:13–15.
[42] Torrance, *Atonement*, p. 323; *Mediation of Christ*, p. 117.
[43] Torrance, *Atonement*, pp. 324–329.
[44] Ibid., ch. 10, 'The Biblical Witness to Jesus Christ'.

understand him that he could make them his authorized representatives, or 'sheluchim',[45] apostles, so invested with his authority that what they said and did should be taken as the words and deeds of Christ himself. In so doing, he did not leave them alone, for he promised to be with them through his Spirit,[46] at work in their word, in personal self-revelation in and through their witness to him. The transition from Christ's immediate self-witness to that of the apostles means that the apostolic word of the New Testament, of Gospels and Epistles together, has to be taken as the word of Christ himself.[47] Torrance speaks of it as 'the apostolic word joined to Christ by the Spirit to become word of Christ' and 'Apostolic scripture is so conjoined to the divine Word as to be the written word of God to man'.[48]

Christ's person: the pattern of grace

Torrance saw very early in his career that the way God has dealt with us in Christ provides the basic pattern for all the ways he interacts with us. In Christ there is a 'hypostatic union' (*a union in one person*) of God and man.[49] There is no such union in any of God's other relations with us, but the way God is related to us in Christ, the relation between his divinity and humanity, Godhood and manhood, is very much an analogy for all God's other relations with us – living Word and written word, Christ and his church, Christ and the individual.[50] The pattern of Christ's person[51] also provides the fundamental pattern for the nature of grace: that God freely gives us all of himself and all of our humanity in Christ and at the same time gifts us our free response. In Christ, he gifts us himself, our humanity and our response, in such a way that our response is at once his doing, his gift, *and* our act, our own free response of faith.

---

[45] Ibid., p. 318.

[46] John 14:18–20; cf. 14:12–14.

[47] Torrance, *Atonement*, pp. 330–333.

[48] Ibid., pp. 331, 335.

[49] See Torrance, *Atonement*, ch. 6, 'The Hypostatic Union'.

[50] Just as the humanity of Christ had no independent existence in itself and was entirely the result of the incarnation (as there would have been no man Jesus if the Son had not become man), so holy Scripture, the church and individual faith could not exist but for the work of Christ (as human beings have no capacity themselves) and their very being is his creation through the Spirit. At the same time, just as the humanity of Christ is real, personal and individual *in* the one person of Jesus Christ, so holy Scripture, the church and individual faith all have free, genuine, personal reality in their relation of union (non-hypostatic) with Christ through the Spirit. On Torrance's ecclesiology, see Kate Tyler, *The Ecclesiology of Thomas F. Torrance* (Lanham, MD: Lexington Books, 2019). See also Joseph H. Sherrard, *T. F. Torrance as Missional Theologian: The Ascended Christ and the Ministry of the Church* (Downers Grove, IL: InterVarsity Press, 2021).

[51] 'Two natures in one person, without confusion, change, division or separation.' For Torrance's reference to this affirmation on the person of Christ from the Council of Chalcedon, AD 451, see Torrance, *Atonement*, p. 197.

As Torrance puts it so memorably, 'All of God means all of man.'[52] Just as the Spirit puts Christ's prayer 'Abba, Father' on to our lips, so he puts Christ's faith into our hearts. It is at once Christ's faith *and* our faith. Both are real and rightly understood, our faith *is* the faith of Christ.[53]

Theologian of the Trinity

The aim of this short chapter has been to provide a way into Torrance's profound theology by focusing on his Christology and his doctrine of the atonement. But in his later years, he was able to develop his understanding of the doctrine of God the Holy Trinity in two major books, *The Trinitarian Faith* and *The Christian Doctrine of God, One Being Three Persons*.[54] Paul Molnar describes Torrance as a 'theologian of the Trinity',[55] and so though I cannot begin to give an adequate account of his trinitarian doctrine here, I must at least outline some further major features of it,[56] making sure technical terms involved are adequately explained.

Three levels of understanding

Torrance understood the trinitarian mystery of God to be revealed in the gospel itself and the consequent doctrine of the Trinity to arise out of the gospel, a point of great importance to him.[57] He identified three stratified conceptual levels in the development of the doctrine historically and in our own understanding of it.[58] First, at the *evangelical* and *doxological* level, it begins with a personal encounter with Jesus Christ, not merely as a private religious experience, but in the community of the church as we 'indwell' the Scriptures. Here through Christ we come to *know* God as our Father through the presence of the Holy Spirit. Second, at the *theological* level, this incipient knowledge of God himself in his self-revelation becomes more explicit through specific concepts the church has developed, employing new terms not found in Scripture such as 'person' or 'Trinity'. Among these is the key term of the Nicene Creed, that the

---

[52] Torrance, *The Mediation of Christ*, p. xii.

[53] See again ch. 13, esp. 204–206, in Molnar and Habets, *Handbook*.

[54] Thomas F. Torrance, *The Trinitarian Faith* (Edinburgh: T&T Clark, 1988); *The Christian Doctrine of God, One Being Three Persons* (Edinburgh: T&T Clark, 1996). See also his *Trinitarian Perspectives: Towards Doctrinal Agreement* (Edinburgh: T&T Clark, 1994).

[55] Paul Molnar, *Thomas F. Torrance: Theologian of the Trinity* (Farnham: Ashgate, 2009).

[56] See the most helpful introduction to Torrance's trinitarian thought in ch. 8 of Elmer M. Colyer, *How to Read T. F. Torrance: Understanding His Trinitarian and Scientific Theology* (Downers Grove, IL: InterVarsity Press, 2001), pp. 285–321.

[57] For Torrance's integration of the doctrines of salvation and the Trinity, see Dick O. Eugenio, *Communion with the Triune God: The Trinitarian Soteriology of T. F. Torrance* (Eugene, OR: Pickwick, 2014).

[58] See Torrance, *Christian Doctrine of God*, pp. 82–111.

Son is *homoousion*,[59] of one being with the Father, and that consequently we must say that Father, Son and Holy Spirit are of 'One Being' (*mia ousia*). What this implies is that what God appears to be in his revelation of himself in Jesus Christ, he truly is eternally in himself. We may therefore utterly trust the revelation of God we have in Jesus. There is no 'dark inscrutable God behind the back of Jesus Christ'[60] who may or may not love us: the love we see in Jesus is the eternal love of God.

At the third level, the *higher theological* level, we come to explore more fully the trinitarian relations immanent in the Godhead. Torrance agrees with the theologian Karl Rahner, who famously laid down the 'rule' that what is called 'the economic Trinity', that is, the revelation of God in the economy of salvation, in what he is in his relations to us, *is* the 'ontological Trinity',[61] what God is in his true eternal Being, in his inner relations. God's self-revelation to us is true to the reality he is in himself. And yet, importantly for Torrance, the eternal reality of God, the 'ontological Trinity', is *not determined by* his revelation in the economy of salvation (the economic Trinity). Here at this higher theological level, the key term is *perichoresis*, the 'mutual indwelling' or 'co-inhering' of the three divine Persons. This requires an 'onto-relational' concept of 'person'; that is, that what the Persons are in their very being is constituted by their relations to each other. Thus the concept of being (*ousia*) cannot be regarded as impersonal or static (as in the metaphysics of Aristotle used by Aquinas) when referring to God, for God's Being is intensely personal Being. God is a fullness of personal Being in himself. Of course, all these terms and all these theological statements fall far short of the reality of the God they are trying to express.

One in three and three in one

A second major feature of Torrance's doctrine of the Trinity is thus to reject along with Karl Barth and Karl Rahner the approach found in Aquinas that gives priority to the divine essence or nature of the One God and only subsequently considers the three Persons. Rather, the dynamic revelation of God to Moses as the I AM, elucidated in the I AM sayings of Jesus, means, following

---

[59] 'Of the same being' or 'having the same being', from the Greek *homo*, 'same', and *ousia*, 'being'.

[60] A phrase well known by Torrance students from his lectures and classes. In his writings he often made the same point in different language. See e.g. T. F. Torrance, *Preaching Christ Today* (Grand Rapids, MI: Eerdmans, 1994), pp. 55–56, where he says that 'there is no unknown God behind the back of Jesus for us to fear; to see the Lord Jesus is to see the very face of God', and warns of coming 'to think of God as some terrifying deity behind the back of Jesus'. See also *The Trinitarian Faith*, pp. 8 and 135.

[61] 'God in his triune very being', from the Greek *onto*, referring to the 'very being' or 'inner reality' of something.

Athanasius, that 'It is more godly and accurate to signify God from the Son and call him Father, than to name him from his works and call him Unoriginate.'[62] In other words, it is more godly and true to approach God from his Son and call him Father than to think of him in terms of his actions and call him 'The Uncaused'. We do not know God by apprehending him *externally* from a distance as the unoriginate originator (uncaused cause) of his creation, but come to know him in his *intimate inner being* from his revelation in his Son. We therefore come to know him as Being-in-communion. This means that he is 'inherently altruistic, *Being for others, Being who loves*', not out of necessity but out of freedom.[63]

Rapprochement between East and West

Third, it is worth noting that Torrance develops his doctrine of the Trinity from the Greek church fathers, who first formulated it, rather than from Augustine and the later Augustinian tradition. His first major monograph on the doctrine is subtitled *The Evangelical Theology of the Ancient Catholic Church*, and is a close and thorough study of the church fathers.[64] However, differing from the Orthodox theologian John Zizioulas,[65] he is critical of the doctrine of the Cappadocians (with the exception of Gregory of Nazianzus) as leaning too far towards tritheism. He prefers the tradition he traces through Athanasius, Epiphanius and Cyril of Alexandria and maintains that we must not come to the doctrine with a preconceived notion of 'person' drawn from our human experience. While clear on the mutual relations within the Trinity, Torrance felt the so-called 'Social Trinity'[66] model proposed in different ways by Zizioulas and Moltmann was tritheistic in tendency and therefore did not endorse it. Though sympathetic to Moltmann's concern that God in Christ truly enters into our suffering, he refrains from any doctrine of divine passibility (that God is able to 'suffer' and hence is changeable) and retains a carefully nuanced

---

[62] Athanasius, 'First Discourse Against the Arians', *Nicene and Post-Nicene Fathers*, 2nd series (Grand Rapids, MI: Eerdmans, 1891; photolithoprinted 1971), vol. 4, p. 326.

[63] Torrance, *Christian Doctrine of God*, p. 131.

[64] As Jason Radcliff has argued, Torrance is not primarily a theological historian but a historical theologian. He presents his own thoroughly documented perspective. See Jason Robert Radcliff, *Thomas F. Torrance and the Church Fathers: A Reformed, Evangelical, and Ecumenical Reconstruction of the Patristic Tradition* (Eugene, OR: Pickwick, 2014). See also Thomas F. Torrance, *Divine Meaning: Studies in Patristic Hermeneutics* (Edinburgh: T&T Clark, 1995).

[65] See John Zizioulas, *Being as Communion: Studies in Personhood and the Church* (Crestwood, NY: St Vladimir's Seminary Press, 1997). Zizioulas came to Edinburgh at Torrance's invitation to teach Christian Dogmatics, but left after a few years to teach in Glasgow and then at King's College London.

[66] The Trinity is conceived primarily in terms of the mutual relations between its members, hence 'social' in being. Such a view makes it easier to appeal to the Trinity as a model for mutual relations of love between human beings, but runs the danger of being tritheistic in tendency, conceiving the Trinity as three individuals and so neglecting the oneness of divine being.

concept of divine impassibility[67] (that God remains steadfastly constant in being).

It was Torrance's enthusiasm for Athanasius and Cyril that led to his warm relations with the Eastern Orthodox churches and to his attempt to reach a consensus between the Reformed tradition and the Orthodox tradition on the doctrine of the Trinity. He initiated a series of consultations in the 1980s and 1990s between the Orthodox Church and the Reformed tradition, represented by the World Alliance of Reformed Churches. This produced an Agreed Statement on the Holy Trinity in 1992 that Torrance drafted following the consultations. Eastern Orthodox and Western traditions stemming from Augustine have been in dispute for a millennium over the *filioque*; that is, the addition by the Latin West of the phrase 'and the Son' to the statement in the Nicene Creed that the Spirit proceeds 'from the Father'. The consultations deliberately did not tackle this disagreement explicitly, but instead tried to get 'behind' the disagreement to work from the underlying agreement of the two traditions. In this they succeeded, and the Agreed Statement anticipated the subsequent argument of many theologians and patristic scholars that the notion of a fundamental difference of approach between the two traditions (the East beginning with the three Persons, the West with the unity of the one Being) was historically wrong. The Agreed Statement that resulted from Torrance's initiative may therefore be said to mark the historic beginning of a new era in relationships between the Eastern Orthodox and Western churches. Their agreement that the being of the Son and the Spirit did not derive from the person of the Father but from the being of the Father is of particular relevance here as it sought to downplay any concept of hierarchy in the Trinity.

Personal memories[68]

My earliest memories of 'TF' (as he was known, to distinguish him from his brother 'JB') are of someone exciting whom my parents looked forward to seeing and who always asked about each of us. It was when I came to study theology under him in New College that I came to appreciate the unique

[67] See Christopher R. J. Holmes, 'Thomas F. Torrance and the Trinity', in Molnar and Habets, *Handbook*, pp. 161–172, esp. pp. 166–167.

[68] Selected from the article 'T. F. Torrance: In Memoriam – a Personal Reminiscence' by Robert T. Walker in *Participatio*, vol. 1, of the Thomas F. Torrance Theological Fellowship online journal, which contains an extensive cross-linked archive of Torrance material, <www.tftorrance.org>. See pp. 39–46 for the full article on personal reminiscences and appraisal of Torrance and his legacy. See also Bruce Ritchie, *T. F. Torrance in Recollection and Reappraisal* (Eugene, OR: Pickwick, 2021). As a riveting appraisal, rich in detail and insight, of Torrance himself, his theology and impact on students, Ritchie's book is probably one of the best and most readable introductions to T. F. Torrance's theology.

intellectual and theological abilities of the person I had known as 'Uncle Tom'. Several characteristics of his life and personality stand out at once: his energy, his learning, his warmth and pastoral concern. He always seemed to get things done at breakneck speed! The energy of his character and mind found vivid expression in his lectures and left his students exhilarated and enthused by the way he connected theological ideas and by the new vistas and horizons he opened up. He read voluminously and would absorb and retain ideas and became recognized as something of a polymath. But he was a man of great personal warmth and pastoral concern who, notwithstanding a demanding schedule, would invariably find time for students in difficulty or in need of pastoral care. I recall the comment of the wife of one senior Scottish churchman that Tom Torrance was the only one of her husband's peers who treated her as an equal.

I recall his focus on the central questions of the faith and how he could enliven discussion and direct it to the dogmatic centre of the Christian faith in a fresh and fruitful way. I recall his commitment to the church and to the parish ministry. I recall too his forthrightness. His own drive, insight and focus on the central issues of theology, together perhaps with his Scottish Presbyterian background and upbringing, meant that TF spoke directly and to the point. He could therefore be rather blunt, and on occasion unnecessarily so. He could unintentionally leave people behind and fail to carry them with him. For many, this would have been difficult, for his biblical understanding and knowledge of church doctrine and its development were bound together in a Christ-centred integration of prayer, worship and biblical theology which did not appeal to many trends of the day.

Among my own many memories, two sets in particular stand out. The first set was his second-year dogmatics lectures at New College, Edinburgh, which I attended in 1967–8. The second was my weekly visits to him in the nursing home during the last few years of his life when he had been incapacitated by a stroke. Both are indelibly etched into my memory. In the first he is in full theological flight: his dogmatics lectures remain by far the most exhilarating and indeed formative intellectual influence in my life. To find myself editing the same lectures years later was not only a privilege but an opportunity to repay in gratitude some of the debt for all I had learnt from him. The second most vivid set of memories of him is in a much more personal capacity, when, unable to walk without support and needing increasing care, he remained alert and gracious to the end. While it was immensely sad to see him so incapacitated and bereft of so many of his usual stimuli, he retained a keen interest in family and friends or other interests, such as the editing of the lectures.

I learned several details I had not known before; for example, that in China he had been widely known by the locals as Tao chee or 'Torrance mischief', a fact that made him chuckle when reminded of it. I also learnt of some of his sporting interests. Apart from horse riding, which he had learnt in China, and skiing in Scotland and Switzerland, he had as a student been a member of the Hare and Hounds, the Edinburgh University Cross-country Running Society, until the effects of a severe bout of flu had led him to take up hockey instead. One of my favourite reminiscences of his was the story of his being issued with badly fitting skis in the army for patrol during the war in Italy. When one of the skis came off and clattered down the hillside alerting the enemy, he had to ski down on one ski avoiding enemy fire!

Throughout his time in the nursing home, I was constantly struck by his interest in others and his Christian patience and graciousness, and I always came away humbled. It is rather appropriate not only that he should die on Advent Sunday but that having been born and brought up in a missionary family in China, where he had always hoped to be a missionary himself, he should find himself at the end of his life in Edinburgh being attended to by a Chinese nurse. She informed us that he had been trying to convert her when he died!

In summing up Torrance's contribution to the church and to theology, the following features are central. First, he was a man of Scripture and prayer. Brought up in an evangelical home to read through the Bible each year, three chapters each day and five on a Sunday, what he called the 'arcane discipline' of reading and prayer sustained his life and ministry. Second, arising out of that, his thinking was centred in the 'scopus' or centre of Scripture, Jesus Christ, and was therefore deeply trinitarian. Third, his originality lay in his ability to see new connections of ideas, many of them deep connections in Christian doctrine arising out of his knowledge of the history of classical theology. In endeavouring to allow Christ (in the Father through the Spirit) to be the open focus of theology, he saw everything else, all Scripture and doctrine, in a wide and comprehensive theological vision. The attempt to relate all of Scripture and doctrine to Jesus Christ had the effect of ironing out underemphases and overemphases in Christian doctrine. This resulted in a fertility and fruitfulness in his theological vision. True, his habit of working very fast and his sheer volume of work and research did leave him vulnerable on occasion to jumping to inadequate or wrong interpretations and failing to be as historically precise as he might have been. His theology and research were inevitably fragmentary and inadequate at points, but their value is not in their completeness as such but in the extent of their basic adequacy and heuristic capability and fruitfulness.

Finally, TF's chief legacy to the church and to theology is the personal theological integration he forged and expressed in his lectures and writings. His most important legacy in my estimate, is his Christian dogmatics, his balanced integration around Jesus Christ of the whole spectrum of doctrine, Christology, soteriology and the doctrine of the Trinity.

11
Lesslie Newbigin

DONALD LeROY STULTS

When identifying and recognizing British theologians who have had a global influence, one cannot count out Lesslie Newbigin. As a global mission leader, Newbigin was drawn into theology both by his own need of a sound theology from which to work, and because the circumstances in which he worked demanded it. He thought, rightly so, that God's mission to the world must originate from and function around certain core theological tenets, tenets that would truly represent God's motive and method, as well as proscribe the manner in which God wishes Christians to relate to each other – in unity, and to the world – in witnessing.

In this chapter we will note his major theological, missiological and methodological beliefs and practices as he confronted the Western world with the gospel, albeit a 'reintroduction' of the gospel. We will attempt to give an overview of Newbigin's theological convictions, the convictions that drove him in his ministry. It will become clear that, even while he was closely associated with the ecumenical movement, Newbigin remained an evangelical.

Life and work

Lesslie Newbigin was born in 1909 in Newcastle upon Tyne in the north-east of England. He was the son of a shipping merchant and had every intention of following in his father's business until he received a call to ministry. His father was, according to Newbigin, active in public life and a deep thinker, 'a devout and deeply thoughtful Christian' who 'was always struggling with the question of how to apply his Christian faith to the day-to-day issues of business and politics'.[1] He seemed to inherit his father's capacity for an energetic life, while his mind dwelt on the deep aspects of his faith.

---

[1] Lesslie Newbigin, *Unfinished Agenda: An Autobiography* (London: SPCK, 1985; repr., Grand Rapids, MI: Eerdmans, 1985), p. 3.

Newbigin was raised in the Presbyterian Church of England but was sent to a Quaker boarding school in Reading, Berkshire, where he struggled with his faith, eventually giving it up and becoming a sceptic. He was particularly influenced by his geography teacher, S. W. Brown:

> For generations of boys who went through his classes, he taught infinitely more [than just geography]. He created a capacity to think, to break out of stereotypes, to explore new ideas and question old ones. He taught us to read voraciously and get to the heart of the argument of a big book so that we could expound and defend it in debate. He made learning a thrilling experience.[2]

While Newbigin was away at school, a friend of his family, Herbert Gray, left a book for him to read when he came home. It was, as Newbigin recalls, 'a lucid and reasonable exposition of the faith. Again I was not persuaded, but I saw that Christian faith was not irrational.'[3] He went to Queen's College, Cambridge, in 1928 as a non-believer but because of reading William James's book *The Will to Believe*, a book he found in his father's library, he did not entirely dismiss faith as irrational. The idea of believing in something rational was very important to him from an early age.

Student life

While at Cambridge, he was uncomfortable with the evangelicals of the Cambridge Intercollegiate Christian Union since they would try to 'get at him' to believe, but he became involved with the Student Christian Movement (SCM). He met students in SCM who were committed to their faith and who were open to difficult questions. Most of all they were willing to accept him just as he was – 'sceptical and basically unconvinced'.[4] He began observing 'the morning watch' – a time of Bible reading and prayer. At that time he did not know whether God existed or not. With the help of William James's book he knew that he was not being irrational 'seeking the help of One of whose existence there was no proof'.[5] He met Arthur Watkins, an older student and captain of the rugby team, who more than anyone else at Cambridge or the SCM introduced and 'drew' him into personal faith. Newbigin realized that a 'profound devotion to Christ was at the heart of Watkins' life'.[6]

---

[2] Ibid., p. 5.
[3] Ibid., p. 6. Newbigin does not give the title of this first book to influence him.
[4] Ibid., p. 10.
[5] Ibid.
[6] Ibid.

Newbigin went on a student mission to the coal mines in Rhondda Valley in South Wales. It was a profound experience that changed his perspective about the gospel. After the miners got hold of some strong drink they began fighting among themselves. Newbigin returned to his tent totally defeated. Their situation seemed hopeless and he did not have the means to cope with it: he felt as if he had nothing to contribute. That night as he lay awake he had a vision of the cross that spanned 'the space between heaven and earth, between ideals and present realities, and with arms that embraced the whole world'.[7] The vision influenced him deeply.

Each summer about a hundred or so students would engage in the Cambridge Evangelistic Campaign, a preaching campaign in the industrial towns of the Midlands and North. The students would engage in open-air preaching and visit the factories during lunch breaks. They needed the ability to communicate effectively while standing on a soap box on a crowded street. They had to be able to endure heckling and also the serious questions that emerged from the crowd of working men and women. It was good training for Newbigin's missionary work in India, where he was involved in street preaching.[8]

Newbigin confessed that he was drawn to participate in these campaigns even before he had anything to give to the listeners, but after his vision in Rhondda Valley, he could (he wrote) 'at least point to the cross of Jesus as the ground of hope for every human being'.[9] While visiting a tenement house where a man was dying with tuberculosis, he realized that he did not have words for the situation because a merely humanistic hope was not enough for something like this. He writes, 'I went back to Cambridge at the end of that vacation a committed Christian.'[10] He was, he admits, an example of a person who had a faith that was seeking understanding.[11] He subsequently threw himself with enthusiasm into the Student Christian Movement. He had observed the devotion of men and women who were committed to a worldwide Christian movement and he experienced a thrilling sense of sharing in this global enterprise.[12] He later served for two years on staff as the secretary of the SCM in Glasgow.

Newbigin moved back to Cambridge to study theology at Westminster College, the Presbyterian college where the principal, John Oman, influenced him, but from his experience in the SCM, he felt that the spiritual preparation of ministers was lacking there. He attended the Edinburgh Quadrennial of the

---

7 Ibid., pp. 11–12.
8 Ibid., p. 12.
9 Ibid.
10 Ibid., p. 13.
11 Ibid., p. 20.
12 Ibid., p. 13

SCM in January 1933, where he heard J. H. Oldham speak, and this profoundly influenced his life, both in 1933 and much later when he retired to Britain in 1974. In his autobiography he reflects on this speech. He writes:

> J. H. Oldham, in a profound address, spoke of the radical departure of Europe from the Christian faith when it followed Descartes and the pioneers of the Enlightenment. In other words – though it was not said so bluntly – the mission field was here in the 'Christian world'.[13]

On a more personal note, Newbigin reveals the state of his faith at this particular time of his life. He writes:

> I knew with an overwhelming certainty that my life was in God's hands, that he and not I had the direction of it, and I would be free of doubt and anxiety. At that moment I did not believe: I knew.[14]

Missionary service and 'retirement'

Newbigin was ordained by the Presbytery of Edinburgh and commissioned by the Church of Scotland to work in the Madras Mission in India. His work between 1936 and 1947 was to serve as a village evangelist, preaching in the streets. After years of working towards the unity of the church he became a bishop in Madurai in the newly formed Church of South India, serving from 1947 to 1959. Subsequently, he became General Secretary of the International Missionary Council and helped it to integrate with the World Council of Churches in 1961. He then served as Associate General with responsibility for the Commission of Mission and Evangelism until 1965, upon which he returned to India and resumed the role of Bishop of Madras until 1974.[15]

Upon his retirement in 1974 he taught at Selly Oak Colleges in Birmingham as Professor of Ecumenics and Theology of Mission until 1979, serving also as the moderator of the United Reformed Church from 1978 to 1979. A small inner-city congregation of the United Reformed Church in Birmingham needed a minister and since he was unsuccessful in finding someone and did not want to see the church closed, he assumed the role from 1979 to 1989. In 1982, while minister of this congregation, he organized the Gospel and Our Culture group to consider what form Christian mission should take in 'pagan Britain'.[16]

---

[13] Ibid., p. 26.

[14] Ibid., p. 19.

[15] Charles West, *Biographical Dictionary of Christian Missions*, ed. Gerald H. Anderson (New York: Macmillan Reference USA, 1998), p. 491.

[16] Ibid., 'Newbigin', p. 491.

Newbigin's penchant for desiring that faith be rational seemed to set him up for the writing he would do in retirement. However, he never allowed his preoccupation with the mind to push aside the spiritual dimension of the faith. They were never at odds with each other, but together provided the impetus to charge forwards in his engagement with the Western world.

Newbigin as a theologian

A. F. Walls asserts that Newbigin was 'probably the most influential British theologian of the twentieth century'.[17] 'Newbigin's theological advocacy brought him to prominence in the International Missionary Council (IMC).'[18] Scott W. Sunquist notes that some of the top theologians of the age – such as Barth, Brunner, Bonhoeffer, Visser 't Hooft, Hoekendijk – were involved in the theological discussions and publishing of theological articles.[19] Later, after the IMC merged with the World Council of Churches, Newbigin became the first director of the Division of World Mission and Evangelism as well as editing the *International Review of Mission*.

Newbigin's interests, style and situation caused his theological approach to be accommodated to the needs of his constituents, from Indian pastors across the spectrum of the ecumenical movement. His earlier writings were more like biblical expositions: *Household of God* (1952), *Sin and Salvation* (1956). His apologetic style began quite early with *I Believe* (1946), and developed later in *Honest Religion* (1966) and *The Finality of Christ* (1969): it bloomed when he focused on his rebuttal of the Enlightenment ideology of the Western world. According to Philip Burton, Newbigin believed that the most genuine theology is practical and pastoral.[20] Geoffrey Wainwright writes, 'For Newbigin, Christian theology was precisely and intrinsically "working theology" – constantly developed and refined and formulated within, and addressed to the daily lives of, Christians and non-Christians.'[21] 'He was constantly reflecting on the pastoral challenges of Christian ministry in light of the gospel.'[22] 'Newbigin theologized in the midst of practice and for its

---

[17] A. F. Walls, 'James Edward Lesslie Newbigin (1909–98)', in Martin Davie, Tim Grass, Stephen R. Holmes and T. A. Noble (eds.), *The New Dictionary of Theology: Systematic and Historical*, 2nd edn (London: Inter-Varsity Press; Downers Grove, IL: InterVarsity Press, 2016), pp. 615–616.
[18] Ibid., p. 616.
[19] Scott W. Sunquist, *Understanding Christian Mission: Participation in Suffering and Glory* (Grand Rapids, MI: Baker Academic, 2013), p. 6.
[20] Geoffrey Wainwright, *Lesslie Newbigin: A Theological Life* (Oxford: Oxford University Press, 2000), p. 397.
[21] Ibid.
[22] Ibid.

better pursuit.'[23] This way of theological thinking is the reverse of typical Western thinking, which is that the task of theology is to begin with theory and inform practice (a dichotomy), while Newbigin believed it should not have this dichotomy. Once we have determined our theological convictions, the interaction with practical ministry refines and develops our theology.[24]

The twenty-five

The World Council of Churches (WCC) was founded in 1947, and in 1952 they held a world mission conference in Willingen in Germany to hammer out the WCC perspective of the Christian global mission. Newbigin reports, 'My main job at Willingen was with the theological group.'[25] He was asked, as a part of this group, to write a 'fresh statement on the missionary calling of the Church'.[26] A committee of twenty-five theologians (including Barth, Brunner, Niebuhr and others) was formed, and to Newbigin's surprise he was included in that group.[27] He was selected to lead the group in future sessions.[28] He was puzzled by this decision but surmised that it was because he was theologically between the Americans and the Continentals, and because he was the only member of the group who was a pastor and not a professor. He wrote to his wife, Helen, from Geneva about leading the group:

> They are exceptionally able people with gleams of vision and favourite theories all of their own, and they are all accustomed to being listened to and not contradicted, but it is very hard to get them to stick to a certain line of thought.[29]

Consistently evangelical

Since Newbigin became totally absorbed with working for the WCC, some may assume that his theology would reflect the attitudes and positions of the more radical and liberal members. That assumption is incorrect and in some ways unfair. Anyone who followed Newbigin along his intellectual and spiritual journey knew that his evangelical views, begun while still a student, never deviated all his life. They were developed and refined along the way but maintained their core ideas. Wainwright asserts, 'The lineament of his thinking . . .

---

[23] Ibid., p. 26.
[24] Ibid., p. 397.
[25] Ibid., p. 138.
[26] Ibid.
[27] Ibid., p. 131.
[28] Ibid., p. 132.
[29] Ibid., p. 139.

remained constant for sixty years, and as his ideas developed and expanded, the fundamental pattern continued to be readily recognisable.'[30] He was entirely capable of working with and alongside persons of many perspectives of the faith without compromising his own evangelical beliefs that profoundly shaped his theological convictions.

Newbigin testifies to the fact that while he was associated with the SCM as a student, his mind was filled with numerous questions, many of which he did not find any answers to at the time. He was determined to discover what he could believe in. He decided to do an in-depth study of the book of Romans, believing that he would find a 'complete and condensed statement of the Gospel'. While at Westminster College, Cambridge, he spent several months intensely studying the Greek text of the book, surrounded by a few major commentaries. He was not so impressed with Karl Barth or C. H. Dodd, but was deeply influenced by reading James Denney:

> That was a turning point in my theological journey. I began study as a typical liberal. I ended with the strong conviction about 'the finished work of Christ,' about the centrality and objectivity of the atonement accomplished on Calvary. The decisive agent in this shift was James Denney. His commentary on Romans carried the day as far as I was concerned.[31]

He appreciated H. H. Farmer, Professor of Systematic Theology at Westminster College, Cambridge, for being accessible for 'face-to-face' discussions, where Newbigin had the freedom to present his 'half-developed' theological thoughts to him and have them thoroughly refined by deep examination while having a rigorous argument with him.[32]

Newbigin's book *Sin and Salvation* contains the heart of evangelical faith, discovered and believed as a theological student in the 1930s, and commended to the West following his return to Britain upon retirement.[33] Interestingly, liberals thought that Newbigin might be a 'fundamentalist', but they failed to see that to be a 'fundamentalist' meant presupposing a disjunction between 'facts' and 'values', the view of modernists and secularists, whom Newbigin argued against. It was the 'integrated vision of the Scriptures and of classic Christian doctrine' that he desired to retrieve.[34]

---

[30] Ibid., p. 26.
[31] Newbigin, *Unfinished Agenda*, p. 30.
[32] Ibid.
[33] Wainwright, *Theological Life*, pp. 390–391.
[34] Ibid.

Newbigin's mission to the Western world

Newbigin's practical ministry experience was primarily in India, but because of his earlier work with the WCC he became acquainted with the theological development of theology in the West. As a missionary he understood that the gospel and theology needed to be geared towards the culture of the audience but never to the point where the essential teachings of the gospel were compromised. While participating in dialogue with Hindus and Muslims in India, he enjoyed the interaction but felt it was important to share the deepest aspects of the Christian faith, especially the significance of the work of Christ's incarnation, death and resurrection. Later he remarked that doing evangelism and ministry in Britain was far more difficult than what he experienced in India. In Britain there was a cold indifference to the gospel that he did not encounter in India.

Many think of Newbigin as an apologist. Wainwright identifies him as a Christian apologist but an apologist on his own terms. Wainwright describes the dilemma Christian apologists face:

> The Christian apologist is caught puzzling over the relation between Christianity and modernity and then cutting through the ambiguities in order to offer in the gospel a new–old alternative to other worldviews that always end up in either self-idolatry or despair, if not both.[35]

Newbigin tried to redefine Christian apologetics. Traditional apologetics had compromised with cultural expectations and therefore did not maintain the integrity of the gospel.[36] Modern culture believes that truth is supported by so-called 'self-evident' truths,[37] so that Christian apologists feel the need to demonstrate the truth of the gospel through self-evident truths. Newbigin did not agree with this method, because the gospel is not based on self-evident truth but on the gospel itself.[38] The Christian apologist, Newbigin believed, must witness to the truth by 'telling the story'.[39]

The reason for Newbigin's insistence on his view of apologetic theology came because his critique of the Western world demanded such an approach. Vinoth

---

[35] Ibid., p. 27.

[36] Donald LeRoy Stults, *Grasping Truth and Reality: Lesslie Newbigin's Theology to the Western World* (Eugene, OR: Wipf & Stock, 2008), pp. 38–39.

[37] Ibid., p. 41; cf. Lesslie Newbigin, *Truth to Tell: The Gospel as Public Truth* (Grand Rapids, MI: Eerdmans, 1991), p. 51.

[38] Stults, *Grasping Truth and Reality*, p. 41; cf. Lesslie Newbigin, *Proper Confidence: Faith, Doubt, and Certainty in Christian Discipleship* (Grand Rapids, MI: Eerdmans, 1995), p. 96.

[39] Stults, *Grasping Truth and Reality*, pp. 41, 43; cf. Newbigin, *Proper Confidence*, p. 94.

Ramachandra, nuclear engineer and Anglican lay theologian, believes that Newbigin 'has mounted one of the most vigorous theological critiques of modern secular culture'.[40] Missionaries are aware that articulating the faith in various cultures will cause the doctrines to be perceived and understood from the perspective of each culture. This does not mean compromise by changing a particular doctrine into inappropriate ideas and systems that contradict the Christian faith. So, the theologian, particularly the theologian in mission, must speak to a culture while confronting those ideas and basic beliefs that contradict the gospel and biblical faith. Each culture has to be taken seriously and the gospel has to be explained in such a manner that it can be understood as it was originally when first spoken and written. This includes Western cultures.

When Newbigin retired back in Britain in 1974, he began to critique Western culture, trying to understand Western culture as it really is. Scott Sunquist gives us an overview of the process that led up to Newbigin's conclusion:

> Mission has come out of the eighteenth and nineteenth centuries, in which it was a special task that some Christians elected to participate in by forming special missional structures. The Missional Church movement of the twentieth century came out of discussions of the ecumenical movement and was energised by Newbigin's challenge in his 1984 Warfield Lectures at Princeton Theological Seminary, which asked the question, 'Can the West be Converted?' The lecture pointed to the missionary nature of the church universal applied to the West. The West had become a mission field in the minds of missiologists as never before.[41]

Newbigin's idea of the West's being a mission field came, he explains, from J. H. Oldham, who spoke at the Edinburgh Conference of 1910. George A. Hunsberger describes the challenge and articulates the question facing missions to the Western world:

> Enlightenment culture . . . places a high premium on the rational, autonomous self, a belief in the inevitability of progress, and confidence in technology and technique for managing the word and constructing social order. The question arises whether, and to what extent, churches in the societies of a waning Christendom have lost their distinctive character

---

[40] Stults, *Grasping Truth and Reality*, p. 2; cf. Vinoth Ramachandra, *The Recovery of Mission: Beyond a Pluralist Paradigm* (Carlisle: Paternoster Press, 1976), p. 144.

[41] Scott Sunquist, *Understanding Christian Mission: Participation in Suffering and Glory* (Grand Rapids, MI: Baker Academic, 2013), pp. 172–173.

as communities of witness by becoming overly accommodated to such cultural assumptions, values, and instincts. This question fuels the challenge put so directly by Lesslie Newbigin to imagine what would be involved in the missionary encounter of the gospel with Western culture.[42]

Newbigin answers the question of how to engage Western culture by insisting that a theological understanding of the situation would be the first priority because this would subsequently allow the reordering of culture.[43] Newbigin writes, 'We need a theological understanding of the issues involved in a global encounter with modernity.'[44] Newbigin did not think that traditional missionary sending agencies in the West understood that their homelands, the Western world with its 'aggressive paganism', was the most serious challenge to the gospel.[45] This implied that Western theology must seriously consider the missionary nature of the church having an engagement with Western culture and thus discard the idea that the church is a static institution of the culture, expected to reflect culture's values.[46]

Reintroducing the gospel to the West

At the time of the Enlightenment, according to Newbigin, there were two belief systems that were introduced to Western culture which resulted in a loss of purpose and in scepticism – humanism and dualism.[47] Newbigin's solution to this was to reintroduce the gospel to Western culture to restore purpose, and to reunite it with true reality through Jesus Christ. This would be accomplished through the church witnessing in the public square about the 'superior rationality of the Christian belief system'.[48]

We need to be clear about the difference between the gospel and Christianity. In 1966 Newbigin emphasized this in a two-part speech to a mission and evangelism conference in Salvador de Bahia, Brazil. He described the gospel not as a religious experience, but as

---

[42] George A. Hunsberger, 'Accommodation', *Evangelical Dictionary of World Mission*, ed. A. Scott Moreau (Grand Rapids, MI: Baker, 2000), pp. 11–12.

[43] Stults, *Grasping Truth and Reality*, p. 26; cf. Lesslie Newbigin, *The Open Secret: Sketches for a Missionary Theology* (Grand Rapids, MI: Eerdmans, 1978), p. 11.

[44] Lesslie Newbigin, *A Word in Season: Perspectives on Christian World Mission* (Grand Rapids, MI: Eerdmans, 1994), p. 194.

[45] Newbigin, *Open Secret*, p. 10.

[46] See Stults, *Grasping Truth and Reality*, p. 23, and Lesslie Newbigin, *Trinitarian Faith and Today's Mission* (Richmond, VA: John Knox Press, 1964), p. 12.

[47] Stults, *Grasping Truth and Reality*, p. viii.

[48] Ibid., p. ix.

a factual statement that God, who is the author, the sustainer, and the goal of all that exists, of all being and meaning and all truth, has become present in our human history as the man Jesus, whom we can know and love and serve; and that by his incarnation, his ministry, his death and resurrection he has finally broken the powers that oppress us and has created a space and a time in which we who are unholy can nevertheless live in fellowship with God who is holy.[49]

In seeking to reintroduce the gospel to the West, some themes in Newbigin's thinking point to the reason for and application of his missional methodology. The first is that the dogmas of the incarnation and of the Trinity constitute the essential starting point for understanding reality as a whole and lead the way 'into a wider and more inclusive rationality than the real but limited rationality of the reductionist views that try to explain the whole of reality in terms of the natural sciences'.[50] Newbigin is clear about the many rationalities in science that seek to explain reality from their perspective. The Christian view in no way negates these rationalities and he acknowledges that their explanations are proper from their own perspective. Newbigin, however, considers them 'narrow' rationalities, whereas the Christian view is 'broader' and more inclusive.

Another idea prominent in Newbigin's thinking is 'public truth'. By that he meant that the gospel is public truth, not a neutral or abstract starting point from which we can defend or commend Christian truth, but a truth that is personal, since it is given by God through Jesus Christ and is by means of revelation, and received by faith. It is truth for all, universal truth that is true for all, and has a place in public conversations: hence it is truth for the public square. It is not just a private affair that individuals embrace as purely subjective, but is personal and subjective while also being universal and objective. It is personal in the sense that it is not merely abstract and propositional:

It is personal because it comes from God … The Incarnation is the supreme example of God's involvement in the material world … The cosmos is not a pure mechanistic universe that slavishly follows rigid laws: it is where God and humanity meet.[51]

Newbigin rejects the subjective–objective dualism of the West. When he engages Western science and scientists, he presses this point, one derived from

---

[49] Wainwright, *Theological Life*, p. 387.

[50] Ibid., p. 366.

[51] Stults, *Grasping Truth and Reality*, pp. 42–43.

Michael Polanyi.[52] Some scientists have claimed to be wholly objective in their work but Polanyi asserts that scientists indwell a scientific tradition that has certain assumptions scientists believe. So, science is a faith commitment.[53] Newbigin calls this a 'fiduciary framework'.[54]

Another key phrase used by Newbigin is 'plausibility structure'. A plausibility structure is defined by Peter Berger as 'a social structure of ideas and practices that create the conditions determining what beliefs are plausible within the society in question'.[55] In Newbigin's book *Foolishness to the Greeks*, he quotes Berger's view that Western culture does not have a plausibility structure. Essentially, Berger says, Western culture has no plausibility structure, the 'acceptance of which is normally taken for granted without argument and dissent from which is regarded as heresy'. Consequently, Westerners are by default required to be heretics.[56] While 'plausibility structure' is related to culture generally, 'fiduciary framework', in Newbigin's parlance, is restricted to the scientific community that accepts certain presuppositions in their work, thus having a belief system that functions as a framework of belief.[57]

Newbigin believed that because there is a variety of Christologies in the New Testament, this represented the fact that there would be a variety of Christologies geared to individual cultures, without compromising the essential gospel. The gospel is translated into receptor cultures (designated the 'Third World' at that time) in the form of preaching, songs, stories and drama. Newbigin calls the process of the gospel going into various lands and cultures, carried there by the New Testament church, and becoming embedded in those cultures as 'inculturation'.[58] The means by which the gospel is embedded into cultures is termed by missiologists 'contextualization'. Newbigin addresses the question of contextualization, something missionaries living cross-culturally think about but not something theologians living in their own culture often think about. They are generally comfortable in their culture and over-accommodate their theology to their culture. Newbigin considers Western culture to be dominated by non-Christian ideology, most prominently Enlightenment thinking. He later described English (and, by extension, Western) culture as pagan: 'England is

---

52 Newbigin, *Proper Confidence*, p. 39.
53 Michael Polanyi, *Personal Knowledge: Towards a Post-Critical Philosophy* (Chicago: University of Chicago Press, 1958), p. 171.
54 Newbigin, *Proper Confidence*, p. 41.
55 Quoted in Wainwright, *Theological Life*, p. 356.
56 Newbigin, *Foolishness*, pp. 10–11.
57 Newbigin, *Proper Confidence*, p. 41.
58 Lesslie Newbigin, *The Gospel and Pluralistic Society* (Grand Rapids, MI: Eerdmans, 1989), pp. 154–155.

a pagan society and the development of a truly missionary encounter with this very tough form of paganism is the greatest intellectual and practical task facing the Church.'[59] Newbigin believed that Christians ought to practise selective accommodation by communicating within Western culture in ways that are understandable to the culture without compromising the gospel. In much the same manner, Christians around the world must communicate within their various pagan cultures.

In the West, there is a problem of having to deal with Enlightenment culture and methodology that makes this communication particularly difficult since it has existed beside Christianity for centuries and has succeeded in permeating every aspect of culture, even the church. The church has become too comfortable in the West and has not realized how it has compromised with Western culture. This led Newbigin to say that 'the idea of a missionary encounter means ... that the Church refute the assumptions of Western culture'.[60] The secularization of culture in the West is a very difficult ideology to deal with and is spreading around the world, creating the same difficulties in a variety of cultures, especially in the major cities, that Christians face in the West. In the end, Newbigin did not like the term 'contextualization', particularly the way it was used by many in the ecumenical movement. They had radicalized the term and made the social and political context the norm for theology. The first indications of this drift towards liberal and humanistic theology began at the International Missionary Council's meeting in Strasbourg in 1960 and subsequently dominated the thinking of the WCC. Newbigin strongly believed that this was inappropriate contextualization because theology was reshaped to promote cultural ideologies.[61]

Newbigin on doctrine

Newbigin held to the ancient creeds, particularly the Nicene Creed, as confessions of faith that preserved and 'safeguarded the identity and ontology of the Godhead', specifically the God of the biblical story – Father, Son and Holy Spirit, the one true God. One can see from reading his earliest writings that he had a firm grasp of the essential doctrines that defined Christianity.[62] His interaction with religious teachers in India helped refine and clarify certain Christian doctrines (such as his Christology) that were to become mainstays for him.

---

[59] Newbigin, *Unfinished Agenda*, p. 249.
[60] Stults, *Grasping Truth and Reality*, p. 24.
[61] Ibid., p. 244.
[62] Wainwright, *Theological Life*, p. 391.

However, his interaction with other thinkers preceded his ministry in India. While on his journey to India from Liverpool to Madras on the ship *City of Cairo*, Newbigin wrote the book *Christian Freedom in the Modern World*, which was a rebuttal of the writings of John Macmurray. Macmurray's writings had helped him greatly and were very influential among Newbigin's SCM friends and colleagues, but he was concerned about the conclusions Christians were drawing from Macmurray's work. Newbigin carefully reread Macmurray and, in doing so, concluded that the problem was 'at the point that had been so central to my thinking: the necessity of an atonement provided by God without which real freedom is impossible'.[63]

Newbigin was a prolific writer and his early understandings of the evangelical faith remained with him throughout his life, but he also developed additional theological convictions in response to the challenges of his ministry in India and Britain. After retiring in Britain in 1974, he used his theological convictions to evaluate the belief system of Western culture in response to its spiritual problems. He focused on developing a theology of mission while teaching at Selly Oak Colleges and pastoring an old inner-city church. A. F. Walls believes that it was during this time that Newbigin wrote some of his finest works, especially as he analysed the post-Christian West and critiqued the influence of Enlightenment ideology on Western thought.[64]

George Hunsberger characterizes Newbigin's writing as essentially theology, produced on the anvil of service in the church.[65] This is the model for theological writing from the apostle Paul, who produced the first theological material while a missionary. Newbigin did not write a systematic theology as a singular work, but was a systematic thinker, not unlike John Wesley, whose theological writings and sermons responded to the deepest questions of the flock he was shepherding.[66] Newbigin asserted that the closest thing he had to a systematic theology was his book *A Faith for This One World?*, a doctrinal study written for pastors in India.[67] Wilbert R. Shenk observes, 'Newbigin's mode of discourse was theological, even though he consistently disclaimed any pretension to being a professional theologian.'[68] As mentioned earlier, the theological convictions Newbigin developed when he was young were carried forward the rest of his life, but were recast into a theology of mission because

[63] Newbigin, *Unfinished Agenda*, p. 39.
[64] Walls, 'James Edward Lesslie Newbigin', p. 616.
[65] Stults, *Grasping Truth and Reality*, p. 28.
[66] Ibid., p. 29.
[67] Ibid.; cf. Lesslie Newbigin, *A Faith for This One World?* (London: SCM Press, 1961).
[68] Wilbert R. Shenk, 'Lesslie Newbigin's Contribution to Mission Theology', *International Bulletin of Missionary Research* (April 2000), pp. 59–63; also in *TransMission*, Special Edition (1998), pp. 3–6.

that is what a confrontation with Western culture necessitated.[69] 'Newbigin's theology is thoroughly missiological, and his missiology is theological.'[70] The historian of missions, A. F. Walls, observed that Newbigin's theology of mission was 'essentially Trinitarian', a 'three-dimensional theology of mission, *proclamation* based on the Father's authority, *presence* rooted in the Son's work and *prevenience* arising from the Spirit's preparatory activity'.[71]

Theology of mission

Rodger Bassham gives an excellent definition of theology of mission: '[It] refers to those theological presuppositions, statements, and principles which critically reflect upon and explicate God's purpose for the church in relation to the world.'[72] This definition captures Newbigin's passion for a theologically guided mission of the church in the Western world. Geoffrey Wainwright points to the central theological conviction that dominated Newbigin's perspective and practice of mission, saying: 'Christ's atoning work constituted the centre set within an increasingly explicit Trinitarian frame persistently directed toward the goal of God's reign.'[73] The core theological conviction that drove Newbigin's theological pursuit was trinitarian doctrine. Kirsteen Kim asserts that Newbigin describes the trinitarian basis of his theology of mission by describing mission as 'bearing the witness of the Spirit', the Spirit thus 'leading the way' for the church to follow in mission. The mission of Christianity and the church is in reality the mission of the Spirit.[74] Newbigin explains it more fully as follows:

> Only a fully Trinitarian doctrine would be adequate, setting the work of Christ in the Church in the context of the over-ruling providence of the Father in all the life of the world and the sovereign freedom of the Spirit who is the Lord and not the auxiliary of the Church.[75]

I have laid the foundations for appreciating Newbigin's understanding of Christianity and a theology of mission. How then does one move from 'knowing' about Christianity to 'becoming' a Christian? In Newbigin's

[69] Stults, *Grasping Truth and Reality*, p. 45.
[70] Shenk, 'Contribution', p. 46.
[71] Walls, 'James Edward Lesslie Newbigin', p. 616.
[72] R. Bassham, *Mission Theology* (Pasadena, CA: William Carey Library, 1979), p. 7.
[73] Wainwright, *Theological Life*, p. 26.
[74] Kirsteen J. Kim, 'The Holy Spirit', in John Corrie, Samuel Escobar and Wilbert R. Shenk (eds.), *Dictionary of Mission Theology: Evangelical Foundations* (Nottingham: Inter-Varsity Press, 2007), p. 164.
[75] Newbigin, *Unfinished Agenda*, p. 199.

presentation (as a part of the document 'I Believe') at a leadership conference in 1945, he said that the 'Christian faith . . . is being laid hold of or by something from beyond oneself'.[76] Later he reiterates this:

> The Gospel comes to us not as a set of propositions which I can lay hold of and so stand as one who knows the truth among the multitude who do not, but rather as a truth which has laid hold on me, though I am still only a groping and stumbling intelligence in no way superior to others.[77]

Newbigin approached the knowledge of God by way of his epistemology and his view of revelation. A. F. Walls sees Newbigin's epistemology as expressed in personal relations, where the knowledge of God is personal knowledge we receive as persons in relationship with God. The knowledge of God, like scientific knowledge, is not something individuals conjure up from within them but is given to them through their interaction with a God who is there and who communicates with humanity.[78]

Newbigin's insights into revelation go back to a paper he wrote in 1935–6. He states that revelation is dependent 'upon two beliefs about the nature of the world and of man', that the meaning of the world is personal and that the meaning of human life is in fellowship.[79] Revelation is mediated through the witness of those who have seen God's actions in history. We know God because he has revealed himself to us. The Bible draws together the acts of God in history, witnessed by those who recorded God's deeds in the Bible. The Bible thus becomes an important avenue of divine revelation, and humanity can come to know God through his self-revelation as found in historical witnesses in the Bible. The self-revelation of God is salvific: knowledge that can lead to salvation. In his dialogue with those of other religions in India, Newbigin heard testimony of how God led people to himself even as they were involved in other religions. God's prevenient grace, applied by the Holy Spirit to the heart of individuals, gave sufficient knowledge of himself to lead these persons to salvation.[80]

After serving in India for many years and listening to the spokesmen for other religions, he learned they believed that ultimate reality is unknowable.

---

[76] Newbigin, 'I Believe,' A Paper Presented at the Regional Leaders' Conference, Held at the American College, Madura, S. India, December 1945 (Madras: SCM Press, Madras), p. 74.

[77] Ibid., p. 75.

[78] Walls, 'James Edward Lesslie Newbigin', p. 616.

[79] Lesslie Newbigin, 'Revelation', unpublished theology paper presented at Westminster College, Cambridge, 1936.

[80] Newbigin discusses revelation at length in A Faith for this One World?

Newbigin asserts, however, that humanity can know ultimate reality because the triune God is ultimate reality. Ultimate reality is therefore personal and not impersonal, as some religions teach.[81] Newbigin posits that God has created a contingent universe, one that is separate from himself but he interacts with and in it.[82] Newbigin always had a concern for a rational understanding of the faith. He writes:

> The basis of any attempt to understand the world as a rational whole is the conviction that man can know and recognise truth, and therefore he can attain to a knowledge of reality which is not merely a private mental construction but a true apprehension of that which is true for all.[83]

Christianity is different from the philosophies of the Graeco-Roman era in that these philosophies expressed truth in timeless statements, while the Bible speaks of truth and reveals God primarily through stories and the confession of witnesses. This does not mean that the Bible is not telling the truth, but only that it tells it in a different manner. Biblical stories are not a special history but take place in the midst of the history of the world.[84] Newbigin says about the Bible:

> Within the Christian tradition the Bible is received as the testimony of those events to which God has disclosed ('revealed') the shape of the story as a whole, because in Jesus the beginning and the end of the story, the alpha and omega, are revealed, made known, disclosed.[85]

Within world history the church is active in ministry and witnessing. Newbigin believes that mission is the very nature of the church. The Christian faith is a way of understanding world history, challenging and relativizing all other interpretations and models of history.[86] Theological colleges and seminaries have often placed missiology in the area of practical theology and not as central to Christian doctrine, but the separation of the church from mission is 'theologically indefensible'.[87] Christian faith, then, involves a theology of mission, and mission is the context within which the most vital theology is

---

[81] Newbigin, *Proper Confidence*, p. 95.
[82] Stults, *Grasping Truth and Reality*, pp. 92–94.
[83] Newbigin, 'I Believe', pp. 75–76.
[84] Newbigin, *Open Secret*, pp. 82, 86.
[85] Ibid., p. 85.
[86] Ibid., pp. 88–89.
[87] Ibid., p. 2.

honed. Theology does not begin with ideas, but with praxis,[88] yet this does not make this theology inferior or secondary to the main doctrines. Theology in and of mission is the overarching principle that unites all theology.

Along with his emphasis on a trinitarian perspective for his theology of mission, Newbigin focuses on other doctrines that are relevant for the church in mission. His soteriology, his emphasis on the Holy Spirit as the dynamic and power of mission, his doctrine of election, and the purpose of the church receive particular attention. His soteriology, influenced as we saw by James Denney, centred on the cross of Christ demonstrating God's judgement of sin and love of humanity. Wainwright highlights the importance of Denney's commentary on the book of Romans in *The Expositor's Greek New Testament*, where Denney affirms 'the propitiatory virtue of the blood of Christ. Christ as a propitiation is the inmost soul of the Gospel for the sinful man'.[89]

This Christology is central. In his discussion of the formation of the canon of Scripture, Newbigin says that it was shaped by the church's understanding of the first witnesses of the life, death and resurrection of Jesus, and how Jesus Christ is the starting point of the church's attempt to articulate a Christology, and it has a 'real destination in universal confession within varied cultures'.[90] Further, 'The controlling belief that shared the selection and handling of material was that in Jesus the meaning of the whole of history is revealed. Within this perspective the Jesus of history *is* the Christ of faith.'[91] In dialogue with persons of another faith, the Christian remains committed to the belief that Jesus is the ultimate authority of the faith.[92] Wainwright rightly asserts that Newbigin held to belief in the finality of Jesus:

> In both practice and theory, Newbigin … remained constant in his attachment to the comprehensiveness, centrality, and finality of Jesus Christ in the areas of creation, redemption, and consummation, while locating Jesus Christ theologically in an increasingly explicit trinitarian framework.[93]

Newbigin resisted the move towards inclusion of an 'inter-faith dimension' promoted by elements in the ecumenical movement that would compromise

---

[88] Ibid., p. 95.
[89] Wainwright, *Theological Life*, p. 31.
[90] Newbigin, *Open Secret*, p. 156.
[91] Ibid., p. 157.
[92] Ibid., p. 164.
[93] Wainwright, *Theological Life*, p. 205.

and essentially deny the centrality and finality of Christ.[94] He firmly believed that Jesus is Lord and this meant that Jesus has a universal claim to ultimate authority and this would ultimately clash with the *cultus publicus*. This happened during Jesus' own ministry within the Roman Empire and will happen in every culture to a certain degree – even (or especially) Western culture. This implies that the gospel is public truth, not just relegated as it is in the West to being a private faith. The resurrection of Jesus from the dead as an event within history cannot be fitted into any view of the world that exists but must become the totally new starting point of a belief that defines and nurtures the gospel in every culture.[95]

Newbigin discusses the role of the Holy Spirit in the work of God in Christ and through the church. This is interconnected with his doctrine of election. Newbigin defines the elect as 'those who are chosen to be bearers of a blessing are chosen for the sake of *all*'. This was the meaning of the calling of Israel and of the church.[96] It was a selection, a few chosen for the sake of all.[97] Newbigin calls this a 'scandal of the particularity'.[98] The doctrine of election is presented in the Bible as 'the story of a universal purpose carried out through a continuous series of particular choices'.[99] The Holy Spirit is the instigator and dynamic energy of mission, the One who inspires, directs and goes before the church in mission. He articulates all doctrines of the faith through his theology of mission.

Those who are chosen form the church, and through it exercise their calling. Newbigin believes that Western theology must rid itself of its view that the church is an institution of culture and therefore should be defined in 'static, institutional terms'.[100] Newbigin notes that a great deal of the substance of the Western church tradition took shape during a period when Western Christendom was confined in an enclosed ghetto that did not allow missionary advancement. Hence, it became static as it looked inward and did not have the challenge of experiencing new venues in other cultures.[101] It is necessary, then, for the church to go against the stream of Western culture and become what the church was meant to be.[102] This can be done only if the church accepts its role of proclaiming the gospel as public truth, participating in the discussions

---

94 Ibid., p. 231.
95 Newbigin, *Journey* (Grand Rapids, MI: Eerdmans, 1972), p. 59.
96 Newbigin, *Open Secret*, p. 32.
97 Ibid., p. 34.
98 Ibid., pp. 66–67.
99 Ibid., p. 68.
100 Newbigin, *Trinitarian Faith*, p. 12.
101 Newbigin, *Open Secret*, p. 4.
102 Ibid., p. 5.

of the public square, even if that is in what the church has viewed as its own territory.[103]

Putting it all together

While many aspects of the doctrines of the church have been articulated repeatedly for centuries, and this needs to continue since cultures and languages change, increasing our understanding and expression of the faith, there is one area of doctrine that has received little theological attention until recently. It has often, even until the present, been seen as a peripheral teaching of the church, often expressed in the form of auxiliaries. That doctrine is the full understanding of the mission of the church. It has begun to gain prominence in the theological world with an increasing interest in theology of mission. When I began my theological studies in the 1960s, I was not aware of the term 'missiology' and did not learn of it until graduate school. A clearer under-standing of the 'mission of God' has led more theologians to explore its theological implications. The mission of God has taken a more central role and, if understood correctly, should be central, being birthed as it was in the writings of the apostle Paul.

Newbigin writes as a theologian while involved in missionary work, with ecumenical responsibilities and while shepherding a local congregation, and not as an academic theologian. While never demeaning academic theologians, he sought to complement their work. At the onset of the ecumenical movement, we noted that he worked with 'The twenty-five', a group of the leading theo-logians in the world, and eventually, because of his leadership and administrative ability, he led the group in their sessions. Such an event was rare, but Newbigin is better known for his writings than his ecumenical leadership. His powerful writings and clear insights into the mission of God raised the profile of missiology in theological circles.

In summary, Newbigin sought for the church to be the church, advocating that the Christian community contend for public truth in the public square before and with the wider community. He was seeking to convince Western culture that the answers to their fundamental ideological problems were to be found in Christian theology, specifically in the doctrines of the Trinity and the incarnation, both of which teach an understanding of reality broader than the narrow parameters of Enlightenment thinking.

© Donald LeRoy Stults, 2022

---

[103] Wainwright, *Theological Life*, p. 349.

12

Colin E. Gunton

JOHN E. COLWELL

For the son of a factory worker, the Athenaeum in Pall Mall was both unfamiliar and somewhat unsettling territory. Back in the 1970s it was still often the case that a prospective research student looked around for a viable supervisor and then registered with the university where that person happened to teach (rather than the other way around). In my search for a possible supervisor I had already talked with three or four possibles (rather than probables) when Raymond Brown, then Principal of Spurgeon's College, suggested I meet with Daniel Jenkins (the United Reformed Church scholar) and he, in turn, suggested meeting at his club. It was quickly apparent that Dr Jenkins was unwilling to take on a research student himself but recommended that I should have a conversation with a young lecturer in the Philosophy of Religion department at King's College London. Colin Gunton's doctoral dissertation had been published earlier in 1978[1] and, reading this prior to our first meeting, I realized our theological commitments (such as I then understood them) cohered. At the time Colin was living in Brentwood and, as I was then minister of the Baptist church in Maldon, it was convenient to meet him at his home (he had a study at the top of the house). I liked him instantly and I suppose he must have liked me since he chose to overlook my glaring theological naivety and suggested I register as a research student at King's under his supervision. It was just as I was leaving that he said, 'By the way, you do have German, don't you?' Seeing the look of horror on my face, he added, 'Oh, don't worry: it only took me three months.' It took me somewhat longer.

Having been raised in a fundamentalist home and having been prepared for ministry at Spurgeon's College, I had little experience of more liberal approaches to theology. Back then there was a single postgraduate seminar at King's for all staff and postgraduate students, and the first seminar I attended was addressed

---

[1] Colin E. Gunton, *Becoming and Being: The Doctrine of God in Charles Hartshorne and Karl Barth* (Oxford: Oxford University Press, 1978)

by Dennis Nineham not long after the publication of the collection *The Myth of God Incarnate*, to which Nineham had been a contributor.[2] As Nineham presented his paper I grew increasingly uncomfortable, increasingly feeling that I had made a serious mistake in registering here, increasingly feeling that I did not and could not belong or thrive in this context. When Nineham finished speaking, Colin Gunton immediately questioned in what sense, if the speaker seriously held the views he had expressed, he continued to term himself 'Christian' (and do remember that Gunton was merely a junior lecturer in the department at this time). He was to make a similar point later at the beginning of his study of Christology:

> it is very difficult to maintain a real continuity with earlier ages unless we can *at least in some ways* affirm their words as our words, even though necessarily we shall not use and understand those words precisely as they did.[3]

Or, as he later expresses it, 'without certain beliefs, about God, Christ, salvation, the church and the work of the Spirit, Christianity would not be recognisably continuous with what it once was'.[4]

Vita brevis

Born in Nottingham at the beginning of 1941, Colin Ewart Gunton attended Nottingham Grammar School, and won a classics scholarship to Hertford College, Oxford, in 1960. Having completed his degree, he transferred to Mansfield College to study theology, completing his doctoral thesis in 1969. That same year he joined the staff at King's College, being ordained in the college chapel as a minister of the United Reformed Church in 1972. King's College was to remain his academic home and he was appointed to the chair of Christian Doctrine in 1984. With remarkable speed the postgraduate seminar changed its character and, in 1988, Colin together with Christoph Schwöbel established the Research Institute in Systematic Theology as a means of organizing conferences and with the outcome of drawing students from around the world to study in what had become an overwhelmingly positive, conservative

---

[2] Dennis Nineham, 'Epilogue', in *The Myth of God Incarnate*, ed. John Hick (London: SCM Press, 1977).
[3] Colin E. Gunton, *Yesterday and Today: A Study of Continuities in Christology* (London: Darton, Longman & Todd, 1983), p. 5.
[4] Colin E. Gunton, *A Brief Theology of Revelation: The 1993 Warfield Lectures* (Edinburgh: T&T Clark, 1995), p. 87.

and orthodox context. To participate in this seminar became an extraordinary privilege and the galaxy of scholars and students who, at various times, passed through King's College was breathtaking: Christoph Schwöbel (already mentioned), Brian Horne, Alan Torrance, Murray Rae, Stephen Holmes, Graham Stanton, Francis Watson, Paul Helm, Jeremy Begbie, Douglas Farrow, Douglas Campbell, Oliver Crisp, Lincoln Harvey – a roll call of what had been or would become key figures in a positive and confessional approach to biblical studies and systematic theology.

Being supervised by Colin was an unfailingly pleasurable, but in some ways perplexing, experience. I would send him something I had written and we would arrange a date to meet (either at King's or at his home). But when we met he would be as likely to want to talk about cricket, gardening, music or maybe the latest theological article he had read and with which he strongly disagreed. Colin could be irascible, vehement in his criticisms and dismissals of certain trends in theology, taking great delight in commenting that a notable more liberal scholar was 'tone deaf'. Indeed, one of Colin's faults (if fault it was) was that he could not (or did not) hide his responses, leaving you in no doubt as to whether or not he liked you, whether or not he considered you theologically able. At the end of our time together discussing the latest Test match or the piece being rehearsed by the Brentwood Choral Society I would hesitantly ask concerning the stuff I had sent him to read. 'Oh, that was fine,' he'd say, 'but there was a hanging gerund on page twelve.' 'Eh!'

Some fifteen or so years later Colin was supervising Stephen Holmes's doctoral research on Jonathan Edwards. Steve had been one of my Master's students when I first began teaching at Spurgeon's College and, seeing his potential, I commended him to Colin for doctoral studies. (Having completed his doctorate,[5] Steve became one of Colin's colleagues at King's before moving to St Andrews.) Steve assured me that nothing had changed in Colin's approach to supervision during the intervening years but that he (Steve) was fairly confident that Colin would have been quick to criticize if there was something problematic in anything we presented. I cannot begin to imagine what Colin would make of the current rubrics of supervision with agreed targets, clear and specific direction and extended written reports on every supervision. At least those successfully supervised by Colin can rest in the knowledge that their doctoral dissertation was their own idea and the fruit of their own work rather than the mere following of the promptings of a supervisor.

---

[5] Stephen R. Holmes, *God of Grace and God of Glory: An Account of the Theology of Jonathan Edwards* (Edinburgh: T&T Clark, 2000).

And for Colin (as for most of us) the experience of supervision, combined with participation in regular postgraduate seminars, provided stimulus and insight that informed his own work. Douglas Farrow's work on Irenaeus, Graham McFarlane's work on Edward Irving, Stephen Holmes's work on Jonathan Edwards, Alan Spence and Kelly Kapic with their work on John Owen – each enriched and enhanced Colin's thought as his thought enriched and enhanced theirs. I used to urge my students not to think of tradition as a separate authoritative book, a rival source to Holy Scripture, but as a very large table around which are seated Christian thinkers of the present and the past who, like us, are listening to Scripture and pondering its significance (or, as I think Rowan Williams puts it, a complex web of continuing conversation). Colin sat at an immense table, a table he shared with colleagues and students, a table at which a host of thinkers of the past had a place – and Colin engaged them all in lively and critical conversation.

Theology through theologians

'One of the ways of learning to write theology is . . . to sit at the feet of other theologians.'[6] A cursory glance at the contents page of the book at the head of which this quotation occurs gives some indication of the richness and variety of voices that informed Colin's thinking: Anselm, Coleridge, Newman, Barth, Jüngel, Augustine, the Reformers, Irving, Dale, Owen, Zizioulas, Niebuhr, Forsyth. Authors, like biblical texts, are vulnerable to differing interpretations and assessments of significance and I realize that other friends and commentators may differ but, for me, the key thinkers who mark the stages of Colin Gunton's thought are Barth, Coleridge, Berkeley (an often overlooked influence), Polanyi, Irving, Zizioulas, Augustine (in an overwhelmingly negative sense), the Cappadocians and Irenaeus – though, as perhaps one would expect, the influences and the stages of thought overlap and do not conform to a strict chronological order.

Anyone familiar with Colin's lectures at King's College will know that he did not just begin with Barth. Interaction with Barth (albeit increasingly critical interaction) was basic to Colin's thinking. As has already been noted, Colin's doctoral dissertation was a comparison of Charles Hartshorne and Karl Barth – a comparison strongly in favour of the latter – and one of Colin's earliest published essays was an exploration of the significance of Barth's

---

[6] Colin E. Gunton, *Theology Through the Theologians: Selected Essays 1972–1995* (Edinburgh: T&T Clark, 1996), p. ix.

location of the doctrine of election within his treatment of the doctrine of God.[7] Karl Barth himself recognized and confessed that the *Kirchliche Dogmatik* represented a new beginning from the *Christliche Dogmatik* that preceded it. What is not always so readily recognized is that chapter 5 of the *Kirchliche Dogmatik*, the beginning of volume 2 part 1, marks a similar (self-conscious or otherwise) new beginning: a definition of God as 'the One Who Reveals Himself as Lord' is here displaced by a definition of God as 'the One who Loves in Freedom' and, effectively, this remains the unpacking of what Barth means by the word 'God' for the remainder of the Dogmatics.[8] For Barth this is who God is as identified in Jesus Christ and it is for this reason that he places the doctrine of election at the heart of his doctrine of God. Here, in the election of Jesus Christ and our election solely in him, God defines himself as the one who loves in freedom. Certainly, this exposition of election is a major and deliberate departure from that of Calvin (and from some who preceded him and many who have succeeded him). Certainly, this exposition will severely discomfort those for whom evangelicalism is primarily the adherence to a tradition rather than a faithful reflection on the gospel. But notwithstanding some of his later criticisms of Barth, this understanding of God as defined in the gospel remained the unequivocal foundation, not just for Colin Gunton's thought but even more basically for his life. The collection *Theology Through the Theologians* already includes an essay on chapter 5 of Barth's *Church Dogmatics* with the phrase 'No Other Foundation' as a part of its title.[9]

Interestingly (but unsurprisingly given the date of the collection), the essay 'Karl Barth's Doctrine of Election as Part of His Doctrine of God' also is republished in the volume *Theology Through the Theologians* but in revised form, chiefly by the addition of a new conclusion:

> God's freedom, the freedom that is prior to but revealed in all his acts outwards, is the personal freedom of the mutually constituting love of Father, Son and Spirit. In that sense, God is the one who loves in freedom. The doctrine of election is thus the expression of his loving freedom, but it derives from his personal being in communion rather

---

[7] Colin E. Gunton, 'Karl Barth's Doctrine of Election as part of his Doctrine of God', *Journal of Theological Studies* 25 (1974), pp. 381–392.

[8] Karl Barth, *Church Dogmatics*, vols. I–IV, ed. T. F. Torrance and G. W. Bromiley (Edinburgh: T&T Clark, 1956–75).

[9] Colin E. Gunton, 'The Knowledge of God: "No Other Foundation" – One Englishman's Reading of *Church Dogmatics* Chapter v', in *Theology Through the Theologians*, pp. 50–69.

than from his being an eternal *decision*. In this way, a 'space' is created between the eternal being of God and all his acts *ad extra*, a space which enables both God and the world to be themselves, in relation but also in distinction.[10]

What had occurred between 1974 and 1996 was the influence of John Zizioulas. As a classics scholar who made the time to read the early Greek tradition of the church, Colin Gunton would have been familiar with a Cappadocian understanding of the Holy Trinity. Pre-empting his Bampton Lectures, his inaugural lecture in the chair of Christian Doctrine bears the title 'The One, the Three and the Many'. Within this lecture Colin engages with John Macmurray, T. F. Torrance, William Hamilton and, in relation to these, Richard of St Victor. Here too Samuel Taylor Coleridge is identified as 'a pivotal figure in the alternative tradition in Western thought', being 'the first to have developed both a trinitarian understanding of God and a relational view of the human person'.[11] But it is the voice of John Zizioulas and an awakening to the significance of the Cappadocians' use of the term *hypostasis* that marks the key turning point in Gunton's theology and the distinctive emphasis for which (probably) he is chiefly known.

Earlier in 1985, Zizioulas, who became a regular participant in the King's seminar, had prepared a paper on 'Ontology and Personhood' for the British Council of Churches Study Commission on 'Trinitarian Doctrine Today' and this was to be followed by his formative work, *Being as Communion*.[12] But though the significance of Zizioulas's influence on Gunton ought not to be understated, neither ought it to be overstated. While his discussion of Western culture in *Enlightenment and Alienation* gives lingering evidence of that hesitation of Barth concerning the term 'person', the book is subtitled *An Essay Towards Trinitarian Theology* and the far more favourable references to Augustine within it relate, in anticipation of Michael Polanyi's theory of knowledge, to knowledge as a gift and the priority of faith.[13]

---

[10] Colin E. Gunton, 'The Doctrine of God: Karl Barth's Doctrine of Election as Part of His Doctrine of God', in *Theology Through the Theologians*, pp. 88–104; cf. 88.

[11] Colin E. Gunton, *The One, the Three and the Many: An Inaugural Lecture in the Chair of Christian Doctrine* (London: King's College London, 1985), p. 12.

[12] John D. Zizioulas, *Being as Communion: Studies in Personhood and the Church* (Crestwood, NY: St Vladimir's Seminary Press, 1985).

[13] Colin E. Gunton, *Enlightenment and Alienation: An Essay Towards a Trinitarian Theology* (Basingstoke: Marshall Morgan & Scott, 1985); cf. Michael Polanyi, *Personal Knowledge: Towards a Post-Critical Philosophy* (London: Routledge and Kegan Paul, 1962).

Trinitarian theologian

For Colin Gunton, as a non-Anglican and committed dissenter, to be invited to give the Bampton Lectures in 1992 represented a break with tradition that provoked ripples of consternation. The lectures were subsequently published under the title *The One, the Three and the Many: God, Creation and the Culture of Modernity*.[14] It was the invitation to give these lectures and their subsequent publication that sealed Colin's standing as a scholar of international repute. As the subtitle to the lectures suggests, there is a continuity of concern here with the issues previously exposed in *Enlightenment and Alienation* but by now Colin is recognizing that the proper theological response to the alienation generated by modernity is relational, an understanding of personhood and particularity rooted in the eternal communion that is Father, Son and Spirit. And here, without equivocation, Aurelius Augustine is identified as the bête noir at the root of Western thought. In Augustine's focus on God's oneness in a manner that qualifies the distinct subsisting particularity of the persons of the Father, Son and Spirit lies the fountainhead of Western society's impasse between the many and the one, between the philosophy of Heraclitus and the philosophy of Parmenides, an impasse fatally resolved in Nietzsche's conclusion that 'the one must be denied in order that the many should be free'.[15] What Western society requires is an understanding of personhood that is essentially relational; a freedom rooted in relational particularity; an understanding of humanity as the image of God reflecting God's being in communion rather than the monism of inwardness. What Western society requires is the gospel thus understood, a focus on the relational three as the resolution to the impasse between the one and the many.

The theological themes developed in these lectures were largely anticipated in Colin's earlier work *The Promise of Trinitarian Theology*,[16] but it is in the Bampton Lectures that this indebtedness to the Cappadocians is more thoroughly worked out in relation to the dynamics of Western society. And here perhaps it is appropriate to distinguish Gunton's emphases from (at first sight) similar emphases that preceded him or developed alongside his own development. Social understandings of the Trinity became something of a theological fashion, a fashion that has more recently been subjected to severe criticism, much of it (in my view) wholly justified. Projectionism remains a constant

---

[14] Colin E. Gunton, *The One, the Three and the Many: God, Creation and the Culture of Modernity. The 1992 Bampton Lectures* (Cambridge: Cambridge University Press, 1993).

[15] Gunton, *One, the Three* (1993), p. 27.

[16] Colin E. Gunton, *The Promise of Trinitarian Theology* (Edinburgh: T&T Clark, 1991).

danger for Christian theology as for any religious thought and it is all too easy to slip from a reflection on human society in the light of God's revealed triunity to a reflection of God's triunity in the light of aspects of human society. This is a move Colin Gunton never makes, nor does he ever give way to the commonly parallel rejections of God's impassibility and constancy (following Barth, Gunton finds the latter term more helpful and precise than the term 'immutability'):

> whatever else the tradition is, it is not naive, and that is why the fashionable assumption that we may simply reject certain of the ancient attributes – for example impassibility – is at best patronizing to a tradition that had good reason to say the things that it did about God.[17]

Or, with reference to divine simplicity:

> There is . . . a positive way of construing simplicity if we think in terms of perichoresis, of the relations of persons. The Father, Son and Spirit constitute one God without remainder because their communion is perfect and unbroken. The being of the Father, Son and Spirit is constituted entirely from being who they particularly are in their relations one to another. The Trinity is indeed not constituted of parts – which can be separated – but of persons, who are distinguishable but not separable, and therefore constitute a 'simple' God.[18]

Again in parallel to Karl Barth, Colin Gunton was passionate about the music of Mozart and this may prove even more revealing of Colin's theological attitudes than those of Barth. It is generally agreed that Mozart pressed the tradition he received to its boundaries without ever transgressing those boundaries (as Beethoven famously was to do in his third symphony). If the Reformation can be understood not as a departure from a tradition but as a reaffirmation of that tradition against the transgression of that tradition – a negative response to the question 'Is the Pope Catholic?' – Colin Gunton's questioning of Augustine can similarly be comprehended not as a rejection of the tradition expressed by Irenaeus, the Cappadocians and Athanasius, but as the reaffirmation of that tradition in response to its qualification by Augustine and his Western successors. Now I might prefer Beethoven, not to say Debussy

---

[17] Colin E. Gunton, *Act and Being: Towards a Theology of the Divine Attributes* (London: SCM Press, 2002), p. 22.
[18] Ibid., p. 122.

or Poulenc – but Colin would dismiss such as romanticism. The point I'm trying to make is that Colin Gunton was deeply orthodox in his theological thinking: he did not consider his criticisms of Augustine (or Thomas Aquinas for that matter) to be a departure from a tradition but the reaffirming of an older tradition for the sake of taking seriously Scripture's witness to the revelation of God as Father, Son and Spirit within the economy of salvation. And in both this affirmation and rejection Colin was passionate, shaking his head in puzzlement at my attempts to rehabilitate Thomas Aquinas and, I suspect, he would express similar incomprehension at Steve Holmes's attempts to rehabilitate Augustine.

As with others, Robert Jenson for instance, Colin Gunton located the root of Augustine's deficiency in his failure to grasp the significance of Basil of Caesarea's distinction between essence (*ousia*) and subsistence (*hypostasis*):

> Because Augustine continues to use relation as a logical rather than an ontological predicate, he is precluded from being able to make claims about the being of the *particular* persons, who, because they lack distinguishable identity tend to disappear into the all-embracing oneness of God.[19]

There is, of course, a logical (or rather, ontological) circularity here: without particularity there can be no relatedness but it is precisely relatedness that establishes particularity: it is the relatedness of Father, Son and Spirit that establishes their particularity in that relatedness: 'The persons are not persons who then enter into relations, but are mutually constituted, made what they are, by virtue of their relations to one another.'[20]

This notion of relationally established particularity is foundational not just to Colin Gunton's account of the Holy Trinity but similarly central to his account of human persons, human freedom and the distinctive freedom of creation itself and of the particulars within it. Just as the Spirit, as the love between the Father and the Son, thereby establishes the distinctive particularity of the Father and Son, so the Spirit establishes the distinct particularity of creation and of the distinct particulars within creation. The freedom of creation in relation to God and the freedom of human persons is Spirit-given. Creation is not a part of God, an emanation from God, or a space within God; creation is distinct from God, particular in relation to God, its distinct particularity (and the distinct particularity of particulars within creation) being

---

[19] Gunton, *Promise of Trinitarian Theology*, pp. 41–42.
[20] Ibid., p. 156.

an outcome of the continuing presence and action of the Spirit. If the Cappadocians are the inspiration (and Augustine the detractor) for Gunton's understanding of the Trinity, then Irenaeus increasingly becomes the inspiration (and Augustine again the detractor) for Gunton's understanding of creation. In this respect too Gunton finds a realist (rather than idealist) interpretation of George Berkeley helpful:

> The aim of Berkeley's polemic against atheism and scepticism was in part to establish the concreteness of the particular. Things are as they are perceived to be because God sees to it that they are. The fact that Berkeley's theory of particulars was taken, for example by the foolish Dr Johnson, to be the opposite of what it set out to be is in large measure the fault of the terminology of idea that he inherited from the tradition of Descartes and Locke. The concrete particulars appear to be unstable and merely occasional moments of perception rather than the substantial entities that Berkeley intended.[21]

These themes are most thoroughly developed in the book *The Triune Creator*,[22] a careful and detailed historical analysis of understandings of creation that traces ideas and developments through Scripture, Hellenism, the concept of a mediated creation in the thought of Irenaeus, the qualification of these ideas through Origen, and the further qualification of these ideas as Western theology develops. The book demonstrates an impressive analytical and critical grasp of the history of Western thought and, alongside the expected criticisms of Augustine, Thomas Aquinas is especially subjected to severe criticism. Perhaps somewhat unkindly, one could summarize the argument of the book by saying that Irenaeus got this right and that it has been downhill ever since! But such a summary, though accurate, would do little justice to the careful discussion and analysis displayed. Gunton had an exemplary gift for being able to penetrate to the heart of an argument and to expose its flaws with laser-like precision. Yes (of course), there can be responses to these criticisms and the host of authors here engaged can be severally defended, but the kernel of Gunton's critical analysis stands with quite devastating effect. For Irenaeus creation is a trinitarian act: the Father creates through the 'two hands' of the Son and the Spirit: creation is mediated, not through Gnostic hierarchies, nor through Platonic eternal forms, but by the Son and the Spirit. Obscure the

---

[21] Gunton, *One, the Three* (1993), p. 199.
[22] Colin E. Gunton, *The Triune Creator: A Historical and Systematic Study* (Edinburgh: Edinburgh University Press, 1998).

trinitarian mediation of creation and creation is reduced to a decision of divine will rather than an outworking and overflowing of divine love. Moreover, as mediated by the Son and the Spirit, creation finds its goal in the Son and through the Spirit – it is in the Son and by the Spirit that creation reaches its goal. Whereas for Augustine an already perfected creation falls from that perfection and regains that perfection through redemption, for Irenaeus (and therefore for Gunton) creation is destined to reach its perfection in Christ and in no other way: creation is God's 'project'. The essentially circular Augustinian notion of creation, fall, redemption has become so commonplace in Western theology that the voices of Colin Gunton and Douglas Farrow need to be greatly amplified if we are to be alerted to this older tradition from which Augustine departs:

> At the fountainhead of the Western treatment of creation is Augustine's subtly altered account of the matter . . . in his theology, the mediation by Christ and the Spirit, as well as the teleological directedness of the creation, play too limited a role, a first effect is that the link, so beautifully maintained in Irenaeus between creation and redemption, becomes weakened to the point of disappearing, so that it is rarely adequately treated in Western theology after this time. And second it comes to be that the theme of love becomes subordinate to that of will. If not in Augustine, certainly in those who learned from him, creation becomes very much the product of pure, unmotivated and therefore arbitrary will, a will that operates equally arbitrarily in the theology of double predestination that became after him so much a mark of the Western tradition.[23]

Back in 1990 Colin had been invited to deliver the Didsbury Lectures at the Nazarene College in Manchester. These four lectures were revised and published under the title *Christ and Creation*[24] and, for those who might get lost in the historical detail of *The Triune Creator*, they outline the same argument with the same conclusions with regard to trinitarian mediation. This booklet also serves to illustrate a dynamic that (perhaps unfortunately) was true of Colin and is similarly true of many of us. As a lecturer Colin was engaging, humorous and accessible. As a writer he could be harder to follow and one can easily become disorientated in the density of his argument. The relative accessibility of the Didsbury Lectures and the Warfield Lectures

---

[23] Gunton, *One, the Three* (1993), pp. 120–121.
[24] Colin E. Gunton, *Christ and Creation* (Carlisle: Paternoster Press; Grand Rapids, MI: Eerdmans, 1992).

(see below) perhaps reflects Colin's awareness of the audience to which they were originally addressed.

Revelation and Scripture

So was Colin Gunton an evangelical? A positive answer to the question is presupposed by his inclusion within this collection but, as the introduction to this volume asserts, it really depends on how you define 'evangelical'. Increasingly in the last few decades evangelicalism has tended to be defined as a conservative tradition: you are an evangelical if you can tick a series of doctrinal boxes (or correctly pronounce 'Shibboleth'). Depending on the boxes chosen (some can be fairly arbitrary) Colin may well fare better than the present author. As I have already recognized, Colin, like Mozart, may have pressed the boundaries of a tradition but he never (to my knowledge) transgressed them. Where he so stridently challenges aspects of the Western tradition with respect to an understanding of the Trinity and of creation it is in faithfulness to an older tradition and in faithfulness to a careful hearing of Scripture. Sadly, Colin died before he could bring a full systematics to publication but his single-volume *Introduction*,[25] organized around the first three articles of the creed (and including a discussion of the church within its discussion of the Spirit), gives some indication of the form such a systematics might have taken and again gives clear evidence of Colin's conservative orthodoxy. Colin was a convinced dissenter, a committed congregationalist and a trenchant critic of Anglicanism. If a theology of creation goes downhill after Irenaeus, then similarly hymnody goes downhill after Isaac Watts. Like Karl Barth, Colin was as suspicious of pietism and romanticism as he was of liberalism and, thereby (and consistent with his understanding of relationality), there would certainly be some more individualistic and self-absorbed forms of evangelicalism for which he would have had scant tolerance.

Some years ago I was discussing a definition of evangelicalism with a former tutor of another evangelical college and we (in part playfully) concluded that evangelicalism was a club into which you were born (or reborn), which was fairly hard to leave (even if you pushed the boundaries), but which was extremely hard to join (or in which to be generally accepted) if it had not been your ecclesiological or spiritual heritage. By such a criterion I would deem Colin to have increasingly identified himself as an evangelical but, again like Barth, to have encountered some difficulty in being accepted into the 'club'.

---

[25] Colin E. Gunton, *The Christian Faith: An Introduction to Christian Doctrine* (Oxford: Blackwell, 2002).

Around the same time as this half-serious discussion, I was moderating the viva voce examination for a PhD, where the candidate had assumed David Bebbington's quadrilateral of Scripture, cross, conversionism and activism as defining of evangelicalism.[26] One of the examiners, a Jesuit, was surprised by the quadrilateral (which he had not encountered previously) since these four commitments, as a Jesuit, would be his own distinctives. This, then, raises the possibility that evangelicalism is defined not just by what it affirms but equally by what it rejects. Here too I deem Colin Gunton to be truly and thoroughly evangelical in his commitment to the Reformation (Lutheran) distinctives of *sola scriptura*, *sola gratia* and *sola fide*. Like Luther and the other Reformers, Colin Gunton listened carefully to the voices of the tradition in interpretation of Scripture but (as has been demonstrated) he was prepared to challenge them. Like Luther he held that salvation was by grace alone and through faith alone, but like Calvin he held that true grace and true faith never remained alone.

Colin Gunton was invited to give the Warfield Lectures in 1993 at Princeton Theological Seminary, the lectures subsequently being published under the title *A Brief Theology of Revelation*.[27] I raved about this little volume (it really is 'brief') when it first appeared and, though Colin disagreed with me, I still consider it to be his best work (although this probably says as much about me and my interests as it does about the book itself). Certainly, like the Didsbury Lectures that preceded it, it is accessible and clearly (though characteristically tightly) argued. In many respects the arguments here were anticipated as far back as *Enlightenment and Alienation* but here those ideas are thoroughly revised with regard to a now mature notion of trinitarian mediation. The argument begins with a rejection of immediacy (or better, unmediated immediacy) and a recognition of the secondary nature of credal propositions: revelation is always a mediated knowledge of God because that is who God is as Father, Son and Spirit, and because this is the manner of God's relatedness to the world. The second lecture carries the subtitle 'Toward a General Theology of Revelation' and revisits the arguments of Coleridge and Polanyi that all knowledge 'is a species of Revelation',[28] and the assertions of Berkeley that all knowledge (all perception) is a gift: 'The doctrine of revelation tells us that we cannot discover certain things unless we are taught them.'[29]

---

[26] D. W. Bebbington, *Evangelicalism in Modern Britain: A History from the 1730s to the 1980s* (Abingdon: Routledge, 1988).

[27] Colin E. Gunton, *A Brief Theology of Revelation: The 1993 Warfield Lectures* (Edinburgh: T&T Clark, 1995).

[28] Ibid., p. 22, citing Samuel Taylor Coleridge, *Collected Letters of Samuel Taylor Coleridge*, vol. 2: *1801–1806*, ed. E. L. Griggs (Oxford: Clarendon Press, 1956), p. 388.

[29] Gunton, *Brief Theology of Revelation*, pp. 58–59.

Lecture Three, with the title 'No Other Foundation', distinguishes general revelation from any natural theology, asserting again that all authentic revelation is revelation of the true God and therefore is mediated by the Son and the Spirit and, consequently, agreeing with Calvin that we need Scripture as 'spectacles' if we are ever to recognize general revelation as revelation: 'The doctrine of general revelation is not therefore something that operates in parallel with biblical revelation, but is derived from it.'[30] Or again, 'God may be revealed in the things that have been made, but it does not follow that the discernment of this truth is achievable by unaided reason alone.'[31]

The fourth lecture discusses the relation between revelation and inspiration. The two must be distinguished:

much of the history of the doctrine of inspiration is in large measure an attempt to equate inspiration and revelation in such a way that the text in some way replaces or renders redundant the mediating work of the Spirit.[32]

Nevertheless, Gunton concludes with Alan Torrance that there must be 'an intrinsic relation between revelation and the words used to enable it to come to expression'.[33] To speak of the inspiration of the Scriptures then, is to affirm Scripture as a mediation of revelation through the inspiration of the Spirit, an inspiration operative in the church both in the human authors of Scripture and in its human hearers. It is precisely this distinction between revelation and inspiration that enables Gunton to affirm the truthfulness of Scripture while avoiding a notion of inerrancy: '[D]ogma and theology are revisable, scripture is in certain respects open to question, but revelation, mediated through scripture, is not.'[34]

The fifth lecture begins with a further protest against that form of immediacy that assumes 'a direct relation to the Scriptures without the mediation of a tradition of interpretation'[35] (the unfortunate habit of not a few who name themselves as evangelicals and act as if they were the first to pick up a Bible and ponder its significance). Tradition, for Gunton, is not an alternative or parallel source of authority but simply the 'process of gift and reception in which the deposit of faith . . . is received, interpreted and handed

---

[30] Ibid., p. 61.
[31] Ibid., p. 55.
[32] Ibid., p. 66.
[33] Ibid., p. 77.
[34] Ibid., p. 81.
[35] Ibid., p. 83.

on through time'.[36] The final chapter revisits and summarizes the previous lectures, leading to this final statement of a trinitarian dynamic of mediation:

> If Christ is the mediator of creation, then he is the basis of created rationality and therefore of human knowledge, wherever and whatever, we might say, of all human culture. But that point must be developed pneumatologically also, so that all rationality, truth and beauty are seen to be realised through the perfecting agency of God the Spirit, who enables things to be known by human minds and made by human hands. Christ is indeed the Truth, but the truth becomes truth in all the different ways in which it is mediated by the Spirit. Pneumatology is thus the key to any adequate theology of revelation and of its mediation.[37]

I have deliberately taken rather longer to outline the argument of these lectures because, theoretically, they represent a focused summary of Gunton's approach to Scripture within the context of his understanding of trinitarian mediation. However, perhaps in this particular respect a person's practice is more eloquent than a summary of that person's thought. From 1975 Colin Gunton was Associate Minister of the United Reformed church in Brentwood. Through his commendation a steady stream of his colleagues and senior students were invited to lead worship and preach at the church and to enjoy Jenny and Colin's hospitality at a lunch to which also other friends from the church were invited (it was usual for eight or even ten folk to sit together for lunch and to enjoy most stimulating conversation). Friendships were thus established with others in the church and Rosie (my wife) and I were often included in party trips to the Open Air Theatre in Regent's Park. More to the point, Colin himself preached at the church on average (I believe) once a month and often commented that you could always spot a theologian who had given up preaching or who had never started. In the course of his Introduction to the second collection of Colin's sermons my friend Steve Holmes recalls Colin once saying to him,

> you should always have three readings from Scripture – Old Testament, New Testament and Gospel – and a psalm at the beginning. After all, it is only when the Bible is read that you can be sure God is speaking to the people![38]

---

[36] Ibid., p. 103.

[37] Ibid., p. 125.

[38] *The Theologian as Preacher: Further Sermons from Colin E. Gunton*, ed. Sarah J. Gunton and John E. Colwell, introduction by Stephen R. Holmes (London: T&T Clark, 2007), p. xiv. See also Colin E. Gunton, *Theology Through Preaching* (Edinburgh: T&T Clark, 2001).

Church theology

Resolutely Colin Gunton held the church, rather than the academy, to be theology's primary and proper context and his theological effort is probably misunderstood unless this most basic ecclesial commitment is recognized. With this in mind it is surprising (to say the least) that the theme of ecclesiology features so little in his published works. The collection *On Being the Church*, jointly edited by Colin Gunton and Daniel Hardy, included a chapter by Colin entitled 'The Church on Earth: the Roots of Community' that subsequently formed chapter 4 of Colin's *The Promise of Trinitarian Theology*.[39] Warning against moving too quickly from an understanding of God to an understanding of the church, whether rooted in God's oneness as a basis for unity or rooted in God's threeness as a basis for 'an ecclesiology of diversity',[40] Colin concludes:

> Whether a community of those who claim the name of church is justified in its claim is a question which may always be asked. But should our criteria be those of monistic, legal and 'organic' structures, or the trinitarian ones concerned with whether a community freely orders and disciplines its life so as to echo the community of Father, Son and Spirit? It is with that directedness to the Trinity that this endeavour to understand something of what the Church is should appropriately come to an end.[41]

The note of hesitation with which this early essay begins is echoed in Colin's far later *Introduction to Christian Doctrine*:

> The Spirit's work is to make real, from time to time and as a divine gift gives rise to human freedom, anticipations of the true community of the last days. In this regard, the church's mistake is too often to claim that these conditions are too directly and by their own inner strength realized in her life and institutions, rather than being anticipated in them only by the gracious and free action of the Lord the Spirit. Many of the worst disasters of that partly sorry story known as church history derive from too confident a claim to realize, now, what can be fully realized only in the kingdom of heaven. The church may be the servant of the kingdom, but

---

[39] Colin E. Gunton, 'The Church on Earth: The Roots of Community', in Colin E. Gunton and Daniel W. Hardy (eds.), *On Being the Church: Essays on Christian Community* (Edinburgh: T&T Clark, 1989), pp. 48–80; cf. Gunton, *Promise of Trinitarian Theology*, pp. 58–85.

[40] Ibid., pp. 71–83.

[41] Ibid., p. 83.

once she begins to think that she is the kingdom she displaces the work of the Spirit with her own rather than receiving her true being as gift.[42]

Perhaps Gunton's fullest account of ecclesiology occurs in the Drew Lecture he delivered at Spurgeon's College in 1999 under the title '"Until He Comes": Towards an Eschatology of Church Membership'.[43] But as Colin notes in the first footnote, the essay could as easily be subtitled 'a conversation with Robert Jenson, with particular respect to the first letter to the Corinthians'.[44] The major omission of this present chapter thus far has been the scarcity of its reference to Robert Jenson. For a time Jenson had been one of the series of supervisors of Colin's doctoral research and the two remained the closest of friends until Colin's death. Indeed, put Colin Gunton, Christoph Schwöbel and Robert Jenson in a room together and it would be difficult to get a word in edgeways amidst the argument and the laughter. Colin and 'Jens' held so much in common – the influence of Barth, an emphasis on the relational particularity of the Father, Son and Spirit; a strident criticism of Augustine. But in other respects they sharply disagreed and that disagreement can probably (and not inaccurately) be reduced to the distinction between the Lutheran and the Reformed. Robert Jenson (who died in 2017) could not unfairly be described as a radical Lutheran in his understanding of the relationship between God and the world, Christ and the church, Christ and Holy Communion. In each of these instances, and consistent with his understanding of mediation, Colin would take Calvin's part in response to the Lutheran part. For Jenson the naming of the church as the body of Christ was a matter of identity: for Gunton such was a metaphor and Jenson's position lapsed precisely into an unwarranted pre-empting of the eschatological future. But this dispute, though intractable, in no way threatened the most loyal respect and affection that bound these two men.

The actuality of the atonement

The other key doctrine with which this volume is intended to be concerned is that of the atonement. Relatively early in his academic career Colin Gunton published an introduction to the theme in which he discusses the leading

---

[42] Gunton, *Introduction to Christian Doctrine*, p. 122.
[43] Colin E. Gunton, '"Until He Comes": Towards an Eschatology of Church Membership', in John Colwell (ed.), *Called to One Hope: Perspectives on Life to Come*, Drew Lectures on Immortality Delivered at Spurgeon's College (Carlisle: Paternoster Press, 2000), pp. 252–266.
[44] Ibid., p. 264, n. 1.

metaphors of atonement that have arisen within the (largely Western) tradition.[45] Following a chapter on the rationalism of our present context and a chapter on the nature of metaphor generally Colin outlines and responds to the themes of victory, of justice and of sacrifice, concluding with a chapter on the atonement in the light of God's triunity and a chapter on the church as the community of reconciliation. The language of the demonic encountered in the metaphor of victory is seen by Gunton as 'an essential way of speaking if we are to understand certain features of our fallen world'.[46] While both appreciative and critical of Anselm, Gunton's discussion of justice leads to an extended and positive engagement with P. T. Forsyth and some questioning of that definition of justice that so often has been assumed in relation to the atonement. While sharing Edward Irving's criticisms of 'mathematical' notions of substitution, Gunton resolutely defends the substitutionary nature of the atonement, not to the exclusion of but rather enabling an understanding of representation:

> we have to say that Jesus is our substitute because he does for us what we cannot do for ourselves. That includes undergoing the judgement of God, because were we to undergo it without him, it would mean our destruction. Therefore the 'for us' of the cross and resurrection must *include*, though it is not exhausted by, an 'instead of'. He fights and conquers where we are only defeated, and would continue to be without him; he lives a just life, where we disrupt the order and beauty of the universe, and where without him we should continue to do so; he is holy, as God is holy, where we are stained, and would continue to be but for him. And just because of all this he bears the consequences of the world's slavery and pollution; and he does it because as the Son he accepts the burden as his obedience to the Father ... It is for such reasons that substitution and representation are correlative, not opposed concepts. Because Jesus is our substitute, it is also right to call him our representative.[47]

These correlating themes of substitution and representation are reaffirmed in *The Christian Faith* as we near the end of Colin Gunton's life and contribution:

> The cross follows the logic of God's providence, of Israel's and Rome's politics and of Jesus' own actions. It is the confluence of divine action and Jesus' human determination to persevere in face of fallen political

---

[45] Colin E. Gunton, *The Actuality of Atonement: A Study of Metaphor, Rationality and the Christian Tradition* (Edinburgh: T&T Clark, 1988).
[46] Ibid., p. 74.
[47] Ibid., pp. 165–166.

and religious forces. As a fulfilment of Jesus' baptism, it represents his full identification with Israel and ultimately with all men and women in their self-inflicted sundering from their creator. That is the realm of death as judgement. The Father abandons Jesus to the cross so that he may share our condition in its uttermost depths.[48]

Amicus memoratus

In April 2003 Colin Gunton and I were together in Newcastle at a theological conference on the theme of the cross. I arrived at the hall early for what was to be the final presentation of the conference and sat at the end of a row, next to the wall. A few minutes later Colin came to sit next to me: 'I really hoped you'd sit somewhere else,' I said (jestingly). 'You'll mutter all through this.'

'All right. If that's how you feel, I'll move,' he said, but by that time Steve Holmes had entered the same row and Colin was hemmed between us. When the lecture ended, Colin turned to me with his customary impish grin. 'I wasn't the only one muttering,' he said. The three of us sat, together with others, talking late into the night, both on the content of the conference and more generally. Apart from a telephone conversation a couple of weeks later, that was the last time I spoke with Colin. He died on Tuesday 6 May that year, aged 62.

My father died in 1996, my mother in 2010, the best friend from my late teens and early twenties (the best man at my wedding) in 2012, but no human death has affected me remotely as deeply as Colin Gunton's. Of course, the suddenness of his death was a cause of immense shock for all who knew and loved him. But, perhaps more basically, the numbing emptiness I felt at Colin's death (and still feel when I reflect on it) was revealing of the degree to which I had come to be reliant on his counsel, his criticisms, his unswerving friendship. Both Sarah and Carolyn (Colin's daughters) independently have rebuked me for speaking of their father's 'untimely' death. Colin was full of life and energy and would have railed against retirement but, more fundamentally, what can 'untimely' possibly signify if we believe in the providence of a loving heavenly Father?

My reaction to his death, however, was compounded by the knowledge that I was due to preach at the church in Brentwood twelve days later (two days before Colin's funeral). Notwithstanding our protests Jenny Gunton insisted that we come, as usual, for lunch that Sunday (displaying the strange calm that so often accompanies sudden bereavement but that speaks also of an unshakeable trust). Jenny, who had worked as a primary school teacher, had taken

---

[48] Gunton, *Christian Faith*, p. 110.

early retirement partly in order to accompany Colin on his frequent teaching engagements overseas and, through her hospitality and regular visits to the department at King's, had become a friend to many of us in her own right. The little church in Brentwood was packed for Colin's funeral (Robert and Blanche Jenson had flown the Atlantic to be there). Colin's coffin was carried to the graveside by Christopher and Jonathan (his sons), Peter (his son-in-law) and Christoph Schwöbel. After the committal I was speaking with Christoph about the void I felt within at Colin's passing. He replied that this surely is what we should expect to feel, believing as we believe and as we had learnt from Colin: who we are as persons is rendered by our relatedness to one another.

© John E. Colwell, 2022

Coda: looking back to look forwards – on the past, present and future of British evangelical theology

Looking back

In several academic and professional fields, retrospectives provide valuable opportunities to look back at significant events, and reconsider and evaluate important works that have been produced. This book serves such a purpose, examining twelve of the key figures most relevant to represent the best of twentieth-century British evangelical theology. Its focus is not to showcase particular historical developments (although these are considered), nor is it to highlight various sociological features of the movement (although these are noted where relevant). Instead, concentration focuses on the theology operative in the work of these twelve exemplars whose ideas helped shape British evangelicalism in the last century, with its remarkable reach throughout the world. Here in this 'Coda', as a Californian who lived, studied and taught in Britain, and serves as the co-chair of the Tyndale Fellowship's Christian Doctrine Study Group, I will try to think finally about how the gospel preached by these twentieth-century theologians faces today the changing context of our twenty-first century. While desiring to be true to the gospel preached by these twelve exemplars, the present context raises questions of the emphases and the presentation of evangelical truth.

The changing context

This project has been a descriptive endeavour, largely celebratory, or at least paying tribute to those who have shaped our thinking. But can such an effort also be critical? This question, admittedly academic, is an important one because the role that theology plays within the life of our institutions and contemporary culture (and also in the very life of the church) is not always clearly understood or agreed.[1] For example, evangelical theology is now done in a context where, since the end of the twentieth century, Britain has become much more obviously a multiracial society and the effects and unintended consequences of colonialism and empire are matters now on the agenda in a multiracial country. While evangelicalism cannot ever lose the biblical call to personal faith, the social context and the social ethics of the community of faith (remembering Wilberforce and Booth) also demand attention. Evangelical theology, the original impetus for world mission in recent centuries, and the inspiration for the anti-slavery movement, surely has much to contribute here.

The popular early twentieth-century notion of Britain as the heart of an empire 'on which the sun never set' is seen by many today as an imperialism akin to oppressive political regimes. But we may note that democratic principles led to the transformation of the empire into the Commonwealth as democratic nation states came to birth while the former 'mission fields' became partner nations with partner churches. Meanwhile, the evangelical student movement that brought numerous university graduates to commit themselves to missions around the world also led to the ecumenical movement, launched in 1910 at the Edinburgh Missionary Conference. This was of deep concern to several theologians profiled in this book (especially Torrance and Newbigin, to some degree Stott and Packer, although opposed by Lloyd-Jones) and changed the face of Christian missions away from the harmful colonial model of missions to encourage greater local development of indigenous leadership to which visiting Christian missionaries would submit.[2]

Beyond the academic question of critique and context, and the desire to locate a usable past from which to draw, there also remains the ecclesial issue. Faith matters. It is passed down and tradition becomes, as it were, a faithful guide. More than the past left in the past, in the rear-view mirror as it were, the chapters of this volume aim to examine twentieth-century British theology – to learn from it, and incorporate its important parts, and also perhaps to recognize what should be discarded. This order is important, however, if evangelical theology is to be done in a manner that displays, as Steve Holmes has argued,

---

[1] See Jason S. Sexton, 'The Critical Study of Religion and Division in the Age of Covid-19', *International Journal of Public Theology* 15.2 (2021), pp. 157–176, <https://doi.org/10.1163/15697320-12341652> (accessed 4 October 2021).

[2] See Lesslie Newbigin, 'Mission to Six Continents', in Harold E. Fey (ed.), *The Ecumenical Advance: A History of the Ecumenical Movement*, vol. 2: *1948–1968*, 2nd edn (Philadelphia: Westminster Press, 1986), pp. 173–197. See also Brian Stanley, *The Bible and the Flag: Protestant Mission and British Imperialism in the Nineteenth and Twentieth Centuries* (Leicester: Inter-Varsity Press, 1990).

'a respect for the past, rather than a freedom to plough our own furrows'.[3] Paying close attention to the features that might be maintained and carefully passed down is of great importance. St Paul's admonition to Timothy is instructive in this regard: 'what you have heard from me through many witnesses entrust to faithful people who will be able to teach others as well' (2 Tim. 2:2, NRSVA).

This stewardship of faith and its inherent transferability are also due to its deposited character: 'the faith that was once for all entrusted to the saints' (Jude 3, NRSVA). As such, the subject matter is not merely academic, but a matter of faithfulness to God and to the life of communities of faith – both to people who wish to belong to this faith at present, and to those who will embrace it in the future. 'There is', Tony Lane reminds us, 'no virtue in reinventing the wheel in every generation and even less in repeating the errors of the past.'[4] Such an approach to tradition and to maintaining the character of the gospel in its sound articulation remains of enormous consideration when determining how best to hand down the Christian faith from generation to generation.

British evangelical theology and academic theology

It is difficult to overestimate the significance of British theology in the modern world, since it arguably constitutes the fountain of English-speaking theology today. This is not merely a historical assertion, but acknowledges that much of the theology happening today (especially in the English-speaking world) has some direct linkage to British theology, and to the figures who have been shaped by British theology at some level. And British evangelical theology – from Wesley and Whitefield down to the current situation with the far reaches of its influence and nodes of institutional intersections – has arguably demonstrated an international significance beyond any other form of Christian theology in Britain.[5]

Theology positions within British universities and institutions of higher learning remain far more robust today than they are in other public university

---

[3] Stephen R. Holmes, *Listening to the Past: The Place of Tradition in Theology* (Carlisle: Paternoster Press, 2002), p. 164. See also Jason S. Sexton, 'Introduction: Recalibrating the Church's Mission', in Jason S. Sexton (ed.), *Four Views on the Church's Mission* (Grand Rapids, MI: Zondervan, 2017), pp. 7–16.

[4] Anthony N. S. Lane, 'Tradition', in Kevin J. Vanhoozer (ed.), *Dictionary for Theological Interpretation of the Bible* (London: SPCK, 2005), p. 812.

[5] See e.g. the historical and cultural significance of the movement in the five-volume History of Evangelicalism series (Inter-Varsity Press). The post-war influence of evangelicalism in the UK as it revolved around the work of the Cambridge-based Tyndale House and Tyndale Fellowship is chronicled in T. A. Noble, *Tyndale House and Fellowship: The First Sixty Years* (Nottingham: Inter-Varsity Press, 2006).

settings through much of the English-speaking world. This is partly because theology is mainstream in the UK, allowing for theology positions (including Cambridge and Oxford Regius Professorships) to be occupied by evangelical theologians. As with any such academic positions, they are open not only to British scholars but to those from overseas, and accordingly are open to scholars producing the best academic work. These are often evangelicals. They are able to appeal to the brightest minds of undergraduate and postgraduate evangelical students who take their faith seriously and pursue academic courses of study at leading British universities.

The ecologies of the theological colleges (training students for professional ministerial degrees), which are often accredited by major British universities, including the Church of England's Common Award accredited by Durham, generate an egalitarian spirit within British theological higher education that often lends towards cross-pollination among these institutions, especially those sharing close geographical proximity, or even actual space, offering cross-institutional degrees. One thinks of Ridley Hall, a Cambridge University affiliate college that trains Anglican ordinands but offers degrees from the University of Cambridge, University of Durham and Anglia-Ruskin University. One thinks of Regent's Park College, or Wycliffe Hall within Oxford University, which grants degrees for both institutions. New College, Edinburgh, is at the same time the Divinity School of the University of Edinburgh and a church college of the Church of Scotland, with the church often having a strong say in some university appointments.

Other major universities such as those south of the border like Durham, Roehampton, Leeds and King's College London, or those in Scotland such as St Andrews or Aberdeen, have had long histories of robust theology faculties where evangelical theologians with deep and personal evangelical convictions have often been found. They attract graduate students of remarkable calibre from around the world who are then able to generate high-quality scholarship from evangelical perspectives. A number of evangelical theological colleges, such as the London School of Theology, Spurgeon's College, Oak Hill, the Highland Theological College, and the Nazarene Theological College, are associated with major universities so are able to offer degree studies and doctoral research.

British evangelical theology around the world

From the mid-twentieth century, graduate students have come from around the world to pursue British PhDs. As serious-minded scholars, many of these have also been leaders passionate about serving the church in their own home contexts. Sometimes through the Langham Partnership established by John Stott,[6] they have had access to resources to come to receive the highest education possible from an evangelical faith perspective and have returned to their own countries with the resource-tools received through a rigorous high-level education. Some of these have come to study with several of the scholars who have contributed essays to the present volume.

Such developments are often the fruit of the positive relationships seen today within Commonwealth countries, having emerged in the twentieth century out of the old empire, and thus demonstrating a reverse-colonialist model. British scholars and theologians thus serve and educate leaders throughout the world who wish to study in the UK (and in this way will always be connected to the UK), and yet with an emphasis towards serving the churches within other social, political and geographical contexts. This open-handedness of British evangelical scholarship has effectively trained hundreds if not thousands of theologians around the world with evangelical faith-based perspectives that allow for careful contextualization.

This emphasis on making education available to students in the Global South and East has meant a host of students from India, East Asia (including China, Korea, the Philippines, etc.), Africa and Latin America, as well as those from the USA, who have received a British theological education before going back to assume leadership positions within the institutions of their own countries. The irony is salient for places such as Asia and Africa, which is where most early Christian theology comes from.[7] But in addition to theologians from around the world being trained in the UK, British theologians also go elsewhere, and the cross-pollination continues. And evangelicals such as H. R. Mackintosh, his student T. F. Torrance and every person profiled in this volume had as a motivating factor the desire to see conversion to Christ happen, and forgiveness extended, and reconciliation to God experienced. This openness to the world for quite a while viewed Western culture as already evangelized, although Torrance and Newbigin were especially aware that new, dominant, post-Christian sets of ideas – whether scientism, postmodernism, secularism or something else – posed new challenges back home.

---

[6] See Christopher J. H. Wright, *The Mission of God: Unlocking the Bible's Grand Narrative* (Downers Grove, IL: InterVarsity Press), by the International Ministries Director of Langham Partnership International.

[7] On African origins of Christian theology, see e.g. Thomas C. Oden, *How Africa Shaped the Christian Mind: Rediscovering the African Seedbed of Western Christianity* (Downers Grove, IL: InterVarsity Press, 2007).

Evangelical theology and British culture

While much of the theology of the twelve theologians profiled in this volume took shape within the framework of traditional systematic theological categories (especially the doctrine of Scripture, Christology, the atonement, the doctrine of salvation and mission), their theologies were deeply shaped by the issues of their day. They were not done in a vacuum. Whether it was Hegelianism, challenges to doctrines of biblical inspiration or sources of authority,[8] or science and the myth of progress,[9] or the rise of social sciences such as psychology,[10] or the real pressures of war time,[11] the British evangelical theology that developed in academic settings and in pulpits was in response to characteristic questions of the context. This demonstrates the significance of culture and context in doing theology.[12] They also demonstrated a self-awareness and proximity that encouraged irenic debates and helped resist the fundamentalism that developed in the USA.

British churches composed of predominantly white people are declining today in attendance, membership and finances, with many closing. Yet within Britain, some of the biggest and fastest growing churches are Pentecostal churches comprised largely of evangelical believers from the African diaspora.[13] But the world of British evangelical theology is wide. It is Scottish, English, Welsh, Northern Irish, Commonwealth countries, immigrants and refugees. It is Langham scholars and postgraduate students who come for a British theological education, and then go elsewhere. British evangelical theology is a very large and growing family, and in the future will almost inevitably be both very different from and similar to what it looked like in the twentieth century.

Looking to the future

There is no doubt about the significant role British evangelical theology played in Britain and elsewhere during the twentieth century, and continues to play in the contemporary world. But with regard to the future, much is changing.

---

8 See chapter 1 above, on Orr and his response to these challenges.
9 See chapter 10, on Torrance on theology and science.
10 See chapter 6, on Sangster: Lloyd-Jones also addressed this.
11 See chapters 6 and 7, on Sangster and Lloyd-Jones respectively.
12 See Graham McFarlane, *A Model for Evangelical Theology* (Grand Rapids, MI: Baker, 2020), pp. 22–25.
13 It was noted in the England football team during England's 2021 European Cup run, the only players who appeared to acknowledge God on the field were black players. See also Julian Coman, 'God-Given Talent: Saka, Rashford and Sterling Blaze a Trail for Black British Christians', *The Guardian*, 17 July 2021 <https://amp.theguardian.com/football/2021/jul/17/god-given-talent-saka-rashford-and-sterling-blaze-a-trail-for-black-british-christians?> (accessed 4 October 2021).

British demographics are changing, especially in the church. As acknowledged in this volume's introduction, evangelical theology in twentieth-century Britain was almost entirely the work of white males. Whether their work served to perpetuate white supremacy amid the ongoing effects of colonialism by which we are all infected remains for further research to address. But with British society and the British churches now being multi-ethnic, British evangelical theology must become so too. With the rich egalitarian tradition going back to the Clapham Sect as the early slavery abolitionists, British evangelicals should welcome this development. British evangelicalism should also welcome the greater presence of women to articulate the future of evangelical theology. Increasingly this theology will traverse the worlds of missiology, theological ethics and political theology, but all of it can certainly incorporate the span of Christian doctrine in conversation with the tradition.

British evangelical theology today continues to be cross-pollinated, not just between England, Scotland, Wales and Northern Ireland, but among evangelicals around the world. This wide community of faith – this evangelical family – requires a responsibility of maintenance (of particular features, distinct traditions, etc.) and clarity of articulation in order to help faithfully proclaim the evangel with the focus on 'Christ crucified' that we have seen in these twelve theologians. Theology, then, is seen as perhaps less defensive and apologetic than it has been, and yet continues to take up the task of rendering an orderly account of the Christian faith with an evangelical fervour and passion that spills out into our everyday practices, and what we might call practical, public and even political theology. As such, this kind of evangelical faith, articulated and expressly lived out, showcases – or rather witnesses – an emergent mode of reasoning that amounts to an exercise not only in wise and critical reception, but also and especially in astonishment, gratitude and righteous actions that do good works in service of the church and the wider world, until the Lord Jesus returns.

Index of names

Note: Contains all personal names except biblical persons. Names of places and organizations are not included. M' and Mc are filed as if spelled Mac.

Æschylus, 41
Akers, J. N., 186
Anderson, G. H., 223
Anderson, M. W., 56, 57
Anselm of Canterbury, 6, 45, 243, 257
Aquinas, Thomas, 214, 248, 249
Aristotle, 214
Armstrong, J. H., 186
Athanasius of Alexandria, 199, 210, 215–216, 247
Atherstone, A., 71–92, 135, 142, 143, 148, 149, 150, 151
Augustine of Hippo, 182, 186, 215, 216, 243, 245, 246, 247–250, 256
Aulén, G., 186

Baillie, B., 143
Balmer, R., 129
Barclay, O. R., 2, 157
Barnes-Lawrence, A. E., 86
Barth, K., 8, 17, 98, 100, 101, 139, 161, 168, 196, 198, 214, 224, 225, 226, 240, 243–245, 247, 251, 256
Basil of Caesarea, 248
Bassham, R., 234
Battles, F. L., 186
Baughen, M., 158
Bauman, M., 201
Baur, F. C., 17, 18, 83
Bavinck, H., 14, 30
Baxter, C., 9
Baxter, R., 177, 185, 187
Bebbington, D. W., 3, 4, 11, 72, 129, 156, 252

Beet, J. A., 85
Beethoven, L., 247
Begbie, J., 242
Berger, P., 231
Berkeley, G., 243, 249, 252
Bevans, S., 174
Beza, T., 184
Black, J. S., 35–36
Blanchard, C. A., 82
Boice, J. M., 186
Bonar, A. A., 87
Bonhoeffer, D., 161, 224
Booth, C., 2
Booth, W., 2, 261
Botting, M., 157
Bowles, C., 157
Bradley, F. C., 52
Bray, G., 9
Brencher, J., 135
Briggs, C. A., 35, 37
Bromiley, G. W., 198, 244
Brooks, T., 190
Brown, R., 240
Brown. S. W., 221
Bruce, A. B., 34–35, 37, 38, 42
Bruce, F. F., 6, 43, 157
Brunner, E., 224, 225
Bulloch, J., 11
Burleigh, J. H. S., 9, 11
Burton, P., 224

Caird, E., 13, 33
Caird, J., 14
Cairns, J., 12, 14

Calvin, J., 2, 8, 30, 55, 141, 162–163, 182, 184–186, 190–191, 198, 204, 205, 244, 252, 253, 256
Cameron, J., 158
Cameron, N., 93
Campbell, D., 242
Candlish, J. S., 34, 36, 38
Carson, D. A., 179, 181
Catherwood, C., 145
Chafer, L. S., 71
Chai, T., 174
Chalmers, T., 2, 3, 34
Chapman, A., 156–157, 158, 159, 160, 163, 166, 172, 174
Charteris, A. H., 17
Cheatle, A. J., 10, 113–132
Chester, T., 157, 159, 160, 161, 163, 165, 169
Chrystal, G. W., 35–36
Clark, M. G., 73
Coffey, J., 142
Coggan, D., 161
Coleridge, S. T., 243, 245, 252
Collins, J., 157
Colquhoun, F., 181
Colwell, J. E., 9, 240–259
Colwell, R., 254
Colyer, E. M., 213
Coman, J., 265
Conn, H. M., 194
Corrie, J., 234
Costas, O., 171
Cranmer, T., 160
Crisp, O., 242
Crowe, P., 159
Cyril of Alexandria, 215–216

Dale, R. W., 141, 168, 243
Dante Alighieri, 118
Darwin, C., 3, 7, 23–24, 122, 173
Davie, M., 224

Davies, H., 127
Dayton, D. W., 2
Debussy, C., 247
Denney, J., 6, 10, 33–50, 53, 72, 96, 100, 104, 107, 111, 141, 167, 226, 237
Descartes, R., 223, 249
Dixon, A. C., 25
Dobschütz, E., 41
Dodd, C. H., 226
Dods, M., 17, 18
Douglas, J. D., 129, 171, 190
Drummond, A. L., 11
Dudley-Smith, T., 120, 148, 155–156, 157, 158, 164, 173

Edwards, D. L., 155, 157, 164, 169
Edwards, J., 2, 140, 144, 182, 242, 243
Einstein, A., 198
Eliot, G., 52
Ensor, R., 115
Epiphanius, 215
Escobar, S., 171, 234
Etchells, R., 9
Eugenio, D. O., 213
Eusebius, 41
Evans, L. J., 35

Farmer, H. H., 226
Farrow, D., 242, 243, 250
Fee, G. D., 181
Ferguson, S. B., 183, 190, 192
Fielder, G. D., 141
Findlay, T. V., 10, 33–50
Finney, C., 2, 3
Flew, R. N., 9
Forsyth, P. T., 6, 7, 44, 47, 51–70, 72, 98, 100, 111, 141, 167, 168, 243, 257
Fraser, H., 14

Gadamer, H-G., 192
Gandhi, M., 173

Garvie, A. E., 118

Geevarghese Mar Osthathios, 171

Geisler, N., 193

George, T., 71, 187, 191

Godet, F., 62, 64, 69

Goodhew, D., 157

Goodwin, T., 190

Gordon, J. M., 33, 34, 37–38, 39, 40, 41, 50

Graf, K. H., 21

Graham, B., 3, 4, 113, 163, 170, 171, 197

Grass, T., 224

Gray, H., 221

Gray, J., 82

Green, M., 9

Greene, W. B., Jr., 26

Gregory of Nazianzus, 207, 215

Grieg, G. S., 183

Griffith, G. O., 44

Griggs, E. L., 252

Gunton, C. E., 8, 9, 54, 240–259

Gunton, Carolyn, 258

Gunton, Christopher, 259

Gunton, Jenny, 254, 258–259

Gunton, Jonathan, 259

Gunton, S. J., 254, 258

Guthrie, D., 43

Habets, M., 203, 207, 209, 213, 216

Haeckel, E., 23–24

Hamer, M., 91

Hamilton, J., 85

Hamilton, W., 245

Handel, G. F., 55

Hannah, J. D., 71

Hardy, D. W., 255

Hardy, T., 52, 88

Harnack, A., 3, 6, 16

Harp, G. J., 71

Harris, H., 153

Harrison, E. F., 181

Hart, T., 51–70

Hartshorne, C., 240, 243

Harvey, L., 242

Hastings, A., 155

Hastings, J., 39, 41

Hegel, G. W. F., 13, 16, 52, 53, 58–59, 95

Helm, P., 9, 242

Henry, C. F., 3, 170, 181

Heraclitus of Ephesus, 246

Herbert, A. G., 186

Herrmann, W., 17, 100

Herschel, J., 122–123

Heslam, P., 15

Hick, J., 241

Hilborn, D., 160

Hill, D., 46

Hindmarsh, D. B., 187–188

Hodge, C., 13

Hoekendijk, J. C., 224

Holmes, C. R. J., 216

Holmes, S. R., 224, 242, 243, 248, 254, 258, 261, 262

Hopkins, E. H., 79

Horn, R., 2

Horne, B., 242

Horne, C. S., 52

Houston, J. M., 162, 163, 177

Hughes, P., 9

Hume, D., 13, 15

Hunsberger, G. A., 228–229, 233

Hunt, W. H., 52

Hunter, A. M., 53

Huxley, T., 88

Ibsen, H., 52

Irenaeus of Lyons, 96, 243, 247, 249–250, 251

Irving, E., 97–98, 243, 257

James, M. G., 118

James, W., 52, 221

Jebb, R., 33, 35
Jenkins, D., 240
Jennings, J. N., 174
Jenson, B., 259
Jenson, R., 248, 256, 259
Johnson, S., 249
Johnston, O., 181
Johnston, R. K., 2, 194
Jones, D. C., 72, 133–154
Jones, D. G., 153
Jones, R. T., 9
Jorgensen, K., 174
Jowett, B., 83
Jüngel, E., 243

Kapic, K., 243
Katerberg, W. H., 71
Kay, W. K., 150
Kaye, B., 181
Kempis, T. à, 169
Ker, J., 13
Kim, K. J., 234
King, M. L., Jr., 170
Kings, G., 171, 172
König, E., 84
Kuyper, A., 14–15, 30

Labberton, M., 4
Lamont, D., 9
Lane, A. N. S., 9, 262
Larsen, D. L., 113
Latimer, H., 160, 161
Lewis, D., 176
Lightfoot, J. B., 33
Lindsay, T. M., 34, 35–36
Lindsell, H., 179
Litton, E. A., 73
Lloyd George, David, 73
Lloyd-Jones, B., 138
Lloyd-Jones, D. M., 7, 8, 126, 127–128,
    133–154, 160, 161, 163, 178, 195, 261, 265

Loane, M. L., 159, 160, 161
Locke, J., 249
Loucks, C. M., 76
Luce, H. K., 163
Lukens, F., 73
Lum, R. A., 71
Luther, M., 1–2, 39, 40–41, 55, 148, 181,
    252

Macaulay, A. B., 56
M'Cheyne, R. M., 87
McCurdy, L., 51
McDonald, H. D., 9
McFarlane, G., 243, 265
McGowan, A. T. B., 11–32, 43
McGrath, A. E., 9, 149, 176, 178, 192, 197
Macgregor, G., 86
Machen, G. J., 3
Mackintosh, H. R., 7, 8, 56, 93–112, 197,
    264
Macleod, D., 9
Macmurray, J., 198, 233, 245
McNeill, J. T., 186
McPherson, A. S., 3
Mantle, J. G., 86
Marsden, G. M., 3
Marshall, I. H., 43
Meeking, B., 171–172
Menzies, M. J., 86
Meyer, F. B., 86
Mickelsen, A., 194
Mills-Powell, D., 173
Milne, B., 9
Milton, J., 52
Moffatt, J., 129
Molnar, P. D., 203, 207, 209, 213, 216
Moltmann, J., 215
Moody, D. L., 2, 3, 81
Mooneyham, S., 170
Moore, E. W., 86
More, H., 3

Morgan, G. C., 7, 81–82, 86
Morgan, J., 82
Morris, L., 44, 46
Mott, J. R., 3
Moule, C. F. D., 157
Moule, H., 86, 157
Mozart, W. A., 247, 251
Murray, A., 86
Murray, I. H., 126, 135, 136, 140, 141, 143, 149
Murray, J., 9
Murray Zoba, W., 176

Nash, E., 156–157
Newbigin, L., 8, 220–239, 261, 264
Newman, J. H., 16, 243
Nicoll, W. R., 37
Niebuhr, R., 225, 243
Nietzsche, F., 52, 83, 246
Nineham, D., 241
Noble, T. A., 1–10, 33, 42, 47, 139, 191, 207, 224, 262
Noll, M. A., 2, 164, 176

Oden, T. C., 264
Oldham, J. H., 223, 228
Oman, J., 222
Origen of Alexandria, 249
Orr, J., 6, 11, 13–32, 72, 265
Owen, J., 140, 177, 178, 243

Packer, J. I., 4–5, 7–8, 71–72, 73, 134, 145, 149, 155, 162–163, 169, 176–196, 261
Padilla, R., 171
Palmer, P., 2
Parmenides of Elea, 246
Payne, D. J., 176–196
Pelikan, J., 2
Pennefather, W., 81
Pfleiderer, O., 17, 18
Plato, 41

Polanyi, M., 198, 231, 243, 245, 252
Poulenc, F., 248
Price, C., 158, 169
Profumo, J., 136–137

Quicke, M., 161

Radcliff, A. S., 199
Radcliff, J. R., 199, 215
Rae, M., 242
Rahner, K., 214
Rainey, D. L., 93–112
Rainy, R., 17, 18
Ramachandra, V., 228
Randall, I. M., 125, 151, 155–175
Rashford, M., 265
Rauschenbusch, W., 3
Raven, C., 157
Redman, R. R., 100, 107, 111
Reid, J. K. S., 11
Reid, T., 13
Richard of St Victor, 245
Ridley, N., 160
Riley, W. B., 82
Ritchie, B., 208, 216
Ritschl, A., 3, 6, 17, 18–19, 55, 56, 100, 106
Rossetti, D. G., 52
Rowland, D., 133
Ryken, L., 176–177
Ryle, J. C., 178

Saka, B., 265
Samuel, V., 174
Sangster, P., 113, 114, 115
Sangster, W. E., 7, 113–132, 265
Sargent, T., 144
Schleiermacher, F., 17, 18, 100, 106
Schlenther, B. S., 133
Schopenhauer, A., 52
Schwöbel, C., 241–242, 256, 259

Scorgie, G. G., 11, 16, 18, 24, 26
Scougal, H., 126
Sell, A. P. F., 11, 55, 93
Sexton, J. S., 260–266
Shaw, I., 174
Shenk, W. R., 233, 234
Sherrard, J. H., 212
Simeon, C., 2, 7, 159, 162, 163, 178
Smail, T., 9
Smith, C. R., 128
Smith, H. E., 157, 158
Smith, H. P., 35
Smith, W. R., 34–36, 43
Socinus (Lelio Sozzini), 56
Soderlund, S. K., 181
Speidell, T., 199
Spence, A., 243
Spencer, H., 123, 124
Spittler, R., 184
Springer, K. N., 183
Spurgeon, C. H., 3, 74, 138
Stanley, B., 4, 170, 261
Stanton, G., 242
Steer, R., 156, 167
Sterling, R., 265
Stewart, L. and M., 26
Stibbs, A. M., 190
Storms, S., 176
Stott, J. R. W., 3, 4, 7, 8, 120, 129, 132, 134–135, 148, 155–175, 261, 264
Stott, Lady Lily, 156
Stott, Sir Arnold, 156
Strauss, D., 83
Struthers, J. P., 33, 37
Stults, D. L., 220–239
Sugden, C., 174
Sunquist, S. W., 224, 228
Swai, E., 128

Talmage, T., 74
Temple, W., 155

Tertullian, 161
Thiselton, A., 9, 192
Thomas, W. H. G., 6–7, 8, 71–92
Thomson, G. T., 9
Tidball, D., 158
Tinker, M., 179
Toon, P., 9
Torrance, A., 9, 242, 253
Torrance, D. W., 198
Torrance, J. B., 9, 199, 202
Torrance, T. F., 8, 9, 93–94, 96, 111–112, 191, 196, 197–219, 244, 245, 261, 264, 265
Torrey, R. A., 25
Treloar, G. R., 3, 72
Trumbull, C., 79, 84
Tyler, K., 212

Vanhoozer, K. J., 262
Veitch, J., 13, 33, 35
Visser 't Hooft, W., 224

Wagner, R., 52, 55
Wainwright, G., 9, 224–227, 230, 231, 232, 234, 237–238, 239
Waldrep, D., 71
Walker, R. T., 9, 197–219
Walls, A. F., 9, 224, 233, 234, 235
Warfield, B. B., 7, 15, 24, 26–27, 28, 29, 30, 35, 42, 72, 79–80, 92, 141, 179
Watkins, A., 221
Watson, D., 9
Watson, F., 242
Watts, I., 251
Weatherhead, L., 113
Webb-Peploe, H. W., 79
Webster, J., 9
Weightman, C., 198
Wellhausen, J., 20, 21, 83
Wells, A., 86
Wells, D. F., 164, 183

Welsby, P., 155
Wenham, G., 181
Wenham, J., 120, 178
Werner, D., 174
Wesley, C., 2
Wesley, J., 2, 113, 116, 117, 118, 122, 124, 125, 126, 233, 262
West, C., 223
Westerdale, T. E., 114
Whale, J. S., 157
White, E. M., 133
Whitefield, G., 2, 178, 262
Whitehead, F., 158
Wilberforce, W., 3, 261

Williams, R., 243
Williams, S., 9, 15, 16
Williams, W., 133, 141, 142, 143, 150
Witherspoon, J., 13
Wolffe, J., 3
Wood, A. S., 9
Woodbridge, J. D., 179, 181, 186
Wordsworth, W., 52
Worrall, B. G., 46
Wright, C. J. H., 156, 159, 174, 264
Wright, D. F., 9, 183, 190, 192
Wright, N. T., 181

Zizioulas, J. D., 215, 243, 245